About the Author

Dr. Purdum is a retired professor from Purdue University's College of Technology where he taught various programming courses. He wrote his first C programming textbook in 1983 and has been using C since the 1970's. He has received numerous teaching awards and is the author of 20 books and dozens of magazine articles, many of which are about programming as it relates to his hobby of amateur radio. He has received three coveted *Cover Plaque Awards* for articles in *QST* from the American Radio Relay League for amateur radio construction projects involving C-based microcontrollers. When asked why his books have been so popular for almost 40 years, Dr. Purdum responded: "I'm dumb enough to appreciate the difficulties beginning programming students face, but smart enough to answer their questions in a way that makes sense." Dr. Purdum continues to support the Open Source movement with his own software and hardware contributions.

To: Hailey, Spencer, Liam, and Luke

Acknowledgements:

No author operates without help from others. Al Peter, AC8GY, has been a valuable EE resource and good friend for years and his efforts have made this a better book. I have also benefited from the following Beta Readers: Rocco Barbaro, Brian Bowling, Martijn Hiemstra, Stephen Martin, Jackie Russell, and Ron Taylor plus several others who read parts of the manuscript. Bev and Joe Kack, John Strack, John Weiner, Katie Mohr, and John Purdum have supported my efforts, too. To each one of them, my sincerely thanks.

Jack Purdum, Ph.D.

Sept., 2020

Table of Contents

(Page left blank intentionally)

Foreword

It's a little embarrassing to say how long I've been messing around with electronics in general and programming specifically. I've been a continually-licensed amateur radio operator for over 65 years and still love the hobby. Indeed, that's probably one of the reasons I got into programming in the first place. Programming seemed to be a nexus for electronics and computers, both of which I enjoy.

The primary goal of this textbook is to teach you the C programming language as it exists in the Arduino Integrated Development Environment (IDE). There are probably 100's of C programming books, including my older *Beginning C for Arduino* book. Still, I think there are some good reasons for choosing this book over the alternatives.

First, I've been teaching C for almost 40 years and have a learned a lot over those years. I have no doubt that there are a bunch of authors who are smarter than I and can probably code circles around me. Indeed, when I had my software company, my lead programmer was one of the brightest people I've ever met and a brilliant programmer. But, he couldn't teach to save his life...everything was "obvious" to him. I made the mistake of assigning an intern to him one summer. Before the day was done, she was in my office in tears telling me he was a horrible teacher, whereupon she stomped out of my office never to be seen again. Truth is, a brilliant programmer is *not* necessarily what you need. I'm dumb enough to appreciate the difficulties of learning a new programming language, but smart enough to figure out an answer that makes sense. I can just about guarantee you that I have seen every student stumbling block there is and have a way of explaining things that makes sense to most people. This book holds the essence of that experience.

Second, this book presents C as it is used for microcontroller programming. Most books assume you're going to use C in a PC or mainframe environment. While the C language is the same for microcontrollers and mainframes, its use and methods of learning are not. My earlier beginning C book concentrated on the Arduino Uno processor for all of the examples and exercises. That was over five years ago and the microcontroller environment has changed substantially. The Arduino family of microcontrollers (e.g., Uno, Nano, Mega2560, and Due) simply have not kept up with the times. For that reason, I've expanded the microcontrollers used in this book to also include the STM32 (aka, "Blue

Pill"), ESP32, and Teensy 4.1 microcontrollers. As you will see in Chapter 1, these additional microcontrollers bring a lot more to the table in terms of speed and resource depth with barely a nudge in their price points. The advantage is that you can leverage your C knowledge by applying it to the microcontroller that makes sense for each specific project.

Third, even though this book can be used with a wider variety of microcontrollers, all of them are programmable using the same Arduino IDE. The Arduino IDE combines all elements of a programmer's tool chain (i.e., editor, compiler, assembler, linker) into one program. This saves you the time and effort of learning new set of programming tools for each specific microcontroller. Even better, the Arduino IDE is a free download!

Fourth, unlike a "straight C" book, we present examples of interfacing with external devices (e.g., LEDs, TFT color displays, sensors, rotary encoders, etc.). We also show you tips and techniques that help you to better utilize the limited resources many microcontrollers face.

Fifth, teaching you C doesn't have to be a boring process. As much as possible, I have tried to make this text read as if you and I are talking face-to-face about programming issues. Sometimes I even ask questions and I really do want you to stop and think about how you would answer those questions if we were in a classroom together. If you see a code listing, I hope you'll take the time to mentally "walk through" the code *before* you read what I have to say about it. This makes you think about what you're doing. It's far too easy to read something and say: "Yeah, I get it." only to close the book and realize you really don't get it. Also, being wrong in some cases is not a bad thing. If you think something will work one way and later my explanation shows you that's not the case, trust me, you will learn that point better having made the mistake. Shooting yourself in the foot once is probably a better safety lesson than telling you a hundred times not to shoot yourself in the foot.

Finally, I hope this book conveys to you the enjoyment and appreciation I have for programming. I truly appreciate reading a beautifully-crafted piece of code. By the time you finish this book, I hope you'll hold the same appreciation. Also, having the ability to make a piece of hardware dance beautifully to the tune of your design...well, it simply is intoxicating!

Assumptions About You

First, I assume you do not have to master C by next Tuesday. A major reason students who try to learn C on their own fail is because they don't invest the time it takes to absorb the material. You *must* invest the time it takes to type in and run the sample programs. You *must* work through the exercises at the end of each chapter. (There are little nuggets of information hidden in some of the programming exercises and you owe it to yourself to ferret out those nuggets.) Effort less than this is just cheating yourself of the learning experience.

Second, you need to invest in some hardware that allows you to both run and experiment with the sample programs. At a bare minimum, you need to buy a microcontroller of your choice (Chapter 1 should help you with that decision), some resistors, LED's, a small breadboard, a rotary encoder, and perhaps a sensor or two. Excluding the microcontroller, the cost should be under $15.

Third, I assume you have absolutely zero programming experience. Actually, this is a good thing, because you come to the table with a brain that is uncluttered and no bad programming habits. I have a different way of teaching C and often get into details that makes students "roll their eyes". Sometimes, I want you to understand what a compiler (or whatever) is doing behind your back. One student countered this depth of understanding by saying: "Yeah, but I don't have to know how to build a car to drive one." When I hear that, I think of the time I was driving about 400 miles north of Toronto and a guy was standing next to his car on the side of the road with the hood up. I'll bet he wishes he knew a little more about what is under that hood. Understanding what is going on "under the hood" in the IDE *will* make you a better programmer. That understanding will make you better equipped to identify, isolate, and fix program bugs (i.e., errors), too.

Fourth, I assume you start at page 1 and read straight through the book. My teaching experience has shown me that laying a solid foundation makes understanding more complex topics much easier. A good understanding of lvalues, rvalues, and the Bucket Analogy makes understanding pointers a breeze. So, content in one chapter may not seem all that useful at the moment, but several chapters later you may have an "Ah-ha!" moment that you would miss if you skipped the earlier chapter. You paid for all of the book, seems smart to me to read all of it.

Finally, take your time reading the book, work with the exercises and try modifying and experiment with the programs. While you may feel that such experimentation will slow you down, it actually does the opposite. Writing, testing, and debugging programs is the *only* way to learn how to program. You'll notice that this book does not have the solutions to the exercises at the end of the book. That's so you won't be tempted to look at the answers before trying to think through and develop your own answer. (You can download the answers, however, from https://groups.io/g/SoftwareControlledHamRadio.) Remember: A wrong answer is not bad, but no answer is. At least you will learn something with the wrong answer. With no answer...not so much.

Use What's Available

Before I start any programming project, I do an Internet search of the project's primary design goal first.
After all, there is nothing wrong with standing on the shoulders of those who have gone before you. Many highly-qualified programmers have made their efforts available through the Open Source community. If a project is Open Sourced, that means anyone is free to use it for their own use. (If you plan to use the code commercially, it's a good idea to contact the author first. It's probably polite not to use the Permission/Forgiveness reasoning with Open Source projects destined for commercial use.)

Appendix A lists some of the sources I've used to purchase microcontrollers, sensors, and components. If you order things online, pay attention to the expected delivery time. Ordering from outside your country can mean up to six or seven weeks before your order arrives. I tend to order microcontrollers 5 at a time, and often do the same for other components (e.g., rotary encoders, voltage regulators, etc.) Quantity discounts may seem unnecessary, but you can always split the cost with other you may know.

Most microcontroller vendors host Forums on the web where you can read answers asked by other users. Usually you have to join the group to be able to ask your own questions. However, there's a pretty good chance that your question, or one very close to it, has already been asked. Reading the answers is also a good learning experience.

Okay...let's get into the fun stuff...

Chapter 1 Getting Started

In this chapter you will download and install the Arduino Integrated Development Environment, or IDE. The IDE contains virtually all of the software tools you need to write microcontroller programs in the C programming language. Years ago when I programmed in the mainframe environment, the software tools embodied in the Arduino IDE would have cost thousands of dollars. The Arduino IDE is provided free by a small group of people dedicated to the Arduino and the Open Source philosophy. The Open Source philosophy is that software resources should be shared freely to the benefit of all. I agree with this philosophy and hope that, when you download the Arduino IDE, you will make a contribution to the group who continue to maintain and improve the Arduino IDE.

Arduino? The name Arduino comes from a bar in Ivrea, Italy. Evidently that bar was a hangout for some of the founders. The bar was named after Arduino of Ivrea, who was the military commander of the March of Ivrea and King of Italy from 1002 to 1014. You should memorize this information as it comes up in cocktail conversation all the time.

Over the years, the Arduino's IDE has grown in popularity to the point that it is one of the most ubiquitous IDE's in use on PC's. Because of its popularity, microcontroller manufacturers outside of the Arduino family have created software "patches" for their microcontrollers so they can be programmed using the same Arduino IDE. Figure 1.1 shows some of the popular microcontrollers that can be used with this book.

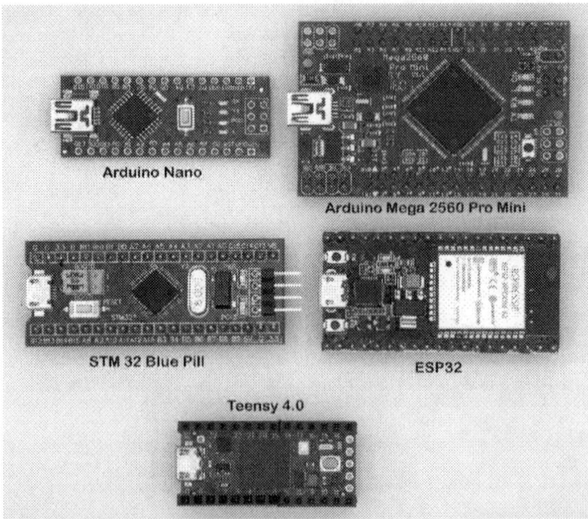

Figure 1.1. Several microcontrollers supported within the Arduino IDE.

By way of reference, the Arduino Nano shown in Figure 1.1 measures 1.75"x 0.75", so all of the microcontrollers (except the Mega 2560 Pro Mini) are fairly small...probably smaller than your thumb. Yet, these small microcontrollers have more computing power than the computers that landed men on the moon.

Table 1.1 lists the primary resources offered by each of the microcontrollers that we used when writing this book. It's important that you understand these resource differences, as they may influence which microcontroller you wish to use, as you start your C programming learning experience.

Processor Bits

A detailed discussion of processor bits and the binary numbering system is presented in Chapter 2. All we need to say at this moment is that, *ceteris paribus,* the larger the number of processor bits, the greater the processing power of the microcontroller. Notice that the Arduino family of microcontrollers listed uses an 8-bit processing architecture while the others are 32-bit. However, notice that the cost is generally less for the Arduino family. For most of the exercises presented in this book (and the programming assignments), an inexpensive Nano is fine.

In Table 1.1, the first row shows that the Arduino microcontrollers use 8-bit processors while the others are 32-bit processors. Perhaps the best way to think about the distinction is to think of how many binary digits, or bits, can the registers and the microcontroller's Arithmetic Logic Unit (ALU) hold. A register is just a special place in the microcontroller where data can be processed (e.g., multiplied, divided, bit-shifted, etc.). The Arduino microcontrollers are designed for 8-bit operations while the registers in the other microcontrollers are designed with 32-bit registers. While the relation doesn't work out perfectly, you can think of a 32-bit processor as performing its data manipulation four times faster than an 8-bit processor.

Table 1.1. Resources by Microcontroller

Resources	**Arduino Nano**	**Arduino Mega 2560 Pro Mini**	**Teensy 4.0**[6]	**Blue Pill (STM32F103)**	**ESP32 NodeMCU WROOM 32**[7]
Processor bits	8	8	32	32	32
Flash[1] (bytes)	32K	256K	2048K	64K - 128K	1.3M[5]
SRAM (bytes)	2K	8K	1024K	20K	380K[5]
EEPROM	1K	4K	64K[2]	?[3]	?[3]

(bytes)					
Processor Clock Speed	16MHz	16MHz	600MHz	72MHz	240MHz[4]
I/O pins	14	54	40	26	25
Interrupts	All 14 mappable, 2 external	6	All digital pins	All 26 mappable	All 25 mappable
Timers	3 (2 8-bit, 1 16bit)	6	16	14	4
SPI	1	1	3	1	2
I2C	1	1	3	1	2
DAC resolution (bits)	10	10	12	12	12
Analog pins	8	16	14	5	15
Price	$3	$8	$20	$5	$10

1. Figures are for total flash memory. Some portion is taken by the bootloader and therefore is not available for program development.

2. The Teensy doesn't actually have EEPROM, *but rather emulates it by setting a block of flash memory aside that can be accessed as EEPROM memory.*

3. Teensy, BP, and ESP32 can emulate EEPROM. See main discussion

4. Can be overclocked to 240MHz.

5. Uses both internal and external memory. These are expected minimums.

6. The Teensy 4.0 (T4) recently became available and is a real powerhouse at a price of $20. We have modified those projects that used the Teensy 3.6 to use the T4. PJRC also just released the Teensy 4.1, which makes more I/O pins available and has an onboard SD card reader for $27.

7. The ESP32 is just being listed here for completeness. See sidebar in the ESP32 section below.

Flash Memory

Flash memory is usually internal to the chip itself. It is where the statements you write in the C programming language are stored after those statements are compiled into binary instructions the microcontroller understands. Flash memory is similar to the memory in a thumb (flash) drive. That is, whatever the binary code values are with power applied to that memory remains the same when that power source is removed. When power is reapplied, the program picks up right where it left off (i.e., its state is the same as when power was removed.)

SRAM Memory

Static Random Access Memory (SRAM), is the memory that holds all of the data values used in your programs. Any variables you define in your program or values you assign into those variables end up being stored in SRAM. However, unlike flash memory which retains its values in the absence of power, SRAM goes stupid (Stupid RAM?) when power is removed. When you re-apply power to SRAM, it contains totally random bit values that you should count on to be garbage (i.e., unusable) values.

Virtually all microcontrollers have lesser amounts of SRAM than flash memory. However, in a very real sense, it is the amount of SRAM, not flash memory, your microcontroller has that determines the maximum program size. Let me explain why.

Suppose we are looking at an Arduino Nano's SRAM organization. A Nano has 32K of flash memory and 2K of SRAM. We can depict the Nano SRAM organization as shown in Figure 1.2.

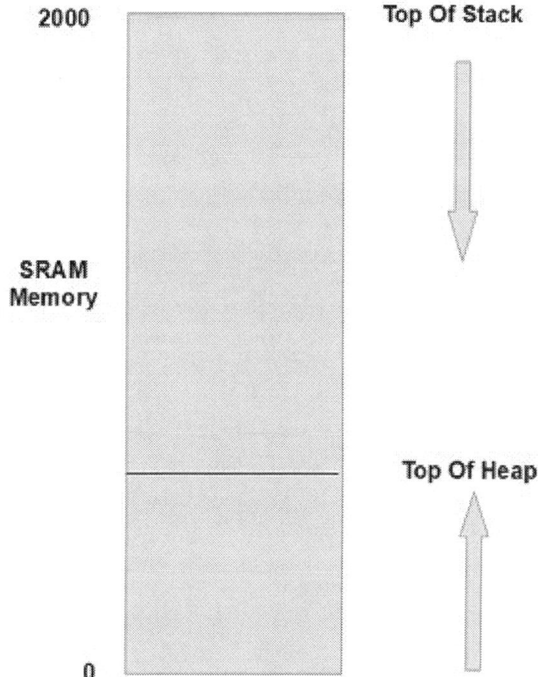

Figure 1.2. Arduino Nano SRAM organization

In very simple terms, there are two types of data in a microcontroller program:

1. global data (available throughout the program)
2. local data (available only within a certain block of the program).

For microcontrollers, global data is stored starting at the bottom of SRAM memory space in an area called the *Heap*. As you add more global data to your program, the Heap memory space being used grows upwards. That is, the Top of Heap grows upwards.

Local data are those data values that come to life as the program runs and they are allocated memory space in SRAM called the *Stack*. As you define more local data as the program executes, the Top of Stack grows downwards. As those local variables are used and then discarded because they are no longer needed, the Stack can slide back up towards the Top Of Stack. In other words, the Stack space being used ebbs and flows as your program executes.

For microcontrollers, global data is stored at the bottom of SRAM memory space in an area called the *Heap*. As you add more global data to your program, the Heap memory space being used grows upwards. That is, the *Top of Heap* (ToH) grows upward.

A common analogy for the Stack is a stack of salad plates you often see at the start of a restaurant's salad bar. When the waitstaff add more plates (i.e., data) to the stack, the bottom of the stack is pushed down by the new plates that are added on top. As people remove plates from the stack, the bottom of the stack moves back up towards the top. The same thing happens in a microcontroller stack. As you add more local variables to the stack, the bottom of the stack gets pushed down.

Guess what happens if you add too many plates to the stack? The bottom of the stack can crash into the Top of the Heap and all of the Heap and Stack data get clobbered, white smoke starts pouring out and fire breaks out in the microcontroller. Naw...just kidding. This event, called a Stack Crash, may go completely unnoticed unless you happen to observe the variable value(s) on the Heap/Stack that just got destroyed.

So, how can you prevent a Stack Crash? Well, the first line of defense is to read the compile statistics that the Arduino IDE gives you after each compilation. (We show this later in the chapter in Figure 1.13.) The compiler tells you how much SRAM space you have used during the compile. However, that statistic can be very misleading because that number is the *compile-time* statistic for SRAM, not its *run-time* statistic. Remember that the Top Of Stack slides down as your program runs and compile-time statistics can't tell you how far down the stack will slide. I've had a Stack Crash occur with only 72% of SRAM being used. Any time your data seems to have a mind of its own, try decreasing the Heap Space variables or use fewer temporary variables if you can. If those actions fix the problem, you probably had a Silent Stack Crash (i.e., no smoke or fire!)

Perhaps now you can better understand why SRAM often becomes a more limiting factor in program size than does flash memory. If your proposed application is data-intensive, try to select a microcontroller that has good SRAM depth.

EEPROM

Electrically Erasable Programmable Read Only Memory (EEPROM) is another form of memory that retains its values when power is removed. However, it is usually a little different than flash memory. First, EEPROM is organized to write smaller packets of data. Second, EEPROM is slower to read and write data than flash memory. Finally, EEPROM has a longer write-cycle lifetime (i.e., usually more than 100,000 write cycles) than flash memory (typically 10,000 write cycles). As a result, EEPROM is often used to store configuration (e.g., port numbers, sensor ID's, font sizes, etc.) and restart data (e.g., last file(s) opened, update values, database or windows handles, etc.).

The Arduino family of microcontrollers have “real” EEPROM memory buried in the microcontroller. All of the other processors used in this book *emulate* EEPROM. This emulation is done by reserving a block of flash memory for simulated EEPROM use only. Hardware and/or software can enforce the EEPROM boundary so that it can only be accessed through EEPROM methods (e.g., *EEPROM.read()*, *EEPROM.write()*). Because emulated EEPROM actually resides in flash memory, it faces the same lower write-cycle lifetime as flash memory. Therefore, EEPROM should not be used for standard program data, but only used for storing data that you wish to preserve between program restarts.

Processor Clock Speed

Every microcontroller has a system clock that determines how fast things can take place within the chip. Indeed, if you look at the specifications for each instruction the microcontroller can process, one of the details usually given is the number of clock cycles it takes to complete that particular instruction. It kinda makes sense, then, that the faster the microcontroller's clock, the faster data can boot-scoot around the system. Looking back at Table 1.1, you can see that the Arduino family has the lowest clock speeds, so they also tend to be the slowest to complete a given task.

So, should you ignore the Arduino family and only buy the Teensy 4 because of its superior clock speed? Not necessarily. If your program deals mainly with human interactions (e.g., an automated test recording system, voting machines, etc.), even the Arduino thinks human input occurs at about the same pace that continents drift apart from one another. On the other hand, if you're updating a graphics display screen based on some complex math computation, you need all the speed you can get so a high clock speed is desirable. There are online videos that show graphics display tests using different microcontrollers.

Often, the clock speed differences are dramatic. For example, I wrote a simple program to see how many times different processors completed a simple loop in one second. The Arduino Nano did 429,830 passes per second. The Seeed Studio XIAO microcontroller (too late to include in this book, but clocked at 48MHz) did 2,383,050 passes per second. The Teensy T4 did 199,980,290 passes per second. You can select the one that best suits your processing needs.

I/O Pins

The I/O pin count refers to the number of Input and Output (I/O) pins that the microcontroller has. In Figure 1.1, most of those "dots" along the edges of the microcontroller are I/O pins. (The pinout figures presented later in this chapter make the pins clearer.) Most of the microcontroller's I/O pins are digital pins. A digital pin can only have one of two values at any moment in time: ON (1) or OFF (0). Usually, a digital pin is used to control (i.e., a write) or sense (i.e., a read) some external device. For example, you might connect a pin to a fire sensor in a bedroom. If the microcontroller reads a binary 0 from the fire sensor, it probably means there is no fire in that room. If the microcontroller receives a 1 from the sensor, time to sound an alarm.

Analog pins are different. Most analog pins are actually part of an analog-to-digital (A/D) converter system within the microcontroller which allows an analog pin to have a range of numeric values rather than just 1 or 0. If the A/D converter has 10-bit resolution, it can produce 1024 (2^{10}) distinct values (i.e., 0 – 1023). You can then map those numeric values to whatever use you need. For example, if an *analogRead()* returns a value of 10 for a volume control device, you might program it to be barely audible. If the value is 1020, the speakers are probably close to self-destruction. The great thing about programming is that you get the final say on how things are interpreted.

Other Microcontroller Characteristics

At this early stage in the book, the other characteristics in Table 1.1 probably won't make much sense if we try to explain them here with no contextual framework to work with. We get into these other characteristics later in the book, but present them here so they are "all in one place". For now, we have enough information available to make a decision on which microcontroller you may wish to buy and experiment with. What we need to do next is get the software you need that enables you to program a microcontroller.

The Arduino IDE

The Arduino IDE is a free software download and is available at the following URL:
https://www.arduino.cc/en/Main/Donate_
This URL starts at a page where you can make a contribution to the team which continue to improve the Arduino IDE. I hope you'll support their efforts in whatever manner you can afford.

Figure 1.3 shows the primary download screen. At the time this book is being written, Release 1.8.12 is the most-current IDE download. On the right side of Figure 1.3 you can see downloads for Windows, Mac OS, and Linux. Select the flavor that suits your programming environment. I used the ZIP file for Windows.

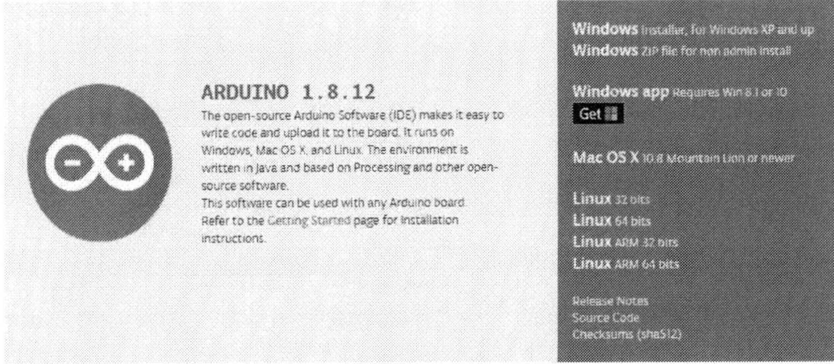

Figure 1.3. The Arduino IDE download page

Once you have selected the version to download, you are asked where you would like to save it. I prefer to keep my older versions of the IDE, just in case I need to "back up" to a previous release. For

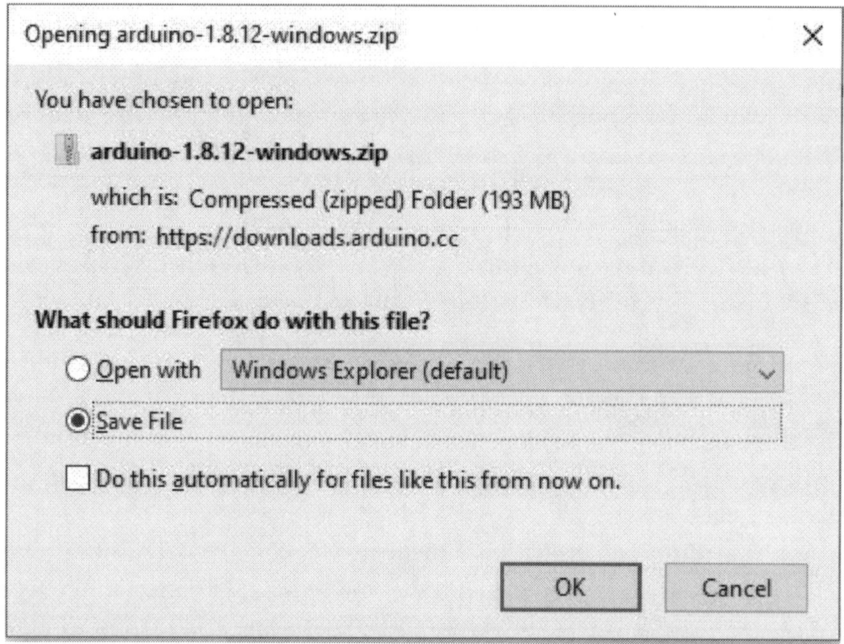

Figure 1.4. Dialog box for saving the Arduino IDE to disk

that reason, the directory I use for each new release is the word "Arduino" followed by the release number. So for this release, my new directory name is *Arduino1.8.12*. Because I downloaded a Windows ZIP file for installation, when the download finished, my *Arduino1.8.12* directory had the IDE stored there as a ZIP file. I then double-click on the ZIP file to unpack the IDE into the *Arduino1.8.12* directory. After the ZIP file is unpacked, you end up with a "double directory" (e.g., C:\Arduino.1.8.12\Arduino1.8.12). Simply copy all of the everything for the "second" directory up to the "first" directory and then delete the "second" directory folder name. If you do this, your C:\Arduino1.8.12 directory will look like that shown in Figure 1.5.

When the computer finishes unpacking the IDE ZIP file, my *Arduino1.8.12* (partial) directory listing looks similar to Figure 1.5. Note that I use drive D for my programming work, but most people probably use drive C. So with that caveat, your directory should look very similar to that seen in Figure 1.5.

One directory you will not have that is shown in Figure 1.5 is the TempSketch directory. I added this directory to hold temporary programs that I might be experimenting with. You really don't have to have this, as the IDE will create a temporary directory for you. However, I find it easier if I know exactly where it is and tie it to the current release. If you

› This PC › DATADRIVE1 (D:) › Arduino1.8.12 ›

Name	Date modified	Type	Size
drivers	2/21/2020 4:48 PM	File folder	
examples	3/11/2020 2:44 PM	File folder	
hardware	3/14/2020 10:41 AM	File folder	
java	2/21/2020 4:49 PM	File folder	
lib	3/11/2020 2:44 PM	File folder	
libraries	3/12/2020 12:52 PM	File folder	
reference	2/21/2020 4:49 PM	File folder	
TempSketch	2/21/2020 5:02 PM	File folder	
tools	2/21/2020 4:49 PM	File folder	
tools-builder	2/21/2020 4:49 PM	File folder	
arduino.exe	2/13/2020 4:32 AM	Application	395 KB
arduino.l4j.ini	2/13/2020 4:32 AM	Configuration sett...	1 KB
arduino_debug.exe	2/13/2020 4:32 AM	Application	393 KB
arduino_debug.l4j.ini	2/13/2020 4:32 AM	Configuration sett...	1 KB
arduino-builder.exe	2/13/2020 4:32 AM	Application	15,971 KB
libusb0.dll	2/13/2020 4:32 AM	Application exten...	43 KB
msvcp100.dll	2/13/2020 4:32 AM	Application exten...	412 KB
msvcr100.dll	2/13/2020 4:32 AM	Application exten...	753 KB
revisions.txt	2/13/2020 4:32 AM	TXT File	93 KB
uninstall.exe	2/21/2020 4:49 PM	Application	404 KB
wrapper-manifest.xml	2/13/2020 4:32 AM	XML Document	1 KB

Figure 1.5. The Arduino1.8.12 directory after unpacking the ZIP file.

examine your Preferences file (e.g., use the IDE's menu sequence of *File → Preferences*), there is a dialog box similar to that shown in Figure 1.6. The first textbox in the Preference dialog box is the directory path where you want your microcontroller programs, called *sketches*, located. As you can see in Figure 1.6, I filled in the path to the *TempSketch* directory I created. Now, by default, any sketch that I may be experimenting with gets saved in my *TempSketch* directory.

Unless you have reason to do otherwise, you might use the same setup parameters I'm using. In some cases, it will make it easier for you to follow some program examples. This is especially true for the *Display line numbers* checkbox. The path name at the bottom of the Preference dialog shown in Figure 1.6 tells you where your Preferences.txt file is stored.

Some people find the default colors used in the text editor difficult to read. If that's the case for you, try changing the colors to better suit your needs. The file you need to change is called theme.txt and it is located in the lib directory (e.g., Arduino1.8.12\lib\theme.txt). Anytime you go messin' around with a program file like this, make a copy of the existing file first (e.g., themeOriginal.txt) and save it in the same directory...just in case. You might want to use a "color picker" (e.g., https://www.w3schools.com/colors/colors_picker.asp) to determine the hex numbers that correspond to your preferred colors. When you're done, save the revised theme.txt file. You need to restart the IDE for the color changes to take effect.

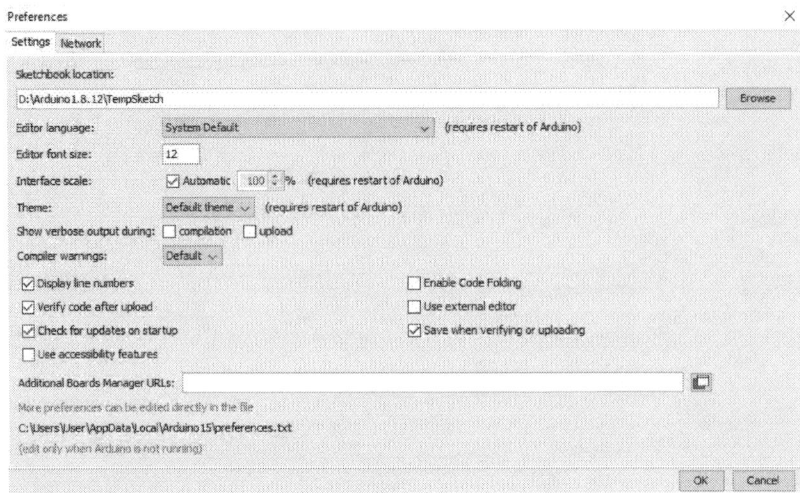

Figure 1.6. The Preferences dialog box.

Loading the IDE

Perhaps the best way to see if the IDE download was installed successfully is to try and run it. Use Windows File Explorer (or whatever your PC uses to launch a program) to move into the *Arduino1.8.12* directory. What you see should look very similar to Figure 1.5. Note that, after the "folder list", the first file listed is the Arduino IDE executable file, arduino.exe. Double-click on that file. You should quickly see the Arduino IDE startup screen, which looks like Figure 1.7. I have labeled some of the more important controls that you will use when writing your programs.

Source Code Window

This is where you write your C language program statements. Because every Arduino IDE program ***must*** have a *setup()* and *loop()* function in it, those are automatically supplied for you whenever you start a new program. If you are working on a program, save your work, and then shut the IDE down, the next time you start the IDE, that last program you worked on is automatically reloaded. Because we just loaded the IDE for the first time, it starts with a skeleton program framework. If I want to save this program, I would click the *File* → *Save* menu sequence and the IDE would write the (skeletal) program to disk.

So, where did it save the file? Because I used the Preferences dialog box to set the Sketch location to the *TempSketch* directory (see Figure 1.6), that's where the new program file is written. But what's the file named?

Look closely at Figure 1.7 near the top of the program title bar or at the program tab above the Source Code Window and you can see *sketch_mar15a*. Because this is the first program (i.e., the "a") I wrote on March 15th, that becomes the primary file name: sketch_mar15a.ino. (It appears that the secondary file name, or extension, "ino" comes from the last three letters in "Ard<u>ino</u>" and is used to associate that file type to the Arduino IDE.) Because every Arduino-based program *must* have the *setup()* and *loop()* functions present somewhere in the source code for the program, the file that holds those two functions will *always* have a secondary file name of "ino".

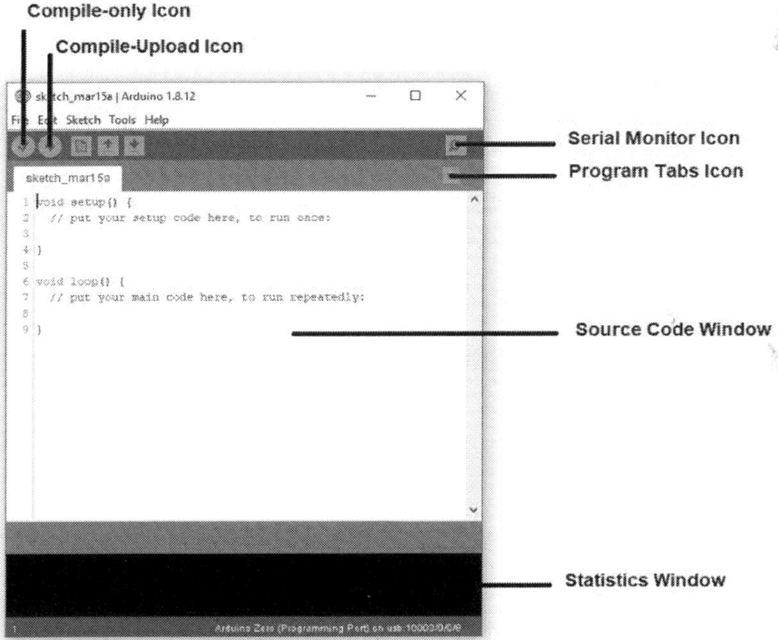

Figure 1.7. The Arduino IDE

Compile-only Icon

Clicking on this icon causes the C compiler (i.e., the Gnu C++ Compiler (GCC)) that is embedded within the IDE to check the program source code for syntax and semantic errors. A *syntax error* occurs when you attempt to use a program statement that does not conform to the rules of the C programming language. A *semantic error* occurs when you attempt to write a program statement that uses the proper syntax, but that statement is used out of context (e.g., incrementing a constant). For example, the rules for the English language say that a sentence needs a noun and a verb. The sentence: "The dog meowed." is syntactically correct, but is semantically incorrect because the context is wrong...dogs don't meow.

The compile-only icon is a quick way for you to check the syntax and semantics of your program. Because you are just starting to learn how to write C programs, you should expect to wade through a bazillion syntax and semantic errors. You should view each of those errors as a learning experience. Some errors may be very difficult to ferret out. (As you become a better programmer, the sophistication of your errors increases.) Often, many will be "Flat Forehead" mistakes—you know, the kind where you slam the heel of your hand into your forehead and ask yourself how you could make such a stupid mistake. All good programmers have flat foreheads and you should expect the same. Whatever you do, don't get discouraged. We've all been there, done that. Welcome to the crowd. Think of it as a rite of passage.

Compile-Upload Icon

The Compile-Upload icon also performs the same syntax and semantic checks as the Compile-only icon. However, if there are no errors, this option takes the compiled code from your PC and, using the USB cable that connects your PC to the microcontroller, moves the compiled code into the microcontroller and starts executing that code.

Most microcontrollers embody a small program, called a *bootloader*, that helps to manage copying the code from your PC into the microcontroller and start the program execution. Some microcontrollers do not have a bootloader and require additional software/hardware to transfer the program. The Arduino Nano Pro Mini, for example, is cheaper than the standard Nano, but lacks a USB connector for program downloads and often has no bootloader. While you can use the Nano Pro Mini, it is less convenient than a regular Nano which does include the USB connector.

Some of the STM32 and ESP32 microcontrollers are sold without a bootloader. Check to see if the bootloader is on the chip before you buy. If you already bought one of these microcontrollers without a bootloader, do an Internet search on “Install bootloader on “ and add the microcontroller type you are using.

Serial Monitor Icon

I'm pretty sure that you will...eventually...write a program that doesn't execute in the manner for which it was designed. That's when you don your detective hat and start looking through your code for the error. (Program errors are called bugs because one of the first computers was brought to its knees when a moth flew inside of it and shorted out its circuitry.) Alas, the Arduino IDE lacks the most important debugging tool available: a symbolic debugger. A symbolic debugger allows you to pause a program in the middle of its execution and examine the values of variables as they exist at that moment. Lacking a symbolic debugger, you are forced to display (i.e., print) whatever data you are interested in via print statements that end up being displayed on the Serial monitor.

When you click on the Serial Monitor icon, the Serial Monitor window opens on your PC monitor, and looks similar to that shown in Figure 1.8. All communication between your program and the Serial Monitor displayed on

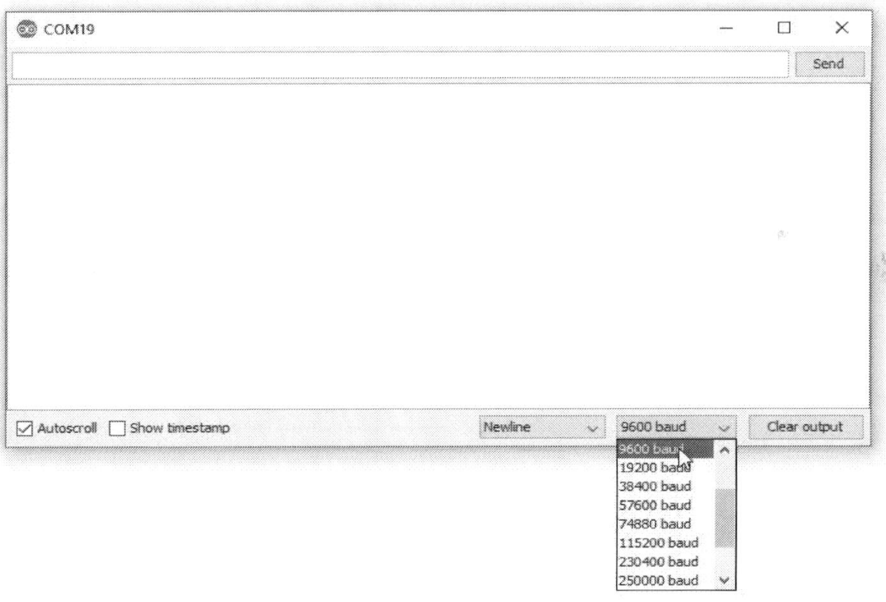

Figure 1.8. The Serial Monitor Window shown on the PC display

your PC is done via the USB cable that connects your PC to the microcontroller. For the two devices to communicate, they need to “talk” at the same rate, known as the baud rate. As you can see in Figure 1.8, the Serial Monitor is capable of using several different baud rates, with 9600 being the default.

Because there is some significant amount of program memory consumed when the Serial Monitor is in use, your programs do not automatically include the code necessary to use it. The statement to activate the Serial Monitor is usually placed in the (required) *setup()* function like this:

```
void setup() {
   Serial.begin(9600);   // Make Serial Monitor object
}
```

Essentially, you could verbalize the single *setup()* statement as: “Create a Serial Monitor object named *Serial* in my program, and initialize it using the *begin()* method so it can 'talk' to the PC at 9600 baud.” Because your program has “begun” the dialog by setting the “talking rate” at 9600 baud and you selected the 9600 baud option on your PC's Serial Monitor window, you have an effective communications link between your microcontroller program and your PC's Serial Monitor window. If the two baud rates don't match, either you will see nothing displayed in the PC's Serial Monitor window or the output will look like a blend of Mandarin and Swahili. We have more to say about the Serial Monitor later in this chapter.

Program Tabs Icon

At the outset, we will be writing fairly short programs that are often easily viewed without scrolling the Source Code Window. However, as program size and complexity increases, scrolling the code becomes more time consuming. This past weekend I reviewed an Arduino program that had 16,000 lines of code.
Scrolling that code from top to bottom was a monumental waste of time.

As your program complexity increases, you will find it beneficial to break the program down into logical, or functional areas. For example, if your program has lots of menu choices, one function code area might be called MenuingSystem. You might have another area named EEPROMManagement, and yet another called DisplayManagement. Rather than glom all of the functional areas into a 16,000 line mess, place each functional area on its own program tab.

Figure 1.9 shows what happens when you click on the Program Tab icon. A small dialog box opens up and you want to select New Tab from the list

of options. Also note the "Ctrl+Shift+N" (command line) notation at the end of the option choice. This is a common notation used with many of the options presented in the IDE. Obviously, if you click on the New Tab option, the IDE creates a new tab. However, you can also press the Ctrl (just below the Shift key on most keyboards), plus the Shift key, and the N key at the same time and the program will likewise create a new tab. Providing these shortcut key options allow you to make menu choices without having to grab the mouse and click on the option.
Once you click the New Tab option, the display changes to that seen in Figure 1.10. Note that, just below the Source Code Window, the IDE is asking you to provide the name by which you want to refer to this program tab. As you can see in Figure 1.10, I typed in "DisplayManagement.cpp". cpp?

Why does the secondary file name (i.e., file extension) end with *cpp*? The reason is because I want the compiler to treat this file as though it is a C++ (i.e., C-Plus-Plus (cpp)) file. It's absolutely fine if the file contains only "pure" C code in it. I just want you to start developing the habit of thinking that the IDE can also handle C++ code as well as straight C code. As a general rule, I only use two secondary file types for New Tabs in my programs: 1) .cpp for code files, and 2) *.h* for header files. (We'll cover header files later on in the book.)

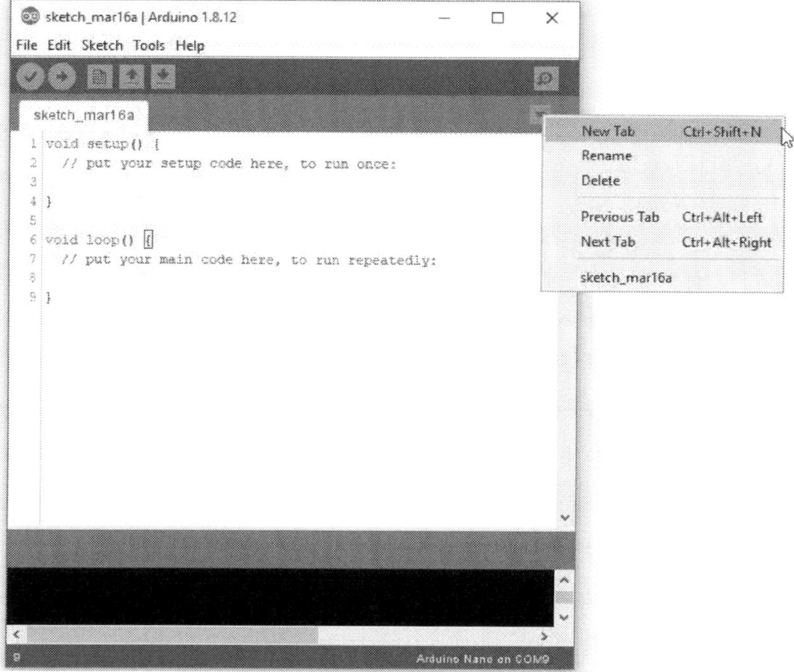

Figure 1.9. Adding a new program tab

Now that I've given my new tab a proper name, I can click on the OK button and make that tab part of my current program. Your display now looks like Figure 1.11. Note how the new *tab name* is now displayed immediately above the Source Code Window with the cursor positioned so I can start writing code for the new file. Anything I write in this new file is saved to disk using the file name DisplayManagement.cpp.

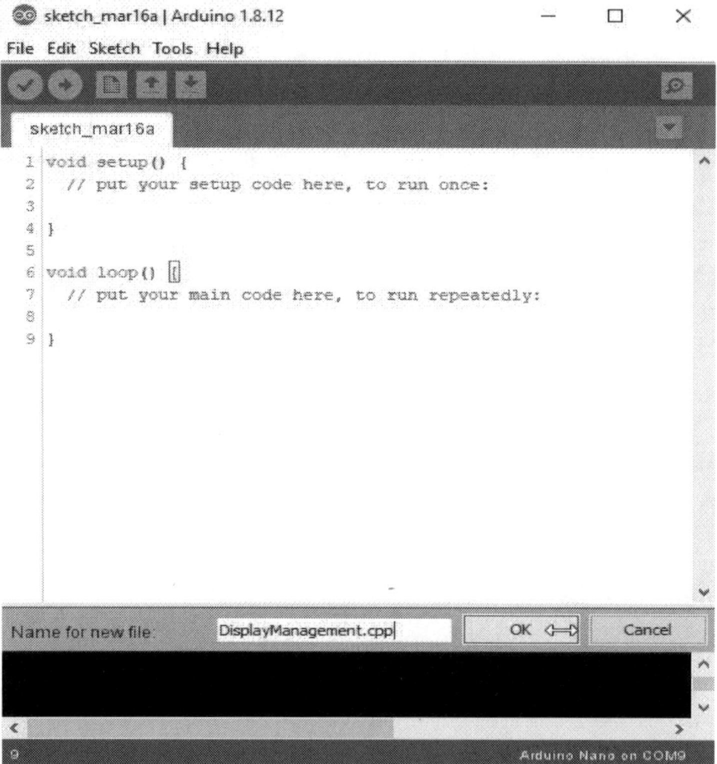

Figure 1.10. Giving a new program tab a name

Saved? Saved where?

It is important to note that all Arduino IDE projects use this *IDE Directory Naming Rule*:

> *The directory name for any programming project MUST match the primary ino filename that contains the setup() and loop() functions*

It is saved in my *sketch_Mar16a* directory in my *TempSketch* folder. If I look on my D drive, I now see:

```
Arduino1.8.12\TempSketch\sketch_Mar16a\DisplayManagement.cpp
                                       sketch_Mar16a.ino
```

Note how the project directory and project file names (the shaded parts above) are the same.

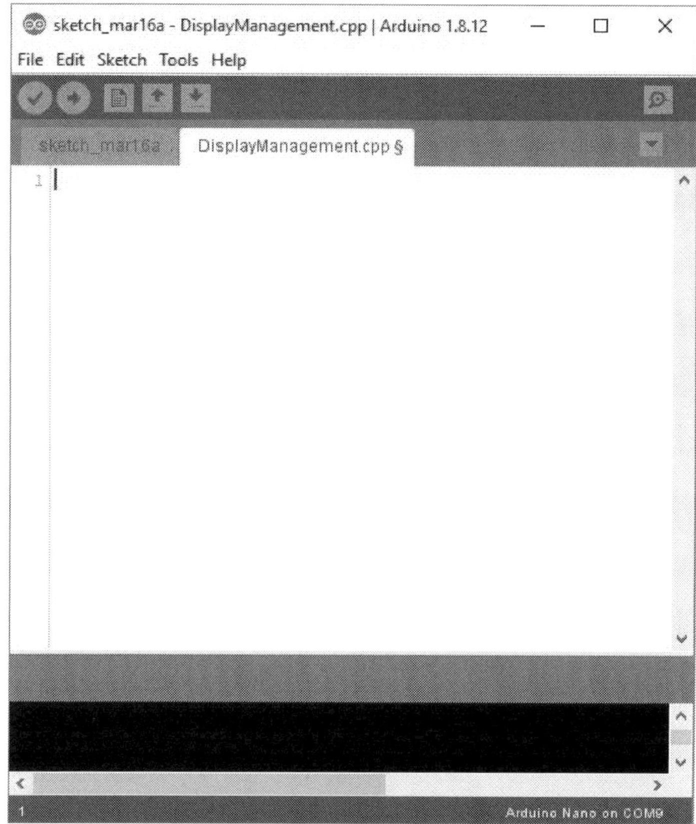

Figure 1.11. The new program tab

That's the rule!

If you have a multi-tab project as shown in Figure 1.11, the left-most tab always identifies the file that holds the *setup()* and *loop()* functions. In addition, that file name must end with a secondary file name of ".ino". If you add new .cpp source code file or .h header file to the project, they will appear in alphabetical order to the right of the project's .ino file. ("Header files" are explained in chapters 4 and 13 that discusses libraries in more detail.)

Statistics Window

A common program to run the first time is the Blink program. It is used because it gives you visual feedback that the program compiled, uploaded, and executed successfully. Let's assume you are using an Arduino Nano board and have the USB cable connected from your PC to the Nano. To load the example Blink program, use the File → Examples → 01.Basics → Blink menu sequence, as shown in Figure 1.12. After clicking on the Blink program option, the IDE loads the Blink program. Your IDE should look similar to Figure 1.13. Note that the first program tab above the Source Code Window has the program name "Blink". You can also see that it contains the *setup()* and *loop()* functions, so the full source code file name must be Blink.ino. Now everything is ready to compile and upload the program to the Arduino Nano board...almost.

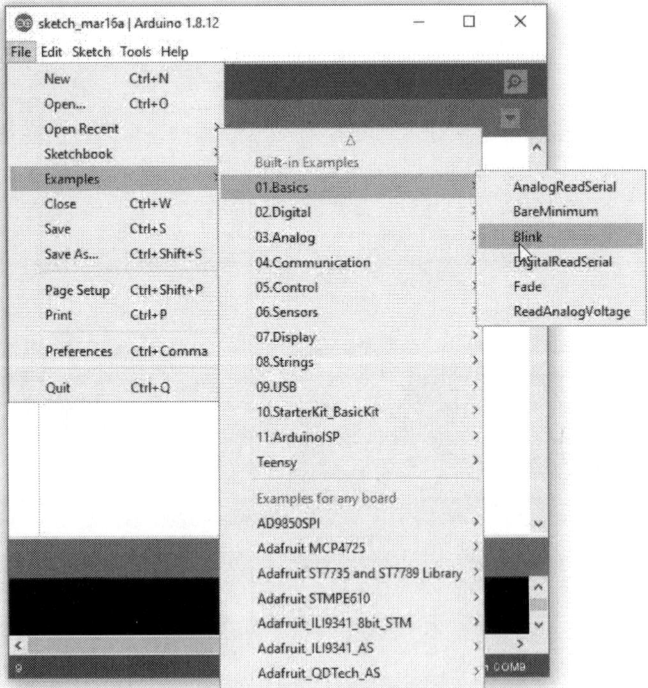

Figure 1.12. Selecting the Blink program example

As you know, the USB cable that connects your PC to the microcontroller provides the communications link for the IDE. All that is fine and good, but perhaps we need to tell the host operating system (e.g., Windows) what port number we will use for this COM (COMmunications) link. To select the port, use the Tools → Port menu selection as shown in Figure 1.14. As you can see, Windows would like us to use the highlighted port, (e.g., COM9 in Figure 1.14), in this instance. Click on the highlighted port and we're ready to go. (If not highlighted, select the last one in the list.) Well, not quite.

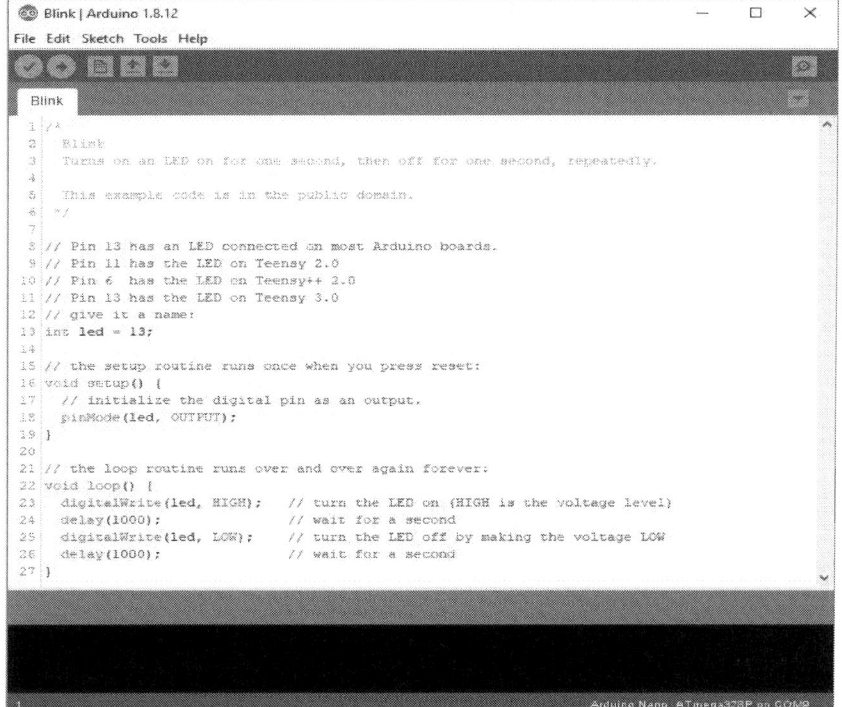

Figure 1.13. The Blink program in the Source Code Window

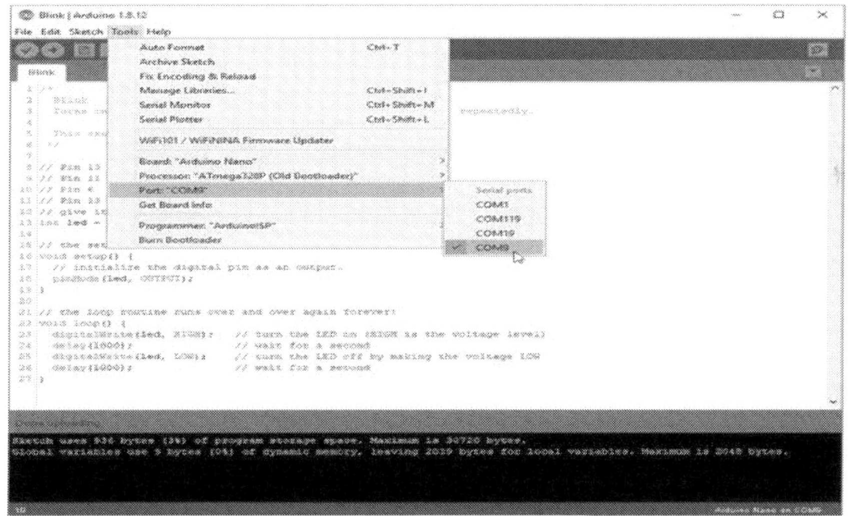

Figure 1.14. Selecting the communications port

So, are we ready to actually compile the Blink program? Yes! Click on the Compile-Upload Icon (see Figure 1.7). You can see a green progress bar near the lower right corner and in a few moments you will see a message above the Statistics Window saying “Done Uploading”, as seen in Figure 1.16.

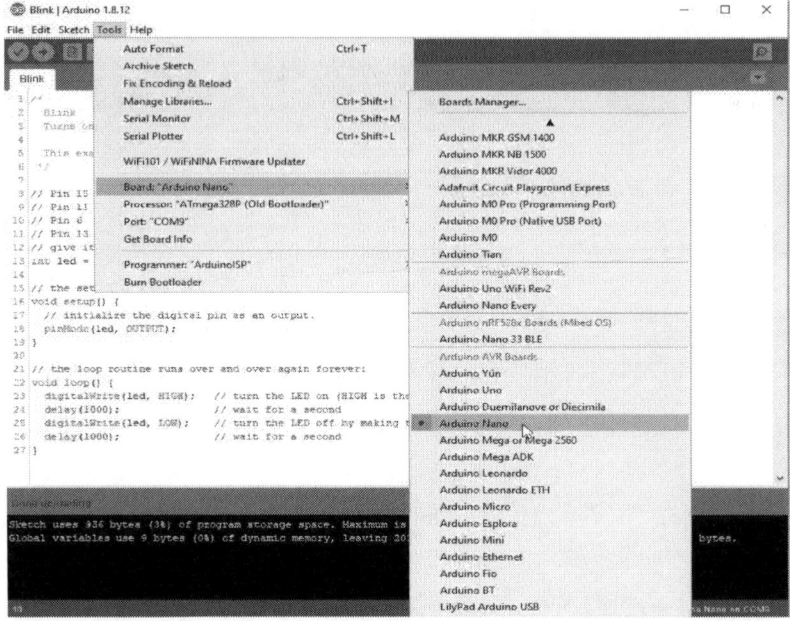

Figure 1.15. Selecting the target microcontroller board

So, are we ready to actually compile the Blink program? Yes! Click on the Compile-Upload Icon (see Figure 1.7). You can see a green progress bar near the lower right corner and in a few moments you will see a message above the Statistics Window saying “Done Uploading”, as seen in Figure 1.16.

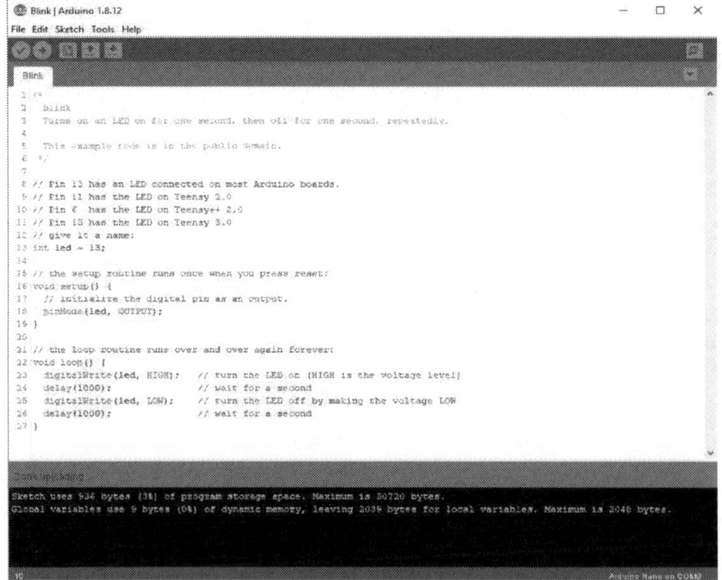

Figure 1.16. The IDE after compiling the Blink program

Congratulations...you just compiled your first Arduino program!

If you look closely at Figure 1.16, you can see that the Blink program used 936 bytes of flash memory and 9 bytes of SRAM. If you look at your Nano, its onboard LED should be blinking at the rate of one blink per second.

You might be saying: "Wait a minute! Table 1.1 says the Nano has 32K of flash memory, which I know is actually 32767 bytes of flash memory. However, the stats say I only have 30720 bytes. Where's the rest?" Milton Friedman taught me a long time ago that there's no such thing as a free lunch. In this case, part of your lunch was eaten by the bootloader that moved all those program bytes from your PC into the proper places in the Nano's memory. There are ways to program the Nano without a bootloader, but that is considerably less convenient.

Actually, some of you are sitting there looking at the green bar waiting for your compiler to finish uploading your program to the Nano. In some cases, you can wait until the cows come home and you'll still be waiting there. What's wrong?

Preparing for Clone Microcontrollers

The Arduino family of microcontrollers are Open Source, which means anyone who wants to can take an Atmel ATmega328 chip and make their own board. Often, these clones use cheaper parts than the original board did. The original interface chip used the *FTDI drivers* and a more expensive chip. The clones substituted a less expensive chip that uses the CH340 device driver. Fortunately, this driver can be downloaded without charge from:

https://github.com/HobbyComponents/CH340-Drivers

Run the install package to install the CH340 device driver. You should reboot your system to make sure your OS knows about the new device driver. In some cases, clone manufacturers not only switched the device driver on you, they also installed an older bootloader in the chip. Consider Figure 1.17. If you have installed the new device driver and restarted the IDE and it still doesn't upload properly, try using the Tools → Processor → Atmega328P (Old Bootloader) option and then click the compile/upload icon again. If that doesn't work, consider learning Python.

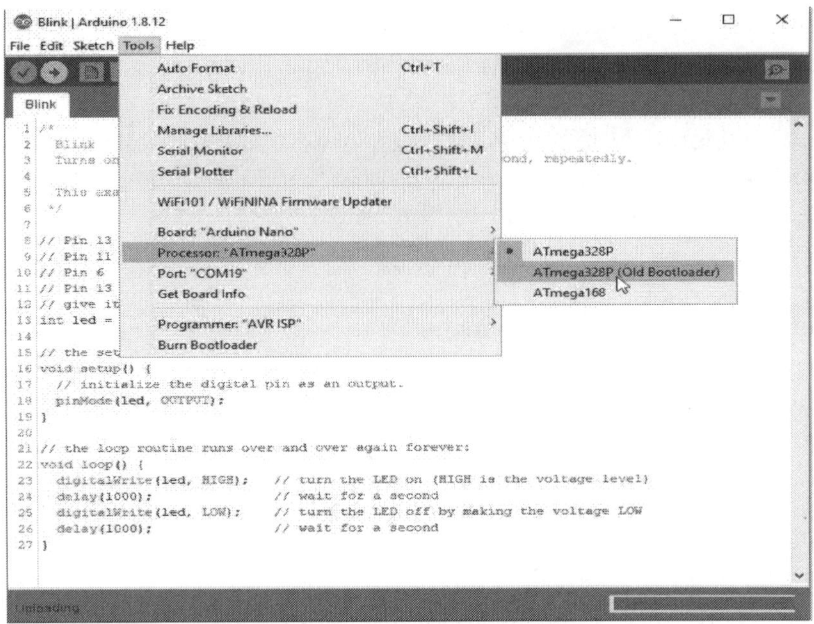

Figure 1.17. Using an old bootloader

All kidding aside, 99.9% of you should be sitting there looking at the Nano which is blinking at you at a one-second rate. As uninteresting at this may seem, it does confirm that you downloaded, installed, and configured the Arduino IDE successfully. That's a good thing. But...what if you want to use a non-Arduino microcontroller?

Installing Software "Patches"

Way back when, the Arduino IDE was designed for the Arduino family of microcontrollers; mainly the Uno and Nano, but supported the other Atmel microcontrollers (e.g., the ATMega2560, Due) as they appeared. What probably wasn't anticipated was the huge popularity of the Arduino IDE environment. In an effort to woo consumers away from the Atmel family of microcontrollers, competing companies developed software "patches" that would allow the user to write programs for their microcontrollers using the Arduino IDE.

Why is a patch needed? The primary reason is because the non-Atmel microcontrollers have vastly different binary instructions to cause something to happen in the microcontroller. All of the microcontrollers have low-level *assembler* instructions like LDI,A (Load Immediate into register A) and LDI,B and ADD,A+B. The problem is that binary numbers for each instruction is different for each microcontroller. So while 0x11010111 (0x indicates hexadecimal, or base 16, notation) might be the binary instruction for LDI,A on the STM32, it may be 0b00110010 for the ESP32, and even something else for the Teensy.

Buried deep within the IDE is a code generator, which is responsible for generating the binary instructions used by each program. The instruction set used by that code generator is going to be very different for each of the various microcontrollers. The purpose of each software "patch" is to install that instruction set that is designed to work with a specific microcontroller. It is these patches that allows the IDE to perform properly across all microcontrollers. Designing, writing, testing, and debugging all of the code necessary to make the IDE work for their microcontroller is not a trivial task. Still, it is in their interest to do so to broaden their market. What is even more amazing to me is that one individual (Roger Clark) would take on this task alone for a specific microcontroller (i.e., the STM32). Still, that's in fact what has happened and we programmers are the winners because of it.

Fortunately, these software patches are free and very easy to install. This section details how to install the software patches for each microcontroller.

STM32 Patch

Actually, you have a choice of software patches for the STM32 microcontrollers. Roger Clark has one that can be downloaded from:

https://github.com/rogerclarkmelbourne/Arduino_STM32/wiki/Installation

This is the first patch I installed and it works great. You should take some time and read the notes Roger has posted there and then follow the link to the download.

You can also choose:

https://github.com/stm32duino/Arduino_Core_STM32

which appears to be updated more regularly and also works well. The link also provides a list of the STM32 boards that it supports. When you are asked to save a patch file, save them in the *Arduino1.8.12\hardware* directory.

If I were doing commercial software development, I'm mindful that relying on a single source for factors of production is usually not a good idea and it appears that this latter source is more of a team effort. However, that in no way belittles the work done by Roger. Pick one and try it out. If you find something you don't like, try the other and see if that clears away your objection.

ESP32 Patch

The company that makes the ESP32 family also has created the software patch for their microcontrollers. You can download the patch at:

https://github.com/espressif/arduino-esp32

and save the generated files to the *hardware* directory. The process is the same for all of the microcontrollers.

Teensy 4.0-4.1 Patch

PJRC is the company that created the Teensy and it is a very nice microcontroller with the fastest clock and the deepest resource pool. It can be downloaded from:

https://www.pjrc.com/teensy/td_download.html

and also save its files to the hardware directory.

When you have finished installing all of the patches, your hardware directory should look like Figure 1.18. Notice that this is what is seen on the path: *Arduino1.8.12\hardware*

› This PC › DATADRIVE1 (D:) › Arduino1.8.12 › hardware ›

Name	Date modified	Type	Size
arduino	2/21/2020 4:48 PM	File folder	
Arduino_STM32	3/12/2020 10:05 AM	File folder	
espressif	3/14/2020 10:42 AM	File folder	
teensy	3/11/2020 2:44 PM	File folder	
tools	3/11/2020 2:44 PM	File folder	
package_index_bundled.json	2/13/2020 4:32 AM	JSON File	10 KB
platform.keys.rewrite.txt	2/13/2020 4:32 AM	TXT File	3 KB

Figure 1.18. The hardware directory

As you can see, there are directories for all four processor families: Arduino, STM32, ESP32, and Teensy. If you follow the Arduino_STM32 directory structure, you will see something similar to Figure 1.19:

› This PC › DATADRIVE1 (D:) › Arduino1.8.12 › hardware › Arduino_STM32 › STM32F1 ›

Name	Date modified	Type	Size
cores	3/12/2020 10:05 AM	File folder	
libraries	3/12/2020 10:05 AM	File folder	
system	3/12/2020 10:05 AM	File folder	
variants	3/12/2020 10:05 AM	File folder	
boards.txt	3/12/2020 10:05 AM	TXT File	56 KB
platform.txt	3/12/2020 10:05 AM	TXT File	10 KB

Figure 1.19. The Arduino_STM32\STM32F1 directory

You will notice that the *Arduino_STM32* directory has a subdirectory named *STM32F1*. There is also one named *STM32F4* that holds the patch for the F4 family of microcontrollers.

If you follow the Espressif directory, you eventually see the files presented in Figure 1.20.

› This PC › DATADRIVE1 (D:) › Arduino1.8.10 › hardware › espressif › esp32 ›

Name	Date modified	Type	Size
.github	11/6/2019 10:39 AM	File folder	
cores	11/6/2019 10:39 AM	File folder	
docs	11/6/2019 10:39 AM	File folder	
libraries	12/24/2019 12:56 PM	File folder	
package	11/6/2019 10:39 AM	File folder	
tools	11/6/2019 10:39 AM	File folder	
variants	11/6/2019 10:39 AM	File folder	
.gitignore	4/9/2019 11:17 AM	GITIGNORE File	1 KB
.gitmodules	4/9/2019 11:17 AM	GITMODULES File	1 KB
.travis.yml	4/9/2019 11:17 AM	YML File	2 KB
appveyor.yml	4/9/2019 11:17 AM	YML File	1 KB
boards.txt	4/9/2019 11:17 AM	TXT File	127 KB
CMakeLists.txt	4/9/2019 11:17 AM	TXT File	8 KB
component.mk	4/9/2019 11:17 AM	Makefile	2 KB
Kconfig.projbuild	4/9/2019 11:17 AM	PROJBUILD File	8 KB
Makefile.projbuild	4/9/2019 11:17 AM	PROJBUILD File	1 KB
package.json	4/9/2019 11:17 AM	JSON File	1 KB
platform.txt	4/9/2019 11:17 AM	TXT File	11 KB
programmers.txt	4/9/2019 11:17 AM	TXT File	0 KB
README.md	4/9/2019 11:17 AM	MD File	4 KB

Figure 1.20. The ESP32 directory

You now have the necessary patches installed for the microcontrollers we use in this book. Now let's take a quick look at the pinouts for the four microcontrollers.

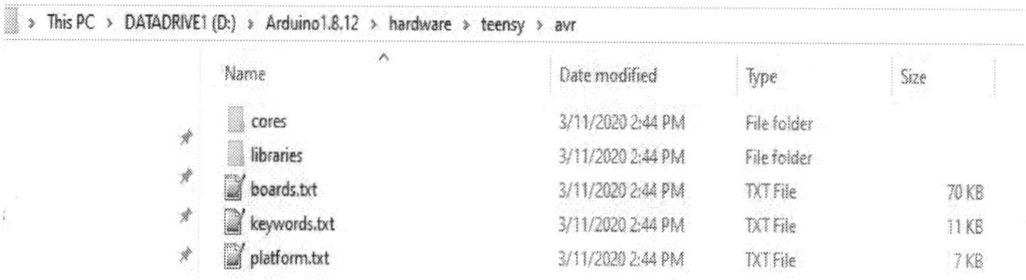

> This PC > DATADRIVE1 (D:) > Arduino1.8.12 > hardware > teensy > avr

Name	Date modified	Type	Size
cores	3/11/2020 2:44 PM	File folder	
libraries	3/11/2020 2:44 PM	File folder	
boards.txt	3/11/2020 2:44 PM	TXT File	70 KB
keywords.txt	3/11/2020 2:44 PM	TXT File	11 KB
platform.txt	3/11/2020 2:44 PM	TXT File	7 KB

Figure 1.21. The Teensy directory

Microcontroller Pinout Images

Each of the four microcontrollers we use in this book has dozens of pinout images online that you can view. After you select a microcontroller to start out your learning experience, I suggest you print out one of these images in full color and use it as a reference when you start programming the I/O pins.

Arduino Nano Pinout

The Arduino Nano is a good microcontroller to start out with because it has a very robust support network, including a huge number of pre-written programs that you can study. Also, you can buy Nanos online for under $5 each. I tend to buy them in lots of 5, but that depends on if you're just learning right now or you plan to build projects where they have a permanent home.

Figure 1.22 shows a pinout for the Arduino Nano. First, the outer-most numbers are physical pin reference numbers for use in your program. For example, pin 2 can be used in your program as a general purpose I/O pin, but it is also one of the two external interrupt pins (i.e., INT0) available on the Nano. (Pin 3 is the second external interrupt pin, INT1.) Pins 0 (RXD) and 1 (TXD) are used to read and write data to the USB serial port (*Serial*).

If you look at the Blink code in Figure 1.16, line 8 in that program says that pin 13 is used to reference the onboard LED. Looking in Figure 1.21, you can see that pin 13 (lower-right corner in the figure) has a box with some “light arrows” in it to show that it is the onboard LED control pin. Line 13 in the Blink program assigns pin 13 to a variable named *led.* Why? Well, if you didn't know anything about the Arduino Nano, which statement makes more sense to you:

```
digitalWrite(13, 1);
```

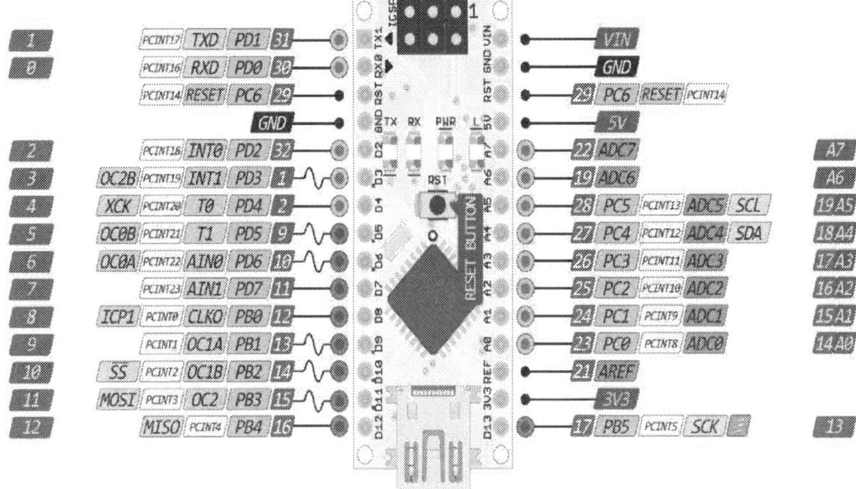

Figure 1.22. The Arduino Nano pinout

or

```
digitalWrite(led, HIGH);
```

The second form is easier to read and understand. It also points out how descriptive variable names and symbolic constants can make it easier to read the code in a program. More on that in Chapter 2 and Chapter 10.

I want you to go to the Source Code Window and place your cursor at the end of line 25 in Figure 1.16, just after the word LOW. Now press the Enter key, which opens up a new line. Now type:

```
Serial.println("The LED is off.");
```

and press the Enter key. Now go to the very end of line 23 (after "level)") and type in:

```
Serial.println("The LED is on.");
```

and press the Enter key. Finally, move to the end of line 18, just after the semicolon and press Enter and on the new line type in:

```
Serial.begin(9600);
```

Your revised Blink program should look like that shown in Listing 1.1.

The shaded lines are the program *Listing 1.1. Modified Blink program*

```
int led = 13;

void setup() {
  // initialize the digital pin as an output.
  pinMode(led, OUTPUT);
  Serial.begin(9600);
```

```
}

// the loop routine runs over and over again forever:
void loop() {
  digitalWrite(led, HIGH);// turn LED on (HIGH is the
                          // voltage level)
  Serial.println("The LED is on");
  delay(1000);              // wait for a second
  digitalWrite(led, LOW); // turn LED off by making
                  // the voltage LOW
  Serial.println("The LED is off");
  delay(1000);              // wait for a second
}
```

statements you just added. Now click on the Compile-Upload Icon. In a few seconds, you should see the LED blinking at a 1 second pace. Now click on the Serial Monitor icon. What do you see? Nope, not going to tell you. Type the code in and test it yourself.

The first statement you added initializes the *Serial* object to communicate with the PC at 9600 baud. Looking at Figure 1.21, that call to the *Serial* object's *begin()* method initializes the communications link using pins 0 (RXD) and 1 (TXD). This means that the *println()* method buried in the *Serial* object transmits your messages to the PC using the Nano pin1 at a speed of 9600 baud. What happens if you change the *Serial.println()* method calls to *Serial.print()* method calls (notice no “ln” before the opening parenthesis)? Nope, not going to tell you...again.

STM32, ESP32, and Teensy 4.0 Pinouts

If you decided you wanted to work with one of these three microcontrollers instead of the Nano, no problem. For something as simple as the Blink program, the code should compile, upload, and run with minor changes. Let's look at the pinouts for these three microcontrollers.

First, note that the STM32 in Figure 1.23 has PC_13 tied to the onboard LED. SO, instead of writing:

```
int led = 13;
```

you need to write:

```
int led = PC_13;
```

Everything else in the Blink program stays the same.

By the way, if you try to save the modified Blink program, you will have to give it a new program name. The reason is because all of the Example programs provided by the IDE are read-only. That is, you cannot make permanent changes to them. If you try to save it, the IDE will ask you for a new program name (e.g., ModifiedBlink) and it will save it to your sketch directory.

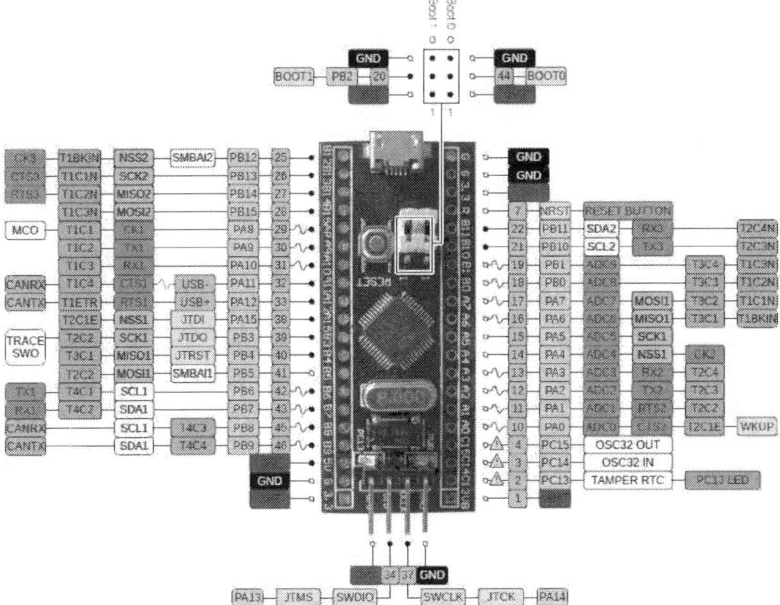

Figure 1.23. The STM32F103 pinout

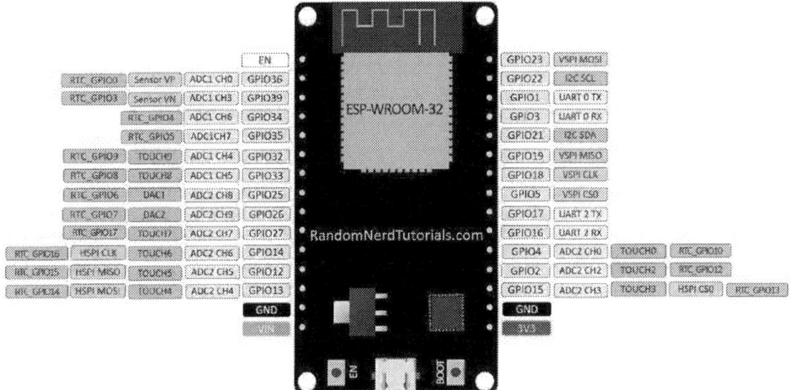

Figure 1.24. The ESP32 pinout

One important difference about these three microcontrollers is they use 3.3V on the I/O pins instead of the 5V the Nano uses. Placing 5V on the pins of these devices very likely will damage the microcontroller. You may need to use a logic level shifter if you're using both 5V and 3.3V in the system. Don't expect a pin on any microcontroller to handle much

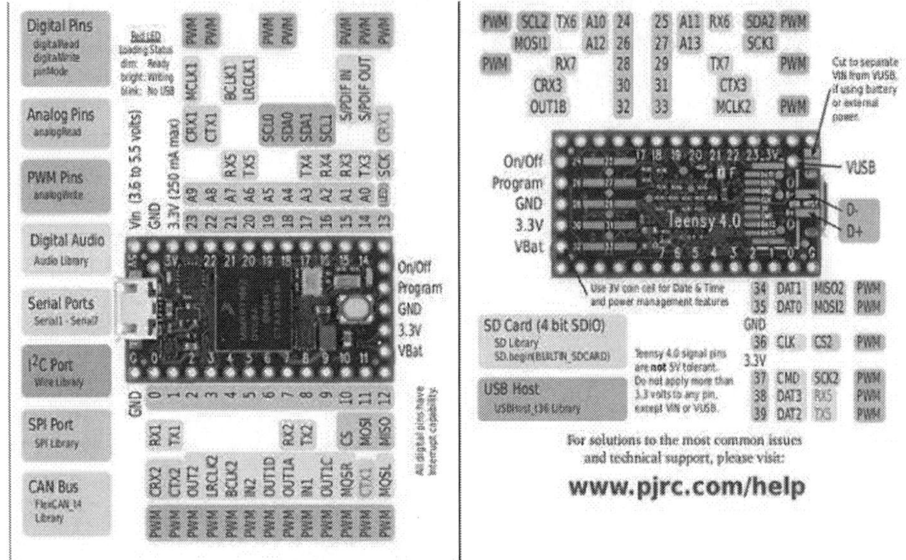

Figure 1.25. The Teensy 4.0 pinout

more than 20mA of current (they are rated above that, but best not to push it). Also, on the Teensy 4.0 on the bottom of the board there is a trace that needs to be cut if you're going to use both external and USB power to the chip at the same time. (The standard USB is 5V.) You get an image card that looks similar to Figure 1.25 when you buy the Teensy and the trace is clearly marked on the card. In the upper-right corner of Figure 1.25 you can see the arrow pointing to the trace. If you're just powering the Teensy from the USB connection, you don't need to cut the trace.

As mentioned earlier, the Blink program may or may not run properly on all of these microcontrollers without some modifications. For example, if you look at the Teensy 4.0, you can see that its pin 13 is connected to the onboard LED so it can run unchanged. Just remember to change the Tools → Board to the Teensy 4.0 and select the proper port. (You need to do this each time you change microcontrollers.)

ESP32

If you look at Figure 1.24, there is no clearly-defined LED in the pin map. Most vendors of the ESP32 send you a pin map when you buy the microcontroller board and it may tell you which pin connects to the onboard LED. (Some vendors don't send pin maps.) Most of the ESP32 microcontroller boards use pin 2 for the LED.

When I started formulating this book, I had used the ESP32 in several projects and found its depth of memory resources, clock speed, and price very compelling. Now...not so much. When I started using it with external sensors and other devices, it proved to be almost impossible to provide a single programming solution for all ESP32 boards. For example, some pins are General Purpose Input (GPI) only type of pins (e.g., GPI34, GPI35, GPI36, and GPI39) while others are General Purpose Input/Output (GPIO) pins (GPIO32 and GPIO33) are connected to the crystal and can only be used for general I/O if you modify the board itself. There are also pins (GPIO0, GPIO2, GPIO5, GPIO12, and GPIO15) that are "strapping pins" that do different things depending upon whether they are pulled high or low. Because of these differences, some board manufacturers simply do not make some of the "weird" pins available (e.g., a 30-pin board) while others assume you are an expert and won't do anything stupid (e.g., a 38-pin board) and there are some who take the middle ground (e.g., a 36-pin board). All these permutations make me very nervous as an author because the chance of failure for anything placed here becomes greater. Fostering failure doesn't seem to be a laud-worthy goal.

Programs that use General Purpose I/O pins will likely run fine as long as you stay away from the "weird" pins. See Table 1.2 for the ESP32 pin uses. If you want to experiment with the ESP32, that's great, but do some research for your project up front. I have added a couple of resources at the end of this chapter to help you in that research effort.

Of the microcontrollers we use in this book, the ESP32 is the least standardized. Some ESP32 boards have 30 pins, some 36, and some 38. Also, not all of the pins can be used for both input and output signals (pins 34, 35, 36, and 39 are input only). Some pins output Pulse-Width Modulation (PWM) signals on a reboot, which may be good or bad for a given situation. On the plus side, it has a lot of memory resources, a pretty fast clock, plus WiFi and Bluetooth capabilities at a competitive price. For the most part, your intended use dictates which microcontroller is best for you.

Unlike the other microcontrollers, the ESP32 boards bring out pins that have very specific functions or cannot be used for other common I/O functions. Some of the unusual aspects of the ESP32 are summarized in Table 1.2. For example, pins 34, 35, 36 and 39 can only function as input pins. General Purpose Input/Output (GPIO) pins 0, 5, 14, and 15 output a PWM signal when a boot is performed. Figure 1.13 shows the pin outs for the ESP32 that we used during development, which is the HiLetgo ESP-

WROOM32. If you looked closely at Figure 1.24 (and you did, didn't you?), you'll notice that there are 19 pins on each side of the board; 38

Table 1.2. General Purpose Input Output (GPIO) Pins for ESP32

GPIO Pin	Input	Output	Description
0	pulled up	OK	outputs PWM signal at boot
1	TX pin	OK	debug output at boot
2	OK	OK	connected to on-board LED
3	OK	RX pin	HIGH at boot
4	OK	OK	
5	OK	OK	outputs PWM signal at boot
6 thru 11	x	x	connected to the integrated SPI flash
12	OK	OK	boot fail if pulled high
13	OK	OK	
14	OK	OK	outputs PWM signal at boot
15	OK	OK	outputs PWM signal at boot
16 thru 33	OK	OK	
34	OK		input only
35	OK		input only
36	OK		input only
39	OK		input only

total. If you read Table 1.2 closely, you noticed that pin 39 can be used as a general I/O pin. Wait a minute...how can a board with 38 pins use pin 39?

It can't.

Actually, most ESP32 boards use the ESP32-D0WDQ6 chip, which has 48 pins, but not all of those pins are brought out on the board. Another popular board is the ESP32 Development board, but it only provides access to 30 pins. While the ESP-WROOM-32 can be purchased for around $10, the ESP32 Development board is about half that price. Originally, we thought the additional cost of the ESPWROOM-32 was worth the added expense. Now we're not so sure, because most of those additional 8 pins are dedicated and cannot be used in a general sense. For that reason, we're now concentrating on the less expensive NodeMCU version of the ESP32.

I did a flat forehead mistake in that I used pins 3-5 while writing a menu demo program. I knew something was wrong because each time the IDE tried to run the program, the Serial monitor would show a reboot and a "Guru" message with a bunch of register information. Fascinated by the Guru messages, it took me way too long to remember that I should not be using those pins for general I/O use. Now I think that maybe the 30-pin versions may not be too bad. In any case, pay attention to Table 1.2 when you are using an ESP32 board.

I couldn't decide on the best way to refer to the ESP32 pins. The reason for the indecision results from several factors. First, there are a number of boards that use the same basic ESP32 chip, but the boards vary on the pins that are brought out for use on the board. As mentioned earlier, some boards in the ESP32 family have 30 pins, some 36, and some 38. Further, the silk screen on the boards also vary. Some use plain numbers (13), other prefix the pin number with a letter (D13).

However, *all* of the boards have an image file that uses the GPIOXX format to identify the pins. For example, in Figure 1.24, the second pin down from the upper left (physical pin 2) is reference as GPIO36 (i.e., General Input/Output Pin 36). This means in your code you could say:

```
#define SWITCHPIN    36
```

which creates a symbolic constant that ties your switch to physical pin 2, but is used in your code as SWITCHPIN, which is tied to I/O port 36. Therefore, to figure out which I/O pin your code should reference, use Figure 1.24 and simply strip away the "GPIO" which leaves the I/O pin number. That I/O pin number becomes your reference for your use of that pin in your code.

Unlike the other controllers, Espressif evidently has not required board makers using the ESP32 to use a standard pin configuration. As a result, the ESP32 you buy may not be able to use the pin out numbers shown in Figure 1.24. It also means you must pay attention to the pin assignments that exist for your particular board. The last set of boards we bought (from HiLetgo) includes a sheet with the mapping of each of the pins. Truthfully, the ESP32 boards are harder to tame, but the resource depth and performance are worth the effort it takes to learn how to use it, especially if you require the built-in BlueTooth or WiFi functions.

Odd...

During development of our first ESP32 project, I would always have to press the Reset pin on the ESP32 board immediately after a compile or it would not upload the code. (It timed out after about 10 seconds of trying to upload the compiled code.) Not a big deal, you just had to make sure you hit the Reset button before it timed out. It was just one of those things you learn to live with. I took my code and breadboard over to friend and colleague Al Peter (AC8GY) for some tests using his "big boy" test equipment. I made a small code change, clicked the compile/upload button and was ready to press the reset button, but the code uploaded without pressing reset. Odd, since AL and I have similar machines running Windows 10. I mentioned this on a web group and one of the members said to connect a 10µF electrolytic cap between the EN (reset) pin and ground. I did and, voila, no more pressing reset. I'm not smart enough to know why this works but figure it's something that's different in the two BIOS's. If you're having a similar experience, try the fix and see if it works.

There are dozens of links that tell you how to download and install the patch for the ESP32, but this one:

https://circuitdigest.com/microcontroller-projects/programming-esp32-with-arduino-ide

is easy to understand and follow. It even gives an ESP32 Blink program that you can use to test whether the installation was installed properly. The method used is a little different than you've seen earlier because it used the Board Manager to install the patch. It works fine. If you would rather use Github like we've done before, you can download the patch from:

https://github.com/espressif/arduino-esp32

Either way works fine.

Once you have installed the patch, connect your ESP32 to the USB cable and try to compile/upload the Blink sketch. You may have to hold the reset button the first time. If you've installed the 10µF cap mentioned in the sidebar, you should not have to press the Reset button again during this session. (You will have to press the Reset button the next time you load the IDE.) Select the *ESP32 Dev* module for the board and select the COM port for uploading the code to the ESP32. Now load and compile/upload the Blink program to make sure everything's working properly.

Additional Libraries

Programming libraries are collections of code that are pre-written, tested, and debugged for you. Libraries allow you to stand on the shoulders of others who have gone before you. Libraries make your programming life incredibly easier than it would be without them. If you look back at Figure 1.18, 1.19, and 1.20, notice that all of them have a *libraries* directory. Suppose you discovered a new library for the STM32 microcontroller and you want to use it in a project. You could use the Library Manager that is part of the IDE. Pish posh...that's like going into a gas station and asking for directions.

Most new libraries are available as a compressed-file (e.g., ZIP) download. I copy the new library file directly into the library's directory of the microcontroller for which the library is designed. For example, suppose there is a statistics library for the Teensy named *Microstat*. I would copy Microstat-Master.ZIP into the *Arduino1.8.12\hardware\teensy\arv\libraries* directory and unpack it there. Chances are, the unpacked directory would be named *Microstat_Master* and would likely hold the following files:

```
docs                    // folder with documentation
examples                // examples on how to use the library
utilities               // other odds-and-ends
MicroStat.cpp           // C-Plus-Plus code file
MicroStat.h             // header file
```

Most libraries match the primary file name of the libraries header file (Microstat.h) to the directory name. I've yet to see a library where the source code files are anything but C++ files using the .cpp file extension. (We have more to say about C++ in Chapter 13.) As it appears on your disk drive right after unpacking, the new entry looks like:

```
C:\Arduino1.8.12\hardware\teensy\arv\libraries\Microstat_Master\
                                                                  docs
                                                                  examples
                                                                  Utilities
                                                                  MicroStat.cpp
                                                                  MicroStat.h
```

The IDE isn't going to like this arrangement because the library's directory has "_Master" in it which doesn't match the header file's primary name(Microstat). To correct this, change the library's directory name to *Microstat*:

```
C:\Arduino1.8.12\hardware\teensy\arv\libraries\Microstat\
                                                                  docs
                                                                  examples
```

```
Utilities
 MicroStat.cpp
MicroStat.h
```

The IDE is happy now because the library's directory name and the header file's primary name match. It's very common for new libraries to tack on the "_*Master*" onto the directory name after unpacking. Just make sure you remove it before you try to use the library. Also, the IDE does not know about the new library until after you close the IDE down and reload it.

Features of and Customizing the IDE

Finally, there are a number of features supported by the IDE that are not obvious from what is visible on your display. We've already mentioned the Preferences option (File → Preferences, Figure 1.6) that allows you to change some of the default settings used by the IDE. In this section we show you some other features of the IDE that you may also wish to use or change. I suggest that you load the IDE and a sample program (e.g., File → Examples → 04. Communications → ASCII Table) and try some of the options discussed here.

Statement Block Identification

As you will learn in upcoming chapters, many keywords and programming structures are associated with an opening brace ('{') and a closing brace ('}'). These brace pairs are used to delimit statement blocks in the program. Figure 1.27 shows an example of this using the skeletal

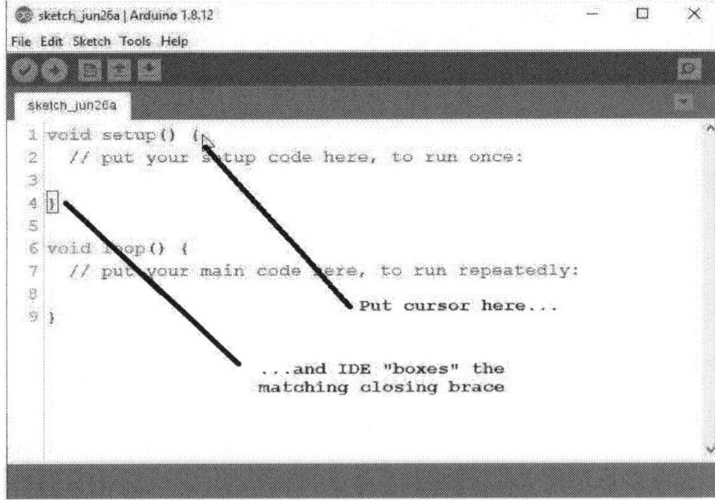

Figure 1.27. Identifying statement blocks.

program that is automatically created for you each time you start a new program.

As you will see in later chapters, the block identification can be used with many C keywords (e.g., *for, while, if, switch*, etc.). Forgetting a closing brace is a common programming mistake made by beginning and seasoned programmers alike. The real problem for the programmer is that the compiler gets so confused that it may issue an error message telling you the error is on line 80, when actually the error is caused by a missing brace on line 50! (The compiler can get *really* confused when you forget to end a statement with a semicolon, too!) Placing the cursor next to opening/closing braces lets you quickly see the statement blocks. Sometimes what you see doesn't match what you intended. Keep this "bracechecking" feature in mind...it can be very helpful when debugging a program.

Auto-Format of Source Code

C is not a "position" language. Unlike some older languages that required certain keywords to be positioned at a certain place in the source code, C is a free form language. By now, you're probably accustomed to seeing the "skeletal" program that the IDE creates for you each time you create a new program. (See Figure 1.25.) C, however, is just as happy if you write that code as:

```
void setup(){} void loop(){}
```

However, the default format is a lot easier to read than the scrambled format above. Using a consistent formatting style for your programs makes it easier for you (and others?) to read your code. For example, suppose you wrote the following code fragment for the *loop()* function:

```
void loop() {
  int i;
  for (i = 0; i < 10; i++) {
    Serial.println(i);
  }
}
```

The compiler compiles the code above just fine (even though it doesn't do much). However, the code is not easy to read, and it would be even more difficult if the code is more complex. The IDE has an auto-format feature that can reformat your code using a style that is used by most C programmers. To activate the source code auto-format feature, place the cursor in the Source Code Window (See Figure 1.7) and simulataneously press the Ctrl and T keys (Ctrl+T). Or you can select the feature from the Tools → Auto-Format menu sequence. Either way, when you're done, the source code will look like:

```
void loop() {
 // put your main code here, to run repeatedly:
    int i;
    for (i = 0; i < 10; i++) {
        Serial.println(i);
    }
}
```

Note how the code is indented one tab stop within the *loop()* function, and the statement controlled by the *for* loop (*Serial.println(i);*) is tabbed in another level within the statement block.

While we're here, I often see students write the *for* loop code as:

```
 for(i=0;i<10;i++){
```

Come on! Why are you squishing everything together? It's not like the "squishy-format" is going to make the code execute faster or save any memory. All it does is make the code harder to read. Put blank spaces around all operators and after semicolons. It makes your code easier to read and that is *always* a good thing.

Changing Tab Stop

The IDE indents statements when the auto format is used according to the number of spaces that are associated with a Tab character ('\t'). For many editors, a tab stop defaults to 8 spaces. For me, that is way too many spaces. Indent your source code a few times within a statement block and pretty soon the text is pushed to the right so far you need to use the scroll bar at the bottom of the IDE to see the end of the line. Not good.

If you're not happy with the number of spaces used by the IDE for a tab stop, change it! Many of the defaults for the IDE are stored in the *preferences.txt* file that was created when you installed the IDE. On my Windows system, the path to my *preferences.txt* file is:

C:\Users\User\AppData\Local\Arduino15

(Your *preferences.txt* might be located on a different path. If so, use your directory search utility to locate the file.) The very first thing you should do when you find it is to make a copy of the file and name it *preferencesOriginal.txt*. That way, you can always "back up" to the default set of preferences. Once the backup file is created, open the original *preferences.txt* file and look for the following line:

```
editor.tabs.size=2
```

and change it to whatever you wish to use as the number of spaces used for a tab stop. I use 2 spaces because I find that it lets me clearly see the indentation, but the indent is small enough it doesn't push the source code too quickly past the right margin.

While you have the *preferencesOriginal.txt* open, look at some of the other defaults (e.g., *editor.caret.blink*) stored in the file that you'd like to change. It doesn't hurt to experiment because your backup file always can be used to restore the default.

When you are finished making the changes, save the *preferences.txt* file. You must now close the IDE and reload it for the changes to take effect.

Modifying the Skeleton Sketch

The IDE has a skeleton program, or sketch, that serves as a starting point when you click on the File → New menu option. This skeletal program was shown in Figure 1.7. However, many of the programs in this book are geared towards teaching you concepts by showing you what's going on using the Serial monitor. This means almost every sketch in this book instantiates (or defines) the Serial object in *setup()* so you can use it to print variable values out while the program executes. This printing of the data is your major debugging tool, too.

Therefore, it would be nice if every program started out with the skeletal program shown in Listing 1.1.

Listing 1.1. A new skeletal sketch.

```
#define DEBUG
void setup() {
#ifdef DEBUG
  Serial.begin(9600);
```

```
    while  (!Serial)              //  Waste  time  until  Serial  is
instantiated
      ;
#endif
}
void loop() {
}
```

The first line, *#define DEBUG* is a preprocessor directive that defines a symbolic constant named *DEBUG*. The details of the compiler's preprocessor is explained in detail in Chapter 10. For now, just assume it means that the compiler knows what *DEBUG* is. The first line in *setup()* is another preprocessor directive (*#ifdef DEBUG*) that says: “Mister Compiler: If *DEBUG* has been defined at this point in the program, add all of the source code lines from this point up to the *#endif* preprocessor directive into the program.” What this does is define the Serial object in your program so you can use it for debugging.

If you comment out the line using the single-line comment pair (//):

```
//#define DEBUG
```

then *DEBUG* is no longer defined in the program. (Comment characters are explained below.) Because the compiler no longer knows what *DEBUG* is, the program lines between the two preprocessor directives in *setup()* are *not* compiled into the program. This has the effect of removing the Serial object from the code without having to actually erase them! This removes a pretty large chunk of code from your program when you're done testing and debugging it. To make this change, you first need to locate the skeletal program on your disk drive. It is stored in the examples directory. If you use Arduino1.8.12 as the root directory on your C drive, look in:

C:\Arduino1.8.12\Examples\01. Basics\BareMinimum.ino

and locate the BareMinimum.ino file. This file is write-protected as it is distributed with the IDE so you can't accidentally change it. If you are using Windows, use Windows Explorer to locate the file and click on it. Now right-click on *BareMinimum.ino* and select the Properties option from the dropdown list. You should see something similar to Figure 1.28. Under the Attributes heading, uncheck the box that makes the file Read-only. Click OK. This changes the file attribute to read-write so you can save the file.

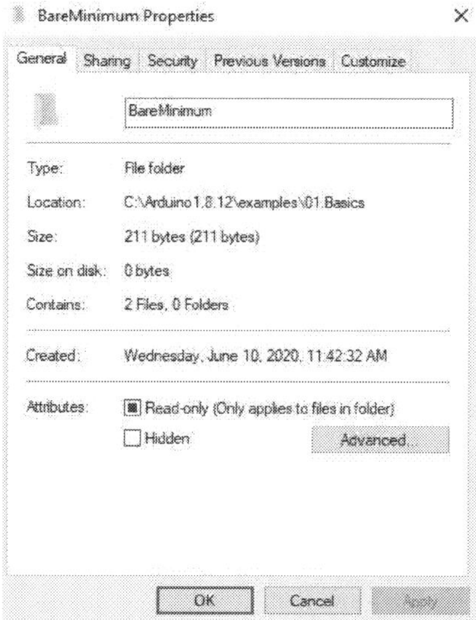

Figure 1.28. The Properties Dialog Box.

Now, using a different text editor (whatever you have, like Notepad), load the *BareMinimum.ino* file and add the lines shown in Listing 1.1 and save the file. Now, load the IDE, select File → New and you should see the modified skeletal program.

This change saves you a few keystrokes each time you create a new program.

Program Comments

In Figure 1.7 this line:

```
// put your setup code here, to run once:
```

appears at the top of the empty *setup()* function. This line is known as a single-line program comment. A single-line program comment can be anything you would like to add to the program source code from a memory-jogger to a URL for further information. Everything from the comment pair, "//", to the end of that line is ignored by the compiler. In other words, a *program comment has absolutely no impact on the memory use or speed of execution for the program.*

You can also have multi-line program comments:

```
/*
```

```
        This is a
        multi-line
        comment
        because it is
        continued on a
        second line.
*/
```

A multi-line program comment begins with the two character "/*" and continues until the compiler finds a balancing closing comment pair, "*/". You could place two sets of single-line comment pair ("//") at the start of the two lines, but the multi-line comments use fewer keystrokes. It's also easier to insert new comments in the middle of an existing comment when multi-line comments are used.

There's another important use of the multi-line comments when it comes to testing and debugging code. Sometimes you'll want to test a section of code using "test data", so you might write:

```
// a bunch of code above isn't being shown...
testPrice    = 5.50;
quantitySold = 100;
salesTaxRate = 0.06;
totalDue = CalculateTotalBill(TestPrice, quantitySold,
salesTaxRate);
```

The first three lines are "bogus" test data that you made up. Perhaps *CalculateTotalBill()* isn't working right and you want to find out why *totalDue* is wrong, so you feed the function your "made up" test data. After you mess around with the code for a while, you think it's right...but you're not positive. In that case, you would add a multi-line comment like this: that case, you would add a multi-line comment like this:

```
// a bunch of code above isn't being shown...
   /*
 testPrice    = 5.50;
 quantitySold = 100;
 salesTaxRate = 0.06;
   */
 totalDue = CalculateTotalBill(TestPrice, quantitySold,
                                salesTaxRate);
```

which has the effect of removing your test data so you can compile the program without it. However, if you are still not getting the correct answer, you can remove the multi-line comment and your test data is restored without having to retype it.

In other words, multi-line comments are a nice way to toggle test code into and out of a program during development with minimal keystrokes.

Some people over-comment their code, which often just adds clutter to the program and the comments get in the way of reading the code. As a general rule, I add comments at the top of a statement block if I think what it does needs to be explained. If it's a really complex piece of code, I may even put in a web URL where the reader can go for more information on what's being done in the program. You will develop a feel for what needs to be commented as you read through the book.

Conclusion

In this chapter you learned about the microcontrollers used in this book. Each one has its own advantages and disadvantages but I still need you to select one that you wish to experiment with in the coming chapters. You have successfully installed the Arduino IDE and have even modified and run a C program.

You might want to select the Arduino Nano to experiment with at this stage because it is inexpensive, the IDE is designed to use it without patches, and there is a ton of software projects available online that you can use to expand your learning experience. (I just search "Arduino Nano Projects" and got over 3.5 *million* hits. I'll bet you'll find one of them interesting.)

Keep in mind that the only way to learn how to program is to write programs. Try writing a program of your own that uses the *Serial.print()* method to print your name on the Serial monitor.

One more thing about the IDE and the compiler. If you copy program text from a magazine or a web posting of some kind, make sure you check out the double quotation marks it uses (i.e., "like these quote marks") because word processors often use what I call "down-turn marks" and the start of the quote and "up-turn marks" at the end of the quote. The compiler doesn't like these...at all. You may get an error message that is a little cryptic, like:

```
stray '\342' in program
```

This (or similar) error message says (in a very obtuse way) that it doesn't know what to do with character 342. Since 342 falls outside the maximum standard ASCII code range (0-127), this must be some kind of special 2-byte code. To fix this, go into the IDE, look for those double quote marks, and simply retype them. Chances are pretty good the error message will go away.

Okay...let the fun begin!

Resources for ESP32:

https://leanpub.com/kolban-ESP32. Good reference book for the ESP32 at nominal cost. https://docs.espressif.com/projects/esp-idf/en/latest/esp32/api-reference/index.html. The manufacturer's reference work for the ESP32. (Free.) Take a look at the SPI interface and SD topics to see some of the complexities that are present.

Do your own Internet searches on the specific use you have in mind (e.g., “ESP32 with SD card”).

Chapter 2 Really Understanding Data

In this chapter, we explore how data are actually stored, accessed, and processed as a program executes. This may seem out of sequence, since Chapter 3 actually covers the various data types C has to offer. There's a reason for this departure from the norm.

You are going to spend a little more time than most texts do "under the hood" to see what the compiler is doing to your programs as they execute. I had one student who thought this level of understanding was unnecessary, stating: "After all, I can drive a car without knowing how to build one." True, but would he feel differently if his car broke down 200 miles north of Nome, Alaska at 4AM when it's -50F outside? Perhaps. I think an understanding of what's going on under the hood makes you a better programmer and I'm pretty certain it helps you detect, isolate, and fix program bugs.

Also, the concepts presented in this chapter will serve you well in topics we discuss later in the book. For example, many students have a difficult time understanding C pointers. Armed with the information in this chapter, pointers become a piece of cake. Also, topics like data casts, scope, and other topics benefit from the concepts presented here. So, enough of the sales pitch. Let's find out what this chapter is all about.

C Program Expressions

If you had to reduce the C programming language to a fundamental element, that element would be a C expression. A C expression has two parts: 1) operands, and 2) operators. You can think of operands as data that are used in the expression. Operators *are the action(s) that are performed on the operands*. For example, consider the following list of expressions:

```
a + b           // An addition expression
val % 2         // A modulus expression
x > y           // A "greater than" relational expression
```

The expressions above are of the general form:

```
operand1  operator  operand2
```

This type of expression is called a binary expression because the expression has a single operator (i.e., + for addition, % for modulus, and >

for a greater-than relational operator) and two operands. A binary operator uses two operands. An operand *is simply a data item used by the operator.* (You will learn that there are unary and ternary operators, too.)

Expressions can be combined, too. For example:

```
a + b + c  x * y - 5
val / 10 * 2 + these % those
```

You can string as many expressions together as you wish. However, multiple expressions need some rules to play by. For example:

```
    5 * 6 / 2 - 1
```

In the expression above, does the answer resolve to 14 or 30? That is, which is the correct resolution:

```
5 * 6 / 2 - 1  =  30 / 2 - 1 = 15 - 1 = 14
5 * 6 / 2 - 1  =  5 * 6 / 1  = 30 / 1 = 30
```

Operator Precedence

As you can see, the order in which you process the expressions and their operators makes a difference in what the result of the expression is. We need rules that tell us how to resolve things when there are multiple operators. Those rules are summarized in Table 2.1, Operator Precedence.

Table 2.1 Operator Precedence[1]

Precedence	Operator	Description	Associativity
1	::	Scope resolution operator	Left-to-right
2	n++ n-- type() type{} func() array[] →	Suffix/postfix increment and decrement Function cast Function call Index subscript Member access	Left-to-right

3	++n --n +n -n ! ~ (cast type) *n &n sizeof	Prefix increment and decrement unary plus and minus Logical NOT and bitwise NOT cast indirection address-of size-of	Right-to-left
4	.* ->*	Pointer to member	Left-to-right
5	j*k j/k j%k	multiplication division modulo	Left-to-right
6	j+k j-k	addition subtraction	Left-to-right
7	<< >>	bitwise shift left bitwise shift right	Left-to-right
8	< <= > >=	less than less than or equal to greater-than greater-than or equal to	Left-to-right
9	== !=	equal to not equal to	Left-to-right
10	&	bitwise AND	Left-to-right
11	^	bitwise XOR	Left-to-right
12	|	bitwise OR	Left-to-right
13	&&	logical AND	Left-to-right
14	||	logical OR	Left-to-right
15	e1 ? e2 : e3 = += -= *= /= %= <<= >>= &= ^= |=	ternary conditional operator assignment compound assignment, add subtract compound assignment, multiply,divide, modulo compound assignment bitwise shift left, shift right compound assignment bitwise AND, XOR, OR	Right-to-left
16	,	comma (expression separator)	Left-to-right

1. A few special operators, mainly used with C++, that are not in this table.

Pretty impressive set of rules, right? Actually, they're not nearly as foreboding as they appear. Let's consider the question that got us here: Which is right? After the compiler has finished

```
x   =   5   *   6   /   2   -   1;
```

Well, it appears that we have four operators in the statement above. (These are shaded to make them easier to see.) They are: 1) assignment, 2) multiplication, 3) division, and 4) subtraction. Let's take that statement and place the operator precedence level below each operator (the larger the precedence number, the lower is its ranking in precedence order):

```
x    =    5    *    6    /    2    -    1;
    15         5         5         6 <----------- Precedence level
```

Uh-oh, two of the operators have "tied" precedence levels (multiplication and division at Level 5). Now what? No problem, that's what column 4 is for in Table 2.1. For a Level 5 precedence level, the expressions group left-to-right. In our statement, that means we resolve the left-most operator (multiplication expression) first (5 * 6 = 30):

```
x    =    30    /    2    -    1;
     15         5         6
```

and then division next (30 / 2 = 15) because it has higher precedence than subtraction:

```
x    =    15    -    1;
     15         6
```

Because the next highest operator precedence is for the subtraction operator, we resolve that expression (15 – 1 = 14):

```
x    =    14;
     15
```

and the assignment operator assigns 14 into X and all expressions in the statement are resolved with x equaling 14. As you can see, any ambiguity in an expression is resolved by the content of the operator precedence table, with the lowest precedence level going first.

Changing Operator Precedence

But what do you do if the correct answer is not given by the natural precedence level? For example, suppose the answer of our test statement should be 30, not 14? In that case, surround the expression that you wish to elevate in precedence with parentheses:

```
x = 5  *  6  /  (2  -  1);
```

The addition of parentheses forces the expression within those parentheses to be resolved first, so the statement becomes:

```
x = 5  *  6  /  (1);
x =    30    /   1;
x = 30;
```

Note that parentheses are used in multiple expressions (e.g., function calls, casts), but their interpretation by the compiler is determined by the context in which they are used. That's why there are both syntax and semantic rules involved when using C. As you gain experience with C, these rules become second nature to you. Meanwhile, keep working on that flat forehead and perhaps dog-ear this page so you can find the precedence table easily.

If the inputs into a complex statement look right, but the answer doesn't agree with your test data, there's a chance that the expression sequencing is not what you think it is. Expression sequencing is *the order in which subexpressions in a statement are resolved.* It is the expression sequencing we need to determine to get the correct value for x. So, if a statement is giving an incorrect answer when the inputs are correct, check the expression sequencing to make sure the statement is correctly written for the task at hand. Often that means breaking a complex expression into smaller, more easily tested, subexpressions. For example:

```
                // I have no clue what this does...
        result = 6.0 * log(7) - sqrt(y) + fabs(x) * pow(n, p);
```

In this statement, it's pretty likely that the result is *float* data type, so to debug it, you might try (I'm assuming that the Serial object is instantiated using something like *Serial.begin(9600);*. The word instantiated simply means that an object or variable has been defined and can be used in the program.):

```
float temp;

temp = 6.0 * log(7); // Doesn't make sense now...
                     // but will eventually!
Serial.print("exp1  temp = ");
Serial.println(temp);

temp = temp - sqrt(y);
Serial.print("exp2  temp = ");
Serial.println(temp);

temp = temp + fabs(x);
Serial.print("exp3  temp = ");
Serial.println(temp);

temp = temp * pow(n, p);
Serial.print("exp4  temp = ");
Serial.println(temp);
```

If you're still getting squirrely results, you may need to examine the individual variables used as parameters in the function calls (e.g., y, x, n, and p). Unfortunately, the Arduino IDE does not (yet) have a symbolic debugger (i.e., a way to inspect variables while the program is running), so the *Serial* object is the easiest way to inspect variables using *Serial.print(variableName).*

Statements in C

A C *program* statement *is one or more expressions terminated with a semicolon.* We just resolved the example statement above that calculated the value of *x* to be 14 (without parentheses)...you did notice the semicolon at the end, right? What's not obvious when processing a simple statement is all the work the compiler is doing behind the scenes to get the statement resolved. This is where we start looking at things "under the hood".

Defining a Variable

One of the most simple statements you can write in C is one that defines a variable. Unlike some languages, *you must define a variable before you can use it.* The following statement defines an integer variable named *val.*

```
int val;
```

At a minimum, defining a variable in C must state its data type (int) and the name, or identifier, of the variable (*val*). Now let's consider what the compiler has to do to make sure you've defined the variable correctly with such a simple statement.

First, the compiler sees the word *int*, so it checks to see what it is. The compiler sees that the word *int* is in its list of keywords so it will check the next expression to see what it is. It sees the word *val* followed by a semicolon, so the compiler knows that it now has the complete statement. In the compiler's rule book is a rule that states that a data type followed by an identifier and then a semicolon is valid syntax for defining an *int* variable.

So far, so good, but there are mistakes that could be made in the statement. You could have misspelled *int* with "unt". You might have violated one or more of the naming rules for C variables (i.e., *4*val*). (The rules for naming variables is covered in Chapter 3.) So far, we've passed the syntax rules, but there are other ways to mess things up.

C Symbol Table

The C compiler needs to maintain information about the variables you define in your program. It keeps that information in an internal data structure called a symbol table. A symbol table is an internal table that maintains all of the pieces of information about each variable. Collectively, that information about a variable creates an attribute list for that variable. An attribute list for a data *item is the collection of the individual pieces of information that are maintained for and describe that data item*. A (greatly simplified) symbol table is presented in Table 2.2. This discussion is significantly simplified, but does illustrate what we need to know about symbol tables. (My software company produced a C compiler and our symbol table had over 20 entries in it for each program identifier.)

Table 2.2 A Simplified Symbol Table

Identifier	Data Type	Scope level	lvalue
k	int	0	200
x	float	1	138
val	int	0	?

When the compiler sees the semicolon, it knows this statement is complete. It's already checked the *int* operand and its context tells the compiler it's parsing a variable definition. (Parse is a programming term for breaking down a statement into its operands and operators.) The compiler must now check to make sure that the identifier you assigned to the variable (*val*) is not already in the symbol table at the same scope level. (We discuss scope in Chapter 4.) Because there is no other *val* defined in the symbol table, that rule is also passed. If there were two *val* variables in the program at the same scope level, you would get a "*redeclaration error of 'val'* " error from the compiler. This makes sense because, when it sees *val* used in a subsequent statement, how would it decide which one to use? (We'll see in a moment that this error message itself is in error!)

It's pretty easy to sit there while you're reading this book and tell yourself: "Yeah, that makes sense." However, it makes a lot more sense if you see the error for yourself. Enter this short program:

```
void setup() {
  // put your setup code here, to run once:
  int val;
  int val;
```

```
}
void loop()
{
  // put your main code here, to run repeatedly:
}
```

and try to compile it. You should see an error message telling you that you've tried to define val twice in the code. While you're there, try changing the name to 4val or some other name that breaks the rules for naming variables. See what error message is issued under controlled conditions like this is a great way to get more "comfortable" with the compiler, even when it get's cranky with you.

Looking at our symbol table, which has only one *val* defined, why does the lvalue column have a question mark in it for *val*?

lvalue??

lvalues

At this instant in the parsing process, our simple attribute list is complete. However, one thing is missing: the variable's lvalue. An lvalue for a data item *is the memory address where that item "lives" in memory*. From the symbol table in Table 2.1, we can see that variable *k* starts at memory address 200 while variable *x* starts at memory address 138. The question mark means the compiler has not yet assigned a memory address to variable *val*.

After all the syntax and semantic checks are passed, the compiler makes the following request to its memory manager: "Hey...memory manager! My programmer needs enough contiguous memory to store an *int* data type. Can you help me out?" (If you're running an Arduino microcontroller, the Memory Manager scans his Available Memory Blocks list for 2 bytes of memory. For all of the other microcontrollers, the Memory Manager is searching for a 4-bytes block of unused memory. Actually, the Memory Manager is not a real "thing" but just a section of code used by the compiler. Well...duh!) We'll assume the Memory Manager scans the unallocated memory list and finds enough memory at address 421. The Memory Manager then sends that memory address back to the compiler and the compiler fills in the lvalue for *val* in the symbol table, as shown in Table 2.3.

Table 2.3 A Simplified Symbol Table

Identifier	Data Type	Scope level	lvalue
k	int	0	200
x	float	1	138
val	int	0	421

You can now say that the variable *val* is *defined* in the program because it has an lvalue. Any data item that does *not* have an lvalue in the symbol table is a *declared* data item. A declared data item is NOT the same as a defined data item. The distinction is important and most programmers are horrible about making the distinction. You, however, will *NOT* be one of them!

Define Versus Declare

Consider the following definitions (which you *MUST* memorize!):

> *define – a data item that has a complete attribute list and a known memory address (lvalue)*
> *declare – a data item that has a complete attribute list, but an unknown lvalue*

Let's give an example that illustrates why the distinction is important. Write a short program and save it as define.ino:

```
int val;         // In primary file define.ino, val is defined here

void setup() {
  Serial.begin(9600);
  val = 10;
  val = val * val;
  Serial.println(val);
  SquareIt();
  Serial.println(val);
}
void loop() {
}
```

Now use the Tab Icon and create a *second* file for this project and name the file *file2.cpp (cpp = C Plus Plus)* . Your IDE should look similar to Figure 2.1.

```
          // This is file2.cpp
int SquareIt()
{
```

```
  val = val * val;
  return val;
}
```

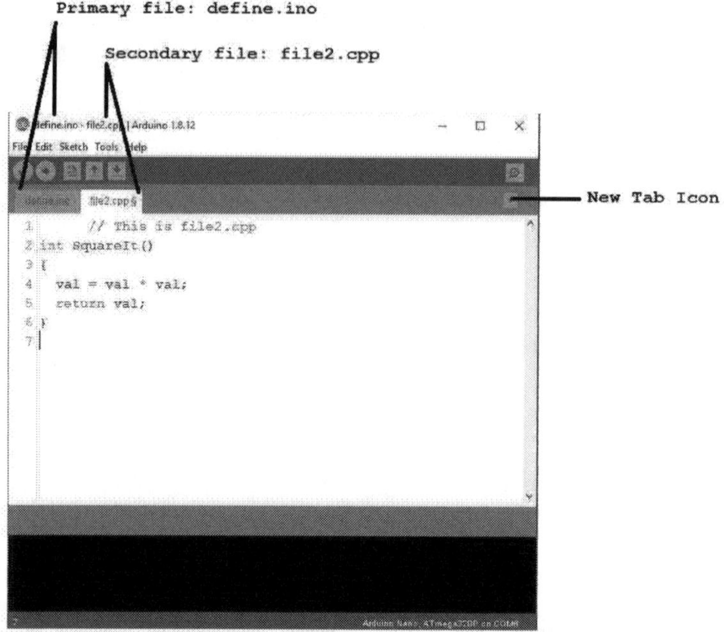
Primary file: define.ino
Secondary file: file2.cpp
New Tab Icon
// This is file2.cpp
int SquareIt()
{
val = val * val;
return val;
}

Figure 2.1. The IDE after creating the define sketch and second source code file.

Now try to compile it by pressing the compile/upload icon. Pretty quickly, you are issued the following error message:

```
'val' was not declared in this scope
```

and the compiler highlights the first statement in the *SquareIt()* function in file2.cpp.

Well, actually, *val* is declared, it's just not defined. In other words, the compiler doesn't know where to look in memory for where *val* lives. This error message should say *val* is not ***defined*** in this scope. Okay, so let's try to fix the error (even though we don't know about scope yet.) Change *file2.cpp* to read:

```
                              // This is file2.cpp
int SquareIt()
{
  val = val * val;
  return val;
}
```

Now, try to compile it. The error message now appears in the define.ino file and says:

'SquareIt' was not declared in this scope

This means the compiler doesn't know what *SquareIt()* is. We can solve this by adding a function prototype for the function. (More on function prototypes in Chapter 6 on writing functions.) See the (shaded) second source code line for the function prototype as added to the *define.ino* primary project file:

```
int val;            // In file define.ino, val is defined here
int SquareIt();     // Function prototype for SquareIt()

void setup() {
  Serial.begin(9600);
  val = 10;
  val = val * val;
  Serial.println(val);
  SquareIt();
  Serial.println(val);
}
void loop() {
}
```

When I try to compile the program now, I get:

multiple definition of `val'

The reason is because both files have *val* defined at the same (global) scope level. So, how can we fix this? In *file2.cpp*, add the word *extern* in front of the first line:

```
     // This is file2.cpp
extern int val;

int SquareIt()
{
  val = val * val;
  return val;
}
```

and compile the program. Not only does the program compile, it gives the correct answer.

Error messages issued by the IDE are often misleading. In other words, the IDE tries to help you by listing the line number and the character position within that line where the error occurred. The problem is that some errors cause the compiler to get so confused it finally gives up, but tells you where is gave up rather than where the real error is. Sometimes you'll get an error message that says the error is on line 60 when in fact it's a missing semicolon at the end of line 35. There's really not much that I can say to help you here, other than "look backwards" from the error if you can't see anything wrong at the point where the error message was issued. All compilers suffer from this shortcoming.

About the only honest answer I can give you is to stick with it. Experience eventually creates a sixth sense about such things. Until then, I would take a medium sized sample program (File → Examples) and purposely mess with the syntax and see what the resulting error message looks like. Remove a brace or semicolon and see what happens. That way you'll have a controlled way of seeing what kind of error messages are generated.

Why Does extern Fix the Problem?

The keyword *extern* simply modifies what would otherwise be a data definition and turns it into a data declaration for the compiler. When the compiler sees the *extern* keyword in *file2.cpp*, the compiler says to itself: "Ok, my programmer is telling me that this variable (*val*) is defined in another file (*define.ino*), but let me use its attribute list from the symbol table here in *file2.cpp* so I can use it (*val*) in expressions in this file."

If you want a simplified way to visualize what's going on, think of the compiler leaving a sequence of question marks after the declared variable (e.g., *val??*) in *file2.cpp* everywhere the variable is used in that file. (The compiler knows the question marks make *val??* stand out because variable names cannot have punctuation marks in them.) After all of the syntax and semantic checks are done, the compiler invokes a new sub-program called the *linker* to stitch the various parts of the program together into a single executable program. By the time the linker gets called into action, all of the lvalues in the symbol table are known. Therefore, when the linker sees *val??* in *file2.cpp*, it replaces each reference to *val* in *file2.cpp* with memory address 421. Now any expression in *file2.cpp* that uses *val* knows exactly where to go in memory to fetch its value.

Note that the reason the keyword *extern* was needed was because *val* was not defined in *file2.cpp*. It was defined in *define.ino*. The keyword *extern* changes the erroneous statement in *file2.cpp* to a data *declaration*, yielding an attribute list that can be used with that variable in that file.

It seems that ninety-nine percent of the programmers in the world treat the terms define and declare as though they are the same. ***They are not***. If we ever get to meet personally and you say you've read my book, I may ask you to tell me the difference between define and declare. People who know me are saying: "Yep...he'd do that." Yep...I would.

lvalues and rvalues

You already know that an lvalue is used to refer to the memory address associated with a data item. The term lvalue is a hang-over from assembly language programming days where a variable's "location value", or its memory address, was often referenced in the program. "Location value" got shortened to lvalue.

While lvalues are very important in the proper functioning of a program, it's equally important to know what is stored at those lvalues. If you use the following statement:

```
long myMills;
```

in a program and the linker puts *myMills* at memory address 150, it's equally important what binary data are held in memory addresses 150-153. What is stored at that memory address is called the rvalue. (The rvalue is also an assembly language term for "register value". Data manipulation, or processing, is usually done in the microcontroller's registers, not memory.) The rvalue of *a variable is the data that is stored at its lvalue*. (Some people find it easier to remember the graphical placement of the lvalues and

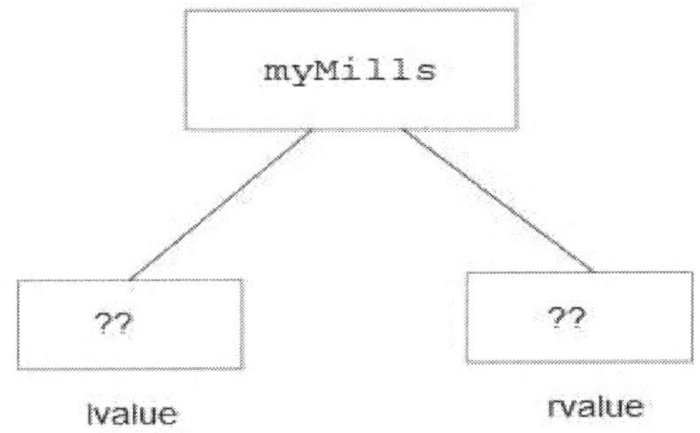

Figure *2.2. The lvalue and rvalue for a variable.*

rvalues as representing the "left value" (lvalue) and "right value" (rvalue) in a figure.) Figure 2.2 is a representation of the lvalue and rvalue of a variable after the compiler has checked the definition statement for errors, but before it has allocated memory for it. Because memory is not yet allocated, we have shown the variable with question marks for both its lvalue and rvalue. (After all, if there's no lvalue, how can there be a meaningful rvalue?)

After a short chat with the Memory Manager, the compiler knows that *myMills* was allocated four bytes of memory starting at, say, memory address 150. Therefore, Figure 2.2 morphs into Figure 2.3, which shows that the lvalue for the variable is now known. So why is the rvalue still unknown? The

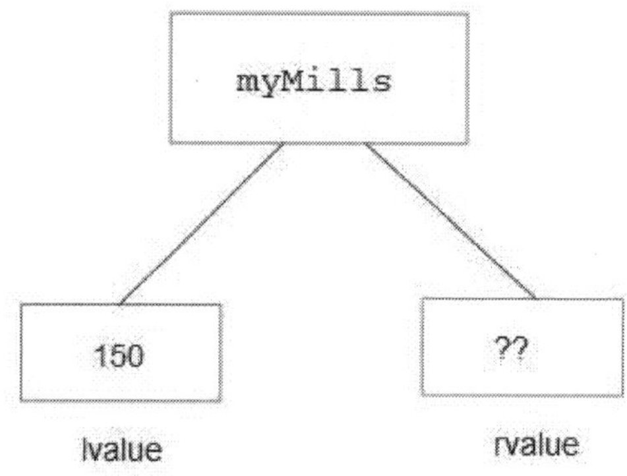

Figure 2.3. A variable's lvalue and rvalue after memory allocation.

reason is because we are not sure what the rvalue is for the variable. True, certain types of data are *assumed* to be initialized by the compiler. (You know the old adage about "assume".) However, it's much safer to assume that any data item contains some random bit pattern of junk in memory until you explicitly change it yourself.

Suppose you want to assign the value 100,000 into *myMills*. The statement to do that is:

```
myMills = 100000L;
```

The 'L' at the end of the statement is the *long* storage suffix, 'L'. (We cover storage suffixes in Chapter 3, but for now just think of it as a "memory-jogger" that the number is a *long* data type. You don't have to add the storage suffix, but I want you to get in the habit of documenting what you're doing with all non*int* data types.) Now, consider all the work the compiler does for you to process such a simple assignment statement.

First, the compiler parses the entire statement looking for errors. Because you defined *myMills* earlier in the program, those checks are successful. Next, it sees the assignment operator. Because the assignment operator works from right to left, it looks at the 100000L operand. The 'L' confirms that this is, indeed, a *long* data type, so the compiler forms the 4-byte binary presentation of 100000L (0b00000000 00001111 01000010 01000000) and forms those four bytes in a microcontroller register. Now the compiler looks in the symbol table for the lvalue for *myMills* and finds that *myMills* is stored at memory address 150. The compiler now directs the microcontroller to move the contents of the register that hold *myMills* rvalue, scoot it across the data bus to memory address 150 and dump those 4 bytes of data into memory, starting at memory address 150. The state of the variable is now as shown in Figure 2.4. Note that the rvalue is no longer unknown since we have used the proper syntax to assign a value into *myMills*.

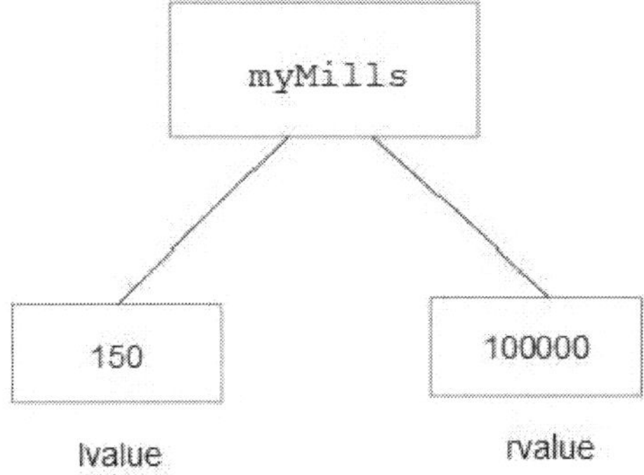

Figure 2.4 The lvalue and rvalue after the assignment statement.

There was a lot of effort expended by the compiler just to get the value into the variable. Suppose you have another *long* variable named *yourMills* defined elsewhere in the program with a lvalue of 200. Now you want to assign it the value of *myMills*. How does the compiler process this statement?

```
yourMills = myMills;
```

Again, our precedence table tells us the compiler must resolve the *myMills* operand first. So, the compiler looks in the symbol table for the lvalue of *myMills* and generates the instructions to go to memory address 150, fetch the 4-byte rvalue stored at that address, scoot it back across the data bus to the microcontroller, and store that rvalue in one of its internal registers. The compiler then looks in the symbol table for *yourMills* lvalue (i.e., 200), and takes the internal register's 4 bytes that is holding the binary representation of 100000L, pushes those data bytes onto the data bus, stopping at memory address 200, and then dumps the 4 bytes into memory at that location. Presto-chango! *yourMills* now has an rvalue of 100000.

Why is it important for you to understand the process the compiler goes through for something as simple as an assignment statement? I honestly believe that an understanding of the process of performing a simple assignment makes you a better programmer. Anything you can do to conserve memory or reduce the binary instructions needed to accomplish a task is almost always a good thing. For example, C allows multiple definitions of identical data types in a single statement, and allows you to initialize them, too. Given that new information, which set of statements would you use:

```
int a, b;
a = b = 0;
```

or

```
int a;
int b;
a = 20;
b = 20;
```

Both yield the same values for *a* and *b* when they have been processed, so which would you pick and why? If you asked yourself: "Which generates less code?", that's a good question to ask. Now I could say I'm not going to tell you in the hope you'd type the code in and find out for yourself, but, alas, I know most of you won't do that. The point here is important enough that I'm going to tell you that both versions generate the same, *identical*, use of flash and SRAM memory—no difference. Knowing that the resource used is unaffected, now which one would you pick and why?

Some of you picked the first version, perhaps because it requires less typing and you have only two program statements instead of four. Penny wise...pound foolish. I'd *always* pick the second version because: 1) it has no effect on resource use, and 2) it better documents my intent, thus making it easier to read. Indeed, I might augment the code a bit with comments so it reads:

```
int a;                  // Sensor on vat A
int b;                  // Sensor on vat B
```

```
a = 20;                    // Starting weight for vat A
b = 20;                    // Starting weight for vat B
```

If the data definitions are on the same line as they are in the first version, it's awkward to add a comment on what each variable is. The same is true for the initial values of the variables. And just as sure as we're sitting here, at some point, those two variables are going to be initialized with different values for each, so you'll need to make them separate statements anyway. The rule: *Always write program code in a way that makes it easier to document, read, and understand the code, especially when it has little or no impact on memory usage or execution speed.*

Another lesson to learn here is: *The compiler is almost always smarter at generating code than you are.* I was less inclined to make that statement 40 years ago than today. The only possible reason you would ever pick version 1 above is because you might think it generates less code. If you're ever in doubt, try coding and compiling the two options and examine the Statistics Window (Figure 1.8) to see if it makes a difference. Even if you save a few bytes, ask yourself if it's worth the documentation and clarity options that you lose. Also, saving 10 bytes by rewriting a line of code that is only executed once is probably not going to be noticed. If those same 10 bytes are in a loop that's executed a million times a second, then it might be worthwhile. Otherwise, forget about it and go for clarity.

In a later chapter, I present an example of coding options where we start with RDC (i.e., Really Dumb Code), progress to SDC (Sorta Dumb Code), and end up with PGC (Pretty Good Code). In that example, changing the code structure can improve resource use. (Those improvements, however, are not the compiler's fault. The improvements are really because of algorithm tweaks we make along the way, not code generation by the compiler.) Still, most of the time, the compiler's going to do a pretty good job of generating the executable code.

The Bucket Analogy

I'm a visual learner, so I'm always looking for ways to visualize whatever point it is I'm trying to teach. The lvalue/rvalue drawing in Figure 2.4 is one example of this penchant. The Bucket Analogy is another representation of the lvalue and rvalue concepts.

Suppose we want to define an *unsigned long* data type with the identifier *processTime*. Also suppose that you need a *char* variable named *whichVat*.

Because we must define a variable before we can use it, you type in the statements necessary to define the two variables:

```
char whichVat;            // letter to identify which
                          // vat in use
unsigned long processTime;// time to cook a vat in
                     // milliseconds
```

You already know the sequence the compiler goes through to define these variables and properly place their attribute list in the symbol table. (You might still review that sequence in your head...it won't hurt that much.) After those two statements are processed, we can picture two buckets having been placed in memory. Figure 2.5 shows how you might visualize the buckets.

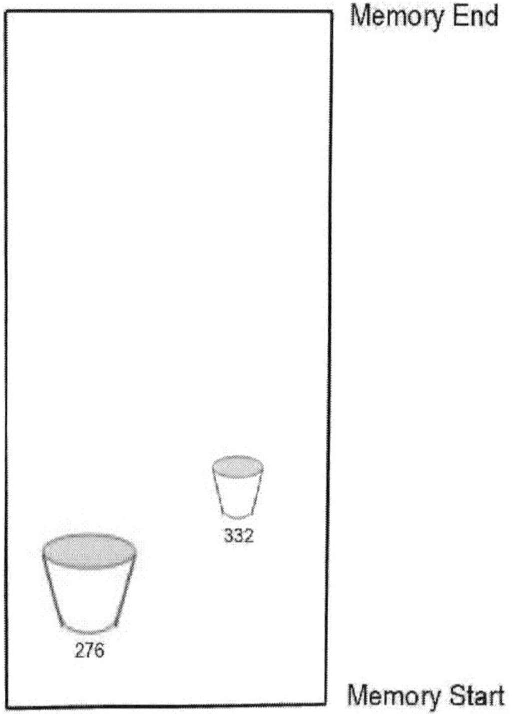

Figure 2.5. Placing the buckets in SRAM memory.

After the compiler has finished processing those two statements, it can assign the lvalues for them in the symbol table. I just arbitrarily assigned an lvalue of 276 for the memory address of *processTime* and 332 for the lvalue of *whichVat*. Note that both of these variables are allocated memory in SRAM. SRAM is where your program's variables (data) are normally stored. The program code ends up in flash memory. You can review Table 1.1 in Chapter 1 to see the sizes of the two types of memory. If you'll recall, the Arduino Uno and Nano only have 2048 bytes of SRAM, while the Teensy 4.0 has one *megabyte*! While you should always be aware of the SRAM usage of your program, it's limitations vary considerably across microcontrollers. The Statistics Windows at the bottom of the IDE shows you your SRAM usage. You should start getting nervous about SRAM storage when usage starts to creep over 70 percent. (I will explain why later in this chapter.)

In Figure 2.5, Memory End for the Uno/Nano is 2K, but is 1MB for a Teensy. Note that in Figure 2.5 we've represented *processTime* with a much larger bucket than *whichVat*. You already know the reason why: an (*unsigned*) *long* data type requires 4 bytes of memory while a *char* only uses 1 byte. Now consider these statements:

```
   whichVat   = 'A';
 processTime = 1000UL:
```

Again, you know the drill: form the appropriate binary values, scoot them across the data bus to their respective lvalues, and dump 4 bytes into *processTime* and 1 byte into *whichVat*. The new state of the SRAM memory is shown in Figure 2.6.

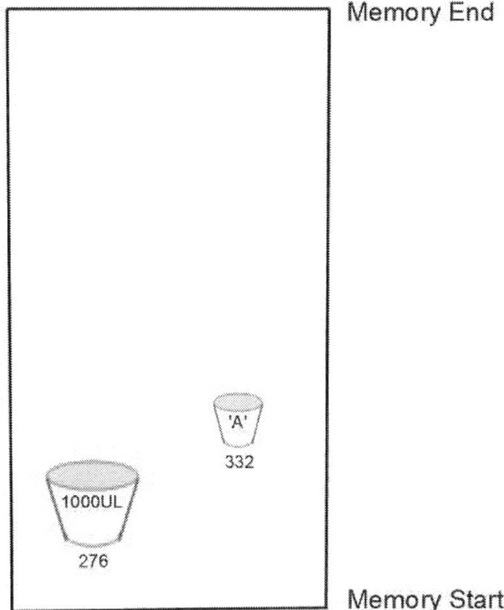

Figure 2.6. SRAM memory after the assignment statements

As a result of the assignment statements, the variables now have known lvalues and rvalues for them. (I have shown the rvalues on the side of each bucket. The actual binary data is "inside" the bucket!) The process just described illustrates two things about the Bucket Analogy:

> *Where – the exact location of where the bucket appears in memory is given by its lvalue*
> *What – the contents of what is inside a bucket is that bucket's rvalue.*

So, if you have the lvalue for a bucket, go to that memory address to find the bucket and peer inside the bucket to see the rvalue of the variable. Simple.

Cast Operator – Why Bucket Size is Important

Suppose we did the following:

```
processTime = whichVat;
```

I'm not saying that the statement makes sense, only that the compiler will let you do it without complaint. After all, both data items are numeric values ('A' is actually 65, and is explained in Chapter 3.) Stated differently, this assignment statement means that we are taking the contents of a 1-byte *char* bucket named *whichVat* and dumping its contents (i.e., its rvalue, or 'A') into a 4-byte *unsigned long* bucket named *processTime*. For this to happen, the compiler must first "fatten up" the *char* data item *whichVat* by adding 3 "empty" bytes to the *char* and then assign that fatter version into *processTime.* After all, the *processTime* bucket expects to hold 4 bytes. (If the compiler didn't fatten things up, there would be one byte for the 'A' and 3 bytes of whatever garbage bit pattern happens to be at those memory locations.) Because this "fattening" conversion is done behind your back with no visible indication that it happened, I call this a silent cast. A *silent cast* takes *place anytime the compiler alters the defined size of a data item into a different size data item without explicit code to make that change*. In this instance, we are taking a small 1-byte data item and bloating it into a 4-byte data item. (Note that the cast operator's precedent level is 3, so a cast is always done *before* the assignment operation takes place.) This silent cast works fine in this instance because you're pouring the contents of a 1-byte bucket into a 4-byte bucket.

Now consider what happens if we reversed the process and did this instead:

```
whichVat = processTime;
```

In this example, if you try to display *whichVat* on the Serial monitor, it displays a backward question mark (i.e., *percontation point*). In this instance, the statement is trying to pour 4 bytes of data into a 1-byte bucket. As a result, 3 bytes are going to get slopped all over the floor. Not good.

We can try to fix this using a cast. The cast operator is *used to change the current data item into the data specified within the cast's parentheses.* The syntax is:

```
(desired_data_type) operand
```

In our example, the cast would be:

```
whichVat = (char) processTime;
```

The shaded part of the statement above is the cast and *processTime* is the operand. To verbalize the statement: "Take the present size of *processTime* and transform it into a *char* data type, and then assign the result into *whichVat.*" If you try the new statement above that uses the cast, the cast makes *no* difference at all to the value of *whichVat*. This is a silk-purse-sow's-ear problem. No matter what you do, the value 1000 is _not_ going to fit into a 1-byte data item...there just aren't enough bits in a byte to represent a value larger than 255. Evidently, the result is a percontation point and 3 bytes of data that are now sloshing around on the floor.

If a cast doesn't make a difference, why bother? Several reasons. First, I picked this example precisely because the cast *doesn't* work. You will see plenty of other examples in this book where the cast does work. Indeed, the cast is necessary to avoid an error message from the compiler in many cases. Second, and perhaps more importantly, it documents your intention. Any time I think the compiler is going to do a silent cast behind my back, I make it explicit with the cast operator. First, using an explicit cast makes a potential silent cast visible and, second, it tells the reader you did the data conversion with intent and that you know what you're doing. Finally, if you go back far enough in time, you can find compilers that complain about both types of silent casts. Most modern-day compilers don't complain. I'm not convinced that's a good thing.

Conclusion

We actually did *not* cover a lot of topics in this chapter, but those topics that were covered did so with considerable detail. And there's a reason for that depth of discussion. Without a doubt, thoroughly understanding the content of this chapter makes subsequent chapters (e.g., pointers) much easier to understand. Please read this chapter again and, if you don't score a 100 percent on the exercises at the end of this chapter, read it again. This chapter's content is that important.

Exercises

1. Define the purpose of a symbol table. At a minimum, what information must it contain and why?

2. If I define a variable in one file, but can't access that same variable in a different file, what's the problem? (You should be able to answer the question in one sentence.)

3. How do I fix the problem in question 2?

4. Define lvalue and rvalue in no more than two sentences.

5. Write a program that defines a *char, int*, and *long* variables. Use the Serial monitor to display each variable's lvalue and rvalue. Use the following skeletal program as a starting point, Hint: *Serial.println(&variable)* uses the address-of operator (&) to display the lvalue of variable.

```
void setup()
{
  char c;
  int j;
  long miles;
  Serial.begin(9600);
  while (!Serial)
      ;    // Faster processors may need time to instantiate the
           // Serial object
   // Add the code to display the lvalues and rvalues here...
}
void loop()
{ // don't need to run anything more than once...
}
```

6. Write a payroll system for a company with 958 employees. (Naw...just kidding.)

Chapter 3 C Data Types

Several years ago, I bought myself a T-shirt that says:

> *There are 10 kinds of people in the world:*
> *Those who understand binary and those who don't*

If this quote didn't crack you up, you gotta read this chapter. If the quote did crack you up, you still need to read this chapter because I have a different way of looking at computer data. This chapter in concert with Chapter 2 lays the foundation that makes later chapters much easier to understand. For example, a lot of beginning C students struggle with the concepts of C pointers. Nonsense! Master chapters 2 and 3 and pointers become a piece of cake.

Part of the difficulty in learning anything new is figuring out where to begin the journey. When I was teaching programming courses, I'd occasionally have 30-minute unannounced programming quizzes to keep the students honest with respect to their assignments. Upon hearing a definition of the programming question, virtually all of the students instantly started banging on their keyboards.

Not good.

The good news is that there were always a few students who would look at the ceiling, scribble some notes on a piece of paper, and then start writing some code. Even though they didn't start writing any code until five or ten minutes later than the other students, they always turned in a worthy answer to the problem, often before the other students. Why?

The reason is because they organized their answer to the problem *before* they started writing a single line of code. A lot of people seem to think movement or activity leads to a solution. Often that's a lot of heat, but no light. It became clear that many students don't have a clue how to organize a solution to a programming problem. That is the purpose of my Five Program Steps. Virtually any program currently running on a computer can be simplified into five steps. These steps give you a starting place in solving any programming problem.

Let's see how the Five Program Steps can simplify things for you.

The Five Program Steps

Step 1: Initialization

The purpose of the Initialization Step is to *establish the environment in which the program runs*. For example, many programs (Excel, Word, the Arduino IDE, etc.) often present a list of the recently accessed files. Internet browsers allow you to define a home page and other "tab topics". A print program often has a default printer that is initialized. A database program often establishes a default network connection. In each program, a list of data files is fetched from somewhere (i.e., a data file, memory, EEPROM, the registry, etc.) and are used to establish a baseline environment in which the program is to run.

Simply stated, the Initialization Step does whatever background preparation must be done before the program can begin execution to solve its primary task. It's the same for microcontrollers. Ports need to be initialized, sensors have to be activated, I/O pins modes set, thermocouples need to stabilize, file handles to SD cards need to be created, plus a myriad of other possible events.

Generally, the program statements in the Initialization Step are only performed once when the program first begins execution. The tasks done in the Initialization Step are often completed before the user sees anything on the display (or other output device). *The code in the initialization step (i.e., the setup() function code for the Arduino IDE) is not executed a second time*, unless the program code is rerun (i.e., the microcontroller is reset or power is lost and reapplied.)

Step 2: Input

Every computer program has a task that is designed to take some existing state of information or data, process that data in some way, and then use or display the new state of that data. If you are writing a fire alarm system, you take the information provided by the fire sensors, interpret their current state and, if there is a fire, do something about it. If the sensor shows no fire, perhaps a second set of sensors are read and the process repeated. Indeed, your program may do nothing for decades but take new readings every few seconds and determine if some remedial action is necessary. Sadly, the day may come when a fire is sensed and remedial actions are taken. Still, the entire process depends upon inputting fresh data from the sensors in a timely fashion.

The Input Step is *the sequence of program statements that are necessary to acquire the information needed to solve the task at hand.* That information, or data, may come from a keyboard, a sensor, a potentiometer, a file handle, a database or printer connection, a Wi-Fi signal...the list of data sources is almost endless. Regardless of the source, the purpose is to provide input that proves useful to the solution of the problem at hand.

Alas, input data can get corrupted. Database and printer connections can fail, sensors go stupid, and users do dumb, unexpected, stuff. Why do drive-up banking windows have instructions in Braille on the driver's side? People often make typing mistakes when entering data. For whatever reason, bad data can get into a program. Implicit in the Input Step is the assumption that the data are "good". After all: garbage in, garbage out. Therefore, it is assumed that the data are *verified* before the program begins to process it.

Step 3: Process

Extending our fire alarm example, once the input from the sensors is received, some body of code must be responsible for determining if the sensors are detecting a fire or not. In other words, the sensing voltage (i.e., temperature) must be read (input), and then interpreted (i.e., the data processed) to determine the current state of the sensors. In a desktop application, perhaps the data input is the price and quantity of some item purchased by a customer. The Process Step may perform the task of determining the total cost of the purchase to the customer.

Note that a program may have multiple Process Steps. For example, with our customer, there may be a process to determine the sales tax due on the purchase. In this case, the process of determining the total cost of the order becomes an input to the process that calculates the sales tax due. Ask yourself this: Should I use one function to compute the total cost of an order and a separate function to calculate the sales tax due. Or, should I combine those two calculations into a single function? (Answers to this and related questions are found in Chapter 6.) The sales and taxes due could be the inputs to yet another process (e.g., customer billing, updating inventory statistics in a database, credit card processing).

Simply stated, the Process Step is responsible for taking a set of verified data inputs and processing them to get a new set of (transformed) data. The planned sequence for moving from data input to data outputs is called an algorithm. An *algorithm is simply a clearly defined sequence of actions that take place in transforming the data.* Algorithms form a plan of attack for transforming data.

Step 4: Output

After the Process Step has finished its work, the transformed data is typically output on some device or sent to some other entity for further processing. In our customer sales example, we might now display the total amount the customer owes us. The Output Step, however, isn't limited to simply displaying the new data. Quite often, the new data is saved or passed along to some other program. For example, a program may accumulate the sales figures throughout the day and then update a database at night so some other program can generate sales/inventory reports for management to review the next morning. In our fire alarm example, the Output Step may cause an LED for a particular sensor to continue to display a green color on a control panel under normal conditions. If a fire is sensed, perhaps the LED displays red so whoever is in charge can see what area of the building is on fire.

The Output Step of one program could be the Input Step for another program. For example, the Output Step might be an average of several temperature readings where, if a certain temperature is reached, two vats of chemicals are mixed together. In this example, the Output Step of the temperature program becomes the Input Step for a vat-mixing program. While that sequence could be done in a single program, there may be reasons why it should be done as a separate process.

Simply stated, the Output Step is responsible for using the results of the Process Step. This utilization could be as simple as displaying the new data on a display device, like your display using the Serial monitor object of the IDE, or passing that new value on to some other program or process.

Step 5: Termination

The Termination Step has the responsibility of "cleaning up" after the program is finished performing its task. In desktop applications, it's common for the Termination Step to perform the Initialization Step "in reverse". That is, if the program keeps track of the most recent data files that were used, the
Termination Step must update that list of files and store it somewhere. If the Initialization Step opens a database or printer connection, the Termination Step should close that connection down so unused resources are returned to the system.

Many microcontroller applications, however, are not designed to terminate. A fire alarm system is likely designed to continue running forever, as long as things are "normal". You don't see (useful) fire alarm systems that quit at 5PM when the employees head home. Traffic light systems don't shut down at 3AM just because there are fewer drivers on the road. Even those systems, however, may need to be shut down temporarily for routine maintenance. For example, if the fire alarm system has a component failure, the Termination Process may try to identify the failed component before the system shuts down for repairs. Perhaps the Termination Process deactivates the alarm system before a maintenance shutdown.

Simply stated, the Termination Step should allow for a graceful termination of the currently running program. The Termination Step should also release any resources it used while it was running. In most of the projects you examine in this book, the Termination Step is not used. It is assumed that the program continues until 1) power is removed, 2) there is a program Reset, or 3) there is a component failure.

Using The Five Programming Steps

It doesn't do much good if you learn The Five Programming Steps, but don't know how to use them. The Five Programming Steps provide a means by which even the most complex program can be broken down into more manageable parts. A good way to start using the Five Programming Steps is to take a sheet of paper, draw and label a column for each of the five steps. Next, go to the Initialization Step and ask yourself: "What resources do I need for this program and what do I have to do to prepare for their use?" If you know you're going to display output on the serial monitor, under the Initialization column you'd write *Serial.begin(9600)*. If you're going to blink an LED, you'd write *pinMode(LED, OUTPUT)*. Mentally, just march through the resources you expect to use and write them down.

When you're done with the Initialization column, move to the Input Step column and ask yourself where is the input data coming from and how do I access it? If you're reading a fire sensor, you might write *digitalRead(FIRESENSOR1)*. If the user is typing in data from a keyboard, perhaps you use the *Serial.available()* method for reading the keyboard. If you're reading a voltage from a device, write down *analogRead(VOLTAGESENSOR)*. Continue to write down all of the input sources and how you are going to verify the data (if needed). After the Input Step column is filled in, move to the Process Step.

The Process Step would list the function calls you need to implement the algorithm you've selected to transform the data. Many of those functions will be from function libraries that someone has already written for you to use in your program. For example, if you are going to use a ladder to get onto a roof, everyone knows that OSHA used to specify the proper angle to be formed between the ladder and the building in terms of transcendental math functions, so you'll need to use the *sin()* function. In other cases, your data are such that you need to write your own function(s) to properly process the data. (Chapter 6 discusses writing your own functions.)

Obviously, you would use a similar procedure for the Output and Termination Steps, too. When you are done, you should have a pretty complete picture of how you're going to tackle this particular programming problem. Indeed, add a glob or two of syntactic C glue to the table and you're ready for testing. Any task, from eating an elephant to writing a program, looks less daunting when it's broken into small pieces. That's exactly what the Five Programming Steps are designed to do.

If someone were to ask: “In just one word, tell me what computer programming is about”, what would you say? For me, that word would be “data”. Data can be sourced from almost an infinite combination of sources, from a simple digital pin to the Large Hadron Collider, perhaps the most complex data source on the planet. Oddly, regardless of its source, data ultimately ends up being fed into the computer in one form: binary. By themselves, computers have the innate intelligence of a bag of hammers. Computers “understand” only two things: On (i.e., 1) and Off (i.e., 0). If you didn't get the joke at the start of this chapter, you're about to learn something new!

Binary Numbers

While you and I grew up in a world that uses the decimal (Base 10) numbering system, computers work in a world where everything is expressed in binary (Base 2) form. Therefore, it's important that we understand how our program data become represented in a program. The primary purpose of this chapter is to show you the basic data types that microcontrollers use in their programs. To understand the C data types more completely, you need to understand binary numbers.

Binary Bits

In the computer world, information is organized in the form of *binary digits*, or *bits*. Each bit can store one of two states: ON (a 1 bit), or OFF (a 0 bit). We call them binary bits because they can only assume one of two states (again, ON or OFF). This also means that computer data manipulation uses Base 2 arithmetic instead of Base 10. (I provide more details on binary numbers in a moment.) While several different ways of organizing bits have been used over the years, the *byte* is pretty-well established as the lowest common denominator for storing computer data. A byte consists of 8 binary digits. (For those who might be interested, a *nibble* is 4 binary digits. Therefore, 2 nibbles equal a byte. Nibbles were actually used at one time to organize data as Binary Coded Decimal, or BCD, data. Still, you'd be shocked to learn how rarely BCD comes up in cocktail conversation.)

Another computer convention is that *counting just about anything related to a computer starts that count with zero, not 1*. Therefore, you can think of a byte as being organized as shown in Table 3.1.

Table 3.1. Bit values

Bits →	7	6	5	4	3	2	1	0
Numeric Interpretation	2_7	2^6	2^5	2^4	2^3	2^2	2^1	2^0
Value	128	64	32	16	8	4	2	1

In Table 3.1, the right-most bit is labeled as bit 0 and is also called the *least significant bit (lsb)* of a byte. The left-most bit, bit 7 (so called because we start counting with 0, not 1) is called the *most significant bit (msb)*. The reason for the least and most significant bit nomenclature is because of value of their exponent value, or power.

For example, suppose bit 0 is turned on. 2 raised to the zero power is 1. Now look at the next bit, immediately to the left of the lsb. 2 raised to the first power is 2. Now consider bit 2, which is 2 raised to the second power, or 2 squared. If its bit is turned on, it has a value of 4. As we march toward the most significant bit (*msb*), the power of each bit is increased by one, which means the value is raised by a power of 2.

So, if you see the binary number 10, what's its decimal value? The decimal value would be 2. Now go back and read the phrase at the start of this chapter. Yep, it's a long way to go for a punch line, but what the heck.

So, how does a numeric value get stored in a byte? Well, suppose you see the following bit pattern in a byte:

```
0b00001010
```

(The "0b" prefix before the actual bit pattern is to tell you the data are being presented in binary, or Base 2, form. Sometimes you may see numbers presented as 0xF5, where the "0x" represents a hexadecimal, or Base 16, numbering system.) From Table 3.1, you can see that the second bit is turned on (since numbering starts with zero, bit "two" is in the "1" column. Therefore, when bit 2 is turned on, its decimal value is 2. Moving to the left, we see bit 4 (i.e., column "3") is the next bit that is turned on, so its representation is the value 8. Therefore, the binary value:

```
0b00001010
```

corresponds to

```
0 + 0 + 0 + 0 + 0 + 8 + 0 + 2 + 0
```

Summing up the bit value yields a decimal value for the byte of 10.

You might be thinking: "Okay, so what? Why do I need to know about binary numbers?" The reason is because there are times when debugging, or troubleshooting, a program is easier when you understand how the data are actually organized in the microcontroller. A second reason is because some external devices, like sensors or alarms, assign meanings to each bit. These individual bits within a byte are often called "flag bits", since they are used to signal whether something is turned on or off. Another reason for understanding the binary numbering system is because there are certain "tricks" you can use if you understand how binary numbers work. For example, suppose you have the number:

```
num = 0b00000101;
```

Using Table 3.1, you should be able to determine that the decimal value of *num* is 5. Now suppose you see this statement in a line of code:

```
newNum = num << 1;
```

While I don't expect you to know this right now, the expression on the right side of the equal sign says: "Shift all of the bits in *num* left 1 position." In other words, the "<<" operator is the "bit-shift-left" operator and the 1 tells the compiler how many positions to shift the bits in *num*. So, if we shift all of the bits to the left one position, *newNum* becomes 0b00001010. Look familiar? Using Table 3.1, you should be able to determine that *newNum* equals 10.

Wait a minute! Bit-shift left 1 position becomes a multiply-by-2 operation! Using a bit-shift operator is about as fast as you can multiply a value by 2 on a microcontroller. Okay, so given that *newNum* is now 10, what does this statement do?

```
num =  newNum >> 1;
```

Yeah, I know...you don't know what “>>” is, but use your imagination. If “<<” is the left-shift, perhaps “>>” is the bit-shift-right operator. (Hint: It is.) It's probably obvious that a shift-right by one bit is a divide-by-two operation. Dividing is one of the slowest math operations you can do on a microcontroller and, if your program is doing a bazillion divide-by-two operations, this little trick can save some significant processing time. (Good optimizing C compilers do this anyway.) There are also some techniques that use bit-masking to communicate with external devices. Without understanding how binary numbers work, you wouldn't understand how these techniques work. Get comfortable with binary numbers...they're your friend.

Numeric Data Ranges

Given that a byte is the basic building block for the data used in a computer, there are limits to the values that can be represented using a byte of binary data. You already know that there are 8 bits in each byte of data, so a single byte can represent 2^8, or 256, distinct numeric values. Some of you astute readers just went back to Table 3.1 and added up all the values represented in the bottom row of that table, didn't you? In doing so, you discovered that the numeric total of the row is 255. You're probably thinking: “Hold on...the sum is 255, not 256. Where's 'the last one'?”

Ahh...Grasshopper: You're forgetting that zero is a numeric value. I was very careful in stating that a byte held 256 “distinct numeric values”. In other words, if the byte has all of its bits turned off, it looks like:

```
0b00000000
```

it has a numeric value of 0. If the byte has all of its bits turned on, it looks like:

```
0b11111111
```

and has a numeric value of 255. As I said earlier, a byte can represent 256 *distinct values*, of which 0 is one of them. Therefore, the numeric range of a single byte is from 0 through 255. This also means that the largest value we can represent with a single data byte is 255.

Extending the Range

Computers would be a tad crippled if they could only count to 255. So, how do we fix that limitation? Simple! Add another byte of memory, but treat the two bytes together as a single piece of data. We can expand Table 3.1 into Table 3.2:

Table 3.2. Bit values for 2 bytes

Bits →	15	14	13	12	11	10	9	8	7	6	5	4	3	2	1	0
Power	2^{15}	2^{14}	2^{13}	2^{12}	2^{11}	2^{10}	2^{9}	2^{8}	2^{7}	2^{6}	2^{5}	2^{4}	2^{3}	2^{2}	2^{1}	2^{0}
Value	32768	16384	8192	4096	2048	1024	512	256	128	64	32	16	8	4	2	1

Using the same logic we did for a single data byte, we can now represent 65,536 distinct values by expanding our storage to using two bytes. If you add up all of the values in Table 3.2, the total is 65,535 so that becomes the largest number we can represent with just 2 data bytes (zero is still important).

Uh-oh! What if the computer needs to process a negative number?

Negative Numbers

Computer language gurus decades ago agreed on a convention for representing negative integer numbers. They agreed that *the* most significant bit (msb) of the data item would be reserved for the sign bit. By convention, if the sign bit is 0, the number can only present positive numbers. If the sign bit is 1, the remaining 7 bits are interpreted as a negative number. For this to work properly, we need to tell the compiler if the data item is a signed or unsigned data type.

This sign-bit convention has a significant impact on the range of numbers that can be represented using either signed or unsigned data. Look at Table 3.1. If we use bit 7 (i.e., the msb) as a sign bit, the largest number becomes equal to the sum of the remaining bits (i.e., bits 6 through 0). Add those up and you get 127, whereas an unsigned byte can range between 0 and 255. Therefore, signed integer numbers have a range that is approximately half that of an unsigned number. (Don't even get me started on the interpretation of unsigned 0 versus signed 0.) Table 3.3 shows the ranges for a variety of integer data types.

The right-most column in Table 3.3 are the predefined *symbolic constants* for the extreme values shown for the data type's numeric range. For example, if you wanted to use the largest number available for a signed *long* data type in a C statement, you could use 2,147,483,647 or LONG_MAX. Most programmers find it easier to remember the symbolic constants than the actual values. You can find these constants in a header file named limits.h. (The exact location will vary depending on your installation. Try: C:\Arduino1.8.12\hardware\tools\arm\arm-noneeabi\include\limits.h.)

Floating Point Numbers and Precision

In Table 3.3, the last three rows are data types that are used to represent floating point numbers. That is, numbers that may have a decimal, or fractional, component. Consider the *float* data type. Table 3.3 shows that a *float* data type can represent a number as large as 3.4 followed by 38 zeros. That's a huge number! The *double* (308 zeros) and *long double* (4932 zeros) data types can represent even larger floating point numbers.

Well...sort of.

You may well be asking yourself how 4 bytes of data can represent a number with 38 digits in it. The magic is done using the IEEE floating point algorithm which is used to represent floating point numbers. In reality, there's some smoke-and-mirrors magic going on behind your back. With a float data type, only the first 6 digits are considered to be precise values. The remaining 32 digits are the computer's best guess as to the rest of the number. Therefore, the precision of a float is taken to be 6 digits. The precision of a number refers to the number of digits that are accurately represented by the floating point data type. For an 8-byte double, you get 15 digits of precision and 293 digits of guesswork. With a *long double*, it's 19 digits of precision and 4913 digits of who-knows-what. If you were a commercial bank, would you want your software to use a *float* data type to count dollars for your customers, or would you use a *long long* data type to count pennies? Think about it.

Table 3.3. Data Type Ranges

C Data Type	Bytes	Numeric Range	Symbolic Constants in limits.h
boolean	1	Logic true, or logic false (1, 0)	
byte	1	0 - 255	
unsigned char	1	0 - 255	UCHAR_MIN, UCHAR_MAX
char	1	-128 to 127	CHAR_MIN, CHAR_MAX
short int	2	-32,768 to 32,767	SHRT_MIN,

			SHRT_MAX
unsigned short int	2	0 to 65,535	USHRT_MIN, USHRT_MAX
unsigned int [1]	4	0 to 4,294,967,295	UINT_MIN, UINT_MAX
int	4[1]	-2,147,483,648 to 2,147,483,647	INT_MIN, INT_MAX
unsigned long	4	0 to 4,294,967,295	ULONG_MIN, ULONG_MAX
long	4	-2,147,483,648 to 2,147,483,647	LONG_MIN, LONG_MAX
unsigned long long	8	-2^{63} to 2^{63} - 1	ULLONG_MIN, ULLONG_MAX
long long	8	18,446,744,073,709,551,615	LLONG_MIN, LLONG_MAX
float	4	1.2E-38 to 3.4E+38	FLT_MIN, FLT_MAX
double	8	2.3E-308 to 1.7E+308	DBL_MIN, DBL_MAX
long double[2]	10	3.4E-4932 to 1.1E+4932	LDBL_MIN, LDBL_MAX[2]

1. The ranges do vary among microcontrollers. More on this later in the chapter.
2. May not be defined for all compilers

Numeric Range Problems

The values shown in Table 3.3 may or may not be correct for the processor you are using while you read this book. If you type in the code presented in Listing 3.1 and compile and run it, you'll see the problem. While I don't expect you to be able to completely understand the program, you can probably guess what's going on. The only weird part might be the *sizeof() operator* which is designed to find the number of bytes allocated *to a data item*.

Listing 3.1. Program to show data storage for types

```
void setup()
{
  Serial.begin(9600);
 while (!Serial)
    ;              // Spin around until Serial object instantiated
  Serial.print("      Bytes for an int = ");
  Serial.println(sizeof(int));
```

```
  Serial.print("      Bytes for a long = ");
  Serial.println(sizeof(long));
  Serial.print("Bytes for a long long = ");
  Serial.println(sizeof(long long));
  Serial.print("     Bytes for a float = ");
  Serial.println(sizeof(float));
  Serial.print("    Bytes for a double = ");
  Serial.println(sizeof(double));
}
void loop()
{
}
```

When I run Listing 3.1 on a Teensy 4.0 microcontroller, the output is:

```
     Bytes for an int = 4
     Bytes for n long = 4
Bytes for a long long = 8
    Bytes for a float = 4
   Bytes for a double = 8
```

However, when I compile and run the same program on an Arduino Uno or Nano, the output is:

```
     Bytes for an int = 2
     Bytes for a long = 4
Bytes for a long long = 8
    Bytes for a float = 4
   Bytes for a double = 4
```

Notice the output differences for the *int* and *double* data types between the two microcontrollers (i.e., the shaded output lines). Why the difference?

Without getting too technical, the Arduinos use an 8-bit architecture while the STM32, ESP32, and Teensy microcontrollers use a 32-bit architecture. Think of the microcontroller as a city and the microcontroller's memory as another city. An 8-bit architecture shoots its data across an "8 foot wide" data bus that is like a small country lane that connects the two cities. A 32-bit architecture is like a 4-lane freeway connecting the two cities. Data can be moved around the system much faster using a 32-bit architecture than an 8-bit architecture. Also, the internal registers in a 32-bit microcontroller are larger than those found in an 8-bit architecture.

The Arduino compiler seems to take a "what's-the-point" attitude with data types that must scoot 8 bytes (or larger data) types around the system (like a *double*). So, rather than disappoint you by flagging those data types as being unsupported by the compiler, the compiler instead chose to pretend they exist but actually compiles them to the next best alternative (i.e., a *double* becomes a *float*). The good news is that by using the *double* data type in your program, you can increase floating point precision if you move the code from an Uno or Nano to a Teensy. The bad news is that your Uno/Nano code looks like it has the precision of a *double* when in fact its precision is limited to that of a *float*.

Keywords In C

There are a number of words that have special meaning in the C language. Each of the data types presented in column 1 of Table 3.3 (i.e., int, char, float, etc.) is an example of a C keyword. *Keywords cause the compiler to take some specific action or process* when that keyword is encountered in a program expression. Because data type keywords (e.g., *char, int, long, float*) are reserved for use by the compiler, you cannot use them as variable names in your own programs.

There are other keywords that do not pertain to C data types that you will also use in your programs. Examples include the keywords *for, if, while, switch, case*, plus a number of others. You will learn these keywords as we progress through this book. You will also learn that, although not keywords in the true sense of the word, there are a lot of function names that you should not use for variable names either (e.g., *delay(), pinMode(), digitalRead()*, etc.). As mentioned in the foreword of this book, by convention I use italics for keywords (e.g., *for*) so you don't confuse them with standard English words when used in the narrative. I also use parentheses and italics when referencing functions, like the *delay()* function.

Given that you shouldn't use C keywords as variable names, it seems a list of C keywords at this point in time might be a good idea. Table 3.4 presents the list of keywords for the American National Standards Institute (ANSI) for C.

Table 3.4. C Keywords

auto	double	int	struct
break	else	long	switch
case	enum	register	typedef
char	extern	return	union

continue	for	signed	void
do	if	static	while
default	goto	sizeof	volatile
const	float	short	unsigned

You will notice that *byte* and *boolean* are not in the list presented in Table 3.4, but they are recognized as keywords by the Arduino GNU C compiler. (The C99 standard for the C language defines a *bool* data type as what's called a macro expansion, but it's not a native keyword.) Therefore, if you plan on writing code that might be moved to a different C compiler, you may wish to avoid the *byte* and *boolean* data types. However, any code compiled with the Arduino IDE's compiler does recognize *byte* and *boolean* as keywords.

Identifiers in C

We can talk about variable and function names in C, but collectively, such names are called identifiers. C *identifiers* are used in a program so the compiler can keep track of the different data items that might be used in a program. I've told you some keywords that you can't use for C variable names, so what is allowed? There are *five general rules for identifiers* in a C program. You may:

1. use the letters 'a' through 'z' and 'A' through 'Z'. (Uppercase letters are distinct from lowercase letters) unformatted
2. use the underscore character ('_') at the start or within the identifier name
3. use the digit characters '0' through '9', provided they are *not* the first character of the identifier
4. not use punctuation or other non-printing characters
5. not use function names that are the same as core library function names (e.g., *delay())*
6. not use math (+, -, etc.) or processing symbols (#, &, *, etc.).

Some examples of valid variable identifiers include:

```
jane   Jane   ohm   volt   Ampere    pressureSensor
```

Note that *jane* and *Jane* are two distinct and different data names. (See Rule 1.) Examples of bad names include:

```
4July  ^top  -negative   +positive    not-good      what?
```

It would be good practice for you to explain to yourself why each of these names does not follow the rules for valid C data item names.

What Constitutes a Good Variable Identifier?

Besides obeying the rules for naming C data items, there are other factors that enter into the mix when naming a data item. First, the identifier should be indicative of what the item represents in a program. For example:

```
inputVoltage  lowpassFilter  toroid2       keyerSpeed
```

Second, while the name should be indicative of what the variable is, it should be short enough that you don't get tired typing it into the program. Most C compilers require the identifier or name of a C item to be unique within the first 31 characters. However, if you're writing programs with variable names that are the same for the first 30 characters, you're either asking for trouble or you're writing a novel. In either case, stop it!

Third, variable identifiers tend to be like nouns in a sentence. A good variable identifier should be suggestive of a "person, place, or thing", as you learned about in third grade English class. The identifier should be descriptive in the sense that it helps you understand its purpose in the program. Function identifiers, on the other hand, are more like verbs in that they describe an action or event associated with the code buried within a function. Function names like *TurnWaterOn()*, *delay()*, *MeasureSWR()* all suggest the task that a particular function might perform.

Also, I avoid function names that might detail the algorithm used by the function. That is, I like *SortData()* better than *DoBubbleSort()*. Detailing *how* things are done in a function locks you into that algorithm even if you discover a better way to sort the data. You might be thinking to yourself: "No worries. I'll just give the new function a new name." True, but now you've forced everyone who uses your function to go through their source code and change the function name.

Not good. The less you "touch" the source code, the less chance there is of screwing things up.

Functions are like Las Vegas: What goes on inside the function is nobody's business but yours...it's a windowless black box with a door for passing data into and out of it. The outside world doesn't need to know anything more about what's going on inside the black box. More on this in Chapter 6.

Fourth, and this is simply a style convention I use, for any function I write I make the first letter of its identifier an uppercase letter. Why? Consider the following: I come back to a program I wrote three years ago and I see *TurnWaterOn()* or *MeasureSWR()* in the code. Because those function identifiers start with an uppercase letter, I *know* that the code for those functions is part of the program source code and that I wrote them. Therefore, using the search facility within the IDE should take me quickly to the source code for either function. On the other hand, because the *delay(), millis(), random()* and a host of other function identifiers start with a lowercase letter, I know immediately that I did *not* write that code. They are likely part of the language core or from one of the libraries. Therefore, searching for their code in this program would be a waste of time. Likewise, most Arduino-compatible libraries use lowercase letters for the functions (or class methods) buried within those libraries, like the *print()* method of the *Serial* object used in Listing 3.1.

Finally, all of my variable names begin with a lowercase letter and then use an uppercase letter for sub-words within the identifier. (I used this convention in the example identifiers above, like inputVoltage.) Such an identifier process uses what is called *camel notation*, probably because the uppercase letters put "humps" in the identifier's name. I use camel notation for both variable and function identifiers. Clearly, it's not a required naming convention, but the practice has served me well over the years.

Additional Data Type Information

This section provides you with additional details about the different types of data that are available to you when using the Arduino IDE and the underlying GNU C Compiler (GCC).

boolean

A *boolean* data type is limited to only two values, or states: *true* or *false*. Although you can use 1 and 0 to represent a *true* or *false* state for the item, using the terms *true* and *false* documents at a glance that the variables are most likely a *boolean* data type. For example, consider this statement which defines a boolean variable:

```
boolean activeMember;
```

Perhaps we are going to monitor this variable to determine if a person is an active member (*true*) or not (*false*). Now suppose we have this code fragment:

```
activeMember = ReadMemberList(membershpNumber);
if (activeMember == true) {      // Are they a member?
   Serial.println("Greetings fellow member!");  // ...Yep

} else {                                       // ...Nope
   Serial.println("Membership cost is $10. Join now!");
}
```

In this example, the code calls a function named *ReadMemberList()* and returns either *true* or *false* depending on their membership status. A message is displayed on the Serial monitor as a result of the *if* statement test. (We cover the *if* statement in Chapter 4, but you can probably get the drift of what the code fragment is doing.)

What if you're pressed for memory and you need to squeeze out every byte you can. You can write the same code block as:

```
if (ReadMemberList(membershpNumber)) { // A member?
    Serial.println("Greetings fellow member!");// Yep
 } else {
    Serial.println("Membership cost is $10. Join now!");//...Nope
 }
```

which gets rid of *activeMember.* It also uses fewer keystrokes to write the code block. If memory is not an issue in the program, which version would you use? I would use the first version because I can test the return value from *ReadMemberList()* with a simple print statement using *activeMember.* Also, I think the first version is easier to read and understand, and that's always a good thing.

I don't find myself using *boolean* data all that often. The reason is because things are rarely just *true* or *false*. For example, a club member could be on the membership list, but they haven't paid their dues yet. Some clubs may keep someone as an active member even though they haven't paid dues because ill health makes it difficult for them to pay their dues. To me, such exceptions mean the membership list might need a classification of on-the-list-but-hasn't-paid-dues. Such situations would be better served with an *int* that would allow for more types of members. If you're pressed for memory, you could save at least one byte by using a *char* instead of an *int*, yet still have enough flexibility for the task at hand.

byte

The *byte* data type is not part of the formal C99 standard, but is useful, especially in an embedded systems environment. The *byte* data type is used to represent *unsigned* data so the msb has meaning beyond being a signed number. Sometimes you might be working with sensors where a particular byte contains status data about the sensor and the msb conveys information about the sensor rather than its signed/unsigned state. Because of this, anytime you have a situation where reading a device returns an 8-bit quantity that holds status information, the *byte* data type probably is the proper data type to use.

Table 3.5. American Standard Code for Information Interchange

Dec	Char	Dec	Char	Dec	Char	Dec	Char
1	NUL	32	SPACE	64	@	96	`
2	SOH	33	!	65	A	97	a
3	STX	34	"	66	B	98	b
4	ETX	35	#	67	C	99	c
5	EOT	36	$	68	D	100	d
6	ENQ	37	%	69	E	101	e
7	ACK	38	&	70	F	102	f
8	BEL	39	'	71	G	103	g
9	BS	40	(	72	H	104	h
10	TAB	41	)	73	I	105	i
11	LF	42	*	74	J	106	j
12	VT	43	+	75	K	107	k
13	FF	44	,	76	L	108	l
14	CR	45	-	77	M	109	m
15	SO	46	.	78	N	110	n
16	SI	47	/	79	O	111	o

17	DLE	48	0	80	P	112	p
18	DC1	49	1	81	Q	113	q
19	DC2	50	2	82	R	114	r
20	DC3	51	3	83	S	115	s
21	DC4	52	4	84	T	116	t
22	NAK	53	5	85	U	117	u
23	SYN	54	6	86	V	118	v
24	ETB	55	7	87	W	119	w
25	CAN	56	8	88	X	120	x
26	EM	57	9	89	Y	121	y
27	SUB	58	:	90	Z	122	z
28	ESC	59	;	91	[	123	{
29	FS	60	<	92	\	124	|
30	GS	61	=	93	]	125	}
31	RS	62	>	94	^	126	~
32	US	63	?	95	_	127	DEL

char

First, let's talk about how to pronounce this word. Some prefer *char* as it sounds when using the word charcoal. Others prefer the word to sound like "care". Personally, when I hear the word, I like it better when visions of a warm, caring, person come to mind rather than a piece of burnt meat. So, I'm sticking with "care"...your choice.

When computers first came onto the scene, developers figured that a signed *char* would provide enough values to represent everything on a keyboard. *The American Standard Code for Information Interchange* (*ASCII*) quickly became the standard for character information in a computer. Table 3.5 shows the standard ASCII codes.

Hmmm...Why does the table end with number 127? Recall that *byte* data is 8 bits (one byte) of *unsigned* data, where a *char* is 8 bits (one byte) of *signed* data. So, if we can't use the msb of the byte, what's the largest value we can represent? (Hint: Look at Table 3.3.)

So, how are ASCII codes used? Suppose you press the letter 'A' on your keyboard. That requires you to press the Caps key along with the 'A' key. So, what happens when you do that? Simply stated, a numeric value of 65 is sent from your keyboard to your computer's processor. At the speed of light, that 65 is translated to a graphic pixel representation of the letter 'A' and that pops up on your display. So, when you are typing at your keyboard, numeric ASCII codes are flying all over the place, but end up on your display as a graphics character based on its ASCII number. Suppose you want to assign the letter 'A' to a char variable. The following statement does that for you:

```
char myLetter = 'A';
```

The *assignment operator* (=) always takes the expression on the right of the operator and moves the result of that expression into the expression on the left side of the operator. (It would be a worthwhile review exercise for you to verbalize the assignment statement above using the terms lvalue and rvalue.) If you followed the statement above with this:

```
Serial.print(myLetter);
```

the letter 'A' would appear on the Serial Monitor. Note that you use *single quote marks* to surround a char data type when you wish to use that ASCII character constant. Note in Table 3.5 that not all ASCII codes "print" something you can see. Indeed, all codes less than 32 are called "non-printing" codes. What does this statement do?

```
Serial.print( (char) 7);
```

(Recall that the underlined expression above is a cast, as discussed in Chapter 2.) We need to put the parenthesized word *char* before the number 7 so the compiler knows we want the number to be treated as a *char* data type rather than an integer number. So, what happened? Anything? After all, it's a "non-printing" character. (You're right, I'm not going to tell you. You'll learn more by typing the code in and running the program yourself. If you hear a ticking sound...run!) What does this code fragment do?

```
char number1 = '5';
char number2 = '3';

Serial.println(number1 * number2);
```

understanding that an *asterisk* (*) is a math operator and means "multiply". I just ran the program and it displayed 2703.

What?

How does 5 times 3 equal 2703? Stop and think. When I press the '5' key, what gets sent to the computer? (Look at the ASCII table.) What about the '3' key? So, the final expression is actually:

```
Serial.println(53 * 51);
```

which is 2703. Now, guess what happens if I do this:

```
Serial.println ( (number1 - '0') * (number2 - '0') );
```

First, the use of *parentheses* around an expression ensures that the complete expression within those parentheses is resolved before any expression(s) outside of those parentheses is evaluated. So, what the compiler ends up doing for you is:

```
Serial.println( (number1 - '0') * (number2 - '0') );
Serial.println( ('5' - '0') * ('3' - '0') );
Serial.println( (53 - 48) * (51 - 48) );
Serial.println( (5) * (3) );
Serial.println(15);
```

and the program prints the numeric value 15 on the display. Subtracting a zero character ('0') from an ASCII digit character (e.g., '5') is a standard coding trick to quickly *convert a single digit character to its numeric value* that can be properly used in an arithmetic expression. That is: 53 – 48 = 5, which is a “pure” number, not a character. It's worth remembering.

Suppose you are processing a questionnaire where the user is asked to enter 'Y' or 'N' in response to the question. Your code does this:

```
char response;

// probably a bunch of other code fits in here...

response = ReadMyKeyboard();   // Assume function to read
                               // keyboard
if (response == 'Y')           // double equal sign tests
                               // for equality
  Serial.println("You voted Yes”);
else
  Serial.println("You voted No”);
```

Unfortunately, every time I run this, despite pressing the 'Y' key, it says I voted No. Why? Well, what happens if I don't have the Caps Lock key on? If I don't have the Caps Lock on, the ASCII code in Table 3.5 says that 121 is assigned into *response*; a lowercase 'y'. However, the *if* test is asking if I entered an uppercase 'Y', or numeric 89. Because those two numbers are different, it says I voted No. Not good.

How can you fix this? One way is to “double check”:

```
                    //double vertical bar is "OR"
if (response == 'Y' || response == 'y')
```

and the code now works fine because the OR operator (“||”) means we check for both possibilities. (Chapter 4 discusses the OR and other logical operators.) However, double-checks are often not the best solution. Instead, we could to this:

```
response = ReadMyKeyboard();        // Assume function to
                                    // read a keystroke
response = toupper(response);       // Convert to upper-
                                    // case if necessary
if (response == 'Y')                // double equal sign
                                    // test for equality
  Serial.println("You voted Yes");
else
  Serial.println("You voted No");
```

In this example, the *toupper()* function (it's actually a macro—more on that in Chapter 10) converts the character entered by the user to an uppercase letter. Now the single test on *response* always yields the appropriate result regardless of the Caps Lock state.

In real life, experienced C programmers would “nest” the function calls so it looks like this:

```
                                    // Assume keyboard read
response = toupper( ReadMyKeyboard() );
```

Note how we collapsed the two statement lines into a single statement. Again, because parentheses force the compiler to call the *ReadMyKeyboard()* first, the program still behaves the same as the version that doesn't nest the function call.

One more little piece of information about ASCII characters. Notice in Table 3.5 that the first printing character is a space character (i.e., ' '). What would happen below if I printed out *myChar* to the Serial monitor?

```
 char myChar;
 char yourChar;
```

```
yourChar = 'P';           // a lowercase 'p'
myChar = yourChar - ' ';
Serial.println(myChar);   // What gets printed??
```

To determine the answer, use the values shown in Table 3.5. And, yep, I'm not telling you the answer.

int/unsigned int

The *int* data type is the real workhorse for most microcontroller projects. One reason *int*'s are so heavily used is because the data used in most microcontroller projects is most efficient when using *int* data. Recall that a 16-bit *int* on an Uno or Nano has a smaller range of values than it does on the 32-bit microcontrollers. Still, even a signed *int* can handle values up to 32,767 and that is often more than enough range for the task at hand. An *unsigned int* almost doubles the range. A second reason is that most of the internal registers in the microcontroller are the same size as an *int* data type of the host language...the data "fits" into a register comfortably, which often means faster processing of the data. What is the output of these statements?

```
int val = 3;
Serial.println(val / 2);
```

Everyone knows that 3 divided by 2 is 1.5. The problem is that integer data types, like int, cannot support decimal values. So, knowing that, is the answer 1 or 2? Math statements involving integer data truncate the result rather than rounding it. As a result, the two statements above yield an answer of 1.

Suppose I give you an *int* variable, *val*, and ask you to determine if the number is odd or even. How would you do it?

Yes, I realize asking for answers like this is unfair because we haven't covered enough to provide an answer. However...that's not the point.

The point is for you to start thinking about the *process* you would use to solve the task at hand. Indeed, that is the difference between a software engineer and a programmer. The software engineer develops a plan for solving a problem. Using the term from Chapter 2, the software engineer develops an *algorithm* designed to solve a problem. That algorithm can then be turned over to a programmer who writes the code to implement the algorithm.

Note that the process for developing algorithms can stand independent and detached from the language used to implement that algorithm. What I want you to do here is *think* about the process you would go through to solve the problem.

The first step in the process of solving the problem is to define what "even" and "odd" numbers are. Even numbers are those numbers that can be evenly divided by 2. What does "evenly divided by" mean? The standard interpretation for an even number is any number divided by 2 that has no remainder. Any number divided by 2 that does have a remainder is an odd number. Therefore, 8 is an even number because 8 / 2 = 4 with no remainder. Likewise, 9 is an odd number because 9 / 2 = 4 with a remainder of 1. Okay, so all we need to do is find an operator that gives us the remainder after division.

As it turns out, C provides a *modulus operator, %,* which *yields the remainder after integer division.* So,

```
   9  %  2 = 1     // 9 is odd
  15  %  4 = 3     // 15 is odd
   8  %  2 = 0     // 8 is even
4096  %  8 = 0     // 4096 is even
```

Having the modulus operator makes our algorithm a piece of cake:

```
if (val % 2 == 0)
  Serial.println("Even");
else
  Serial.println("Odd");
```

Again, because programmers (*especially* C programmers) tend to type as little as possible, they would likely rewrite the same code fragment above as:

```
if (val % 2) // Explicit test for equality missing
  Serial.println("Odd"); // Messages are now reversed
else
  Serial.println("Even");
```

How does this work? The *if* statement evaluates the expression between its parentheses (*val* % 2). If the result of that evaluation is non-zero, the expression is taken to be logic *true* and the next statement is processed. If the expression evaluates to 0, it is taken to be logic *false* and the *else* statement block is executed. So, if *val* is 9, 9 modulo 2 is 1, which evaluates to logic *true* and the code prints that the number is odd. That's why we had to reverse the print statements. Think about it.

Another thing to keep in mind is that the range of an *int* can vary among microcontrollers. For the Arduino family of microcontrollers, an *int* uses 2 bytes for storage, while the 32-bit microcontrollers use 4 bytes for storage for an *int*. You can see in Table 3.3 the impact that difference has on the range of data an *int* can process. Again, an *unsigned int* simply extends the numeric range of the *int*. You rarely need the extended range of an *unsigned int,* but it's there if you need it.

Again, it's not fair to be asking you to use information you don't yet have, but the fragments are simple enough to illustrate the point. The key thing to know about the *int* data type is that it represents whole numbers only, and it has a finite range of permitted values. As a result, there is a huge difference in the range of an *int* on an Arduino and that for the other microcontrollers. All bets are off if the value of an *int* overflows or underflows its range. If you see white smoke coming from the microcontroller...nah, just kidding. It's pretty hard to hurt the microcontroller with program code, so don't be afraid to experiment.

long/unsigned long

The *long* data type is also used for integer data, but sometimes with greater range than an *int*. All of the microcontrollers used in this book reserve 4 bytes for a *long* data type and, hence, have the same numeric range. Therefore, a *long* on a Teensy and a Nano require the same storage. However, because an *int* and a *long* both require 4 bytes of storage on a Teensy, their range is the same for either data type. Because a *long* is an integer number, it cannot represent fractional values. Any integer division that results in a remainder is truncated, not rounded.

If you look at enough Arduino code (e.g., the Blink sample program), you will likely see something like this:

```
delay(1000);
```

The *delay()* function is used to delay, or pause, the program for some specified period of time. The length of that pause is determined by the *argument* (i.e., the number 1000) that is passed to the *delay()* function. Okay, so what is the data type of the number 1000? Because it is not a variable, but rather a numeric constant in the program, if you know nothing about the *delay()* function, there's no way for you to know how the compiler is going to interpret that constant.

If you look at the references that are available for the Arduino IDE (e.g., https://www.arduino.cc/reference/en/language/functions/time/delay/) you can find one under the Time heading that tells you about the *delay()* function. As it turns out, the argument that is passed to *delay()* is an *unsigned long* data type expressed as milliseconds, although you can't tell that just by looking at the function call.

Or can you?

One of the things beginning students fail to see is the value of documentation in your code. Think of *documentation as anything that you can do to make your code less difficult to read and understand by the person reading the code.*

Data Type Suffixes

Back in the old days when my software company was making programming tools, including a C compiler for MSDOS, all "unadorned" program constants were assumed by the compiler to be *int* data types. Therefore, the 1000 in our *delay(1000)* function call would be treated by the compiler as an *int*. But you just learned that the argument to *delay()* should be an *unsigned long* data type. For reasons we explain in Chapter 7, nothing good happens when you send 2 bytes of *int* data to a function that is expecting to get 4 bytes of *unsigned long* data. How can you fix this? Simple: You use a data type suffix:

```
delay(1000UL);
```

A data type suffix is a short, alphabetic, notation at the end of a numeric constant that defines the data type of that constant. Notice the shaded "UL" at the end of the argument constant in the statement above. A data type suffix makes it unambiguous that the 1000 numeric constant is to be parsed by the compiler as an *unsigned long*.

Truth be told, today's compilers are smart enough to know that *delay()* expects an *unsigned long* as its argument, so why bother? Alas, it's also true that the compiler is smarter than we are. If it wasn't, how could it catch all of those syntax and semantic errors we make?
Nope...data type suffixes are there for *your* benefit when you read the code a year from now. Indeed, they are a form of documentation.

Recently I was looking at a program with 25 source code files and thousands of lines of code and right in the middle of one of the files is this statement:

```
check = 340l;
```

I thought to myself: "Man, that's a strange constant. I wonder what *check* is and why does it have the value of 3401?" Actually, the programmer's heart was in the right place because *check* was a *long* data type. Unfortunately, C allows both uppercase and lowercase letters for a data type suffix. Folks, that's an "ell" at the end of 340 above, not a 1 digit. This would have been much better documented using an uppercase 'L':

```
check = 340L;
```

The data type suffixes are presented in Table 3.6. In every case, I urge you to use the uppercase version

Table 3.6. Data type suffixes

Data Type	Data Type Suffix
int	None (assumed data type)
unsigned int	U, u
long int	L, l
unsigned long int	UL, ul
long long int	LL, ll
unsigned long long int	ULL, ull
float	F, f

of the data type suffix even though lowercase suffixes are allowed. With floating point constants, however, I find I don't use the F suffix very often:

```
average = sum / 100F;      // Note the 100F
```

Instead I'd use this:

```
average = sum / 100.0;  // decimal with floating point numbers
```

I think the second version using the decimal notation (i.e., the ".0") for a floating point constant is more clear. A quick look at the first version makes me think the constant represents 100 degrees Fahrenheit. If the floating point constant has a fractional value (e.g., 3.14), the decimal point has to be used anyway. Using the decimal notation is a good, consistent, way of documenting and flagging floating point constants.

float/double

Floating point numbers can use the *float* or *double* data type. The main differences between the two floating point data types are the digits of precision that each represents (6 versus 15) and the memory required (4 bytes versus 8 bytes) to store them. For the Arduino family, *float*s and *double*s both use the same 4 bytes of memory for storage, yielding the same 6 digits of precision. (See Table 3.3.) As a result, the numeric range is the same for both data types. So, why even bother using the *double* data type?

There are several possible reasons for using a *double* data type, even when not supported by the compiler. First, using the *double* data type documents that you would *like* to have the greatest precision possible for your floating point numbers. If you're doing least squares regression analysis on US GNP data expressed in dollars, the enhanced precision is noticeable. Second, if you port your code to a different processor (e.g., the Teensy) that does support the "larger" *double* data type, you automatically get greater precision in your results without making any changes to the code. Getting more precise results with no code changes is almost always a good thing. Third, the new processor (e.g., a Teensy T4) might have a hardware floating point processor buried inside of it. This means that floating point processing is done in hardware rather than software. This change makes the floating point processing significantly faster, again without any code changes on your part.

Buried in the *math.h* header file (e.g., on Windows, try the IDE's *hardware\tools\avr\avr\include* subdirectory path) are some floating point constants and macros you might find useful. For example:

#define M_PI	3.14159265358979323846	/* pi */
#define M_LN2	0.69314718055994530942	/* log_e 2 natural log 2 */
#define M_LN10	2.30258509299404568402	/* log_e 10 natural log10*/
#define fabsf	fabs	/* The alias for fabs(). */
#define fmodf	fmod	/* modulo for fp numbers */

Some of these constants are defined for the *long double* data type and their extended precision, but they can still be used even with *float* data types. To be able to use these constants, simply put this line near the top of your source code file:

```
#include <math.h>
```

The line is a preprocessor directive (discussed in Chapter 10) and tells the compiler to read in the content of the *math.h* header file into the program. By doing this, the compiler now knows about the symbolic constants (e.g., M_PI) defined in the *math.h* header file.

void

The *void* keyword is semantically considered a data type, but is really little more than a placeholder where you might find a "real" data type under different circumstances. In terms of understanding, think of the words "no usable data" as a replacement for *void.* If you look at the skeletal program in Listing 3.1, you see

```
void setup()
{ // some more lines...
}
void loop() [
// more lines
}
```

Note that both the *setup()* and *loop()* functions are preceded with the keyword *void.* The definition of every function must be preceded with a function data type specifier. A *function data type specifier states the data type that function is designed to send back to that part of the program code that called the function*. The *setup()* and *loop()* functions are not designed to return any useful data. What this means is that statements like the following:

```
   myData    = setup();
   yourData = loop();
```

make no sense because neither function is designed to return a value that can be assigned into any variable. Other functions, like *sqrt(x)* from the math library, on the other hand, are designed to return a value:

```
float sqrt(float val) { // code to calculate square root of val
}
```

In this instance, the *sqrt()* function was written to return a *float* data type which is the square root of the argument that is passed to it (i.e., it finds the square root of *val*). Notice the *float* keyword at the start of the first statement line above. So, a statement like:

```
float answer = sqrt(25.0);
```

would end up with *answer* holding

the numeric value 5.0.

Anytime you see the word *void* in a C expression, just think of the word "nothing" and you'll probably understand the context in which the keyword *void* is used.

Some documentation sources describe data types using terms like *uint8_t*, *uint16_t*, or similar types. These are used by the compiler for generating the proper code for the program. These are not hard to figure out (*uint8_t* is an *unsigned* 8-bit integer data type). They are used to unambiguously define a data type. For example, an Arduino *byte* is not a formal data type in the C standard, but is the same as an unsigned 8-bit integer (*uint8_t*).

enum Data Type

An *enum* is a user-defined data type that can only be used with integral data types (i.e., no floating point numbers). The *enum* list is created when it is declared. The standard example is an *enum* list that describes the days of the week:

```
enum weekDays {
   sunday, monday, tuesday, wednesday, thursday, friday, saturday};
//   0        1       2         3          4         4       6      enum values
```

Note that this statement is a data *declaration*: It has an attribute list in the symbol table, but no memory has yet been allocated. By default, the first member of the *enum* list (i.e., *sunday* in the declaration above) has the value of 0 and each member in the list is incremented by 1. The comment line below the enum declaration shows the values assigned to each *enum* member. (You can alter this default sequence if you wish, as we show below.)

To have a variable that you can use in your program, you must define (i.e., instantiate) an *enum* variable:

```
enum weekDays myWeek;
```

The statement defines *myWeek* as an *enum* variable that you can use in your programs. Consider Listing 3.2 below. When you run the program, the output displayed is

```
whichDay = 4
```

because the *enum* member named *thursday* is the 5th member in the list (counting in C always starts with 0 by default, remember?).

Listing 3.2. Program illustrating enum values

```
void setup() {
  Serial.begin(9600);
  enum weekDays {sunday, monday, tuesday, wednesday, thursday,
                 friday, saturday};
  enum weekDays myWeek;
  int whichDay;
  whichDay = thursday;
  Serial.print("whichDay = ");
  Serial.println(whichDay);
}
void loop() {
}
```

Remember that *enum* members are constants and, therefore, cannot be changed during program execution. This statement

```
tuesday = 11;   // error: lvalue required as left operand of assignment
```

draws an error message because the *enum* was declared with the constant value of 2 for *tuesday*. You cannot reassign it during program execution. (This is an example of a *semantic error*.) Suppose I change the *enum* declaration to:

```
enum weekDays {sunday='A', monday, tuesday, wednesday, thursday,
               friday, saturday};
```

Note that I changed the first constant in the *enum* list as shown by the shaded expression above. What happens to the program output in Listing 3.2? More specifically, what's the value of *friday*? You're right...I'm not going to tell you. It's short program, type it in and play with it. What if I changed the declaration again to:

```
enum weekDays {sunday='A', monday, tuesday = 10, wednesday,
                           thursday, friday, saturday};
```

What is the value for *thursday*? What's the value for *monday*?

#define versus enum member

Suppose I have this declaration in the code

```
enum weekDays {sunday, monday, tuesday, wednesday, thursday,
               friday,saturday};
int whichDay;

// ...a bunch of code...
 whichDay = tuesday;
```

As you saw earlier, *whichDay* has the value of 2 because that's the value of *tuesday* in the *enum* list. Now, suppose I do this (notice that I commented out the first program statement):

```
// enum weekDays {sunday, monday, tuesday, wednesday, thursday,
                  friday, saturday};
int whichDay;

#define tuesday 2

// ...a bunch of code...
 whichDay = tuesday;
```

What is the value of *whichDay*? (Note that an *enum* variable is not defined.) Obviously, it's 2. Okay, so if *tuesday* is a named constant from an *enum* list and a *#define* can be used to define a symbolic constant, aren't *enum* members and symbolic constants the same thing?

Nope...not by a long shot.

A *#define* results in a simple *textual substitution* by the preprocessor pass. In the example above, the compiler would never even see *tuesday.* The compiler would only see '2' everywhere *tuesday* <u>used to be</u> in the source code before the substitution took place.

An *enum*, on the other hand, is a real named constant that has a memory address and exists in the compiler's symbol table. If the Arduino IDE had a symbolic debugger, which allows you to inspect each variable as the program runs, you'd be able to see *tuesday* when it's part of an *enum* list. You would never see it with a *#define;* there is no memory allocated for it, the compiler can only see the text character '2'.

So, which should you use in your programs? Since the Arduino IDE doesn't have a symbolic debugger, I think a symbolic constant works just fine. If I were to use an *enum* list, I would likely make all of the member names in uppercase letters to look like the constants that they are. I think making them uppercase makes them stand out as constants. Choose whatever makes you happy.

Storage Class Specifiers

We are not ready to study storage class specifiers yet, but I wanted you to at least be aware of them. The storage class specifiers are: *auto*, *register*, *extern*, and *static*. All four of these storage class specifiers are C keywords, so you cannot use them as identifiers. You may see statements like:

```
extern int myPort;static float pinOffset;
```

Note how the storage class specifiers precede the actual data type of the variable being discussed. Storage classes do impact the way the data are stored or interpreted in a program. Actually, the *auto* and *register* storage class specifiers have pretty much gone the way of the dodo and are rarely used anymore. However, *extern* and *static* are very important concepts that we discuss at several different places later in the book. For now, just don't use the storage specifiers as names for variables or functions.

C string data

So far, we have covered the numeric data types that can be used in a C program. However, not everything in the world is numeric data. Sometimes we need to manipulate textual data, like names and addresses or stuff you might enter into an Internet search engine. In C, textual data is referred to as string data. It's called *string data* because textual data is often represented as a "string" of alphabetic *char* data arranged in a way that makes sense to the user.

Data Arrays

Okay, so how do you "string" a sequence of characters together? Simple. You create an array of characters. For example, suppose I want to define a character array large enough to hold my name. I could do it with the following definition:

```
char myName[12];
```

This statement defines a sequence of 12 consecutive *char* data bytes that can be referenced using the identifier *myName[]*. How would this look in memory? The statement above says the compiler will allocate enough memory for 12 *char* data types somewhere in memory. Let's assume the 12 bytes start at memory address 100. Because each *char* only uses one byte of memory, the *myName[]* array would look like:

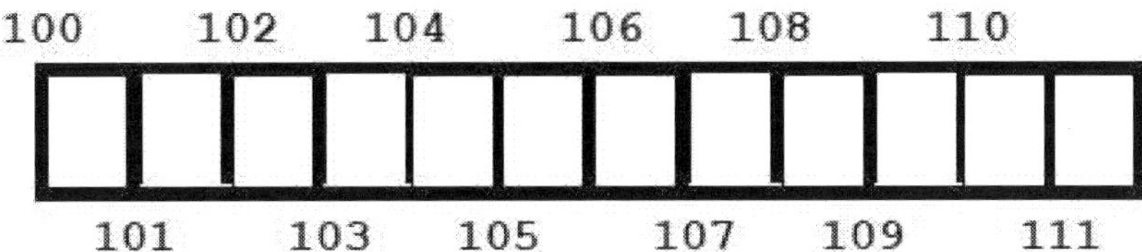

There are three basic ways to get my name into the *myName[]* array. First:

```
myName[0] = 'J';    // A single quote mark is a single character
myName[1] = 'a';
myName[2] = 'c';
myName[3] = 'k';
myName[4] = ' ';    // and so on...
```

This method is the most painful because it requires so much typing. Much less painful is:

```
char myName[12] = "Jack Purdum"; // double quote marks
                                 // is a string
```

Or

```
char myName[] = "Jack Purdum";  // Note empty brackets
```

Either of these variations produces the same data item, but notice that the second version omits the array size specification between the opening and closing array brackets. We can do this because the compiler is *really* good at counting things. The compiler can figure out the number of bytes of storage it needs by counting the letters in the *string literal* (i.e., the stuff between the double quote marks, "Jack Purdum"). Note that string literals use double quote marks, but single-byte character literals use *single quote marks* (e.g., 'A'). (The difference is important.)

The third way to move my name into the *myName[]* string array is with the statement:

```
strcpy(myName, "Jack Purdum");
```

The *strcpy()* function is a standard C library function that comes with the Arduino (and almost any other) C compiler. The *strcpy()* function copies the contents of the second argument (i.e., “Jack Purdum”) into the string array that is the first argument (i.e., *myName[]*).

What happens if you didn't define *myName[]* with a dimension big enough to hold all the characters in my name? No problem, the *strcpy()* function still writes my complete name into memory. Of course, whatever data item happens to be at memory address 112 in SRAM just got trampled to death during the string copy process. Even worse, you may never know it happened! Indeed, I had a similar error in a statistics package my company sold and it was three years, and thousands of customers later, before that bug manifested itself. C comes to you without training wheels. And, yep, the devil's in the details.

Suddenly, you're saying to yourself: “Wait a minute! Your name only has 11 characters in it, including the space character. However, you defined the array to store 12 characters. Why?” To understand why, let's look at the memory image after we have initialized it with my name:

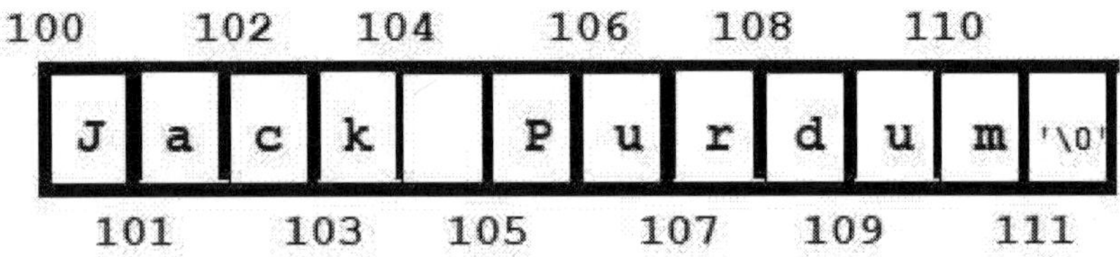

Okay, what's that doohickey at the end of my name, in byte 111? That is called the *null* character and is a single-byte character formed using a backslash followed immediately by a zero ('\0'). (In memory, the null character is usually represented by binary zero, 0b00000000.) The null character is used as a *sentinel marker* and marks the end of the string associated with this variable. When your program runs, the code knows the starting memory address (lvalue) of the string variable (e.g., *myName[]* which starts at memory address 100). So, if your program wants to display my name on the screen, the compiler goes to the lvalue of *myName[]* (memory address 100) and starts spinning through those memory addresses and moving those data bytes to the display. However, when it reads the null character, it knows it has reached the end of the string, so its job is finished. That is, the null becomes the *sentinel that determines the end of the string data.* For that reason, *all string arrays*

must be 1 byte larger than the largest string that array is expected to store. If you are processing a string variable that you forgot to add the null character to the end of it, again, no problem. It will just keep trucking through your memory until it finds a byte that has the value of binary 0 or runs out of SRAM. Unfortunately, there's no way of knowing how much memory the code spins through before it finds a 0!

If you look in Table 3.5, you'll see that the very first character in the table is called NUL (or null when spelled out) and is associated with the decimal value 0--usually. (The pre-XJ11 C compiler vendors were free to define what null would be and I know of one C compiler that used decimal 255 for the null character. I don't know of any modern-day C compiler that doesn't use 0 for null.) In any event, if you define an array that isn't big

Table 3.7. C string processing functions (partial list. See string.h)

String Function	Description
void *memchr(const void str[], int c, int n)	Find first occurrence of c within n bytes of str
void *memcmp(const void s1[], const void s2[], int n)	Compare n bytes of s1[] with s2[]
void *memcpy(const void s1[], const void s2[], int n)	Copy n bytes from s2[] into s1[]
void *memmove(const void s1[], const void s2[], int n)	Like memcpy(), but allows strings to overlap
void *memset(const void s1[], int c, int n)	Set first n bytes of memory in s1[] to c
void *memchr(const void *str, int c, int n)	Find first occurrence of c within n bytes of str
char *strcat(char dest[], const char src[])	Concatenate src to dest
char *strncat(char dest[], const char src[], int n)	Concatenate up to n chars from src to dest
char *strchr(const char str[], int c)	Search for the first occurrence of c in str
int *strcmp(char str1[], const char str2[])	Compare str1 to str2
int *strncmp(char str1[], const char str2[], int n)	Compare the first n bytes of str1 to str2
char *strcpy(char str1[], const char str2[])	Copy str2 into str1
char *strncpy(char str1[], const char str2[], int n)	Copy n bytes from str2 to str1
int strcspn(char str1[], const char str2[])	Get length of str1 which consists entirely of

	chars not in str2
int strlen(const char str1[])	Get the length (i.e., chars) in str1
char *strpbrk(char str1[], const char str2[])	Find first char in str1 that matches any char in str2
char *strrchr(const char str1[], int c)	Find last occurrence of c in str1
char *strspn(char str1[], const char str2[])	Find length of segment in str1 made of all chars in str2
char *strstr(char str1[], const char str2[])	Find first occurrence of str1 in str2
char *strtok(char str1[], const char delimiters[])	Break str1 into substrings based on delimiters[] found in str1

enough to hold the string data being stored in it, you're going to clobber whatever might be stored in the next memory address and that is almost never a good idea. If you ever have a program bug where the data seems to have a mind of its own, the first thing I would check is to make sure you're not over-writing your *string space*. I used the *strcpy()* function in an example above, and it is but one of many string processing functions that are sitting there waiting for you to use. Some of them are presented in Table 3.7. Other lists can be found by searching "C string processing functions" online.

Note that some of the *mem?()* functions duplicate the task done by other *str?()* functions. Putting all differences aside, usually the *str?()* functions are a little more bulletproof than the *mem?()* functions. Okay...if they do the same job, why would you ever want to use the "riskier" *mem?()* functions. Well, that's sorta like asking why did you ever take the training wheels off your bicycle? Because the *mem?()* functions assume you know what you're doing, they don't have any "protective code" in them (i.e., making sure the source and destination strings don't overlap). Because the protective code has been stripped away, the *mem?()* functions are about as small and as fast as they can be.

C++ String Class data

Not a big fan. Don't misunderstand me. C++ is a powerful language built on the *Object Oriented Programming* (OOP) paradigm and I'm a huge fan of what OOP brings to the table. In fact, the last chapter of this book discusses how to implement some of the better elements of OOP into your C programs. That said, the C++ *String class* is often an (unreliable) H-bomb-to-kill-an-ant approach to a programming problem. (Notice that a capital 'S' is used when talking about C++ Strings and a lowercase 's' when discussing strings derived from C *char* arrays.)

Another issue is that the String class seems to have a problem with its *garbage collection* (i.e., reusing idle memory resources). C++ Strings are dynamically allocated and, in our microcontroller world, there is no Real Time Operating System (RTOS) like Linux or Windows running in the background to handle those dynamic memory allocations and deallocations. Likewise, when the String memory is supposed to be released, it appears that some of that memory doesn't find its way back into the resource pool, resulting in wasted memory "gaps".
Not good...especially in an environment where memory is measured in kilobytes instead of gigabytes. Finally, many beginners like the String class because its (supposed to) work like strings in other languages. In other words, preference for String data seems to be a crutch left over from some previous programming experience.

For these reasons, I don't even want to discuss C++ Strings. If you're interested, there are a bazillion online references that you can use. I'd just rather see you invest your time in using string data built from C *char* arrays than some (potentially unreliable) String class. Chances are pretty good that your code will be slightly smaller, faster, and likely more reliable, than if you had used the String class.

Arrays in C

We talked earlier in this chapter about *char* arrays and how you can use them to store textual data. However, C allows you to define arrays for any data type. Consider the following statement:

```
int myData[4];
```

Let's further assume that we are defining this array for the STM32F103 microcontroller (aka, "Blue Pill"). Because the Blue Pill uses a 32-bit architecture, each *int* requires 4 bytes for storage. So, if the compiler places our array starting at memory address 200, each "box"

lvalue

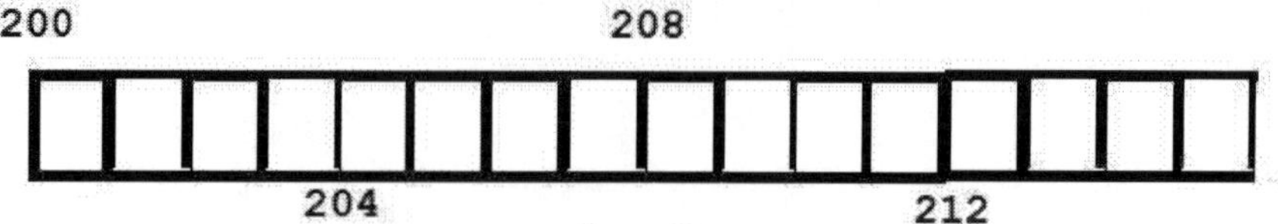

represents one byte in the *myData[]* array. Therefore, *myData[0]* occupies memory addresses 200 through 203, *myData[1]* uses addresses 204 through 207, and so on. This also means that the lvalue, which forms the base address of the array, is memory address 200. Note that *the lvalue of an array is the same as the name of the array by itself.* Therefore, if I write this statement:

```
long lv = myData;    // Note no array subscript!
```

and printed *lv* on the Serial monitor, it would display 200...the lvalue of the array. (Knowing this can be useful when we start talking about pointers.)

Can you figure out why the data type of the array is so important to the compiler? Anytime you access a specific element of the *myData[]* array, the compiler must calculate the proper memory address where that element begins. It does this using a formula similar to this:

*elementAddress = lvalue + (elementIndex * size of dataType)*

So, to find the starting address of *myData[2]*, we have:

```
elementAddr = baseAddr + (elementIndex * size of dataType)
myData[2]   =    lvalue + (        2         *        4)
myData[2]   =       200   +        8
myData[2]   = 208
```

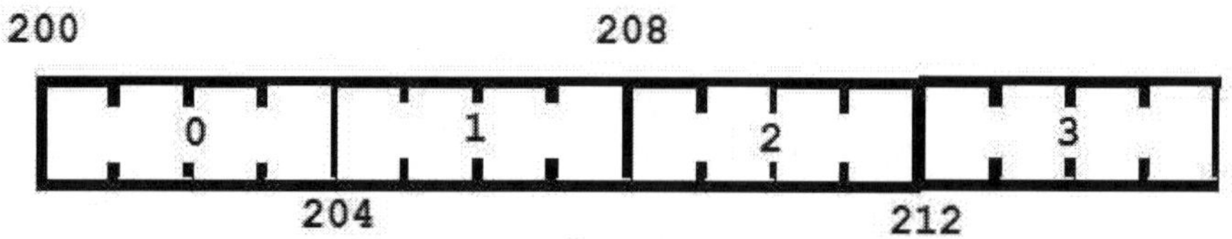

As you can see, *myData[2]* starts at memory address 208.

What if you have a table of data? In that case, you would need an array with 2 dimensions. What if you were printing an object on a 3D printer? Then you need to store the X, Y, and Z coordinates. What if you're writing a game that has objects flying around, but the time they reach a specific coordinate space is also important. Then you need to track X, Y, Z, and Time.

```
int myTable[5][10];                     // A table
int myObject[5][10][20];                // A 3D object
int myTarget[100][100][200][400];       // A 3D object in space-time
```

I tried to think of a good example with 5 dimensions and got nothing but a headache. I'm not sure if the spec has changed, but you are limited to arrays with up to 255 ranks. (Has anyone *ever* needed an array with 255 ranks?)

Some generalized characteristics about arrays:

1. The number of "units" in an array is called the number of *elements* in the array

2, The *array index* tells us which element of the array is being referenced.

3. Array index numbers always start with 0, *not* 1

4. Using an array index that is larger than the number of elements in the array never works, even though the mischief it causes may not be obvious

5. An array name used by itself without any array brackets (i.e., *myData* and not *myData[0]*) always resolves to that array's starting address in memory (i.e., its lvalue).

6. An array element count obeys the N – 1 Rule.

The N – 1 Rule for Arrays

The *N – 1 Rule* for arrays states:

> *The highest valid index number for an array is the array dimension minus 1.*

For example, if you define an array as:

```
long bigArray[10];
```

You have 10 elements defined for the *bigArray[]*, but the N – 1 Rule dictates that the largest valid array index for *bigArray[]* is 9 *(bigArray[9])*. That is:

N – 1
10 – 1

9

The reason is because the valid array elements are *bigArray[0]* through *bigArray[9]*. Before you finish this book, at some point you will do the equivalent of something like:

```
bigArray[10] = 2500L;
```

Sadly, even though an index value of 10 falls outside the array as you defined it and it just blew away whatever was in memory after the end of the array, you might never know it. Such errors may go unnoticed for years, which is why they are so hard to detect.

Initializing Numeric Arrays

There are several different ways that you can initialize a numeric array in C. First, you can do it elementby-element as we did for *char* arrays earlier in the chapter:

```
int myArray[10];
myArray[0] = 1;
myArray[1] = 2;
myArray[2] = 3;
   // and so on as needed...
```

Another way to initialize an array is in conjunction with its definition:

```
int myArray[10] = {1, 2, 3}; // Use initializer list
```

Notice that the last initializer value in an initializer list (3 in this example) does not have a comma after it. Now, the question becomes: If we have defined the array to have 10 elements and we only have initialized the first 3, what is contained in the remaining 7 elements? As usual, it depends. If the array is defined within a function block (i.e., local scope which we discuss in Chapter 6), array elements are assumed to be garbage.

If the definition of *myArray[]* appears outside of any function (i.e., global scope), the remaining 7 elements *are supposed to be initialized to 0*. As far as I know, all of the post-ANSI (American National Standards Institute) C compilers do initialize the (globally-defined array) elements to 0. However, there are some pre-ANSI compilers that do not do global initialization. Perhaps the safest route is to assume all array elements, regardless of scope, are garbage. If you changed the array definition to this:

```
int myArray[] = {1, 2, 3};        // Use initializer list
```

myArray[] now only has 3 elements. Because the array size between the brackets is left empty, the compiler counts the number of values in the initializer list and reserves that many elements for the array.

Quite often you will define an array within a function block, yet you want each element to start with a known value. In other words, you still want the array to start in a known state, but without having to define it outside of the function. If you look at some Arduino code on line, you might see something like this:

```
int myArray[10];
for (int k = 0; k < 10; k++) {
  myArray[k] = 0;
}
```

I realize we haven't discussed *for* loops yet, but my guess is you understand what's going on in this code fragment. The *for* loop define a counter variable named *k* and initializes its starting value to 0. The next expression asks if *k* is less than 10, which it is. Since the middle expression of the *for* loop evaluates to logic *true* (i.e., k is 0 now, so it is true that it is less than 10), it proceeds to the next statement. Because *k* is presently 0, the statement controlled by the for loop becomes:

```
myArray[0] = 0;
```

which means the first element of the array is assigned the value of 0. The last expression in the *for* loop, that weird *k++*, simply adds 1 to *k* so that it now becomes 1 instead of 0. Program control then goes back to the middle expression and asks if *k* is (still) less than 10. Because k is now 1, we excute the same statement as before, but the value of k is now changed to 1:

```
myArray[1] = 0;
```

I think you can see that we end up with all of the elements of *myArray[]* equal to 0 after the *for* loop finishes its task.

The *for* loop code is what I call PGC, or Pretty Good Code. The reason is because most C programmers would write the *for* loop using this code:

```
memset(myArray, 0, sizeof(myArray));
```

The *memset()* function takes a chunk of memory and initializes that chunk to a given value. In our case, the chunk of memory is the block of memory that has been allocated to *myArray.* The value to use for the initializer value is 0. The last argument to the *memset()* function uses the *sizeof()*

operator. The *sizeof()* operator uses the symbol table to determine how many bytes are allocated to *myArray[]*. If you were writing the code for an 8-bit processor, each *int* would use 2 bytes, so the 20 bytes of memory (i.e., 10 elements at 2 bytes each) are all initialized to 0. If you are using a 32-bit processor, the memory block would be 40 bytes long, but would still contain all 0's for those 40 bytes.

It is safe to use *memset()* only when all of the bytes allocated to the array are identical. This means you cannot use it to initialize each element of a 10-element array to 1. Why not? The reason is because a 2byte *int* looks like this when its value is 1:

```
00000000 00000001
```

If we try to use *memset()* to set the elements to 1, it would look like this:

```
00000001 00000001
```

Instead of setting each array element value to 1, using *memset(myArray, 1, sizeof(myArray))* sets each element value to 257. Not good. Always keep in mind that *memset()* has no Kevlar in it and has no bullet-proof protection from misuse. If you always remember that *memset()* can only work at the byte level, you should be okay.

Conclusion

We covered a lot of important stuff in this chapter, so take your time and perhaps go back and just lightly review what's presented here. All concepts presented in each chapter are like another row of cement block when building the foundation of a home. Doing a sloppy job on one row threatens the entire structure, not just that row. Review the material and enjoy the ride.

Exercises

1. What are the Five Program Steps?
2. How might the Five Program Steps be useful to you?
3. What is an algorithm?
4. Good variable names are like _____ while good function names are like _____?
5. How would you describe a "good" variable or function name?
6. What is "camel notation" and why should you use it?
7. In this code fragment:

char memberNames[100][20];

```
long bigNumber;
strcpy(memberNames[0], (char *) "Terry Strickland");
bigNumber = memberNames;
Serial.println( (long) bigNumber);
```

a. What can you tell me about the *memberNames[][]* array?
b. What does *&memberName[0][0]* mean?
c. What does the Serial monitor display?

8. What happens with this expression:

```
Serial.println( 2251UI);
```

9. How would you write a statement that would display the name of the 50th member in #7?
10. If x = 24, what does the expression x << 2 do?

Chapter 4 Making Decisions

We've already mentioned that computers are really good at counting. Microcontrollers are too. Still, if all microcontrollers could do is count stuff, they would be considerably less useful. The real power of computers and microcontrollers is derived from their ability to alter the otherwise linear flow of a program's execution based on the data that they are processing. For example, if a fire sensor does not sense a fire, nothing is done. However, if that same sensor detects a fire, the software can sound fire alarms, dial 911 with an automated message, turn on the sprinkler system, and perhaps a dozen other tasks all in a matter of milliseconds. In other words, microcontrollers can make decisions and alter the course of program action(s) based upon the information the microcontroller is reading. The fun part: We get to make the microcontroller dance to whatever tune we choose to play! Warning! The ability to control what a microcontroller does is more than just fun...it's addicting!

In this chapter we explore how microcontrollers can make decisions based on the data they are processing. However, if decisions are being made on the basis of input data, we need to be able to compare data. Like we just mentioned, a fire sensor has to be able to compare a "no-fire" state to that of a "pants-on-fire" state. A microcontroller might be responsible for turning on the air conditioning if the temperature sensor says the temperature reading is above 75 degrees. Therefore, we need to discover the operators that C uses to evaluate expressions and make decisions based on the outcome of those comparisons.

Relational Operators

You already have seen a list of the relational operators in Table 2.1 of Chapter 2. The relational operators are repeated in Table 4.1. (All of the relational operators associate from left to right.) Note that the equality operators have a slightly lower precedence than the other relational operators. Sometimes forgetting the difference in precedence levels for the relational operators can lead to some frustrating debugging sessions.

Table 4.1 Relational Operators

Operator	Meaning	Precedence
>	Greater than	8
>=	Greater than or equal to	8

<	Less than	8
<=	Less than or equal to	8
==	Equal to	9
!=	Not equal to	9

Each of the relational operators in Table 4.1 requires two operands. Therefore, relational operators are *binary operators. The purpose of relational operators is to make comparisons between two operands.*

The general syntax for a *relational expression* is:

operand1 **relational-operator** *operand2*

The result of a relational expression is either logic *true* or logic *false*. For example:

Operand1	Relational Operator	Operand2	Result of Comparison
5	>	4	logic *true*, 5 is greater than 4
5	<	4	logic *false*, 5 not less than 4
5	==	4	logic *false*, 5 is not equal to 4
5	!=	4	logic *true*, 5 is not equal to 4

As shown here, the relational operators are used to compare operands. The result of a relational expression always resolves to either *true* or *false*. The result of a relational expression is a boolean *true* or *false*; it is not numeric. Okay, so how can we use the relational operators? The simplest comparison statement is the *if* statement.

The if Statement Block

The *if* statement block has the following syntax structure:

```
if (relationalExpression) {
   statement(s);
}
```

We can illustrate the program flow that results from an *if* statement block using the diagram shown in Figure 4.1. The relational expression in an *if* statement block creates two paths that the program can take, depending upon the outcome of the comparison test created by the relational expression. Note the opening brace ('{') at the end of the *if* statement line and its matching closing brace ('}') which marks the end of the *if* statement block. The braces are the delimiters that, together, form the *if* statement block. The *if* statement block *includes all of the statement(s) that appear between the braces and are controlled by the relational expression.*

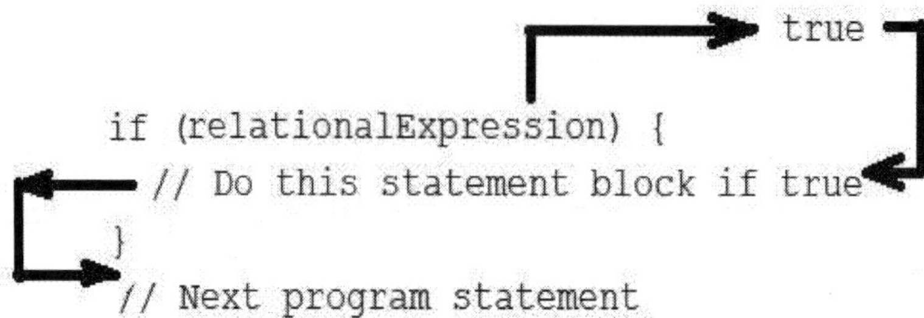

Figure 4.1. Possible execution paths created by an if statement

If the outcome of the relational expression contained within the parentheses following the *if* keyword in Figure 4.1 is logic *true*, the statement(s) within the *if* statement block are executed. This is the path shown in Figure 4.1. If the outcome of the relational expression is logic *false*, all of the statements within the *if* statement block are bypassed and the first statement following the *if* statement block is executed. For example:

```
j = 8;
// some program statements...
if (j == 8) {
   Serial.print("j equals 8");
}
```

Because *j* is equal to 8, we use the *Serial* object to display the message. If *j* is any other value, the statement(s) between the opening and closing braces are ignored.

We can summarize the *if* statement block's program execution paths as follows:

> *true*: all statement(s) within the *if* statement block are executed
> *false*: all statement(s) within the *if* statement are skipped

You're probably saying: "Okay...I'll bite. Why are you parenthesizing the word "statement(s)" when talking about the *if* statement block?" The reason is, when the *if* statement block contains a single program statement, you can omit the braces that delimit the *if* statement block. Consider the following code snippets:

```
if (x == 2) {
   Serial.println("x equals 2");
}
```

and

```
if (x == 2)
   Serial.println("x equals 2");
```

Notice that the second version does not have the delimiting braces for the *if* statement block. However, because the *if* statement block only controls a single statement, both versions are syntactically identical and both execute in the same way.

Why Use Statement Braces When They Are Not Required?

So, given that you don't "need" the braces when the *if* block contains a single program statement, why type them in? There are several reasons. First, because the *Serial.print()* statement is your primary debugging tool, you may need to insert a debug statement in the *if* statement block to inspect some program variable. For the debug statement to be controlled by the *if* block, you're going to have to add the braces to the *if* statement block anyway. Second, always adding the braces to delineate the *if* statement block lends a consistency to your coding style. Programming style consistency makes it easier to read, test, and debug the code. Third, forget the first two reasons and always add the *if* statement block braces.

Let's write a short program to illustrate the *if* statement block. Figure 4.2 is a screenshot of a simple program example of the *if* statement.

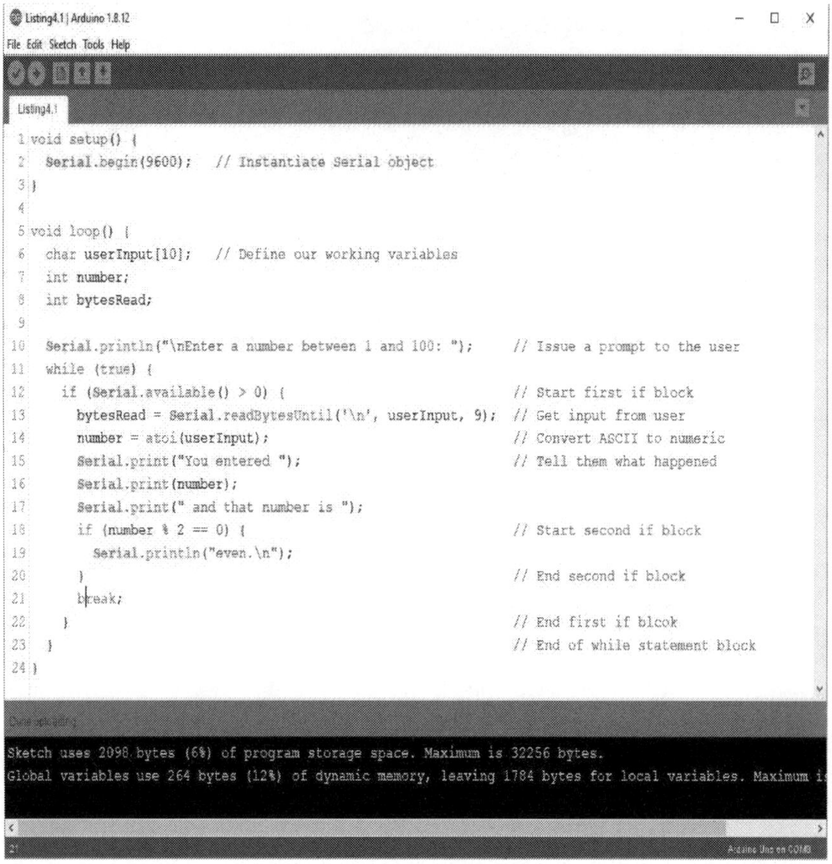

Listing4.1 | Arduino 1.8.12

File Edit Sketch Tools Help

Listing4.1

```
void setup() {
  Serial.begin(9600);   // Instantiate Serial object
}

void loop() {
  char userInput[10];   // Define our working variables
  int number;
  int bytesRead;

  Serial.println("\nEnter a number between 1 and 100: ");      // Issue a prompt to the user
  while (true) {
    if (Serial.available() > 0) {                              // Start first if block
      bytesRead = Serial.readBytesUntil('\n', userInput, 9);  // Get input from user
      number = atoi(userInput);                                // Convert ASCII to numeric
      Serial.print("You entered ");                            // Tell them what happened
      Serial.print(number);
      Serial.print(" and that number is ");
      if (number % 2 == 0) {                                   // Start second if block
        Serial.println("even.\n");
      }                                                        // End second if block
      break;
    }                                                          // End first if blcok
  }                                                            // End of while statement block
}
```

```
Sketch uses 2098 bytes (6%) of program storage space. Maximum is 32256 bytes.
Global variables use 264 bytes (12%) of dynamic memory, leaving 1784 bytes for local variables. Maximum i
```

Figure 4.2. screenshot of if statement program.

Let's walk through the program code line-by-line. (You can activate line numbers for your programs by loading your Preferences dialog box [*File → Preferences* or Ctrl-comma] and then checking the *Display line numbers* option and clicking OK to save the change.)

A Code Walk-through

Let's do a code walk-through on the code in Figure 4.2. *A code walk-through is a process where you examine each line of code, statement by statement, looking for program bugs or errors in the design.*

Code walk-throughs were a regular event at the software company I owned. Typically, I would give a coding assignment to a small team of programmers with a deadline a couple of weeks away. The walk-throughs were always on Friday mornings and every programmer was required to attend. (It was a small company and I never had more than eight programmers.) If the code walk-through did not uncover any program bugs or design flaws, I would buy beer and pizza for lunch and _all_ of the programmers would get the afternoon off.

Sounds expensive? Not by a long shot. I can't tell you how many times I saw all of the programmers at work on Thursday night pouring over the code and preparing the team for their code walk-through. The results were nothing but terrific. First, it fostered a "we're-all-in-this-together" team spirit. I think it helped them to work well together, too. Second, it exposed the entire team to a different element of the project at hand. Because my company was small, if someone was sick or on vacation, it left a noticeable hole in the manpower. The walk-throughs helped when someone had to jump in and take over until the other programmer returned. Finally, they seemed to like working there because they knew that good work was rewarded. The lost man hours from Friday afternoon off was trivial compared to the benefits it brought to the company.

Nope, code walk-throughs are a good thing on multiple fronts.

In Figure 4.2, line 2 instantiates (i.e., defines an object so you can use it) the *Serial* monitor which is used to collect input data from the user or to display program output. The default communication (baud) rate between your microcontroller and PC is 9600. Note that this statement appears in the *setup()* function. In Chapter 3 we told you that the statements in *setup()* are the first statements that are executed in your programs. We also stated that *setup()* typically holds the program's Initialization Step—those things that are done to establish the environment in which the program runs. Often, the *setup()* code completes its tasks before the user even knows the program is running. This is a pretty simple program, so line 2 does set things up for the rest of our program. Once line 2 has been processed and the *Serial* object instantiated, program control is immediately transferred to line 6 in the *loop()* function. If you are running a fast microcontroller, like the Teensy 4.0 (often referred to as the "T4"), the instantiation of the *Serial* object takes a relatively large amount of time. In fact, if you had a *Serial.print()* statement where line 3 is, there's a pretty good chance you'd never see that line displayed on your monitor. The reason is because the T4 is so fast that it blows right through line 2 and into line 6 in *loop()* before the *Serial* object finishes its instantiation. If you need to "see" something immediately after the *Serial.begin()* statement, you often see this statement before any program statements that use the *Serial* object:

```
while (!Serial);
```

Although we are not yet ready to discuss the *while* keyword yet, the *! Serial* (i.e., NOT *Serial*) expression forces the program to "waste time" until the *Serial* object is available for use (i.e., instantiated) in the program. (This is sorta like waiting for NOT *Serial* to become YES *Serial*.)

Lines 6-8 in *loop()* define several variables that are used in the rest of the program. Because *setup()* took care of Step 1 (Initialization) of the Five Program Steps, we're ready for Step 2, Input. Line 10 issues a prompt that tells the user the nature of the input data we want them to enter.

Line 11 uses the *while* statement block to control the rest of the program. The expression that controls the *while* loop has been defined to always be logic *true*. This means that, unless something else happens in the statements controlled by the *while* statement block, our program is stuck here until: 1) power is lost, 2) a component fails, 3) the user does a reset of the microcontroller, or 4) the cows come home. More on this in a few moments.

Line 12 uses an *if* statement block to see if there is any input available from the Serial object. If the function call to *Serial.available()* returns 0, that means that there is no input data available for use in the program. Because the *if* statement block is logic *false* and the closing brace for this *if* statement block is line 22, all of the statements between line 12 and line 22 are skipped and control is sent to line 23. However, line 23 is the closing statement brace for the *while* loop, so the code jumps back to line 11. Once again, because the *while* expression is always logic *true*, control proceeds to line 12 to see if anything has become available from the *Serial* object yet. Indeed, the program is going to bounce back and forth between lines 11 and 23 until the user decides to pay attention and type something into the program.

Type something into the program...where?

We've talked about the Serial monitor before, but have never provided much in the way of details about how to use it. Figure 4.3 shows the Serial

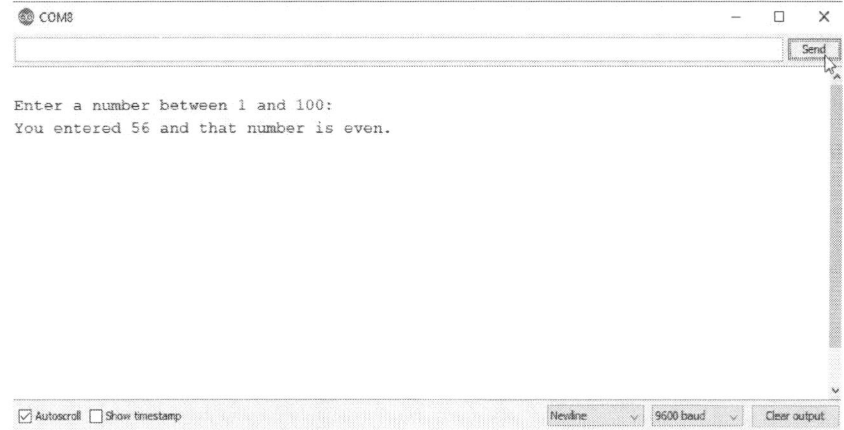

Figure 4.3. The Serial monitor

monitor as our program executes. At the top, you can see COM8 displayed in the title bar. This tells you that my computer selected COM port number 8 for the communications link between the microcontroller and my PC. You must always select a COM port for the IDE to use by the Tools → Port menu option. Select the port that is associated with the Arduino IDE. Immediately below the title bar is a very wide, albeit skinny, text box that you can use to type in data that is to be used by the program.

Once you've finished typing in the data, you can click the Send button that appears at the right edge of the text box, or you can just press Enter. The Enter key works because the option for how the input from the text box is terminated is set to "Newline". (You can see its dropdown box at the bottom of Figure 4.3.) This is the default termination method, but others exist. This option does *not* include the newline character ('\n') as part of the final data input; the newline is stripped from the input stream before it gets to your program and can be used. The other termination options provide the means for including the newline character as part of the input stream should you need it.

If you did type in a number and press Enter (or click Send), that information is sent over the USB cable via the COM port and shoved into the *Serial* object's input buffer. (Think of the term *buffer* as being *a small amount of memory reserved for some type of data.*) When that data arrives in the buffer, a notification is sent to the *Serial.available()* method and that method call returns a non-zero value. Because the *if* expression using *Serial.available()* is now a positive number, the *if* expression in line 12 evaluates to logic *true*, and the *if* statement block is executed starting at line 13.

Reading Input Data from the Serial Object

The *Serial* object provides several different methods for reading input data. The statement in line 13:

```
bytesRead = Serial.readBytesUntil('\n', userInput, 9);
```

says: Use the *readBytesUntil()* method until the user types in a *newline character* (i.e., '\n' which is generated by pressing Enter or clicking Send) or the user has typed in 9 characters, whichever comes first. Collect that user input and store it in the *userInput[] char* array and return a count of the number of characters the user entered, *not* including the newline character." Suppose you typed in the number "26". The progression to resolve the expression looks like this:

```
bytesRead = Serial.readBytesUntil('\n', userInput,
                                                 9);
bytesRead = Serial.readBytesUntil('\n', "26", 9);
bytesRead = 2;
```

So, the *bytesRead* variable holds the number of characters you typed in for the input data. (Try adding a *Serial.print()* statement to confirm that *bytesRead* equals 2. Experimenting is always a valuable learning experience.) If you think about it, line 13 is Step 2, Input, of the Five Program Steps.

"Hold on! Why did you use 9 in the *readBytesUntil()* statement when you defined the array to hold 10 characters?" Good question. Remember our discussion of string data? How does the compiler know when it reaches the end of the string? It does so using the *null* sentinel character that appears at the end of the string. Since we need the *null* to find the end of the input data, it seems like we shouldn't allow the user to enter more than 9 characters, right? In programming, the devil's in the details.

Line 14 uses the *atoi()* function (i.e., ASCII to integer) to convert the string characters "26" you typed into the Serial monitor's input buffer and ended up in the *userInput char* array. (Remember that "26" are characters and are actually ASCII codes 50 and 54. See Table 3.5.) The *atoi()* function converts the character digits 50 and 54 to the integer value 26 and assigns that value into *number.* It would be good practice for you to verbally walk through line 14 describing what is taking place using the terms "lvalue", "rvalue", "register", and "data bus" as you do. (For reasons I don't understand, physically saying the words out loud rather than just "thinking" them seems to make a more concrete learning experience. For this reason, you may want to read this book alone in a fairly sound-proof room!)

Line 14 is Step 3, Processing, of the Five Program Steps because it takes the raw input data (character digits) and converts them into an integer value.

Lines 15-20 are Step 4, Output, of the Five Program Steps. Line 18 does have an *if* statement block that determines whether we display the “even” message or not, but it is still part of the Output Step. Line 21 contains the *break* keyword. We have a complete discussion of *break* in Chapter 5. For now, consider that the purpose of *break* is to transfer program control outside of the current loop statement block. The controlling loop statement is the *while* in line 11. Move the cursor in the Source code window to the end of line 23, right next to the closing brace of the *while* statement block. You should see a small rectangle surrounding the opening brace of the *while* statement block at the end of line 11. Now move the cursor to the end of line 11, next to the opening brace of the while statement block. You should now see the small rectangle around the closing brace in line 23. This “near the brace” tip makes it easier to see the start and end of any programming block. We've mentioned this tip before, but we want to make sure you use it to “see” the various code blocks in a program. (Move the cursor to the end of line 24. What happened?)

Figure 4.3 shows the output from the program after I typed in the number 56. The program works as we designed it, so it's an example of SDC...Sorta Dumb Code. That is, it works as planned, but we can make a few changes to reflect we have learned thus far.

Some Program Tweaks

Suppose we add these lines near the top:

```
(Line 0: )#define INPUTBUFFSIZE 10 // NOTE: No
                                    // semicolon
Line 6:   char userInput[INPUTBUFFSIZE];
Line 13:
bytesRead = Serial.readBytesUntil('\n', userInput,
                              INPUTBUFFSIZE - 1);
Line 18:  if (number % 2) {
Line 19:    Serial.println("odd.\n");
```

Note that we had to change the string constant in line 19 because of the logic change in line 18. Think about it until that last sentence makes sense.

The #define Preprocessor Directive

Line 0 adds something called a *symbolic constant. A symbolic constant is simply a name you wish to use for something in a program*. Perhaps the most common use is to apply symbolic constants to numeric values. The *#define* preprocessor directive tells the preprocessor pass to go through the source code file and everywhere it sees INPUTBUFFSIZE, replace that symbolic constant with 10. (By convention, I use all capital letters for symbolic constants as it makes them stand out from the rest of the code. You don't *have* to use capital letters for symbolic constants...unless you were a student in one of my programming classes.)

The Preprocessor Pass occurs before the compiler ever examines the program source code. All preprocessor directives start the line on which they appear with a # symbol. There are a number of Preprocessor Pass directives you can use, of which #define is just one. *#define causes a <u>textual</u> replacement of the symbolic constant (i.e., INPUTBUFFSIZE) for whatever follows on that line after the symbolic constant (i.e., 10).* If you look at the new lines 6 and 13 and pretend you're the preprocessor pass, you will end up with the lines exactly as they appeared before.

Why Use Symbolic Constants?

If the code the compiler sees is exactly the same as it was before we use symbolic constants, why bother? Most of you are too young to remember when the speed limit on all Federal highways was reduced from (usually) 70 miles per hour to 55 miles per hour. This was done in response to the gas shortages of the early 1970's. Failure to lower the speed limit meant you lost your federal dollars for highway construction and repair.

Somewhere in Texas, the state decided to repair a number of speed sign posts as long as they had to change the signage anyway. In the process, a number of the signs were erected 6" too low to meet Federal highway requirements, forcing the state to go back and install new sign posts. Someone remarked: "Good thing the State made the changes. Had the Feds done it, they would have lowered the road 6". Some element of truth there...

All across the nation, thousands of programs had to be changed to reflect the new speed limit change. It would seem that it would be a simple matter of using your search-and-replace feature of your program editor and search for 70 and replace it with 55. Sadly, there could be dozens, perhaps hundreds of places in a complex program where the speed limit might be referenced, from calculating fines and recording the data to citing section and paragraph numbers in the traffic laws. Doing a global searchand-replace could make:

```
        Section 19-7020. Driving Under The Influence
```

now appear as

```
      Section 19-5520. Driving Under The Influence
```

which is probably not the desired change. The Rule is simple: *Never* use global search-and-replace in a program. It almost always comes back to bite you later on. Inspect each potential change before you commit to it.

Now that you know about symbolic constants, you would have written the original software to have defined a symbolic constant and the start of the program:

```
#define FEDERALSPEEDLIMIT 70
```

After the change in the law, you could go to the same line and replace it with:

```
#define FEDERALSPEEDLIMIT 55
```

recompile the program and take the rest of the day off. By using a symbolic constant from the get-go, one simple change and you're done! No error-prone search-and-replace and the potential for disastrous changes along the way.

Magic Numbers

When I look at the source code of a program, and you see a numeric constant, like 100, in it, I always wonder why "100" is so special. It would have been nice if the coder had thought enough to give me at least a hint as to what the numeric constant means.

Think about symbolic constants any time you are writing code that requires the use of a constant. For example, I was recently working on a project where we had to sample the Standing Wave Ratio (SWR) on an antenna system. Because I wasn't sure how many samples would be required for an acceptable measurement, I decided on 100 samples as a starting point. This resulted in the following symbolic constant:

```
#define SWRSAMPLES 100   // SWR sample size
```

Later in the program there were a number of places where the constant was used:

```
float samples[SWRSAMPLES];

 // more code...

 sum = 0.0;
 for (i = 0; i < SWRSAMPLES; i++) {
  samples[i] = ReadSWR();
  sum += samples[i];
 }
 averageSWR = sum / SWRSAMPLES;
```

and so on. As we gained experience with the electronics, we needed to assess the impact of changing the sample size on the final performance. All I needed to do was change the 100 in the definition of the symbolic constant, recompile the program, and I could quickly see the impact on the results. So, one reason to use symbolic constants instead of hard-coding magic numbers like 100 into the program is because they make program changes so much easier and less error prone. Anytime you have a magic number that you think might change in the future, consider using a symbolic constant.

Another reason for using symbolic constants is that they can help document what the code is doing. Which makes more sense to you without reading additional code:

```
    for (i = 0; i < 100; i++) {
```

or

```
    for (i = 0; i < SWRSAMPLES; i++) {
```

As a general rule, replacing numeric constants with a symbolic constant helps place some context on the code. Whenever possible, get rid of magic numbers in your code. They almost always make your code less flexible and more cryptic. We introduce other preprocessor directives throughout the book as they are needed and follow with a more complete discussion of the directives in Chapter 10.

if-else Statement Blocks

The fact that our program does not display anything when the user enters an odd number is a major design flaw in the code. Even adding the program tweaks, our program is still SDC because nothing happens when the user types in an odd number. We could add another *if* statement block to fix that:

```
if (number % 2 == 0) {
  Serial.println("even.\n");
}
if (number % 2 == 1) {    // Start 2nd if block
  Serial.println("odd. \n");
}
```

Even though this would fix the problem that there is no output when the number entered is even, it's still not a good solution to the problem. The reason it's not a good solution is because the two *if* blocks more-or-less have the same purpose: checking whether the number is odd or even. The design also means that the code performs an unnecessary relational test each time. What we need is a better way to process the "either/or" nature of that test.

We can improve the program by letting a single *if* expression control both (i.e., logic *true* or *false*)

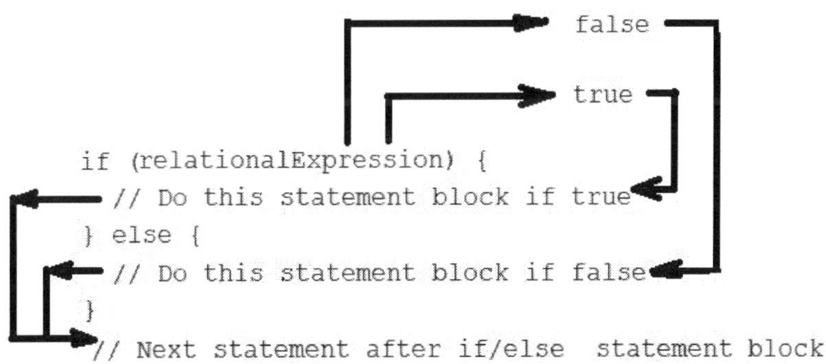

Figure 4.4. Possible execution paths created by an if statement

outcomes of the test. This is easily fixed using the *if-else* statement. Figure 4.4 shows the program flow for an *if-else* statement block. The *else* clause simply recognizes that any relational test can only have two outcomes, logic *true* or *false,* and provides an execution path for the logic *false* statement block. If the *relationalExpression* evaluates to logic *true*, the *true* path is followed to the statement block immediately below the *if* statement. When all of the statements in the *true* statement block have been executed, program control skips over the *else* statement block and resumes execution with the first statement following the *if/else* statement block.

If *relationalExpression* evaluates to logic *false*, the statements in the *true* statement block are skipped and the *else* statement block is executed. When the *else* block finishes, program control resumes at the next program statement.

Now we can replace lines 18-20 by adding the following new lines in their place:

```
if (number % 2) {        // Start second if block
  Serial.println("odd.\n");
} else {
  Serial.println("even.\n");
}                     // End else clause and if block
```

Now the program produces output regardless of whether an odd or even number results. Another win is the fact that we can display the correct answer using a single relational test...no more redundant tests!

I'd say we've progressed to PGC, Pretty Good Code. Still, after entering about three or four numbers, the program has all the interest of watching a nail rust. Let's add just a wee bit of interest.

Adding LEDs to the Odd-Even Program

First, let's think about what we want our modified program to do. We want the program to still output the result to the Serial monitor, but in addition, we'd like to add two LEDs to the program. One of the LEDs should light when the user enters a even number and the other LED lights on an odd number. If you have different colored LEDs, so much the better.

Obviously, for this to work as designed, the Uno needs to interface with external devices (the LEDs). In order for the Uno to interface with the LEDs, the Uno needs to know which pins you plan on using to attach the LEDs to the Uno.

Often I talk about this or that program being used with an Uno or Nano. Unless I say differently, the program also works with the STM32, ESP32, or the T4. Keep in mind, however, that the other three microcontrollers are using 3.3V for the logic levels rather than 5V like the Uno. In this program where an LED (or other external device) is used for the program output,

LEDs designed for 5V still work, but may not be as bright as they would be on a 5V system.

Because an ON or OFF state is fine for the LED indicators, just about any digital pin can be used. Keep in mind that the amount of current a digital pin can handle is pretty limited. Although they are supposed to handle up to 40mA max, I try to operate well below that level. A dropping resistor should be used in any circuit that attaches an LED to a microcontroller pin. Figure 4.5 shows how I chose to wire the circuit. I chose to use pins 10 and 11, although there's no real technical reason for that choice of pins.

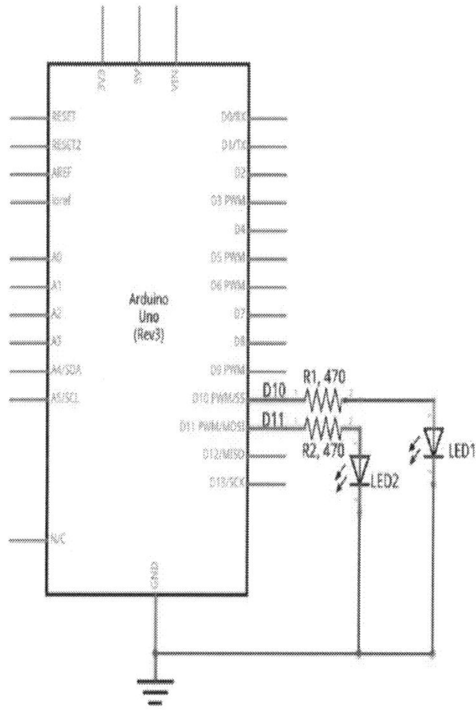

Figure 4.5. Schematic of Odd-Even Program

However, on the Uno or Nano, it's often desirable to stay away from pins 0 through 3. Pins 0 and 1 are used for Serial communications (COM) between your PC and the microcontroller via the USB port. (You can use these two pins for digital I/O if no serial communications are needed when the program runs.) I also avoid pins 2 and 3 if I can, as those are the only two external interrupt pins available on the Uno/Nano and, who knows, I may need them later on. I opted to use 470Ω resistors for R1 and R2, although any value between 200-800Ω should work fine.

Okay, so much for the hardware. We also need to make some software changes so the microcontroller knows that the LEDs are part of the program. The complete listing can be seen in Figure 4.6. The code is similar to the code presented in Figure 4.2, but modified to use the LEDs.

Listing4.1 | Arduino 1.8.12

File Edit Sketch Tools Help

Listing4.1 §

```
1  #define ODDLED     10
2  #define EVENLED    11
3  void setup() {
4    Serial.begin(9600);          // Instantiate Serial object
5    pinMode(ODDLED, OUTPUT);
6    pinMode(EVENLED, OUTPUT);
7  }
8  void loop() {
9    char userInput[10];    // Define our working variables
10   int number, bytesRead;
11
12   Serial.println("\nEnter a number between 1 and 100: ");      // Issue a prompt to the user
13   while (true) {
14     if (Serial.available() > 0) {                              // Start first if block
15       bytesRead = Serial.readBytesUntil('\n', userInput, 9);  // Get input from user
16       userInput[bytesRead] = '\0';                            // Make it a string
17       number = atoi(userInput);                               // Convert ASCII to numeric
18       Serial.print("You entered ");                           // Tell them what happened
19       Serial.print(number);
20       Serial.print(" and that number is ");
21       if (number % 2) {                                       // Start second if block
22         Serial.println("odd.\n");
23         digitalWrite(ODDLED, HIGH);                           // Turn on odd LED...
24         delay(2000L);
25         digitalWrite(ODDLED, LOW);                            // ...and turn it off
26       } else {                                                // Second if block else clause
27         Serial.println("even.\n");
28         digitalWrite(EVENLED, HIGH);                          // Do the same for even LED
29         delay(2000L);
30         digitalWrite(EVENLED, LOW);
31       }                                                       // End else clause and if block
32       break;
33     }                                                         // End first if block
34   }                                                           // End of while statement block
35 }
```

Figure 4.6. The LED Program Listing.

A Code Walk-Through

Lines 1 and 2 define two symbolic constants, one for each of the LEDs used in the program. Again, I use uppercase letters for the two symbolic constants because I think it makes the code easier to read (e.g., *digitalWrite(ODDLED, HIGH)* versus *digitalWrite(10, HIGH)*).

The next new code appears in lines 5 and 6. The *pinMode()* function is a part of the core library of functions that come with the IDE. *Each core library function is designed to perform some small task.* The task for the *pinMode()* function is to define how a given microcontroller pin is to be used in the program. For example, the statement:

```
pinMode(ODDLED, OUTPUT);
```

tells the compiler that we want to use microcontroller pin number 10 (ODDLED) for data output (OUTPUT). The symbolic constant OUTPUT is defined for you in the core libraries. The *pinMode()* function allows us to execute a *digitalWrite(ODDLED, HIGH*) statement, which causes the microcontroller to place 5V (i.e., HIGH) on pin 10. (If you are using one of the other microcontrollers, logic HIGH is 3.3V.) You should have one *pinMode()* function call for each pin you use in a program.

Nothing else really changes until execution gets to line 21. The expression *number % 2* produces a 1 remainder for any odd number, causing execution to follow the logic *true* path for odd numbers. Line 22 displays the "odd" message on the display screen. Line 23 performs a *digitalWrite()* which places 5V (HIGH) on pin 10, thus turning on ODDLED. The *delay()* function at line 24 is another core library function which, in this case, pauses program execution for 2000 milliseconds (i.e., 2 seconds). After that pause, a second call to *digitalWrite()* is done, but this time it sends a digital LOW value, or 0V, to pin 10, which causes the LED to turn off.

You should be able to do your own code walk-through for lines 26-31, and I hope you do that (out loud!) Because of the *if-else* statement block, a given user number causes a different clause of the *if -else* block to execute based on the numeric value of the user's input. That is, the microcontroller decides which statement block to execute based on the input it is given. That's kinda neat!

What about the *break* statement at line 32? (We discussed the *break* keyword earlier in this chapter and provide more details in Chapter 5.) The *break* statement causes program control to "break out" of the *while* loop (line 14) thus sending program control to line 35. Line 35, however, is the closing brace that marks the end of the *loop()* function. Because the *loop()* function is designed to execute forever, you can think of program control being sent back to line 13, which causes the program to ask the user for a new number to evaluate. If you think about it, this means our Odd-Even program continues to run forever or until: 1) you remove power, 2) a component fails, or 3) you press the Reset button on the microcontroller. Almost all microcontroller programs omit Step 5, Termination, in their design.

Are you happy with the program now? You shouldn't be, because we still have a "magic number" in it— the *delay(2000L)* function call. While you're writing the code, do you think you might get tired of waiting 2 seconds on each run during testing. (Hint: Yes.) Therefore, I would probably add:

```
#define PAUSE 2000L
```

at the top of the program and change the function calls to *delay(PAUSE);* The *PAUSE* symbolic constant makes it easier to find a delay value that suits my preferences.

Okay, the *if-else* statement block nicely handles the "either/or" situations, but all program tasks cannot be reduced to such simple "either/or" terms. What then?

Cascading if-else Statement Block

A couple of hundred years ago, after two lectures covering the material presented in this chapter, I gave an in-class programming quiz that asked the students: "If you had specific tasks that were to be done on each day of the week, how would you write the code to call a function for each day's task (e.g., *DoMondaysTasks()*)?" One of the answers was the following code snippet:

```
if (strcmp(today, "Monday") == 0)
  DoMondaysTask();
if (strcmp(today, "Tuesday") == 0)
  Do TuesdaysTask();
if (strcmp(today, "Wednesday") == 0)
  Do WednesdaysTask();
// … and so on...
```

What grade would you give the student? I gave him an F because he should have known better. While he didn't try to contort the solution into an *if-else* answer, the code still fell far short of the mark. The code snippet is a great example of RDC. Why?

First, even though not syntactically required, I demand my students to use statement blocks braces on all *if* statement blocks. DING – minus 10 points.

Now, step back and think about the code as written. On average, the code makes three unnecessary *if* relational tests in finding the right function to call. The "average day" over a long period of time is Thursday. So, in the process of finding the correct day, the code performs 3 relational tests (i.e., Monday through Wednesday) before finding the target day of the week. Given the structure of the question, I let these three relational tests slide. (We'll see a better way shortly.) However, despite the fact we have found the correct day, the code *continues* to perform tests on Friday, Saturday, and Sunday even though we *know* they cannot be the target date. To make the point even more clear, assume the target day is Monday. The code continues to perform six more unnecessary tests even though we've performed the correct function call. Stupid code. (Yes, I'm being kind of judge-y.)

It is this type of situation that the *if-else* statement block is designed to address. (This programming construct doesn't really solve the problem illustrated here, but it's a step in the right direction. More on this later in this chapter.) One solution is to create a cascading *if-else* statement block. *A cascading ifelse statement block is formed by adding new if-else blocks to form a chain of if-else relational tests.* An example helps to illustrate the concept.

Listing 4.1 is very similar to the code in Figure 4.2 for the first 9 lines. It's what appears in Listing 4.1 between lines 10 through 50 that is new.

Listing 4.1. Day-of-the-Week Program (partial) Listing.

```
Serial.println("\nEnter a number between 1 and 7: "); // Issue
prompt
while (true) {
  if (Serial.available() > 0) {             // Start first if block
                                            // Get input from user
    bytesRead = Serial.readBytesUntil('\n', userInput, 9);
    userInput[bytesRead] = '\0';            // Make a string
    number = atoi(userInput);     // Convert ASCII to
                                  // numeric
    Serial.print("You entered "); // What happened
    Serial.print(number);
    Serial.print(" which is ");
    if (number == 1) {            // Start cascading if-else block
      Serial.println("Monday.\n");
    } else {
      if (number == 2) {
        Serial.println("Tuesday.\n");
      } else {
        if (number == 3) {
          Serial.println("Wednesday.\n");
        } else {
          if (number == 4) {
            Serial.println("Thursday.\n");
          } else {
            if (number == 5) {
              Serial.println("Friday.\n");
            } else {
              if (number == 6) {
                Serial.println("Saturday.\n");
              } else {
                if (number == 7) {
                  Serial.println("Sunday.\n");
                } else {
                  Serial.println("Invalid number. Re-enter number
1-7:\n");
                }
```

```
                    }
                }
            }
        }
    }
}               // End of cascading if-else block
break;
  }
}
```

If you walk through the code fragment shown in Listing 4.1, you will see that a cascading *if-else* statement block simply "nests" multiple *if-else* blocks together. So, what do we gain with this weird looking data structure? Well, you should walk through the code and find out.

Suppose you enter the digit '3' in the Serial monitor's input stream. The first *if* statement performs an equality relational test of 3 against 1. Because that expression resolved to logic *false*, the *else* portion of the *if-else* block is executed. However, note that with a cascading *if-else* block, each *else* clause is actually another *if* statement that performs another test for equality. Therefore, the *else* clause actually ends up executing an equality test of the number entered against 2 (i.e., Tuesday). Because the test against 2 also fails, the next *else* clause is executed. However, this third relational test is the number entered against the constant 3. Because the result of the relational test is logic *true*, the message "Wednesday" is displayed on the Serial monitor.

Now, here's the most important part: Because the last relational test was logic *true*, no more *if* clauses are tested. You can think of program control as "bumping down" the cascade of empty closing braces to the *break* statement. In other words, all of the code after the successful match for "Wednesday" is skipped, making our program execute just a tad faster than it did before.

Me? I hate cascading *if-else* blocks. My reason is not a good one, but I *really* dislike the way a properly formatted cascading *if-else* block marches off the screen to the right if you have enough tests used in the block. (Recall that pressing Ctrl-T while the cursor is in the source code window re-formats that code into a commonly-used coding style. Because I like that style, I reformat often.) However, the formatting of cascading *if-else* blocks means I must now hit the source code window's scroll bar to reveal the code that's hiding "past" the right edge of the screen. I also find it difficult to read cascading *if-else* blocks.

Not a fan.

You say: “Well, then don't reformat your code and just write it “straight down the page”. Yes, I could do that, but then I lose the benefits of well-formatted, easy-to-read, code everywhere else in the program.

Again, not a fan.

Still, complaining about something without having a better alternative is sorta like chasing windmills. If you have a better way to do anything in life, you don't have to yell about it. Just tell people what the alternative is and they will gladly accept it if it is better. There is a better way.

The switch-case Statement Block

A long time ago I was hired by a software firm as a consultant to evaluate the firm's banking package. During that review, I came across a cascading *if-else* statement block consisting of 31 possible test branches. As it turns out, there was a task function assigned to each day of the month in an attempt to spread out the processing burden at day's end. Essentially, the code looked like:

```
if (dayOfTheMonth == 1) {       // Start of cascading if-else block
  DoDay1();
} else {
  if (dayOfTheMonth == 2) {
    DoDay2();
  } else {
    if (dayOfTheMonth == 3) {
      DoDay3();
    } else {       // ...and so on through DoDay31()
```

I was asked to do a code walk-through with the entire programming staff. I singled out the cascading *if-else* block, mainly because that section of code had been placed at a point where it was executed *for every account in the bank*. On average, it meant that each month, 15 unnecessary relational tests were performed for every account. I estimated that the unnecessary checks amounted to a 7+ hour monthly charge-back for any medium-sized bank running the software. For some banks, that could be over $100,000/year. When I said this was one of the best examples of RDC I had ever seen, I noticed that almost everyone in the room winced. I figured it was just because I was pointing out that their code had some ugly warts on it.

Wrong.

The chunk of code that I was talking about was written by the very same person who hired me as a consultant and everyone in the room but me knew it. I was fired a few hours later.

Again, it's not fair to complain if you don't have a better idea. I do...the *switch-case* statement block. The general syntax for the *switch-case* statement block is:

```
switch (expression1) {
case expression2:
  // statement(s)
  break;
case expression3:
  // statement(s)
  break;

  // ...more case blocks as needed...
default:
  // statement(s)
  break;
}
```

There are a couple of unusual things about the *switch-case* statement block. First, *expression1* after the *switch* keyword can only be an integral data type: no floating point numbers, no strings. Character constants (e.g., 'A') and integer data types (*byte, int, long*) are permitted for use in expression1. Character string constants (i.e., “A”) are not permitted (notice the double quote marks indicating a string constant).

The second different aspect of the *switch-case* is that the *case* expressions are terminated with a colon (:), not a semicolon like most C statements.

Third, each *case* block ends with a *break* keyword. No statement block braces are needed with a *case* statement block. (You can think of the colon as being the equivalent of an opening statement brace and the *break* keyword serving as the closing statement block brace.)

A fourth difference is the use of the *default* statement block, which is, by convention (not required), placed at the bottom of the *switch-case* statement block. The *default* statement block is a catch-all block. That is, any expression1 value that does not match a *case* statement value is processed by the statements in the *default* statement block. Even though a *default* block is not required, I use it as a debugging aid. Listing 4.2, discussed below, helps explain how I use the default block.

So, how does the *switch-case* statement block work?

The variable used for expression1 controls all of the possible outcomes of the *switch* block. For example, using our day-of-the-week example presented in Listing 4.1, *number* would be the variable used for expression1. In that example, each *case* would then represent a day of the week. We can recode Listing 4.1 to use the *switch-case*, as shown in Listing 4.2.

Listing 4.2. Using the switch-case statement

```
Serial.println("\nEnter a number between 1 and 7: "); // Issue
prompt
while (true) {
  if (Serial.available() > 0) {          // Start first if block
                                         // Get input
    bytesRead = Serial.readBytesUntil('\n', userInput, 9);
    number = atoi(userInput);            // Convert ASCII to
numeric
    Serial.print("You entered ");        // Tell them what happened
  }
  Serial.print(number);
  Serial.print(" which is ");
  switch (number) {         // opening brace of switch block
    case 1:
      Serial.println("Monday.\n");
      break;
    case 2:
      Serial.println("Tuesday.\n");
      break;
    case 3:
      Serial.println("Wednesday.\n");
      break;
    case 4:
      Serial.println("Thursday.\n");
      break;
    case 5:
      Serial.println("Friday.\n");
      break;
    case 6:
      Serial.println("Saturday.\n");
      break;
    case 7:
      Serial.println("Sunday.\n");
      break;
    default:
      Serial.println("Invalid number. Re-enter number 1-7:\n");
      break;
  }            // closing brace of switch block
  break;
}
```

The program in Listing 4.2 performs exactly the same as the (ugly) cascading *if-else* statement block shown in Listing 4.1. However, the performance is just a little bit more efficient than before. The reason is because of the way the code is generated for a *switch* block. The cascading *if-else* block forces us to bump down the relational test chain until we find a match. Those bogus relational tests do nothing but waste time for us. The *switch-case* is different.

When the compiler sees a *switch-case* block, it creates what's called a jump table. *A jump table is a series of memory addresses where program control can "jump" to resume program execution.* To illustrate, suppose the *Serial.println()* statement for Monday resides at memory address 800. Let's further assume that the *Serial.println()* statement for Tuesday resides at memory address 840. Finally, let's assume that all the other memory addresses for the *Serial.println()* statements are 40 bytes more than the previous one (unlikely, but easier to grasp). In memory, the jump table for the *switch* would look like:

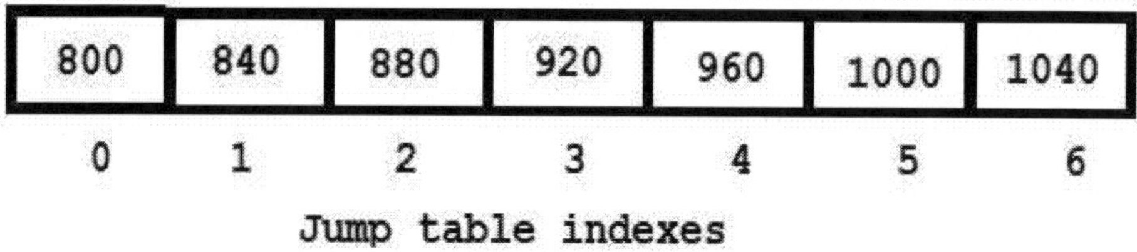

Now, let's suppose you enter the number 7, which corresponds to Sunday. Instead of bumping along doing 6 relational tests in an *if-else* block, the *switch* determines that entry 7 (the index number into the array is 6 because arrays start with element 0) in the jump table is the memory address where the program should continue executing. So program execution would instantly continue at memory address 1040. No time is wasted bumping along executing relational tests looking for a match. When the matching block of code finishes executing, the code sees the *break* keyword and sends program control to the first statement following the closing brace of the *switch-case* block.

So, why do I term the cascading *if-else* block as SDC but the *switch-case* as PGC? First, and the main reason to use the *switch-case* block, is execution efficiency. The *switch-case* block avoids unnecessary relational tests. One jump instruction and we're into the code we need to execute...boom! We're there! Imagine the efficiency gain in the banking software example! Second, I find the *switch-case* much easier to read. It's simply less cluttered and I don't have to scroll horizontally to see all the code in a lengthy code block. Finally, the *switch-case* usually generates a little less program code. (For Listing 4.2, the code size decreased from 2448 bytes to 2270 bytes.)

The default Keyword

As mentioned earlier, the *default* keyword in a *switch-case* block is a "catch-all" for a value that does not match any of the *case* expressions. Over the years, I'd guess 90% of the *switch-case* code I've read never even had a *default* block.

Big mistake.

Omitting the *default* block means you own enough hubris to assume you have covered *every possible value* that might show up at the *switch* expression1 in the program. Really? So, if the MSB gets stuck due to a hardware failure in an *unsigned* data type and, all of a sudden your positive-numbers-only data type in the *switch* expression is negative, it's not a problem? Even when I write the best possible code I can, I still call it Pretty Good Code and not Absolutely Perfect Code because I'm just not sure I've thought of every possible hiccup my code might see. My guess is, you shouldn't be so sure either.

So, if we're going to use the *default* statement block, let's use it to our advantage. I usually write a *default* block with this general form:

```
default:
   Serial.print("I shouldn't be here: line 48 in file listing4-2,
                number = ");
   Serial,println(number);
   break;
```

Printing out the value of the offending variable that controls the *switch* block has saved me a ton of debugging time over the years. This is especially true for those bugs that are intermittent. I would urge you to always add a *default* block whenever you use a *switch-case* block.

The Ellipsis Operator (...)

Sometimes writing a *case* block for all possible values is a little daunting. For example, suppose you want to assign grades to an assignment where 90-100 is an A, 80-89 is a B, 70-79 is a C, and so on. Because a grade of 60 or higher is a passing grade, using a *switch-case* would require 40 case blocks. Not good. Fortunately, C provides us with the ellipsis operator (...) to cover such situations. The general syntax is:

```
case expression1 … expression2:
```

The ellipsis operator is simply three period characters in a row. What is less obvious is that you need to have a space character before the first period and another space character after the last period of the ellipsis operator. Failure to do so will produce a syntax error. For our grading program, we could code the snippet as:

```
switch (score) {
  case 90 … 100:
    grade = 'A';
    break;
  case 80 … 89:
    grade = 'B';
    break;
    // and so on...
```

NOTE: The Arduino IDE does support the ellipsis operator although I cannot find it as part of the C Standard language definition. The ellipsis can also be used in functions to denote a list of unspecified function parameters. I find that using the ellipsis with functions is a train wreck looking for a place to happen. While I feel you are safe using the ellipsis in a *switch-case* block, I am not comfortable using it in function definitions. For that reason, I don't even want to discuss it. (If you're into train wrecks, look it up online.)

Complex if Statement Blocks and Logical Operators

Sometimes a single test expression doesn't fulfill the needs of the test. For example, to drive a car in my state you have to be age 16 or older and have passed the written and driving tests. Therefore, you could write this as:

```
if (age >= 16) {
  if (testsPassed == true) {
    Serial.println("You're old enough to drive and you've passed
your tests!");
  } else {
    Serial.println("You must pass the written / driving exams.");
  }
} else {
  Serial.println("You're not old enough to drive.");
}
```

Programmers always look for ways to lessen the amount of typing they have to do, so programming languages created logical operators to allow programmers to build complex logical expressions without using nested *if* test expressions.

For example, consider the algorithm to determine if a year is a leap year:

> *A year that is divisible by 4 is known as a leap year. However, years divisible by 100 are not leap years while those divisible by 400 are.*

You could implement this algorithm as a series of simple *if* statement blocks, but it can be shortened considerably by using the logical operators. Let's examine the logical operators first and then return to the leap year problem.

Logical AND (&&)

Logical tests are often expressed in terms of truth tables. A *truth table is nothing more than a description of all of the possible outcomes (or states) that can result from a set of test expressions*. Table 4.2 shows the truth table for the logical AND operator.

Table 4.2. Logical AND truth table.

Expression 1	Expression 2	Result
True	True	True
True	False	False
False	True	False
False	False	False

Table 4.2 shows that only when both expressions are logic *true* can the result of the compound test be logic *true*. The operator for logical AND is the double ampersand, &&. So, if you have a compound *if* test:

```
if (expression1 && expression2) {
   // Execute this statement block only if both expressions true
}
```

the AND operator requires both expressions to resolve to logic *true* for the result to be *true*. For example, suppose we want to determine if you should be allowed to drive a car. Perhaps expression1 is the state's age requirement that you be at least 16 years old. Expression2 is a license test that requires you to pass a written and driving test. We might summarize this as:

Table 4.3. Logical AND truth table for driving a car.

Age >= 16	License test	Result
True (Age >= 16)	True (passed both tests)	True
True (Age >= 16)	False (failed one or both tests)	False
False (Age < 16)	True (passed both tests)	False
False (Age < 16)	False (failed one or both tests)	False

Table 4.3 shows all of the possible outcomes for the driving age and license test expression in the Result column. Logic AND is fairly restrictive in that it requires all test expressions to be logic *true* for the result to be logic *true*. We might write the if test as:

```
if (age >= 16 && drivingTestPassed == true && writtenTestPassed ==
true) {
  Serial.println("Here's your driver's license!");
}
```

While there is no language limitation on how many test expressions you can use in a complex *if* test, I find it hard to read *if* statement tests that have more than four logical tests. Use whatever you're comfortable with. You can always add a “trailing” *if* test if needed.

Logical OR (||)

A logical OR test says that the result of a compound expression is logic *true* if <u>*either*</u> test expression is logic *true*. The symbol for the logical OR operator is two vertical bars, || (i.e., the “pipe” symbol above the Enter key.) The truth table for the OR operator is shown in Table 4.4.

Table 4.4. Logical OR truth table.

Expression 1	Expression 2	Result
True	True	True
True	False	True
False	True	True
False	False	False

Because a logical OR statement is logic *true* when either expression is logic *true*, only when both expressions are logic *false* is the result logic *false*. We can write this as:

```
if (expression1 || expression2) {
   // Execute this block if either expression is true
}
```

For example, some amusement parks restrict who can ride on certain rides. Sometimes they require you to be over 48 inches tall (so safety bars are snug), but allow you to ride if you're over 16 years old even if you're less than 48" tall. (I don't know why.) We might write the OR truth table as:

Table 4.5. Logical OR truth table for park rides.

Age >= 16	**Height >= 48**	**Result**
True (Age >= 16)	True	True
True (Age >= 16)	False	True
False (Age < 16)	True	True
False (Age < 16)	False	False

In Table 4.5, as long as one of the test expressions is *true*, the person can get on the ride. Only when they are too young AND too short are they denied access to the ride. As a result, logic OR tests have more expression combinations that result in a logic *true* result.

Logical NOT (!)

The logical NOT operator is the exclamation mark (!) and is used to reverse the current logic state of an expression. Because the NOT operator is a unary operator, it is used with a single expression. This makes its truth table pretty simple, as seen in Table 4.6:

Table 4.6. Logical NOT truth table

Expression1	**! Expression1**
True	False
False	True

The logical NOT operator acts to toggle the current logic state of the expression.

Let's modify the old Blink program slightly to use the logical NOT operator. The modified Blink program is shown in Listing 4.3.

Listing 4.3. Blink using logical NOT

```
// int LED = 2;       // Use with ESP32
// int LED = PC_13; // use with STM32
int LED = 13;         // For Arduino and Teensy 4.0 boards
int state;
void setup() {
   pinMode(LED, OUTPUT);
   state = 1;
}
void loop()  {
  if (state == true) {
    digitalWrite(LED, HIGH);    // turn the LED on
  } else {
    digitalWrite(LED, LOW);     // turn the LED off
  }
  delay(1000L);                 // wait for a second
  state = !state;               // toggle its state...
}
```

Now do a code walk-through on Listing 4.3. I'm testing this on an Arduino Nano, but you can change the LED pin to whatever board you are using. (See comments at the top of the listing.) I use a variable named *state* to tell me if the LED is on or off. The *if* statement block says to turn the LED on if *state* is logic *true*, otherwise turn it off. Because *state* is initialized to 1 in *setup()*, it is viewed as logic *true* in the *if* statement block on the first pass through *loop()*. This means the *digitalWrite(LED, HIGH)* statement is executed, turning the LED on. The call to *delay()* means the program pauses for 1 second while the LED is on.

The next statement immediately toggles the *state* variable, so it is now logic *false*. We then bounce back to the top of *loop()* for another *if* test. However, since *state* is now false, we call *digitalWrite(LED, LOW)* which turns the LED off. The call to *delay()* means the LED remains off for 1 second. The code then toggles *state* again, setting it to logic *true*. The user's perception, therefore, is for the LED to blink on and off. It is the logical NOT operator that is responsible for the blinking LED. The program continues to blink until: 1) power is removed, or 2) there is a component failure.

Could we make the code even smaller? What if I change *loop()* to the following:

```
void loop()  {
  if (state == true) {
    digitalWrite(LED, HIGH);     // turn the LED on
  } else {
    digitalWrite(LED, LOW);      // turn the LED off
  }
  delay(1000L);                  // wait for a second
  state = !state;                // toggle its state...
}
```

Do another code walk-through and mentally run the program. What happens? Fact is, it runs exactly the same as before, but we lopped off the entire *if* statement block. Whadya think about the change?

I don't like it.

The reason I don't like it is because I think the code in Listing 4.3 is easier to read. True, if you are an experienced C programmer, the shortened form takes a few microseconds more to figure out, but not much. My point is, if saving a few microseconds for an experienced programmer is all that's gained, why make it more difficult to read for less experienced coders? It has zero impact on the way the program executes.

I can hear you saying: "Yeah, but the shorter form uses less code and, therefore, runs faster." Not so fast, Bucko! For the Arduino Nano, *both* versions use *exactly* the same flash and SRAM memory space! That tells me *both* versions are going to run at the same speed. (The 1 second delay in the program makes the execution speed a non-issue.) It also tells me that the GCC compiler is pretty smart! If you test it on the other microcontrollers, you find out...something. (Yep, not going to tell you...again!) Moral of the story: Don't judge a program by its cover. Test *both* versions before jumping to any memory or performance conclusions...always!

Leap Year

Ok, I said we'd implement the leap year algorithm:

> *A year that is divisible by 4 is known as a leap year. However, years divisible by 100 are not leap years while those divisible by 400 are.*

Our first try is shown in Listing 4.4.

Listing 4.4. A program to determine if a year is a leap year.

```
int GetYear();        // Function prototypes
```

```
int MyLeapYear(int year);
void setup() {
  Serial.begin(9600);
}
void loop()
{
  int leapYear;
  int myYear;

  myYear   = GetYear();
  leapYear = MyLeapYear(myYear);
  Serial.print("In ");
  Serial.print(myYear);
  Serial.print(" February has ");
  Serial.print(28 + leapYear);   // don't do this with
                                 // standard library
  Serial.println(" days.\n");
}

/*****
  Purpose: Is it a leap year?

  Parameter list:
    int year           the year to test

  Return value
    int               0 if not a leap year, 1 if it is
*****/
int MyLeapYear(int year)
{
  int leapYearFlag = 0;

  if (year % 400 == 0) {            // Evenly divisible by 400?
    leapYearFlag = 1;
  }                                 // Yep, ok so far
  else if (year % 100 == 0) {       // Evenly divisible by 100?
    leapYearFlag = 0;               // Yep, not a leap year
  }    else if (year % 4 == 0) {    // Evenly divisible by 4?
    leapYearFlag = 1;               // Yep, ok
  }    else {
    leapYearFlag = 0;
  }    return leapYearFlag;
}
/*****
  Purpose: to collect a year to test

  Parameter list:
    void

  Return value
        int           the year to test
*****/
int GetYear()
{
  char buffer[10];
  int charsRead;
  int year;
```

```
   Serial.println("\nEnter a year (NNNN):");
   while (true) {
     if (Serial.available() > 0) {
      charsRead = Serial.readBytesUntil('\n', buffer,
                                sizeof(buffer)- 1);
       if (charsRead == 4) { // Expecting year = NNNN
         buffer[charsRead] = '\0';//buffer now a string
         year = atoi(buffer);
         break;
       }          // end if (charsRead...
     }            // end if (Serial.available()...
   }              // end while (true)...   return year;
}
```

The code should be pretty easy to read, but perhaps the *GetYear()* needs some explanation. The function prints a prompt on the Serial monitor asking for the user to enter a year, after which we enter an infinite *while* loop. The first *if* statement queries the *Serial* object waiting for the user to enter a year and press the Enter key. If there is something in the Serial buffer, the *readBytesUntil()* reads that input data until the user presses the Enter key. The Enter key sends a newline character ('\n') to the buffer which ends the input. If the user typed in 2000 and pressed the Enter key, the *Serial buffer[]* array looks like:

2	0	0	0	'\n'

Because the newline character is acting like a sentinel to mark the end of input, it is not counted in the character count variable, *charsRead.* Indeed, the newline character is stripped from the buffer.

Therefore, the return value from *readBytesUntil()* is 4. The next statement uses *charsRead* to place a null character into the input buffer array, *buffer[]*, which now looks like:

2	0	0	0	'\0'

which means we can treat the *buffer[]* array as a character string array. We then call the standard library function, *atoi()* (ASCII to integer), to convert the ASCII text that was entered by the user into an integer number, which we then send back to the user.

We then call *MyLeapYear()* to determine if that year is a leap year or not. As you might guess, there are existing functions that determine if a year is a leap year, but there's a nuance of difference with the one presented here. Virtually all of the existing leap year library functions return a

Boolean value (i.e., *true* or *false*) whereas my function returns 0 or 1. There is a difference.

Prior to the X3J11 C standard, Boolean values could be whatever the compiler vendor wanted them to be and I know of one compiler that used 1 for *true* and -1 for *false*. By returning a numeric value rather than a logic value, you can directly add the return value to 28 to find out the number of days in February for the year in question. This allows us to abstract from the numeric value of *true* and *false* (which you shouldn't consider anyway) and doesn't require a cast to convert the logic value *true* or *false* into numeric 1 or 0. Still, no self-respecting C programmer would write the *MyLeapYear()* as presented above. They would use our newly-discovered logical operators and write it as:

```
int MyLeapYear(int year)
{
  if (((year % 4 == 0) && (year % 100 != 0))|| (year % 400 == 0))
    return 1;
  else
    return 0;
}
```

Note how we can combine logical operators into a complex *if* statement with multiple test expressions. This would be a more common way to write the function. Do a code walk-through on the shortened version and you should be able to convince yourself that it produces the same result. For me, it's easier to read this complex *if* statement than stumble through the SDC in *MyLeapYear()* function shown in Listing 4.4. Select what works for you.

Conclusion

In this chapter we have explored how you can write code to alter the linear processing sequence that would transpire if programs could not make decisions based on input data. The basic building blocks for computer decision making are the relational operators and the operands they operate on. Coupling the relational operators with the various decision expressions (*if, if-else, switch-case*) provides you with the decision making capabilities you need.

In the next chapter you will see how to take advantage of the fact that computers never get bored.

Exercises.

1. Why might you quibble with the following code snippet?

```
if (random()) {
  x = 50;
}
```

2. What does this do?

```
if (j = k) {
   DoStuff();
} else {
   DoOtherStuff();
}
```

3. What might happen if you attach a digital microcontroller pin directly to an LED?
4. Write a program that simulates tossing a coin 10,000 times and then report the number of heads and tails. You should use the *random()* function that is part of the IDE's core libraries.
5. Why might the *switch-case* be a better programming choice than the cascading *if-else* block?
6. Write a single statement that converts a digit character (i.e., '1') into its equivalent numeric value (i.e., 1, with no quotes and can be directly used in a math expression).
7. Some physical fitness centers only allow adult female members to join their club no matter how hard I tried to join. Assuming they consider age 16 or higher to be an adult, write a complex *if* test that allows a person to join. If you used an AND operator, can you reverse it to use an OR operator?

Chapter 5 Program Loops

Earlier I said that microcontrollers were really good at counting. Another nice thing about microcontrollers is that they have the attention span of a gnat, so they don't get bored. No attention span, there's nothing to distract them, unlike humans who do get bored. Microcontrollers are happy doing the same thing over and over, and that's a good thing because we do ask both computers and microcontrollers to do repetitive tasks. For example, you might have an alarm system in your home where the microcontroller sends a query signal to a door or window sensor asking if it is open. It wouldn't be terribly useful if it did this query only once a day. Instead, the microcontroller probably has a sequence where every sensor is continuously monitored. Even if your home has 100 sensors scattered throughout the house, the microcontroller can probably poll each sensor dozens of times every second.

If a burglar is going to get through that door undetected, he'd better be pretty fast on his feet. Fact is, you've already written programs that use loops. Every Arduino-based C program must have the *loop()* function present, which is a loop. If you look in the main.cpp file (hardware\arduino\avr\cores\arduino), you will find this code fragment:

```
int main(void)
{
  init();
  initVariant();

#if defined(USBCON)
  USBDevice.attach();
#endif

  setup();

  for (;;) {
    loop();
    if (serialEventRun) serialEventRun();
  }
  return 0;
}
```

Do the underlined statements look familiar? Any "standard" C program always starts with the function named *main()*, which we can see at the top of the code fragment. The compiler makes a few housekeeping function calls, and then calls your version of *setup()* and executes the code it finds there. Next, the program enters a *for* loop and calls your version of *loop()* in your program and spins around in that loop forever.

So, let's see how we can use loops in our own ways.

Well-behaved Loops

Before you go running off to write some looping code, it's a good idea to appreciate that not all loops do what we want them to. Most of the loops you write are designed to end at some point. If you have 100 sensors to read in your house, you want that loop to stop after reading sensor 100 and start over with sensor number 1 and start querying them again. Letting the sensor-read loop run amok and try to read sensor 23,213 probably doesn't make much sense. Before we ask what characteristics do well-behaved loops have, perhaps we should ask what is a program loop. A program *loop is a structure that is designed to execute one or more program statements and, after executing the last statement in the loop, decide whether or not to go back to the first statement and repeat the execution of the loop statements.*

1. Initialization of a Loop Control Variable

In our loop definition, we stated that the loop structure must "decide" whether to make another pass through the loop or not. For the loop to decide whether to make another pass means that a loop must have some data item that controls how many passes to make through the statements contained within the loop.

Decision control also means that the data item controlling the loop must start in a known initial state. The controlling data item is often an *int* variable that is initialized to 0. However, because there are different flavors of loops in C, there are different ways to *initialize the control variable.*

We will see some of those initialization constructs later in this chapter.

Many C programmers know that their particular C compiler initializes certain variables to 0 when they are defined, so when they're ready to enter a loop, they assume the control variable has been set to 0. It is probably safe to make this assumption 99 times out of 100. However, given the luck some of us seem to have, that one time somehow ends up in the code that controls the launch codes for our nuclear arsenal. So, let's play it safe and *always explicitly initialize the loop control variable.*

2. Loop Control Test

The fact that the loop control variable needs to decide whether to make another pass through the loop code implies that the control variable is tested against some target variable or value. The target variable might be the number of members in a club, or it might be the state of a variable returned from a function call. The need for a comparison means that there is a relational comparison between the current state of the control variable and the termination state for the loop. For example, if we are updating a club membership list, the termination state might be the number of members in the club. For the home sensor alarm case, the termination state would be after visiting sensor 100.

Note that this condition also means that, at some point, the relational test must return a logic *false* to terminate the loop. If the test expression is not falsifiable, the loop never ends. A *loop that runs forever is called an infinite loop.*

3. Changing the State of the Loop Control Variable

The state, or value, of the loop control variable must change at some point in the loop structure. Think what would happen if it didn't. If we enter the loop and the relational test in Condition 2 is logic *true*, we execute the statements. If we never change the value of the variable that controls the loop, we'd spin around in the loop forever. In our membership and home sensor examples, all we need to do is increment the sensor or member counter variable that controls the loop. Incrementing the loop counter changes its state so, eventually, the loop control test says we've made enough passes through the loop and it's time to stop.

These three conditions for a well-behaved loop probably seem rather abstract right now, but I think it will all make sense after we discuss the exact nature of the various loop structures.

The for Loop

The first loop structure we'll examine is the *for* loop. The general syntax for a *for* loop is:

```
                                              // Opening brace
for (expression1; expression2; expression3) {
    // loop body, or statement(s) controlled
      // by the for loop
}                   // Closing brace of for statement block
```

The *for* keyword is followed by an opening parenthesis, '(', followed by an expression list that is separated by semicolons (';'). The last expression is followed by the closing parenthesis, ')', a space, and then an opening brace ('{') that marks the start of the statements that are controlled by the *for* loop. The *for* loop block ends with the closing brace ('}') of the *for* statement block. The *loop body of the for loop is the statement(s) that appear between the opening and closing braces.*

What I like about *for* loops is that the three conditions for a well-behaved loop are normally found in the three expressions contained in the opening and closing parentheses. Expression1 initializes the control variable, expression2 performs a relational test on the control variable, and expression3 changes the state (i.e., value) of the control variable. Consider our home alarm system. You might code the *for* loop as:

```
int count;
int alarmStatus;

for (count = 0; count < 100; count++) {
  alarmStatus = ReadSensor(count);
  if (alarmStatus != 0) {     // Uh-oh, not good
    SoundAlarms();
  }
}
```

In this code fragment, expression1 is the *count = 0* expression. Because variable *count* is used to control the loop, expression1 initializes *count* to a known value, 0 in this example. Expression2 is the relational test on the control variable, *count*. If the outcome of the relational test is logic *true* (i.e., *count* is less than 100), program execution goes to the first statement in the loop body and makes another pass through the loop body. In this example, we show the loop body code making a call to read a sensor and, depending on the sensor's state, the code sounds the alarms or prepares to make another pass through the loop.

Here's the thing that's a little less than obvious when you look at a *for* loop. After the last statement in the loop body finishes executing, program control is transferred immediately to expression3. *After the initial start of the loop, expression1 is never executed again.* That makes sense if you think about it. Why would you initialize the same loop a second time? You'd never get past the first pass through the loop.

When control is transferred to expression3, the *count++* expression is processed. What does expression3 do? We discuss the "++" operator later on, but for now, the operator simply increments *count* by 1. That is, the *count++;* statement is the same as *count = count + 1.*

Okay, so here's the next weird part. Once expression3 is resolved (i.e., its value increased by 1), program control immediately goes back to expression2 again. This also makes sense when you think about it. Because expression3 changes the state, or value, of the variable that controls the loop (*count*), it only makes sense to process expression2 again to see if we should make another pass through the loop body.

As you can see, we continue to plow through expression2, the loop body statement(s), and expression3 until *count* equals 100. At that time, expression2 evaluates to logic *false* (*count* is no longer less than 100), and program control is transferred to the first statement *following* the closing brace of the loop body. Figure 5.1 shows how the logic flow works with a *for* loop. In Figure 5.1, we enter the loop at Start loop. Looking at our code fragment, expression1 is *count* =

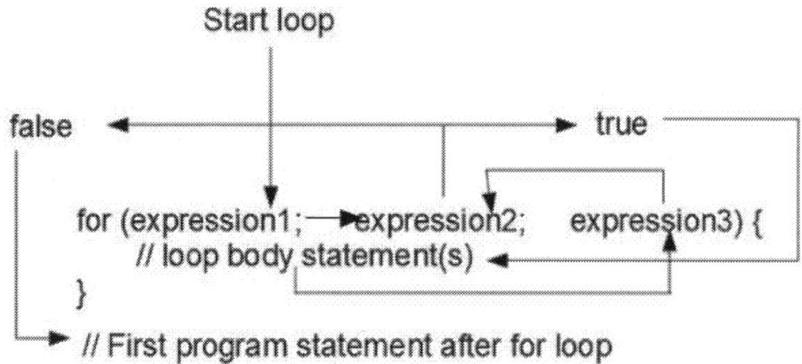

Figure 5.1. The flow of a for loop

0; which is the first condition of a well-behaved loop: The controlling variable used in the loop needs to be initialized. In our example, *count* is initialized to 0. In other loops, the initial value might be to start at the largest value and count down to 0. Either way, *expression1 initializes the variable controlling the loop.*

Once expression1 is evaluated, control is immediately transferred to expression2 for evaluation. In our snippet, the expression was *count < 100*. Since *count* was just initialized to 0, expression2 resolves to logic *true (i.e., count* is less than 100). In Figure 5.1, because expression2 is *true*, program execution follows the *true* path and executes the first statement in the *for* loop body. Note that, if you (for some strange reason) initialized count to 100 in expression1, the statements controlled by the *for* loop would never be executed. The reason is because a value of *count* equal to 100 makes expression2 *false*, and the program would bypass all of the statement(s) in the loop body.

When the last statement in the *for* loop body finishes executing, control immediately transfers to expression3. In our snippet, expression3 simply increments *count* by 1 (*count++*). Note that the increment of *count* changes the state of the variable that is controlling the *for* loop. Therefore, as soon as *count* is incremented in expression3, program control moves to reevaluate expression2 to see if *count* is still less than 100. Because *count* is now 1, which is still less than 100, expression2 evaluates to logic *true* and control goes into the loop body again for another pass through its statements.

This process continues to spin through this same loop path until *count* is incremented by expression3 to equal 100. Now, expression2 evaluates to logic *false*, and the program control path follows the *false* path in Figure 5.1 to the first statement following the closing brace of the *for* loop body. The loop is, indeed, a well-behaved loop.

While almost any *for* loop can be rewritten to use one of the other loop structures, I like *for* loops because all of the necessary and sufficient conditions for a well-behaved loop appear on the same line in one compact set of expressions.

Listing 5.1 presents a short program that illustrates a *for* loop. This is actually the same loop we discussed earlier, except I changed the maximum number of passes through the loop to 50. One thing

Listing 5.1. Program using a for loop

```
void ShowCount(int number)
{
```

```
  Serial.print("The current value is: ");
  Serial.println(number);
}

void setup() {
  int count;
  Serial.begin(9600);

  for (count = 0; count < 50; count++) {
    ShowCount(count);
  }
}

void loop() {
}
```

to note is that we used a function that we wrote to display the value of *count*. We get into functions in greater detail in Chapter 6, but notice how the parameter used in the function call to *ShowCount()* is the variable named *count*, but when that parameter shows up in the code we wrote for *ShowCount()*, the parameter is called *number*. How can that work? Easy. In this case, we don't care what the name of the parameter is, only its value.

When we call the *ShowCount()* function in the *setup()*, it is the *rvalue* of *count* that is sent to *ShowCount()*. What really is happening here is that, when *count* appears within the parentheses of a function call, it's like the microcontroller sends a photographer out to the lvalue of *count* (i.e., the memory address of *count*'s bucket), sticks the camera over the edge of the bucket, takes a picture of its rvalue, and then scurries back to the microcontroller. Therefore, it is a *copy* of the rvalue of *count* that is sent to *ShowCount(),* not the "real" *count*. This process is sometimes referred to as *Pass by Value*. Therefore, when the copy of *count* arrives at *ShowCount()*, we simply refer to the "photograph" as *number* and use it to show the current value of *count* on the *Serial* monitor.

So, Listing 5.1 is a good example of SDC. While it's not PGC, why does it only rate as Sorta Dumb Code? Two reasons. First, we didn't document the code at all and, second, we used a magic number in the code. Listing 5.2 cleans things up a bit. Listing 5.2. A PGC version of Listing 5.1.

Listing 5.2. Better version of Listing 5.1.

```
#define MAXPASSES     50  // Restrict number of loop iterations
```

```
/*****
  Purpose: To show the current value of number on the Serial
           monitor

  Argument list:
    int number

  Return value:
    void

  CAUTION: None
*****/
void ShowCount(int number)
{
  Serial.print("The current value is: ");
  Serial.println(number);
}

void setup() {
  int count;
  Serial.begin(9600);

  for (count = 0; count < MAXPASSES; count++) {
    ShowCount(count);
  }
}
void loop() {
}
```

First, we got rid of the magic number in the *for* loop by defining the symbolic constant *MAXPASSES* at the very top of the program. Try changing its value from 50 to something else, recompile, and upload to confirm the number of passes does change.

Second, we added a function header that tells what the *ShowCount()* function does, the outside help it needs passed to it to perform its task (i.e., *number*), and its return value. Because this function doesn't send a value back to *setup()*, the function type specifier (discussed in Chapter 6) is set to *void*. We'll let the details wait until the next chapter.

I encourage you to type the code in for Listing 5.2 and play around with it. What would happen if you passed *count* * *count* as the argument for *ShowCount()*?

Increment and Decrement Operators

Our *for* loop example used *count++* for expression3. We mentioned that the expression *count++* was syntactically equivalent to *count = count + 1*. Actually, that assertion is only partly true.

Type in the program presented in Listing 5.3.

Listing 5.3 Exercising the Increment and Decrement Operators

```
void setup() {
  int number;
  int result;

  Serial.begin(9600);
  number = 5;
  result = number++;              // Increment/decrement
  Serial.print("number = ");
  Serial.print(number);
  Serial.print("   result = ");
  Serial.println(result);
}
void loop() {
}
```

Given what I just told you, do a walk-through on each line in *setup()* and state out loud what each statement does and the result you expected. (It would be *really* impressive if you used lvalues and rvalues as you verbalize what's going on in the program. This will help you solidify your understanding of what's going on "under the hood".) What are the values of *number* and *result* when the program ends? I really hope you did type in the program and run it. If you did, you'll see that *result* equals 5 and *number* equals 6. "What! But...but...you said that *count++* was the same as *count = count + 1*."

I lied.

Postfix Increment (++) and Decrement (- -) Operators

If you look at the Precedence Table 2.1 in Chapter 2, you'll see that the precedence level for the postfix increment operator (*number++)* is very high at precedence level 2. Conversely, the assignment operator (=) is a rather lowly precedence level 15. Also, keep in mind that the postfix operators are unary operators. That is, *unary operators only use one operand.* Therefore, the *number++* expression has only one operand named *number* which is acted upon by the ++ operator. The wrinkle, however, is the *timing* of the increment operation.

What actually happens *with a postfix operator is that the operator does its job after the expression that uses its operand takes place*. What this means is that the assignment of *number* into *result* takes place before *number* is incremented. That's why these two operators are called postfix operators: Their operands are used before the postfix operator acts upon them. Looking at Listing 5.3, in the statement:

```
result = number++;    // Increment
```

and before *number* is used, it has an rvalue of 5. Because the "++" operator is a postfix operator, the compiler knows to use *number* in the "next" expression to be resolved. In this example, that expression is the assignment operator. Therefore, the compiler moves the rvalue of *number* (5) into the rvalue of *result*. Only *after* that assignment operator has been resolved does the compiler go back and increment *number*. The end result is *number* is displayed as 6, but *result* is displayed as 5. Read this paragraph as many times as it takes to completely understand the sequence of what is taking place. We use these operators *a lot* so it is important that you fully understand the sequence that takes place as the expressions are resolved. Suppose we change that statement to:

```
result = number--;      // decrement
```

The statement now uses the *postfix decrement operator*. The sequencing is the same as the postfix increment operator, except this time the decrement operator *decreases the value by one after the expressions are resolved.* Walk through the modified code and prove to yourself that *number* now equals 4 and *result* still equals 5. Again, verbalize what's going on and repeat the walkthrough until you are positive you understand completely what is taking place.

Prefix Increment (++) and Decrement (- -) Operators

The prefix increment (++) and decrement (- -) operators are different because the operator sequencing is such that the increment/decrement takes place *before* the operand is used, hence the use of the term prefix when referencing these operators. In Listing 5.3, change the line to read:

```
result = ++number;      // Pre-increment
```

and recompile/run the program. What happens? Now change the line to use the prefix decrement operator. Now what happens?

Using the prefix increment operator means that *number* is incremented *before* it is used in the assignment expression. Because the increment operation takes place before the operand is used, both *number* and *result* have the same value, 6 when the statement finishes. The prefix decrement operator has the same sequencing, so *number* and *result* have the same value, 4.

Go back to Listing 5.2 and look at expression3 in the *for* loop, *count++*. What happens if you change that expression to *++count* (i.e., change from postfix increment to prefix increment)? After that change recompile/upload and run and you may be surprised to discover that... Nope, not going to tell you. You already have typed in the program, right? So just make the change and find out for yourself. After all, you're the one trying to learn this stuff, so you need to do your share of the work, too...right?

It would be worth your time to experiment with Listings 5.2 and 5.3. The increment/decrement operators are used a lot in C programming, so understanding them completely is to your benefit.

Complex Expressions in a for Loop

Suppose you want to find the sum of the numbers 0 through 100. The program presented in Listing 5.4 does that.

Listing 5.4. Sum the value 0 through 100

```
#define SUMLIMIT 100
void setup() {
  int i;
  int sum;

  Serial.begin(9600);

  sum = 0;                                // Initialize starting value
  for (i = 0; i < SUMLIMIT; i++) {
    sum += i;
  }
  Serial.print("sum = ");
  Serial.println(sum);
}
void loop() {
}
```

Notice how we initialized the value of *sum* to be zero before entering the *for* loop. The reason is because any variable defined within a function, like *sum*, has an rvalue that is whatever random bit pattern happens to exist at its lvalue. The pure statistical chance that *sum* equals 0 at that point is roughly 0.0000152. If *sum* is a 4-byte *int*, that probability drops to 0.0000000002328. Therefore, it seems like a better plan is to assign *sum* a value of 0 before we use it rather than to hope its rvalue is 0.

If you type in the code, and compile/upload and run the program, it prints out the sum 4950. That's not the right answer...RDC. I know that the answer should be 5050. What went wrong?

The problem is that the program design is supposed to find the sum of the numbers 0 *through* 100, not *up to* 100. What we actually have in Listing 5.4 is a program that sums the numbers 0 through 99. So, how would you fix the program?

As is so often the case in programming, there are multiple ways to skin this cat. One way is to change SUMLIMIT to 101. I'm not crazy about this solution because, quite often, the *#define* for the symbolic constant is not visible in the section of code that's creating the problem. This often results in making erroneous assumptions about the symbolic constant. Also, the value 101 just seems weird.

Another possible solution is to change expression2 in the *for* loop to:

```
i < SUMLIMIT + 1
```

I *really* don't like this because *SUMLIMIT* is supposed to be a symbolic *constant*, but here we are trying to change that constant before we compare it to variable *i*. If you're going to change its meaning, why make it a symbolic constant in the first place? (Recall that the addition operator, +, has a higher precedence level (i.e., 6) than the less-than relational operator (i.e., <). You did memorize the Precedence Table, didn't you? That's okay, I've been using C for over 40 years and I still have to look up the operator precedence levels. However, you might want to dog-ear the page that has Table 2.1 on it.)

I'd rather see the relational operator change than the symbolic constant, so I'd probably use:

```
i <= SUMLIMIT
```

If you make this change and recompile the program, it displays the correct answer, 5050.

Subexpressions in C

This discussion started because we were asking about the starting value for *sum*. However, the syntax for expression1 of the *for* loop allows us to use subexpressions if we choose to do so. A *subexpression is simply the replacement of one expression with a comma-separated list of two or more new expressions*. Allowing subexpressions in expression1 means that we can rewrite the *for* loop as

```
for (sum = 0, i = 0; i < SUMLIMIT; i++) {
```

Therefore, we can get rid of the statement immediately before the *for* loop in Listing 5.4 and move the initialization of *sum* into expression1 as a comma-separated subexpression. The interpretation of expression1 is unchanged: both subexpressions are used to initialize the value of a variable used in the *for* loop. Because expresion1 is executed only once, it has no real impact on the processing of the loop.

Once again, I'm not a fan of this expression change.

The main reason I rarely use this syntax form is because it makes it harder to find the initialization of *sum* versus what it used to be when that initialization took place in its own statement. The second reason I don't favor the subexpression form of initialization is because I can't add a clarification comment on the same line where the initialization takes place. The subexpression muddies the waters if I want to comment on the initialization of *sum*. Finally, the code generated by the compiler is likely to either be identical or so slightly changed that it will have no noticeable impact on the performance of the program or its resource use. The change doesn't even save any typing! So, any time a program option results in code that is harder to read (either because it's less visible or makes it harder to comment it) and understand, always go with the option that makes the intent of the code more clear.

Okay, one more program. What does the program in Listing 5.5 do?

Listing 5.5. A program that does something.

```
#define SUMLIMIT 100

void setup() {
  int i;
  int square;

  Serial.begin(9600);
  square = 0;
  for (i = 0; i = SUMLIMIT; i++) {
    square = i * i;
```

```
    Serial.print("square = ");
    Serial.println(square);
  }
}
void loop() {
}
```

If you said the program displays the square of all numbers between 0 and 100, you'd be wrong. Really...why? Take a closer look at expression2. Now go back to the beginning of this chapter and reread condition 2 for a well-behaved loop. Condition 2 states that *the relational test must be falsifiable*. Now look at expression2. *Expression2 is not even a relational test, it's an assignment expression.*

This is an example of a flat-forehead, wait-'til-the-cows-come-home, program. We've created an infinite loop that continuously displays the value 10000. The program does a really thorough job of calculating the square of 100, but nothing else. You probably jumped to conclusions of what the program does because the *Serial.print()* calls lead you in that direction. That mistake is not uncommon. If I had a nickel for every time I muttered "The code can't be doing that!" to myself, I'd be sipping a pina colada on a beach somewhere. This is one of those flat-forehead mistakes you *will* make at some later time. Flat foreheads are the expected result of the C learning process.

When to Use a for Loop

As we said at the start of this chapter, there are several different C loop structures available to you. How do you know which one to use? If the only tool you have is a hammer, it shouldn't be too surprising that every problem looks like a nail. In other words, you can mangle the other loop structures to perform the same tasks as a *for* loop, but *for* loops are especially suited for problems that involve some form of counting. Most *for* loops initialize some type of counting variable and proceed to process a series of statements that use that variable to solve some specific task. You will see more *for* loop examples scattered throughout this book.

Empty Expression2

Just for grins, go back to the first page of this chapter where we showed you the content of the main.cpp source code file. Look at the *for* loop there:

```
      for (;;) {
```

What!? This *for* loop has omitted all three expressions needed for a well-behaved *for* loop, yet here it is controlling every program you develop in the Arduino IDE. What's going on? By default, any relational expression that is empty (i.e., missing) is taken to be logic *true* by default. This means that expression2 in the *for* loop in main.cpp is always *true*. Think about it. It means that we're going to spin around calling the *loop()* function found in all Arduino IDE programs forever. And isn't that what we said about the Five Program Steps for microcontrollers...Step 5, Termination, is usually not part of a common microcontroller program. What if I change main.cpp and added this line at the top of the source file:

```
#define EVER   ;;
```

and then changed the *for* loop to:

```
 for (EVER){
```

What happens? (I probably should have named this chapter section *Fun with Symbolic Constants*. Yep, I am a geek with a weird sense of humor.)

Nested Loops

You can have loops within loops if you need them. For example, suppose you have a simple 3x3 matrix and want to display its contents. The following code fragment shows how to display the values using nested *for* loops:

```
int j, k;
int matrix[ROW][COL] = {
  { 1, 2, 3 },
  { 4, 5, 6 },
  { 7, 8, 9 }
};

for (j = 0; j < ROW; j++) {
  for (k = 0; k < COL; k++) {
    Serial.print(matrix[j][k]);
  }
  Serial.print('\n');
}
```

Note how the *j* loop walks through the rows, while the *k* loop walks through the columns. Together, nested loops allow you to easily display the contents of the matrix. When I ran the actual program, the output looks like:

```
123
456
789
```

Processing nested loops is no different than what you do with a single loop. You can nest the loops as deeply as you need.

The while Loop

The *while* loop has the following syntax structure:

```
while (expression2) { // Opening brace '{' is start of loop body
     // while statement body
}                     // Closing brace '}' is end of loop body
```

Notice that I've labeled the test expression used in a *while* loop as expression2. The reason is because expression2's purpose is identical to expression2 in the *for* loop. That is, expression2 is a relational test that determines whether another pass through the *while* loop's statement body is to be made. What happened to expressions 1 and 3? Well, they technically are not required, although well-behaved *while* loops require you to write them anyway. Listing 5.6 should help explain how the *while* loop is used.

Suppose you need to write a program that searches a string for a specific character. When the program finds the target character, it displays the index that corresponds to that character's position in the string array. (A more realistic task would be to search a membership list for a specific member number. The principle is the same in Listing 5.6, but is less cluttered.)

Listing 5.6. Find a specific character in a string

```
void setup() {
  char msg[] = "abcdefghijklmnopqrstuvwxyz12345*6790";
  char target = '*';
  int index;

  Serial.begin(9600);
  index = 0;          // expression1
  while (msg[index] != target) {  // expression2
    index++;          // expression3
  }
  Serial.print("Found character ");
  Serial.print(target);
  Serial.print(" at index ");
```

```
  Serial.println(index);
}
void loop() {
}
```

In the program, I initialized the *msg[] char* array to hold a bunch of characters. Notice the asterisk (*) between the 5 and 6 digit characters. I also assigned *target* to be an asterisk *char*, as that's our target character for the search. We then define *index* and instantiate the *Serial* object. Just before we start the *while* loop, we set *index* to 0 so that the loop begins its search at the first character of the *msg[]* array. Hmmm...that looks suspiciously similar to expression1 of the *for* loop. The reason they look so similar is because they are; they serve exactly the same purpose. Expression1 defines the starting condition of both loop types and is the control variable for the *while* loop.

Next, we enter the *while* loop and evaluate expression2. In this program, expression2 does a relational comparison between the current character we're looking at (i.e., *msg[0]*) and the target character (*). Because the two *char*s are not equal (i.e., the != operator), expression2 is logic *true* and means program control is transferred to the first statement in the *while* loop body. In this example, there is only one statement in the *while* loop body: *index++*. Hmmm, again...that looks much the same as expression3 of the *for* loop. Yep, and once again, they serve the same purpose: to alter the state of the variable that controls the *while* loop. If the code didn't increment *index*, we spin around comparing msg[0] (i.e., 'a') to '*' forever, thus creating an infinite loop.

If you do a code walk-through, you should be able to figure out that a match is found at an *index* value of 31. So, how would you grade our little program. Is it easy to read? Does it perform its task? I think it does, so I'll give it an SDC ranking—Sorta Dumb Code. Why?

The reason is because we've written the code on the assumption that there is always going to be an asterisk in the string. On a larger scale, that assumes we will always find the member number in the membership list. Probably not a safe assumption.

Indeed, when I removed the asterisk from the *msg[] char* array, the program found the asterisk at index 467. This seems a little high since there are now only 35 characters in the array. Rather than count the characters myself, I just added these two statements to the code:

```
Serial.print(" len = ");
Serial.println(strlen(msg));
```

The purpose of the *strlen()* function is to find the number of characters in a string. But then, you already know that from our earlier discussion about C strings in Chapter 3, right?

So, why an *index* number of 467? Think about it. Since expression2 didn't see a match in the first 35 characters in the *msg[]* array, the program incremented *index* again and took a peek at whatever *followed* the last character ('0') in the string *char* array. You already know that the 36th *char* is going to be the *null* sentinel character for the string ('\0'). Since the *null* is not a match either, *index* is incremented to 37 and we look at whatever is stored in memory *after* our *msg[]* array! Remember that computers have the innate intelligence of a bag of hammers. Because *you* told it to keep indexing and testing, that's exactly what it does. Eventually, at an index value of 467, expression2 found a byte in memory that equaled the numeric value 42. Guess what the numeric value for an asterisk is in the ASCII table? Bingo...42! In other words, our code plowed through 432 bytes of junk before it found a byte with the value of 42.

Yep, if you ever wished that someone or something would just do exactly what you told it to, you're gonna love programming!

When to Use a while Loop

As we mentioned before, almost any *for* loop can be coded using a *while* loop, but that kind of defeats the purpose of having a choice of loop structures. Usually you will find it easier to use a *while* loop when the task at hand involves searching through a data set for a particular value. In such cases, once the target item is located, the loop is terminated (we'll discuss how to do that in a moment). Therefore, as a general rule, *while* loops are good in searching a large data set and terminating the loop when the item is found. A *for* loop, on the other hand, often involves counting or processing data to the end of the data list as dictated by expression2.

do-while Loops

The third type of program loop is the *do-while* loop, which has the following syntax structure:

```
do {          // Opening brace '{' is start of loop body
```

```
    // statement(s) of loop body
  } while (expression2);      // Closing brace '}' is
                              // end of loop body
```

As was the case with the plain *while* loop, expressions 1 and 3 are also missing from *do-while* loops. In fact, the *while* and *do-while* loops are identical, except that in a *do-while* loop, the relational test is performed after a pass through all of the statements enclosed by the starting and ending braces of the loop body. That is, the relational test is performed at the "bottom" of the *dowhile* loop body. Note what this means: regardless of the current logic state of expression2, *<u>at least one pass</u> is made through the statements in the loop body of a do-while loop.*

Listing 5.7 illustrates how a *do-while* loop might be used. The task is to get a digit character from the user. The program issues a prompt telling the user what is expected and then a *do-while* is used to get that input from the user.

Listing 5.7. Getting specific input from the user

```
void setup()
{
  Serial.begin(9600);
}
void loop()
{
  int number;

  Serial.print("\nEnter a digit character 0 - 9: ");
  do {
    number = Serial.read() - '0';   // Cheap convert
                                // ASCII to numeric
  } while (number < 0 || number > 9);// correct input?
  Serial.print("You entered: ");
  Serial.print(number);
}
```

The *while* segment of the loop at the bottom:

```
  } while (number < 0 || number > 9);    // correct input?
```

uses an additional operator in expression2. The two vertical bars, ||, represent the logical OR operator. (A full discussion of the logical operators appears later in this chapter.) Verbalizing the two subexpressions in expression2, they say: "If the character entered is less than 0 or the character is greater than 9, the user needs a do-over". Stated differently, anything other than a digit character results in logic *true* for expression2, which causes another pass through the *dowhile* loop body. Think about it.

Another interesting aspect of Listing 5.7 is that there is no explicit expression3. The fact that a *do-while* forces at least one pass through the loop ensures that *number* gets assigned a value of some sort. The fact that *number* ends up with an initial value kind of means it's like expression1 in that it initializes the control variable, *number*. After all, the code does a do-over until the user gets it right with respect to *number*.

goto Loops

Telling a beginning student about the *goto* keyword is seen by some programmers as the highest form of programming heresy. The reason is because *goto* loops can create "spaghetti code" where program flow is very difficult to follow. Still, just like a nuclear bomb is a tool you don't want to use, it's there if you must use it. So it is with the *goto* statement: 99.9% of the time there's a better way to code the program than to use a *goto* statement. Still, ignoring that the *goto* exists is like postponing the Birds-and-the-Bees discussion with your kids until they've reached the age of 30. They're going to find out long before that anyway, so you might as well talk about it yourself.

The syntax for the *goto* loop is:

```
label:
      // statements in goto loop body
      goto label;
```

Consider the code in Listing 5.8. If the code in Listing 5.8 looks familiar, it should. It behaves just like Listing 5.1.

Listing 5.8. Loop using a goto statement

```
/*****
  Purpose: To show the current value of number on the Serial
monitor

  Argument list:
    int number

  Return value:
    void

  CAUTION: None
*****/
void ShowCount(int number)
{
  Serial.print("The current value is: ");
  Serial.println(number);
}
```

```
void setup() {
  int count = 0;              // expression1

  Serial.begin(9600);

startLoop:                    // Target label for goto
    ShowCount(count++);       // expression3
    if (count < 50)           // expression2
       goto startLoop;
}

void loop() {
}
```

In Listing 5.8. the initialization of the loop takes place where we define *count* because we initialize it as part of its definition. The loop body starts with the function call to *ShowCount()*. In this sense, it's like a *do-while* because we process the loop body statement before we test to see if we're done with the loop. Note that we use the postfix increment operator on *count* (i.e., *count++*) in the function call to *ShowCount()*. So, because *count* is initialized to 0 before the loop starts, what value is passed to *ShowCount()* on the first pass through the loop? *ShowCount()* receives the value 0 on the first pass through the loop because we are using a postfix increment operator. As soon as that function call is executed, then *count* is incremented by 1.

The *if* statement block checks to see if *count* is less than 50. Because *count* is less than 50, the *if* expression evaluates to logic *true* and the *goto startLoop* statement is executed. The *goto* statement directs program control to resume at the label defined as *startLoop*. You should be able to convince yourself that this example behaves much the same as the code in Listing 5.1. There is one major difference possible with a *goto* statement. The label for the *goto* doesn't have to be used to form a loop. You could place the *goto*'s target label hundreds of lines later in the code. In other words, the *goto* statement does provide a way of "skipping over" large chunks of code. Such use is usually not a good idea and is exactly why the *goto* keyword is rarely mentioned in polite coding circles.

The break and continue Keywords

The *break* and *continue* keywords are used with different loop structures. We examine the *break* statement first.

The break Statement

You have already seen the *break* keyword used with the *switch-case* statement block. In the *switch-case* statement block, the *break* keyword was used to immediately transfer program control to the first statement following the *switch-case* statement block. We can illustrate the use of the *break* statement as it pertains to loops by changing Listing 5.6 a little. The new code is presented in Listing Listing 5.9.

Listing Listing 5.9. Using the break statement

```
void setup() {
  char msg[] = "abcdefghijklmnopqrstuvwxyz12345*6790";   // search
  char target = '*';      // target character
  int elements;
  int i;

  Serial.begin(9600);
  elements = strlen(msg);// How many chars to examine?
  i = 0;
  while (i < elements) {
    if (msg[i] = target) // The right one?
      break;             // Yep, so quit looking
    i++;
  }
  if (i != elements) {            // We found a match!
    Serial.print("Found character ");
    Serial.print(target);
    Serial.print(" at index ");
    Serial.println(i);
  } else {
    Serial.println("Sorry...no match");
  }
}
void loop() {
}
```

We pointed out that the code in Listing 5.7 assumes a match is always found. A small change in the algorithm can improve the performance of that code. Do a mental code walk-through on Listing Listing 5.9 and you can see that the shaded lines are the important code changes. The first change finds the length of the input string via a call to the *strlen()* function. The second change says that, if we find a match on the target character, use the *break* keyword to transfer program control to the first statement following the loop body that encloses the *break* statement. The *if* test allows us to break out of the *while* loop upon a successful match without having to examine every element in the *msg[]* array.

If there is a match between the current character being examined (*msg[i])* and the target character ('*'), the *break* statement transfers control to the *if* *(i != elements) if* statement which is outside the loop. If a match is found, the value of *i* will be less than the length of the input string (*length*). Therefore, the final *if-else* statement block can test *i* against *length* and display the appropriate message. The fact that the user sees a success/no-success message makes this version better than Listing 5.7.

I encourage you to type in Listing Listing 5.9 and run it. If you do, you'll discover the program doesn't work properly! Why? Ask yourself what this statement does:

```
if (msg[i] = target)                    // The right one?
```

The *if* statement is using the *assignment* operator (=) when it should be using the relational operator (==) to test for equality. The result of this error is that on the very first pass through the loop, the assignment expression results in a non-zero value (i.e., interpreted as logic *true*) for the *if* expression, and the *break* statement is executed because the code thinks there was a match. Not good. You *will* make this kind of error many times during your learning process, thus contributing to your flat forehead. The bad news: such mistakes never end...I still make such mistakes!

The continue Statement

There are times when an event occurs in a loop and you want to "record" that event, but continue processing the loop. That's the purpose of the *continue* statement. For example, suppose you are a bank manager and you need to find out how many customers have a line-of-credit limit greater than some target amount. Consider this code fragment:

```
int index    = 0;
int memberCount = 0;

while (index < LOANMEMBERS) {
  if (memberListCreditLimit[index] > TARGETAMOUNT) {
    memberCount++;
    index++;
    continue;
  }
  Serial.print("member ");
  Serial.print(index);
  Serial.println(" does not meet criteria.");
  index++;
}
```

The code is a little contrived, but it illustrates what the *continue* statement does. In the *while* loop, if the current bank member has a credit limit that exceeds *TARGETAMOUNT* (why a symbolic constant?), the code increments the *memberCount*, increments *index* so we can look at the next bank member, and then executes the *continue* statement. *The continue statement sends program control to the relational test that controls the loop to see if another pass is needed.* In this code fragment, the relational test (i.e., expression2) is the *index < LOANMEMBERS* expression. Notice how the *continue* statement allows us to skip over the code that tells the user a member doesn't meet the test criteria.

Even though the *continue* statement may be used in any loop structure, the truth is that the *continue* statement isn't used very often. Still, you can hang the *continue* statement tool on your tool belt in some less accessible segment of the belt since it won't be used that often.

Loop Example Using loop()

Back in Chapter 3, Table 3.5 presented a table of the ASCII codes that are typically used in many IDE programs. In writing this chapter, I was using the STM32 microcontroller and came across the following example program presented in Listing Listing 5.10, written specifically for the STM32 and distributed as part of its patch code installation.

Listing 5.10. Display the ASCII table.

```
/*
  ASCII table

  Connect to the Maple Serial using the Serial Monitor, then press
any key and hit enter.

  Prints out byte values in all possible formats:
   as raw binary values
  as ASCII-encoded decimal, hex, octal, and binary values

  For more on ASCII, see:
       http://www.asciitable.com
       http://en.wikipedia.org/wiki/ASCII

  No external hardware needed.
   created 2006   by Nicholas Zambetti
modified 18 Jan 2009   by Tom Igoe

  <http://www.zambetti.com>

  Ported to the Maple 27 May 2010   by Bryan Newbold
*/
void setup()
{
```

```
  Serial.begin(9600); // Ignored by Maple. But needed by boards
using hardware serial
  // via a USB to Serial adaptor
  // Wait for the user to press a key
  while (!Serial.available())
    continue;

  // Prints title with ending line break
  Serial.println("ASCII Table ~ Character Map");
}

// First visible ASCII character: '!' is number 33: int thisByte =
33;
// You can also write ASCII characters in single quotes.
// for example. '!' is the same as 33, so you could also use this:
int thisByte = '!';

void loop() {
  // Prints value unaltered, i.e. the raw binary version of the
  // byte. The serial monitor interprets all bytes as
  // ASCII, so 33, the first number,  will show up as '!'
  Serial.write(thisByte);

  Serial.print(", dec: ");
  // Prints value as string as an ASCII-encoded decimal (base 10).
// Decimal is the default format for Serial.print() and
  // Serial.println(), so no modifier is needed:
  Serial.print(thisByte);
  // But you can declare the modifier for decimal if you want to.
  // This also works if you uncomment it:
  // Serial.print(thisByte, DEC);

  Serial.print(", hex: ");
  // Prints value as string in hexadecimal (base 16):
  Serial.print(thisByte, HEX);

  Serial.print(", oct: ");
  // Prints value as string in octal (base 8);
  Serial.print(thisByte, OCT);

  Serial.print(", bin: ");
  // Prints value as string in binary (base 2); also prints ending
  // line break:
  Serial.println(thisByte, BIN);

  // If printed last visible character '~' or 126, stop:
  if (thisByte == 126) {    // could also use if (thisByte == '~')
{
    while (true) {   // This loops forever and does nothing
      continue;
    }
  }
  // Go on to the next character
  thisByte++;
}
```

I encourage you to spend some time looking at the code, keeping in mind that I want you to “grade” this example when you're done studying it.

Even better, copy the code, compile and run it after you have studied its use. What do you think about the code?

First of all, the comments get in the way of reading the code. For example, I've repeated a section of the code in Listing Listing 5.10 here:

```
Serial.print(", dec: ");  // Prints value as string as an ASCII-
                          // encoded decimal (base 10).
                        // Decimal is the default format for
                          // Serial.print() and

                          // Serial.println(), so no modifier
needed:
Serial.print(thisByte);   // But you can declare the modifier for
                          // decimal if you want to.
                        // This also works if you uncomment it:
                        // Serial.print(thisByte, DEC);
Serial.print(", hex: ");  // Prints value as string in hex (base
16):
Serial.print(thisByte, HEX);
```

Which code fragment is easier for you to read and understand? I may be biased, but I like my commented version better because the comments don't obfuscate the C source code. In other words, commenting *style* makes a difference, especially when you are debugging a program.

My real complaint with the code, however, is the structure of the program. First, keep in mind that most users of a program are not going to plow through the source code to learn how to run it. Indeed, part of your job is to write code that can be run *without* seeing the source code. Admittedly, this is an STM32 example, so the author expected the person using it has read the source code.

I didn't.

I was overconfident, saw the ASCII Table title, and I was off to the races. I loaded the source code, compiled/uploaded it for the STM32, and waited to see the ASCII table appear on the Serial monitor.

Nothing...

Finally, after I convinced myself that the code was locked up, I started looking in *loop()* to see where it was hanging up. Wrong place! Only after I remembered that I didn't see *anything* on the Serial monitor did I go back and look in *setup()*. It was a perfect flat-forehead moment...Unlike everyone else on the planet, this author chose this method to wait for the Serial object to get instantiated:

```
while (!Serial.available())
  continue;
```

Typically, everyone else on the planet writes this "wait" code using:

```
while (!Serial)
    ;
```

In Listing Listing 5.10, this code calls the *available()* method of the *Serial* object. This requires the user to move the cursor into the textbox at the top of the *Serial* monitor's dialog box and press the Enter key. Doing this means there is a character (i.e., the newline character '\n') "available" in the *Serial* buffer. The newline character causes the *Serial.available()* expression to return logic *true*, but the NOT operator (!, discussed in the next section) immediately changes the state of the expression to logic *false*, causing the *while* loop to end and execution proceeds with the rest of the program.

The cows almost got home before I saw what was going on. (And you thought I was infallible! So much for that little halo of light.) The reason this is a bad example is because code execution gives no clue what's going on or why the program appeared to be locked up. Treat this section as a teaching moment and try to help the hapless user as much as you can in running your programs.

Short-Circuiting

Loops often are the largest time consumers in most programs. Anything we can do to shorten the processing time in loops often pays off in noticeable time savings. The logic AND and OR operators can be used to gain a small speed advantage under certain circumstances. *Short-circuiting means taking advantage of the logic operator expression evaluation order in such a way that it lessens the execution time of the complex expression.* For example, consider the logic AND operator. All of the outcomes of a complex expression are going to be *false* unless both operands are *true*. Now suppose you know from experience that expression1 is logic *true* 99 percent of the time, but expression2 is *false* 60 percent of the time. The AND and OR operators both evaluate from left to right (see the Precedence Table 2.1), so if expression1 is almost always *true*, that means that expression2 is going to be the "most responsible expression" in determining the outcome of the complex expression.

Because expression1 is true 99 percent of the time, the compiler must evaluate expression2 in virtually every instance.

But, what happens if we place expression2 to the left of expression1? Because 60 percent of the time expression2 is *false*, and a *false* expression in an AND operation results in a logic *false* result for the overall logic test, moving expression2 to the left of expression1 means it's evaluated first. Think about what this little change does. Optimizing compilers know that a logic *false* result in a complex logic AND test means a logic *false* result, *the compiler doesn't even need to bother testing the remaining test expression(s)* (e.g., the original expression1). Now, because you reversed the order of the expression tests, 60 percent of the time the second expression doesn't even need to be tested. In a long loop structure, this little time slice savings can add up. Save a million instruction cycles here, save another million instruction cycles there, pretty soon it can add up to a noticeable speed improvement.

Complex Logic Evaluations

You can combine as many logic operators as you want in a complex expression. To illustrate, the algorithm for determining if a year is a leap year is:

> if year is divisible by 400 then is a leap year
> if year is divisible by 100 then not a leap year
> if year is divisible by 4 then is a leap otherwise not a leap year

You could string this determination of a leap year into *if* statement blocks, but you'd likely end up with a cascading *if* block, which I (and many other C programmers) don't like much. Plus, C programmers avoid unnecessary typing. The result might be something like Listing Listing 5.11.

Listing Listing 5.11. *Is it a leap year?*

```
/*****
  Purpose: To determine if the year is a leap year
       if year is divisible by 400 then is a leap year
       if year is divisible by 100 then not a leap year
       if year is divisible by 4 then is a leap year
       otherwise not a leap year
 testdata: 2020 is a leap year, 2017, 2018, 2019 are not

  Argument list:
```

```
    int year        the year under test

  Return value
    int             1 if it is a leap year, 0 if not

  CAUTION:
*****/
int IsLeapYear(int year)
{
  Return (int)(((year % 4 == 0) && (year % 100 != 0)) ||
                 (year % 400 == 0));
}
void setup() {
  Serial.begin(9600);
}
void loop()
{
  char buffer[8];
  int bytesRead;
  int daysInMonth;
  int year;

  Serial.print("\nEnter the year to test: ");
  while (true) {
    if (Serial.available() > 0) {         // They typed something
      bytesRead = Serial.readBytesUntil('\n',buffer,
                                         sizeof(buffer)-1);
      buffer[bytesRead] = '\0';
      year = atoi(buffer);
      daysInMonth = 28 + IsLeapYear(year);
      Serial.print("\nFor the year ");
      Serial.print(year);
      Serial.print(", February has ");
      Serial.print(daysInMonth);
      Serial.println(" days.");
      break;
    }
  }
}
```

I implemented the leap year algorithm in a single complex expression:

```
(((year % 4 == 0) && (year % 100 != 0)) || (year % 400 == 0))
```

Note the multiple use of the logic operators (the shaded blocks above) in the *return* statement expression. Take a few moments to review the algorithm and its implementation in Listing Listing 5.11 until you're sure you understand how the multiple logic tests are being resolved. I should warn you that my leap year function is different than the leap year function found in most libraries. The reason is because most leap year functions return logic *true* or *false* for the result of the function call.

My version returns an *int*. By returning an *int* instead of a *boolean*, I can do this:

```
daysInFebruary = 28 + IsLeapYear(year);
```

without drawing any fussy warnings from the compiler, since I'm using the return value as an *int*, not a *boolean*. (Some compilers complain if you pour a *boolean* bucket into an *int* bucket even though that won't slop data on the floor.) If I want to, and because the return value from my function is 0 (not a leap year) or 1 (yep, it is) as an *int*, I can still use the return value in an *if* statement test, too. Seems like a win-win to me.

Conclusion

Program loops are one of the most powerful features of a computer program. C gives you a variety of loop structures from which to choose. Most *for* loops are used to plow through a known number of passes through a loop. Both the *while* and *do-while* loops are most often associated with a search for some target data item in a large list and breaking out of the loop when the target is found. Spend some time experimenting with the programs presented in this chapter and, perhaps, write some of your own.

Exercises

1. Fix the *while* loop program in Listing 5.7 so that, if the target is not found, the program informs the user that the target is missing from the input string.

2. Write a program that simulates tossing a coin 10000 times and reports a count for the number of heads and tails. You need to use several of the random number functions.

3. Explain the difference between pre- and post-increment and decrement operators. If the increment/decrement is on a statement line by itself, do the pre/post operators make any difference?

4. Initialize a character array with your favorite quote and search for a particular letter within that quote. When you find that character, change it to a new character that you got from the user at the start of the program using the Serial object.

5. Using the same quote from #4, write a program that counts how many characters are in the quote.

6. Using the same quote from #4, write a program that counts the number of vowels that are in the quote and displays their counts at the end of the program.

7. Why should you avoid the *goto* statement?

8. Pascal's Triangle has some interesting properties (https://www.mathsisfun.com/pascalstriangle.html). Write a program that builds the triangle through 8 levels. (Little harder than you might think.)

Chapter 6 Functions

It's pretty hard to write a microcontroller program without using functions of some sort. You have been using functions since the first chapter of this book. In this chapter, we provide information to help you understand and use functions written by others and to write your own functions.

What is a Function?

A function is a small body of code that is designed to perform a specific task. For many of the tasks that your specific program needs to handle, chances are pretty good that someone else has already written a function for that task. Many simple programs often amount to collecting these pre-written functions, arranging them in the order you want, and then you writing the syntactic glue that holds them together into a program. For that reason, any time I wish to start a new programming project, my first step in the process is an Internet search for the task(s) at hand. After all, it's a lot easier to stand on the shoulders of someone else than it is to duplicate their efforts and write everything from scratch. Also, published function code (e.g., Open Source code) likely has been tested and debugged, saving you even more time. (Alas, not all publicly-available functions are bug-free. But even less-than-perfect functions are a starting point.)

Throughout this book, there are three "sub-types" of functions that you use in your programs:

Core functions – these are functions that are "built into" the IDE. For example, you have used *delay()* and *pinMode()*.

Library functions – a collection of task-related functions. We divide these into two groups:

1. Libraries distributed with the Arduino IDE
2. Libraries not distributed with the IDE

Custom functions – Libraries you write yourself

In this chapter, we are going to concentrate on the third type of function; the functions that you write. (We have a lot more to say about function libraries in Chapter 12.) To help you to write your own functions, I am going to suggest some guidelines that should help you write functions that are easier to write, test, debug, use and maintain. These guidelines are not etched in stone and are not necessarily syntax rules. However, these guidelines are distilled from writing C functions for more than 40 years and they have served me well over the years.

Function Guidelines

The purpose of these guidelines is to help you write functions that are easy to use and understand, and to help make them more "reusable" in other programs. Writing reusable functions is a balancing act between code that is flexible enough to find use in other programs, yet specific enough to solve the task at hand. Writing reusable functions is a laudable goal, but not easily achieved. While it may take a little more effort up front to write reusable functions, that effort pays off in the long run when you develop new programs.

Function Header

When I had my software company, I required all of my programmers to use the function header style presented in Listing 6.1. If I found *any* code, even code that wasn't ready for a code walk-through, that didn't have this style of header file for each function they wrote, the penalty was beer and pizza for everyone in the company at their expense. It was rare for any individual to buy beer and pizza more than once. The required function header style is presented in Listing 6.1.

Listing 6.1. Style for function headers

```
/*****
    Purpose: This function is used to (fill in the description
here. If the function is very complex, you are expected to provide
a URL where one could look up the details.)

Argument List:
   int bytesToWrite   the number of bytes to write to the file
   char text[]        the string holding the bytes
   char fileName[]    the file to receive the data bytes

Return value
    int      the bytes successfully written to file, -1 on error

    CAUTION: function assumes the file is already open
*****/
int FileWriteBytes(int bytesToWrite, char text[], char fileName[])
{                    // opening brace of function body
      // function body
}                    // closing brace of function body
```

Everything between the "/*****" and the "*****/" is viewed by the compiler as multiline C comment. Recall that a multiline comment starts with a "/*" character sequence and ends with a "*/". Because the header is viewed as a comment by the compiler, the fact that it's fairly long has absolutely no impact on the performance of the function or its generated code. As a result, there is nothing to be gained by being terse in the function header's verbiage.

Within the function header, the first section is used to describe the purpose of the function. The function header Purpose field describes the task the function is designed to address. If the function is based on an algorithm that requires more than general programming knowledge, I often add a URL for the source I used when writing the function. This is useful when you come back to the code a year later to reuse it but can't remember some specific detail about the algorithm. Also, if anyone wants to question you about the source of the algorithm for legal reasons, it can be extremely helpful to have the URL handy.

Why Not Just "/" and "*/" for the Function Header?*

First, the longer sequence of asterisks makes the start and end of a function header more easily spotted when reading a program listing. Second, and more importantly, I used the exaggerated function header markers as sentinels in a support program I wrote.

The support program would open and read all of the source code files associated with a given project. Upon seeing the "/*****" sentinel, I knew that I was about to read the start of a function header. I used two macros (i.e., small functions in their own right) that come with the IDE to write information to a new file. The first macro, __FILE__, is the name of the current source code file that my program is reading and the second macro, __LINE__, is the line number in that source code file where the current function header is located. (The macros are covered in Chapter 10.) The program would write the source code file name and the line number to a text file that was being managed by my program.

Next, I would write the entire content of the function header file to the new text file. I would write everything in the function header up to the closing sentinel marker, "*****/". After reading the closing sentinel marker, the program then copied the next full line of text, which is:

```
int FileWriteBytes(int bytesToWrite, char text[], char fileName[])
```

to the text file. The program then wrote two newline characters ('\n') to the text file and resumed reading the source file, looking for the next function header.

After all of the project files had been processed in this way, the last task for the program was to sort each header into alphabetical order based on the header's function name. The new, sorted, list of function headers was then written to a new text file. I ran the utility program once a week, usually on Friday afternoon.

Why?

When the utility program finishes, you end up with a printable file that is the documentation for all of the functions your staff has written for the project, the file where that function is defined, and its line number within that file. If a new programmer was added to the project, the printed documentation for the functions helped that person get up to speed more quickly than if they had to search the source files themselves. That's why I was so strict in the enforcement of the style, plus it lends to the consistency of the code, making it easier to read.

You may be sitting there thinking: “I don't plan on having a staff of programmers working for me. The code I write is just for m, so why waste time writing a function header?” Probably true, but does it mean that, a year from now, the comments won't be helpful to you? Thirty years ago, I wrote a function that was capable of doing large number factorials, and recently someone wrote to me asking how I did it. I still have the source code for my statistics package (Microstat) and I was able to go to that function, read the header, and tell them about Stirling's Approximation. (This was before the Internet even existed, so there was no URL in the header, just a footnote-style reference.)

Right now, you may not *think* you need to write function headers, but it takes very little effort to do it, so why not use them? You may well find that they are quite useful at some point in the future.

Function Names

There are several things I consider when giving a new function a name. First, functions often denote some form of action that is to take place in the program. As I mentioned before, variable names are like nouns; they describe a person, place, or thing. Functions are more like verbs; they suggest an action that is to take place or a question the function answers (i.e., *IsLeapYear()*). For these reasons, I try to *select a function name that suggests the purpose of, or the action taken by, the function*.

Second, the function name should *not* indicate how things are done within the function. To the outside world, the function is a black box with a door. There are no windows for a nosy programmer to pry into the inner-workings of your function. To me, *SortData()* is a better function name than is *BubbleSort(), ShellSort(),* or *InsertionSort()*. *SortData()* tells the user the *purpose* of the function, while the other two names tell *how* to sort the data. Frankly, the algorithm used in the function is none of the user's business. The only time the algorithm should become their business is if the algorithm performs poorly or incorrectly.

The reason I feel names that reflect the purpose of the function are better is because it gives me the freedom to change the algorithm without feeling guilty about it. If I wrote an *InsertionSort()* function and later decided that a Shell sort is better given the data at hand, I would feel obligated to write a new function named *ShellSort()* and change the program code everywhere I call *InsertionSort()*. The *SortData()* function name allows me to implement any algorithm I want and still get a good night's sleep.

Function Names and Case

Worrying about the case of letters within a function name sounds kinda trivial at the outset, but there is a reason why it isn't. First, functions that are part of the Arduino core function library (e.g., *delay(), pinMode(), digitalRead()*, etc.) all begin the function name with a lowercase letter. Likewise, C++ libraries typically use lowercase letters for their class methods (e.g., Serial.*print(),* Display.*setCursor(),* etc.). (Class methods serve the same purpose as functions. The primary difference is that methods exist within a class object.) By using an uppercase letter at the start of the functions you write, you can tell at a glance that the function is one that you wrote and have direct access to its source code.

After the first letter in the function name, use an uppercase letter for all "sub-words" in the function name (e.g., *IsLeapYear()*). This convention makes it easier for the reader to discern the purpose (or action) that the function serves. This form of using uppercase words within an identifier is called *camel notation*. We discussed (and use) camel notation for variables, too, but we always start variable names with a lowercase letter. There is usually no confusion between library function names, which also start with a lowercase letter, because functions names are used with parentheses most of the time. (Using a pointer to call a function is one exception.)

Some people like to use the underscore character instead of case changes in their function and variable names (e.g., is_leap_year(), my_fire_sensor). I'm not a big fan. My main objection is personal: I don't use the underscore character very often but when I do, it slows my typing down. Second, camel notation uses fewer characters. At the margin, it means I can fit more code on a single line without the need to fallen into the old-dog-new-tricks rut. I like this rut. The rut serves its purpose, and I won't be changing it anytime soon. You do what suits your preferences.

Function Signatures

The line immediately following the closing comment sentinel in Listing 6.1 is:

```
int FileWriteBytes(int bytesToWrite, char text[], char fileName[])
```

This is the function signature for the function named *FileWriteBytes()*. A function signature has three main parts:

1. the function type specifier (*int*)
2. the function name (*FileWriteBytes*)
3. the function parameter list (int bytesToWrite, char text[], char fileName[])

Figure 6.1 identifies these three parts of the function signature.

Function Return Value

The purpose of the *function type specifier is to tell the user what kind of data this function is designed to return to the caller.* The *Return value* field in Listing 6.1 tells the user what the data type is for the function type specifier. Listing 6.1 and Figure 6.1 show the function type specifier to be an *int* data type. If no data are returned from the function, the function type specifier must still be given, but its data type would be *void.*

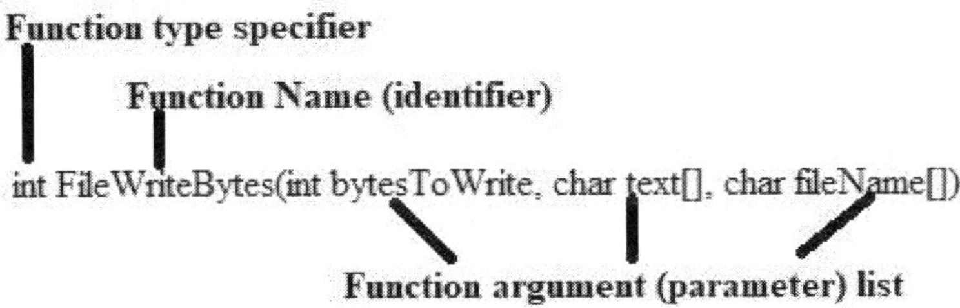

Figure 6.1 Parts of a function signature

The function type specifier determines the data type that is returned from calling the function. Keep in mind that, for non-*void* function type specifiers (e.g., *char, int, long*, etc.), *only one value can be returned to the caller.* For those functions defined with a *void* function type specifier, no value can be returned from the function call.

Function Identifier

FileWriteBytes() is the name of the function in Listing 6.1. We've already discussed function names and why I use the style that I do. Start with a capital letter for the functions you write and use camel notation within the function name.

Function Argument (Parameter) List

The purpose of the *function argument (aka, parameter) list is to pass to the function the data it needs to perform its task.* Most of the time, functions do need data passed into them, but sometimes the function doesn't need outside data in the form of a parameter list. In those cases, the opening and closing parentheses of the function parameter list can be left empty, or you could write the term *void* between the parentheses.

Function Prototypes

When C was first developed, it didn't have some of the safeguards that it does now. Indeed, one of the points of contention in writing a standard for C was one group wanted to make C a "safer" language and the other who liked C's compact, know-what-you're-doing, style. For example, C does not check your use of arrays at runtime to see if you are trying to access array elements that are past the end of the defined array. Some languages, like Java, do such safety checks. That led some C purists to say that Java is C with training wheels.

Another safeguard that did make it into the standard was a check on the function's parameter list. This check makes sure that the data the programmer is passing into the function is the same data type(s) the function is expecting, as detailed in the function parameter list. All kinds of subtle bugs can creep into the code if the function is expecting you to pass in a 1-byte *char* data type and you pass in a 4-byte *long* instead. (Setting up the microcontroller registers and the stack to do a simple function call is pretty complicated. See: https://zhu45.org/posts/2017/Jul/30/understanding-how-function-callworks/#calling-a-function.)

To help solve this problem, the C standard incorporated function prototypes. To create a function prototype for any function, simply copy the function's signature and add a semicolon at the end of the signature. The function prototype for *FileWriteBytes()* is:

```
int FileWriteBytes(int bytesToWrite, char text[], char fileName[]);
```

Note the semicolon at the end of the function signature. Convention places function prototypes at a point in the program that is before that function is used in the program. As a result, you usually find function prototypes near the top of the source code file or in a header file. This placement ensures that the compiler sees what the function's signature is before you use it. By reading the function prototype for a function, the compiler can place the function type specifier, ID, and data types of the parameter list in the symbol table. Then, when you use that function, the compiler can check the attribute list of the function in the symbol table to make sure that you're passing the correct data type(s) to the function. The programming term for this data type checking is simply referred to as "*type checking*". While type checking can't stop you from shooting yourself in the foot, it does give you a set of steel-toed boots to help lessen the pain.

What is a "Good" C Function?

We've already commented on several function elements that are good *style* for writing C functions, like the function header and prototyping. However, there are a number of things that also make for a good C function.

Good C Functions are Cohesive.

A *cohesive C function is a function that performs a single task, and does it efficiently.* If you write a function and cannot tell me what it does in two sentences or less, chances are pretty good it is not a cohesive function. With respect to efficiency, in this context it means the function is written in such a way that it doesn't waste memory resources nor does it dawdle while using those resources. A cohesive function gets the job done...quickly and efficiently.

Over the years, I've seen students try to write the Swiss Army knife equivalent of a function. That is, they want the function to handle two (often more) tasks in a single function call. Such an attempt almost always results in a function that is neither cohesive nor efficient. There are a number of traits that almost always suggest a non-cohesive function.

First, non-cohesive functions tend to have a function body with more source code lines than expected. It's pretty unusual for a cohesive function to take more than a screen-full of the IDE's source code window. There are, of course, exceptions to the small function body norm, but they are less common.

Second, Swiss Army knife functions often have complex and bloated parameter lists. The sole purpose of a function parameter is to give the function the outside data it needs to perform its single task. If you see a bunch of variables being passed into a function as parameters, chances are that one or more of those variables are "flag" variables. *Flag variables are variables that reflect the current state of something in the program* (e.g., *valveState*, *mySwitch*, etc.). Based on the values of the flag variables, the function attempts to perform multiple tasks within a single function call. This rarely works out well and almost always results in a non-cohesive function.

When it comes to the length of a function parameter list: *the longer the parameter list of a function, the less likely it is that the function can be reused in other programs.* It always seems that multi-task functions might incorporate one task you need to perform, but not the other(s). As a result, at best you strip out the code you need, and use that code as the starting point for your own new (hopefully single-task) function.

Good C Functions Avoid Coupling

Function coupling refers to the need of one function's task-solving ability being dependent upon some other function. A dead giveaway of function coupling is when you make a code change in one function and that change triggers the need for a code change in a different function. For example, if you have a data structure that gets saved to an SD card in your system and you decide to add a new field to that structure, does that one change ripple through a half-dozen other functions?

True, you cannot avoid function coupling completely. For example, if you are writing data to a file stored on an SD card, you need to first open the SD card for writing. It is common to see an SD data recorder have functions for *SDOpen()*, *SDRead()*, *SDWrite()* and *SDClose()*. You might be asking: "Why not just make *SDOpen()* and *SDClose()* part of the *SDRead()* and *SDWrite()* functions?"

Well, you could, but if you do that, you're going to have to bury that same open/close code in *both* read and write functions. Duplicating code is almost always a bad idea for several reasons. First, duplicate code means more code to write, test, debug, and maintain. Second, you've made the function less cohesive by giving it another task to perform. Third, any error processing code needed when the SD open/close process fails must also be duplicated in both the SD read and write functions. Fourth, opening and closing SD data files is a relatively slow process and is avoided as much as possible. The more common approach is to open the file once and leave it open the entire time the program needs to use that data. The SD card is then closed when the reads/writes have been completed. Finally, code duplication sets off a "*Trickle Effect*" where a bug fix or change in one function trickles into the body of code for another function. Nope, code duplication is rarely a good idea.

Good Functions Avoid Global Data

We haven't really discussed what global data are, but do so in the next couple of pages. Stated simply, think of global data as data that is accessible to every element of a program. Because global data are usable by every other function in the program, global data do couple what's done in one function to those other functions that also use that same data. We'll see why this is a bad thing shortly.

Good Functions Are Clearly Written

Unfortunately, it appears that some programmers see function writing as a chance to show off and end up writing code that is very difficult to follow. A requirement of a clearly-written function is documentation. A complete function header, like the one described in Listing 6.1, is the first step in documenting a function.

Program comments are a second requirement. I saw one file with dozens of function definitions in it and it did not have one comment in the file. Not good. On the other hand, I actually saw this in a published piece of code:

```
i = i + 1;   // This statement increases variable i by 1.
```

Really? Do they think a C programmer can't figure this out without the comment? This person had a comment on every line in the program. That kind of comment density is clutter rather than clarification, and actually hinders reading the code. Generally, a short comment at the top of a multi-line section of code that performs a specific action, or a comment that explains particularly complex processing, are good comment candidates. Strike a balance between meaningful comments that help the reader understand the code and those that simply add clutter.

Good Functions are Organized

I've already said that good functions are clearly written, which implies that they are organized. The form of organization I'm referring to here relates to how you organize multiple functions in a program.

Function libraries are already organized into a set of task-oriented functions (e.g., the Tone, Wire, EEPROM, and other libraries and the functions contained therein). However, as you gain experience, your programs will increase in complexity and size. Indeed, I have seen one program with over 10,000 lines of code all contained in one single INO file! Moving from the top of that file to the bottom was a career rather than a task, and a monumental waste of time.

Instead of crushing everything into the *.ino file, break the program up into task-oriented C++ (cpp) files and use a new program tab in the IDE for each one of those files. The Five Program Steps is a starting point for thinking about the functions in each file. For example, if you are writing a home alarm system, you might experiment with the following Organizational List as a starting point for your own programs:

1. Initialization – HomeAlarm.ino
2. Input – MenuAndSensorInput.cpp
3. Processing – SensorProcessing.cpp
4. Output – DisplayManagement.cpp
5. Termination – (usually there isn't one, but perhaps you have power loss restart functions or other functions necessary to restart the program?)
6. HomeAlarm.h – header file for function prototypes, symbolic constants, global data, etc.

Breaking a large program into some form of logical organization makes it easier to test, debug, and maintain the program. See Figure 6.2. (The file names located on the tabs above the Source Code Windows are not in the order presented in the list above. The reason is because the IDE *always* places the INO file on the left-most tab. The remaining source code files are in alphabetic order.)

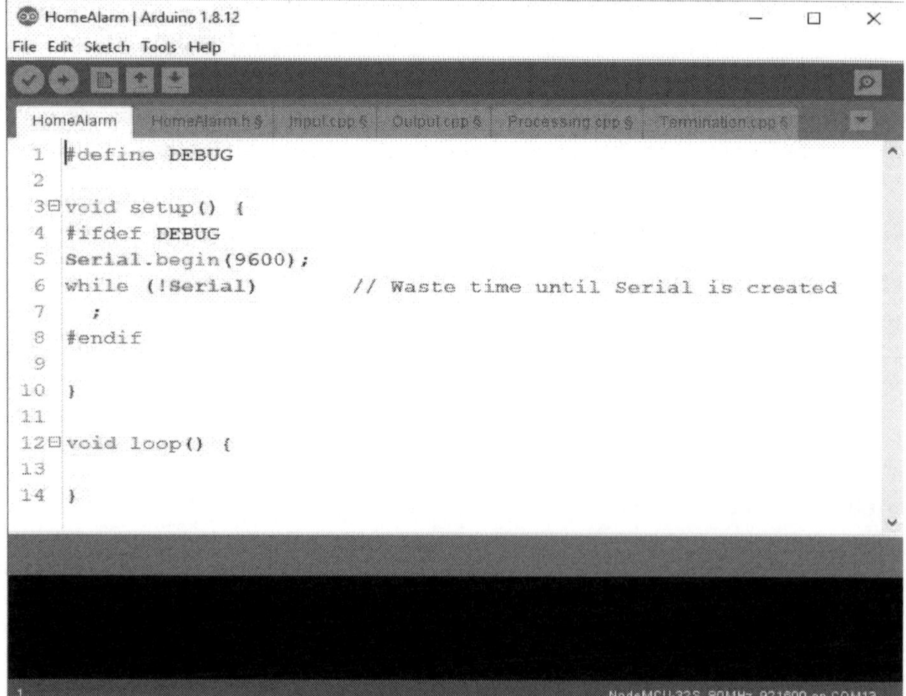

Figure 6.2. Using task-oriented source files. (Note tabs above Source Code Window)

Creating project sub-files (see Figure 1.9 in Chapter 1) organized along task responsibilities makes it much easier to work on a project. Expanding the Organizational List shown above can help in designing and writing the program, too. For example:

1. Initialization – HomeAlarm.ino
   SetDefaultHomeTemperature()
   SetDefaultEntryDelay()
   SetDefaultLightingOffDelay()
   Set911EmergencyPhonePort()
   SetEmergencyCallNumber()

and so on. Once you have filled in the function names for each of the sub-files, writing the program is reduced to filling in the function code and adding a little syntactic glue to hold everything together. This is *not* the same thing as flow charting, which uses graphic symbols to connect lines and show program flow dynamics. This is much simpler and requires less time to construct. Prep work like this doesn't take much effort, but really makes program development considerably easier.

Scope

The scope of a data item is critically important to how you can access and use that data item. *Scope refers to the visibility and life of a data item.* Scoping rules can affect the way you write functions, so this is an appropriate place to discuss scope. When I first started using C back in the late 1970's, I learned that there are three levels of scope. Today, I'm not so sure. I now think there are four scope levels. We discuss each of these below.

Global Scope

A data item with global scope lives and is visible from its point of definition to the end of the source code file in which the item is defined. The program example in Listing 6.2 helps to understand global scope.

Listing 6.2. Program to illustrate global scope

```
#include <limits.h>

int number;                  // Variable defined with global scope

void setup() {
  Serial.begin(9600);

  number = 10;
  Serial.print("In setup(), number = ");
  Serial.println(number);
}
```

```
void loop() {
  if (number == INT_MAX)
  {
    number = 0;
  }
  Serial.print("in loop(), number = ");
  Serial.println(number++);
}       // Close brace of loop() body and last statement in file
```

In Listing 6.2, variable *number* is defined near the top of the program. (The limits.h header file is included so we can use the maximum allowable value for an *int*, *INT_MAX*, in the program. I did this because that value varies among the processors you can use.) Because *number* is defined outside of any function, *number* "comes into scope" the instant the compiler finishes compiling the line where *number* is defined and remains "in scope" to the end of the current source code file. *Global scope means that every statement in this program, starting with the semicolon at the end of the statement that defines* number *through to the end of the source code file, has full access to* number.

Okay, so why is scope important to the functions I write? Think about it. Suppose you write your own function in the file and place its definition somewhere after the end of *loop()*. If your function needs to use the value of *number* for some reason, do you need to pass *number* in as a parameter? No, you don't. Because *number* is defined with global scope, it is already visible and accessible to the code in your function. That is, even though your "black box" function has no windows in it, your function can "see" and use *number* because it has global scope by being defined outside of any function.

Cool! If that's the case, why are we wasting our time passing data into a function as a parameter? Just define all of our variables with global scope! True, but there's a rather nettlesome problem.

Think of the global definition of a data item as the same as placing a program prostitute at the top of the file. With that done, you then give each statement in the file $500. Nine months later, she gives birth to a program bug. Which program statement is the dad?

If a variable is defined with global scope and all of a sudden it assumes an unexpected value, which statement is causing the problem? Because global data are everywhere accessible from their point of definition to the end of the source file, isolating the statement that is causing the bug can be very difficult. Indeed, isolating a program bug is 90% of the debugging effort with 10% going to actually fixing the bug. This also means that any short term benefit you might gain from a shorter function parameter list by using global data is more than offset by the difficulty in isolating and fixing program bugs.

Nope, making everything a global is *not* a good idea. Okay, so what is the solution? Well, for starters, write code with no bugs in it. Since that's probably not going to happen anytime soon, the next alternative is to narrow the scope of the variable.

Function Scope

A data item with function scope is visible and lives from its point of definition to the end of the closing brace of the function block in which it is defined. Listing 6.3 is almost identical to Listing 6.2, except we moved the definition of *number* into *setup()*. Because the definition of *number* is done within the *setup() function*, it no longer meets the requirements for global scope (i.e., defined outside of any

Listing 6.3. Program to illustrate function scope

```
#include <limits.h>

void setup() {
  int number;                                    // function scope

  Serial.begin(9600);
  number = 10;
  Serial.print("in setup(), number = ");
  Serial.println(number);
}

void loop() {
  if (number == INT_MAX) {                       //Uh-oh...problem
    number = 0;
  }
  Serial.print("in loop(), number = ");
  Serial.println(number++);
}
```

function). Because the definition of *number* appears within *setup()*, *number* now has function scope. Now compile the program. You can't. The reason is because the use of *number* in *loop()* draws a "*'number' was not declared in this scope*" error message from the compiler. (Man, that's like fingernails on a chalkboard to me! It should be: '*number*' was not defined in this scope.) The error is pointing out that *loop()* doesn't know about *number* because it has function scope and *loop()* can't "see" into *setup()*. Indeed, the statements in *loop()* may as well put their $500 in a savings account because the hooker is completely invisible to them.

Guess what just happened to your ability to isolate and fix a program bug? Because *number* is now only visible and viable within *setup()*, clearly any unexpected value for *number* must be occurring within the *setup()* function. Therefore, any variable with function scope is going to be easier to debug than a similar variable with global scope. This is also why you use function parameters when you write a function. Because function parameters have function scope, tracking down weird values becomes easier with function parameters rather than using global data.

The process of reducing the visibility of a data item is called data encapsulation. As you can see, encapsulation makes writing stable programs much easier. Indeed, the concept of data encapsulation was a primary driving force behind the creation of C++. More on that in Chapter 12.

Well, if narrowing the definition of a data item from global scope to function scope is helpful, can we squeeze scope any more? Yep, we can.

Statement Block Scope

A data item with block scope exists and is visible from its point of definition to the end of the statement block in which it is defined. Listing 6.4 is similar to the previous two listings, except we are using a *for* loop to control the display of *number.*

Listing 6.4. Program to illustrate block scope

```
#include <limits.h>

void setup() {
  Serial.begin(9600);
}

void loop() {
       // block scope
  for (int number = 0; number <= INT_MAX; number++) {
    if (number == INT_MAX) {
      number = 0;
      break;
    }
    Serial.print("in loop(), number = ");
    Serial.println(number++);
  }
  Serial.print("Finished INT_MAX passes, number reset to ");
  Serial.println(number);
                       // Uh-oh
```

```
}
```

Note that expression1 of the *for* loop defines *number*. Now compile Listing 6.4. Well, you can't. The reason is because *number* in the last statement line issues the same (incorrectly-worded) "*'number' was not declared in this scope*" error message from the compiler. Because *number* is defined in expression1 of the *for* statement block, *number* ceases to exist after the closing brace of the *for* statement block. Because the last *Serial.print()* statement attempts to use *number* when it is out of scope, the compiler must issue an error message. That's the bad news.

The good news is that, if anything had gone wrong with *number* during program execution, we have *significantly* narrowed down the list of statements we need to check during the debugging process. As a general rule, the more restrictive the scope, the easier it is to debug a program.

Inter-file Scope

Most programmers are comfortable with the three scope levels we've discussed. However, I now feel that there is a fourth level that needs to be included in any scope discussion. For lack of a better term, I'm calling the new scope level: inter-file scope. *Inter-file scope applies to data items defined in one file, but only declared in another file*. To illustrate inter-file scope, consider Listing 6.5. For you to see what's going on, call the first file *InterfileScopeDemo.ino* and call the second file *MySquare.cpp*. Put both code files in the same project directory named InterfileScopeDemo. When you open the project, you will see two program tabs just above the Source Code Window.

Listing 6.5. Program to illustrate Inter-file scope

```
====== First code file : InterfileScopeDemo.ino =====

int number;                      // Global scope

void setup() {
  Serial.begin(9600);

  number = 10;
  Serial.print("in setup(), number = ");
  Serial.println(number);

}
void loop() {
  for (number = 0; number < 50; number++) {
    Serial.print("The square of ");
    Serial.print(number);
    Serial.print(" is ");
```

```
      Serial.println(MySquare());
    }
}
====  Second code file : MySquare.cpp =======

/*****
  Purpose: To square the value of number

  Argument list:
    void

  Return value:
     int           the square of umber

  CAUTION:
*****/
int MySquare()
{
  return number * number;
}
```

When you try to compile this program, the last line in the second file (e.g., *MySquare.cpp*) issues the same "*'number' was not declared in this scope*" error message as before. The only real difference is that this time, the error is in a second source code file.

Odd...*number* has global scope in the INO file, but we still get the error message in the second file that is trying to access *number*. Why? Re-read the definition of global scope:

> A data item with global scope lives and is visible from its point of definition *to the end of the source code file in which the item is defined*

In other words, *number*'s scope ends with the end of its source file (in this example, the end of the *InterfileScopeDemo.ino* file). The second source code file, *MySquare.cpp*, has no clue what *number* is. Well then, how can we fix this file-limited scope problem so we can use *number* in the second file? After all, if we stick another *int number;* statement at the top of the second file, the compiler would be forced to issue a *multiple definition of `number'* error message. A true dilemma: two choices, both bad.

Try adding this line as the first statement in the second MySquare.cpp file:

```
extern int number;
```

Hmm...still no joy because you get a '*MySquare*' was not declared in this scope error message. The reason is because the function *MySquare()* used in *loop()* is also unknown to the compiler. As we discussed earlier, this is exactly the problem a function prototype is design to solve. Recall that a function prototype is nothing more than the function signature with a semicolon at the end. So, at the top of the *InterfileScopeDemo.ino* file, right below the definition of *number*, place:

```
int MySquare();              // Function prototype
```

and compile. TaaDaa! The program compiles and functions as it should. So, why does the keyword *extern* solve the scope problem for *number*.

What extern does

When the compiler is checking the syntax in the second file (MySquare.cpp) and it sees the *extern* keyword, it says to itself: "Ok, my programmer wants to use *number* in this file, even though *number* is defined in some other file. So, I'll construct an attribute list for *number* so my programmer can use it in this file and I'll just leave a couple of question marks where he references it and let the linker worry about the lvalue for *number*." Read that quote enough times that it makes sense, as understanding the process the compiler is using with respect to the *extern* keyword is important.

Now another pass of the compile process is made by a program called the linker. It is the linker's responsibility to stitch all of the code presented in the two program source code files into a single executable program. So the linker needs to get any library code used in the program (e.g., code for the Serial object) plus any other routines the program uses and resolve the lvalues (memory addresses) of where those parts are going to live in memory. So, because the linker knows the lvalue for *number* from the symbol table, say memory address 602, it finds all of the question marks associated with number in the MySquare.cpp file and replaces them with 602. Now the code in the MySquare() function knows exactly where the bucket for *number* is in memory and can fetch its rvalue anytime it needs to. Pretty cool!

Therefore, the *extern* keyword is a means by which a variable with global scope in one source code file can be extended across separate data files and be used in a different file.

Define versus Declare...Again.

I said earlier that programmers use the word declare when it should properly be define. If the two terms were truly the same, you would not need to have the word *extern* in the C list of keywords. Just remember: you use *extern* to create the attribute list of a variable that is defined in another file. Likewise, a function prototype is also an attribute list masquerading as a function signature. You need to use a function prototype when the compiler can't "see" the code in the function body that actually defines the function.

Calling a Function and the Backpack Analogy

At various points throughout this book we have said the program "calls a function". Despite using that term multiple times, we have never fully discussed what calling a function means. In this section we discuss calling a function using my Backpack Analogy.

The Backpack Analogy and Function Calls

Suppose you are the person who is responsible for the line-by-line execution of a program. Assuming that the program hardware is all in place, when power is applied to the microcontroller, you put on your backpack and trundle off into the first statement in *setup()*. Visualize the program as a long sidewalk stretching out in front of you towards the horizon and each cement sidewalk slab is a program statement. You look down and see that you are standing on sidewalk block 2500 and written on the surface of that slab of concrete is:

```
pinMode(13, OUTPUT);
```

You write down the number 13 and OUTPUT on a piece of paper and stuff it into your backpack. You also memorize the next block number, 2501, so you know where you are in the scheme of things. Because the linker was here before you, you pull out your program map and look up the lvalue of *pinMode()*. Suppose you find the entry: **pinMode, 3128** written on your program map. Then, faster than a speeding bullet and able to leap multiple slabs in a single bound, you jump and land on cement slab 3128, which just happens to lead to the front door of a windowless black box with the name *pinMode()* etched above the front door.

You walk up to the front door, knock, and instantly the door opens, a hand flashes out, grabs your backpack, and slams the door in your face. You stand at the front door of the function for as long as it takes for the function to execute whatever code is hidden from you inside that black box. A few milliseconds later, the door opens again, the hand flashes out, replaces your backpack, and slams the door in your face...again. One millisecond after that, you're in the air again, mid-jump. You do a quick check in your backpack and see it's now empty. Hmmm, evidently *pinMode()* needed that information for something.

Now you perform a mid-air flight adjustment so you land *exactly* on slab 2501, which is the next instruction to be done *after calling the pinMode() function*. In other words, *calling a function means executing the code associated with that function and then returning to the program instruction that immediately follows that function call.*

Another function call should help nail things into place. Suppose you're on slab 2730 and you see:

```
mySquareRoot = sqrt(x);
```

Looking in your linker list, you see **sqrt, 4890**. Things are just a little different on this function call to *sqrt()*. Because *x* is a variable and not a constant or symbolic constant, you need to visit the lvalue for *x*, gather up the 4-byte rvalue stored there (because the symbol table knows that *x* is a *float* data type), and stuff a copy of those 4 bytes into your backpack. (Being nosy, you look at the rvalue and see that it's 25.0). Now that your backpack has what you need, you jump to slab 4890 and knock on the *sqrt()* door. Same thing happens again: door opens, hand flashes out, grabs the backpack, slams the door, a few milliseconds pass, door opens, hand flashes out again and replaces the backpack, and you're kicked into the air. This time when you look inside the backpack, instead of it being empty like it was before, you see four bytes, but they now hold the number 5.0 instead of the original 25.0.

You do another mid-air correction and land on square 2731. However, this time the instruction is to resolve the assignment operator expression on slab 2730: After all, the function call was only part of the instruction on slab 2730. Now you need to remove the 4 bytes in your backpack and hand them to *mySquareRoot*. The *mySquareRoot variable* goes across the data bus to its lvalue, and dumps the 4 bytes into *mySquareRoot* bucket. Processing the assignment statement associated with the function call ends up changing the rvalue of *mySquareRoot* to 5.0. You can now proceed to slab 2732 and do whatever statement you find there.

Assume your stroll down the sidewalk continues to slab 2810, the last statement in *setup()*. The last instruction on slab 2810 is *loop();*. The linker list has an entry that says **loop, 2811**. You jump (one slab!), knock on the *loop()* door, and brace yourself for the obnoxious hand again. But...this time the door opens and you are invited into the *loop()* black box. Once inside, stretching before you is another sidewalk, each slab with its own instruction, and so you continue your journey.

Eventually, the sidewalk ends. That is the sidewalk ends with the last instruction at the bottom of *loop()*. But, before you take a breather, you are instantly transferred back to slab 2811. Your journey is yet another walk down the entire *loop()* sidewalk...again! This is like the movie Groundhog Day. And so it is for you until 1) power is removed, 2) a component fails, 3) a reset is performed, or 4) cows come home.

A Shortcoming of Functions

Suppose you want to know how many times a function is called while the program executes. To keep things simple, we'll use the following code fragment:

```
void FunctionOfInterest()
{
   int functionVisit;                    // Define functiomVisit

   functionVisit++;                      // Increment it...
   Serial.print("functionVisit = ");  // How many visits?
   Serial.println(functionVisit);     // rest of function code...
}
```

Now, each time the function is called, *functionVisit* is incremented and we display its value. How well is this going to work? What is the scope of *functionVisit*? So *functionVisit* "comes to life" each time the function is entered and contains whatever random bit pattern (i.e., garbage) happens to exist at its newly-created lvalue. We have no clue what that value is, the next statement increments *functionVisit* by 1 and we display the result. When we hit the closing brace of the function, what happens to *functionVisit*? It goes "out of scope" and dies.

The next time we visit the function, this process repeats itself again. As a result, can we ever really know how many times we visited this function? (Hint: No!)

Each time you enter a function, the variables with function scope are redefined. Because they are redefined each time we visit the function, the same variable is assigned a new lvalue. Therefore, you cannot preserve the value of *functionVisit* between function calls. Variables with function scope lose their value when the function ends. Can you fix this limitation? Well, you could define *functionVisit* outside of the function, giving it global scope. That would work, but that does little good other than to lower the hooker unemployment rate. Resorting to global scope just means you just created another source for bugs.

The static Keyword

We can solve this problem by telling the compiler to treat *functionVisit* in a special way by using the keyword *static*. Note the modified code fragment:

```
void FunctionOfInterest()
{
  static int functionVisit = 0;    // Define-initialize variable
  functionVisit++;                  // Increment it...
  Serial.print("functionVisit = ");// How many visits?
  Serial.println(functionVisit);    // rest of code...
}
```

The *static* keyword lets the compiler create *functionVisit* with function scope, <u>*but*</u> allows it to retain its value between function calls. *A static variable defined within a function allows it to persist its rvalue between function calls.* A *static* variable behaves like a global variable in that it retains its value, but the *static* variable acts like a function scope variable in all other respects. That is, *functionVisit* cannot be accessed outside of the function. (In technical terms, *static* data are allocated storage in a memory space called the Heap, while non-*static* function-scoped variables are allocated on the Stack. We cover these details in Chapter 7.)

Note that you must initialize a *static* variable with whatever starting value you want as part of its definition. That's why the code fragment above initializes the rvalue of *functionVisit* to 0 as part of its definition. That definition statement is only read/acted upon when the program first starts. After that, any visit to the function simply ignores the *static* statement. It's like that statement is not even in the function on the second and subsequent visits.

I urge you to write a little program using the code fragment above to confirm how *static* variables work.

Conclusion

Functions are the building blocks of most programs. Well-designed functions can be reused in other programs. There are literally thousands of functions available to you online as part of the Open Source movement. Always begin the design of a new program by searching to see if all or part of that new program has already been written. There is no shame in standing on the shoulders of others. If those programmers didn't want you to use their code, they wouldn't have donated it to the Open Source movement.

You also learned about scope in this chapter. Using scope to hide, or encapsulate, your data can really make program debugging an order of magnitude simpler. While many people think encapsulation is strictly an Object Oriented Programming concept, it is not. Using restrictive scope levels in plain old C does wonders to encapsulate and protect your data. Try to scope all data at the most restrictive level that makes sense. Doing so makes it much easier to test and debug a program.

Exercises

1. In two sentences or less, define what a function is.

2. What guidelines should you follow when writing a new function?

3. What is a “good” function and what are its characteristics? What is a “bad” function?

4. What are the advantages of a fixed style for writing functions?

5. Write a function that, when passed a number corresponding to a month, the function returns the name of the month as a string. So if you pass the number 5 to the function, it returns “May”. You cannot use if or switch/case statements in the function.

6. Write a function that checks to see if the character passed to it is a digit character. If it is a digit character, it returns that digit character as its equivalent int value. That is:

```
int number = MyIsDigit('7');
```

returns the integer value 7 which is then assigned into number. The function returns -1 on error.

7. Write a function that has two function arguments: a char array as a string, and a char. The function searches the string for the presence of char. If it finds the character in the string, it returns the index of the position of that char in the string.

```
int index = FindToken("Wherever you go, there you are.", ',');
```

would see index equal to 15 after the call. If the character is not found, it returns -1.

Chapter 7 C Pointers

Perhaps the most powerful feature of the C programming language is pointers. While many languages have the power for you to shoot yourself in the foot, pointers give you the power to blow your entire leg off. Because of the raw power of pointers, many popular languages either don't support pointers at all (e.g., Java) or only let you use them in a very limited way (e.g., C#). Telling me I can't use pointers is like saying I have to keep training wheels on my bike forever.

Personally, I think most people go wrong using pointers because they don't really understand what pointers are, what they do, or how to use them. The good news is; pointers are going to be a snap for you because you've been thinking about program data in a way that makes pointers easy to understand. If you have experience with a language that doesn't support pointers, you're going to wonder how you lived without them. The proper use of pointers can result in faster, more efficient, programs.

As you read this chapter, your first memory peg for pointers is this: *Pointer "tools" are equally as concerned about where the data are (i.e., an lvalue) as they are about what the data are (i.e., an rvalue).* Stated a little differently, up to this point, you have been concerned about the contents of a data bucket. Now you're going to find out that pointers are also concerned about where that bucket is.

Why Pointers?

Before we get started, let's consider a problem that pointers can help solve. Consider Listing 7.1. Walk through the code before you type it in and mentally "compile" and execute the code.

Listing 7.1. A Simple What-Happened program

```
void setup() {
  Serial.begin(9600);
}

void loop()
{
  int val;
  val = 100;
  Serial.print("Before function call, val = ");
  Serial.println(val);
  SquareNumber(val);
```

```
  Serial.print("After function call, val = ");
  Serial.println(val);
}

/*****
  Purpose: To square a number

  Argument list:
    int val       the number to square

  Return value:
    void

  CAUTION:
*****/
void SquareNumber(int val)
{
  val *= val;
  Serial.print("In SquareNumber(), val = ");
  Serial.println(val);
}
```

The program is pretty simple. In *loop()*, an *int* variable named *val* is defined and then assigned the value of 100 and we display that value. Then the code calls a function we wrote called *SquareNumber()*, passing *val* to it as part of its parameter list. In the function, we take the value of *val* that was passed to *SquareNumber()*, square it, and then display its value of 10000. The function code then ends and program control is sent back to *loop()* where we again display *val*.

When you run the program, this is what you'll see:

```
Before function call, val = 100
   In SquareNumber(), val = 10000
 After function call, val = 100
```

You might be saying: "Wait a minute! We squared *val* in the function and even showed that it has the value of 10000, but then when we return to *loop()* from the function call, *val* is still 100. What happened?"

Think about it. What is the scope of *val* as defined in *loop()*? Yep, *val* has function block scope, so where is it visible? The variable *val* is only visible within *loop()*. Recall when we discussed functions *we said that the arguments passed to a function are copies of the rvalue of the variable(s).* We used the term *call by value* to reinforce the idea that rvalue *copies* were being sent to the function. We further strengthened the analogy with the backpack concept. Each time a parameter was passed to a function, we stated that you copied the value onto a piece of paper and stuff it into your backpack.

If we really want *SquareNumber()* to change the "real" *val*, what does *SquareNumber()* need to know? *SquareNumber()* could only square the "real" value of *val* back in *loop()* if it knew where *val* lived in memory. In other words, *SquareNumber()* would need to know where *val*'s bucket is in memory (i.e., its lvalue). Think about that for about an hour.

If you typed in the program in Listing 7.1, you know it runs forever. As an exercise, recode the program so it only runs 1 time, but keep the processing and output code in *loop(),* not *setup().* Try to keep the code as simple as possible.

Okay, let's check that out. Listing 7.2 provides a way to confirm what we just said above.

Listing 7.2. Checking out lvalues for val

```
void setup() {
  Serial.begin(9600);
}
void loop()
{
  int val;
  val = 100;
  Serial.print("\n\nBefore function call, val = ");
  Serial.println(val);
  Serial.print("                     lvalue = ");
  Serial.println((long) &val);
  SquareNumber(val);
  Serial.print(" After function call, val = ");
  Serial.println(val);
  Serial.print("                     lvalue = ");
  Serial.println((long) &val);
}

/*****
  Purpose: To square a number

  Argument list:     int val       the number to square

  Return value:
    void

  CAUTION:
*****/
void SquareNumber(int val)
{
  val *= val;
  Serial.print("   In SquareNumber(), val = ");
  Serial.println(val);
  Serial.print("                     lvalue = ");
  Serial.println((long) &val);
}
```

The Address-of Operator, & (ampersand)

The code in Listing 7.2 uses a new operator called the address-of operator as indicated by the single & symbol. The *address-of operator, &, is used any time we need to reference the lvalue of a data item*. It is a unary operator. Obviously, the default behavior for a variable when used in an expression is to use its rvalue. We've used the rvalue for relational operations, bitwise operations, logical tests, and in assignment statements. The rvalue of a variable has been ubiquitous in most expressions.

That's about to change.

Using *the '&' before the name of the variable allows us to change that default behavior and fetch its lvalue instead of its rvalue*. In Listing 7.2, we use a cast operator when we print the lvalue of a data type. The reason is because the *println()* method is designed to display the rvalue for the data types and doesn't know exactly how to display an lvalue. (Part of that confusion stems from the fact that memory addresses storage sizes differ on 8-bit versus 32-bit architectures.)

When you run the code in Listing 7.2, this is the output it generates (your values will likely be different, but similar):

```
Before function call, val = 100
                   lvalue = 8697
   In SquareNumber(), val = 10000
                   lvalue = 8695
 after function call, val = 100
```

Look at the lvalues for *val* in *loop() (2298)* compared to the lvalue in *SquareNumber()* (2296). The lvalues are different. (Did I run this example on an 8-bit or 32-bit processor?) The different lvalues are because the *val* in *SquareNumber()* is a copy of *val*. How do we know it's a copy? We know *val* is a copy precisely because the variable has a different lvalue in *loop()* and in *SquareNumber()*. Think about it, because *SquareNumber()* doesn't know the lvalue of *val* in *loop()*, there is no way for *SquareNumber()* to permanently change the rvalue of *val* in *loop()*. They are two totally different *val*'s in memory with different lvalues: the "real" *val* in *loop()* (at memory address 2298) and the "impostor" clone of *val* in *SquareNumber()* (at memory address 2296).

You're complaining: "But...but...what if I <u>want</u> *SquareNumber()* to permanently change the value of *val*?" Welcome to the world of pointers! Pointers are "good stuff", so let's jump right in!

Defining a Pointer

Because a pointer is a different type of data than anything you've studied thus far, the syntax necessary to define a pointer must also be different. Figure 7.1 shows the syntax for a pointer definition.

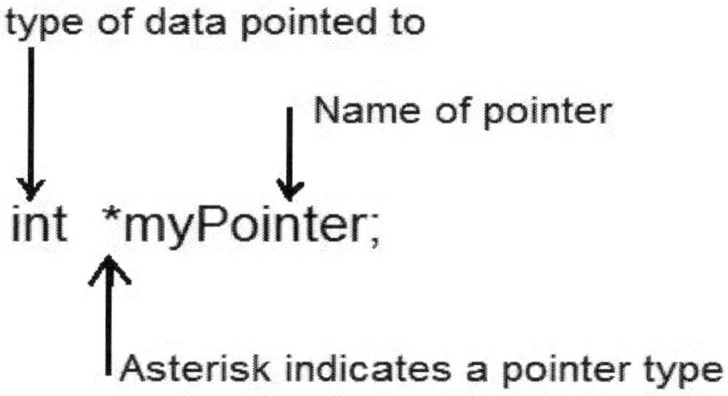

Figure 7.1. *Pointer syntax to define an int pointer*

Every pointer definition needs the three elements shown in Figure 7.1. However, I'm going to discuss the three elements of a pointer definition in a "right-to-left" parsing order. The reason for this order will become clear shortly.

1. The name of the pointer

The name can be whatever you want it to be, as pointer names follow the same naming rules as any other C variable. Some programmers start their pointer ID's with *ptr:*

```
ptrSensorData       ptrStateCapitals    ptrQSignals   ptrSisters
```

Years ago, I used to prefix my pointer variables with *ptr*, but I rarely do that now. My feeling is that the reader is going to know it's a pointer because of the way the variable is used in the code. After all, the prefix on a variable name rarely makes any difference as long as you know what the variable is. True, naming small celluloid balls filled with nitroglycerin *pingPongBalls* might not be a good idea, but the specifics of pointer names holds the same sway as any other variable name. It seems more important that the ID be associated with the *purpose* of the pointer, not the fact that it is a pointer. After all, you had a reason for using a pointer rather than some other data type.

2. The asterisk denotes that this variable is to be used as a pointer

Pointer variables behave differently than "regular" variables. By placing an asterisk ('*'), called the *indirection operator*, at the proper place in the definition of the pointer variable, the asterisk tells the compiler to record that this variable has the pointer attribute set in the symbol table entry. The pointer attribute alters the way the compiler treats pointer expressions and how those expressions get resolved.

Some of you might be thinking: "Hold on! The asterisk is used for multiplication. How can we use it to indicate indirection, too?" Remember way back when we said there were syntax *and* semantic rules? Well, semantic rules mean that the context in which you use an asterisk allows the compiler to figure out which interpretation to use for the asterisk. Since you cannot use a multiply operator in a data definition, that's one way the compiler knows how to process the statement. The other (more obvious?) reason is that multiplication requires two operands because it is a binary operator. The indirection operator is a unary operator. Because the asterisk has different interpretations based on its context, it's called an overloaded operator. *An overloaded operator is an operator whose use in an expression depends upon its syntax and semantic context.*

Note that C doesn't really care about the precise position of the asterisk, as long as the asterisk appears after the data type specifier for the pointer and before the name of the pointer variable. Note the asterisk placement in the variable names below

```
int* ptrTemp;        // Immediately after the type specifer
int * ptrBarom;      // Midway between type specifier and name
int *ptrDewPoint;    // Immediately before name
```

I hope you don't pick the middle version above: it looks too similar to a multiplication expression even though it can't be one. The first one is less desirable because, if you want to define two *int* pointers:

```
int *ptr1, ptr2;
```

is wrong, because only *ptr1* is a pointer. *ptr2* is a plain *int*. This is also why I tend to place one data definition per line.

If you forget the asterisk, the definition looks like any other "normal" variable definition. However, forgetting the asterisk means you will not be able to successfully perform pointer operations on the variable. C doesn't really care which form you use in a pointer definition. Personally, I kinda like the last version which ties the asterisk and the pointer name closely together. There is no theoretical reason for my preference. The last form is how I learned to define pointers almost 40 years ago, so it's an old-dog-new-trick thing with me. Just remember the asterisk is a data modifier and not part of the variable name. Pick whatever makes you happy, but use it consistently.

3. The data type associated with the pointer

This part of the pointer definition statement is <u>*critical*</u>, which is why I saved it for last. Listing 7.3 presents some details about the common data types we've discussed earlier. Recall that *sizeof()* is an operator, even though it looks like a function call. The *sizeof()* operator tells you the number of bytes of memory that are used by the variable enclosed

Listing 7.3. Details about common data types

```
void setup() {
  char c;                    // some standard data types
  int val;
  long yawn;
  float x;
  char  *charPointer;           // some matching pointers
  int   *intPointer;
  long  *longPointer;
  float *floatPointer;

  Serial.begin(9600);

  Serial.print(" char is ");            // char stuff
  Serial.print(sizeof(c));
  Serial.print(" bytes with an lvalue of ");
  Serial.print((long) &c);
  Serial.print(" and its pointer takes ");
  Serial.print( sizeof(charPointer));
  Serial.println(" bytes.");

  Serial.print("  int is ");            // int stuff
  Serial.print(sizeof(val));
  Serial.print(" bytes with an lvalue of ");
  Serial.print((long) &val);
  Serial.print(" and its pointer takes ");
  Serial.print( sizeof(intPointer));
  Serial.println(" bytes.");

  Serial.print(" long is ");            // long stuff
```

```
  Serial.print(sizeof(yawn));
  Serial.print(" bytes with an lvalue of ");
  Serial.print((long) &yawn);
  Serial.print(" and its pointer takes ");
  Serial.print( sizeof(longPointer));
  Serial.println(" bytes.");

  Serial.print("float is ");              // float stuff
  Serial.print(sizeof(x));
  Serial.print(" bytes with an lvalue of ");
  Serial.print((long) &x);
  Serial.print(" and its pointer takes ");
  Serial.print( sizeof(floatPointer));
  Serial.println(" bytes.");
}
void loop() { }
```

within its parentheses. Now do a code walk-through for Listing 7.3. What should the output look like? Now compare the results of your code walk-through with the actual output of Listing 7.3:

```
 char is 1 bytes with an lvalue of 8698 and its pointer takes 2
bytes.
  int is 2 bytes with an lvalue of 8696 and its pointer takes 2
bytes.
 long is 4 bytes with an lvalue of 8692 and its pointer takes 2
bytes.
float is 4 bytes with an lvalue of 8688 and its pointer takes 2
bytes.
```

The first part of the program output is consistent with what you learned in Chapters 2 and 3 about data types. However, you might also be wondering: "What's with the *sizeof()* values for the pointer variables? They are all the same. Why? After all, they are pointing to different data types which have different bucket sizes, so why aren't their sizes different?"

The reason all pointers use the same amount of memory regardless of what they point to is because:

Pointers don't store ordinary numbers or rvalues, they only store lvalues.

When you go into memory looking for a pointer's bucket, once you find it and look inside, if it is a valid pointer, the ONLY thing it should ever hold is a memory address (i.e., an lvalue) or NULL (i.e., '\0'). *The size of a memory address on any given processor is the same regardless of the type of data it points to*. This means that all pointers require 2 bytes on an Arduino Uno or Nano because of their 8-bit architecture. All of the other microcontrollers have 32-bit architectures and have 4-byte pointers. Remember:

> *All pointers on any given architecture use the same amount of memory, regardless of the type of data they point to.*

Please: Read this paragraph over and over...then read it again.

Pointer Type Specifiers and Pointer Scalars

Earlier in this chapter you saw the following data definitions:

```
char  *charPointer;      // some matching pointers   pointers
int   *intPointer;
long  *longPointer;
float *floatPointer;
```

The data type specifiers (i.e., *char*, *int*, *long*, and *float*) shown here are extremely important in all pointer definitions, because the data type specifier dictates the *only* type of data that can be used with its pointer. If you define a *char* pointer and then try to use it with an *int* (or any other) data type, nothing good is going to happen. (Details as to why mixing data types is bad is explained later in this chapter.) The really bad news is that, many times, using the wrong pointer may or may not show itself immediately. Eventually, however, mismatched *pointer data types* fail, sometimes spectacularly! So, the rule is simple:

> *Only use pointers on data that match the pointer's data type specifier when it was defined*

Okay, you've memorized the rule, but it is important that you understand *why* the pointer's data type is so important.

Pointer Scalars

In Chapter 3, Table 3.2, I presented a stripped-down symbol table showing a few of the attributes that might be maintained in a symbol table. At that time, I admitted that the symbol table in Table 3.2 was greatly simplified. Another potential column in a more realistic symbol table would be a column labeled *Scalar*. If that column is filled in, it could be interpreted that any data item with a non-zero scalar column is a pointer variable. The number in that column would be the scalar associated with the pointer. *A pointer scalar is the number of memory bytes allocated to each data item associated with the pointer.* If you have a list of pointer definitions like:

```
char  *charPointer;      // some matching pointers
int   *intPointer;
long  *longPointer;
float *floatPointer;
```

the *char* pointer has a scalar of 1 byte, an *int* (on an Uno) is 2 bytes or 4 bytes on the other microcontrollers, a *long* is 4 bytes, and a *float* is also 4 bytes. In other words, *the pointer scalar is tied to the data type specifier in the pointer definition*. Well, then why talk about a pointer scalar? After all, right now it looks like the scalar is equal to one of the C data types.

However, scalars are different than native data types. The reason is because you might see a pointer definition like:

*OneMembershipRecord *member;*

So, what is the scalar size for *member* as recorded in the symbol table? The point is: A pointer can point to anything, not just a "native" data type. It can point to structures, unions, or objects of a C++ class. Evidently, somewhere there is a declaration of what a *OneMembershipRecord* is and it could be hundreds of bytes long. Okay...so what? Well, suppose you have initialized the *member* pointer to point to your membership record in memory and I tell you to get the rvalue of your membership record. What information do you need to fetch your rvalue? Do you fetch 1 byte, 10 bytes, 233 bytes...how many? Well, a quick peek into the Scalar column of the symbol table for member and guess what you find? As we stated before, the Scalar column holds the number of bytes associated with the data item being pointed to! In other words, a pointer scalar tells you how many bytes to fetch to properly retrieve an rvalue for that data type. Think about that sentence...

So, the lesson here is that *the pointer scalar associated with the pointer tells us the size of the bucket in memory that is being pointed to.*

Pointers and Arrays

We can use arrays to better illustrate why pointer scalars are so important. Consider the following three arrays:

```
char  myLetters[5]; // lvalue = 2100
```

```
int    myNumbers[5];          //          = 2200 (assume
                         // it's a Nano)
float myData[5];         //          = 2300
```

Let's assume the compiler placed these arrays at memory addresses 2100, 2200, and 2300. We could represent their elements in memory as follows:

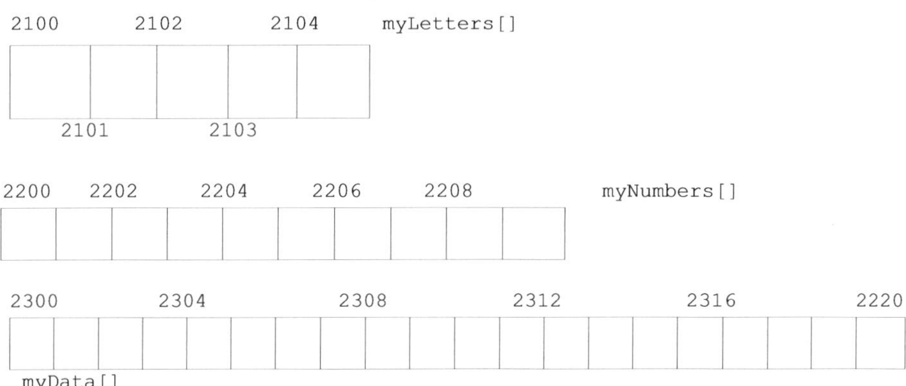

Notice that, for the *char* variable, the addresses change by 1-byte increments for each element. For the *int* array, each element is associated with a 2-byte change on a Nano (4 bytes on the others). Finally, for the *float* data type, each array element needs a 4-byte change. All three arrays have 5 elements, but they require differing amounts of memory. You can think of the memory numbers above each cell as the "memory edges" for each element of their respective array.

Now, look at the program presented in Listing 7.4. Mentally walk through the code and picture what the output should look like. Now, compare your

Listing 7.4. Displaying the contents of several arrays

```
void setup()
{
  char myLetter[] = {'A', 'B', 'C', 'D', 'E'};
  int myNumber[]  = {1, 2, 3, 4, 5};
  float myData[]  = {1.0, 2.0, 3.0, 4.0, 5.0};

  Serial.begin(9600);    // Set baud rate for Serial object
  while (!Serial) ;      // Initialize the Serial object
  for (int i = 0; i < 5; i++) {
    Serial.print(myLetter[i]);
    Serial.print("    ");
    Serial.print(myNumber[i]);
    Serial.print("    ");
    Serial.println(myData[i]);
  }
}
```

```
void loop() {
}
```

vision of the program output with what is actually printed:

```
A   1   1.00
B   2   2.00
C   3   3.00
D   4   4.00
E   5   5.00
```

If you got it right, good on ya! If you got it wrong, no problem. Ask yourself where you went astray and, then, don't do it again!

Now, let's modify Listing 7.4 to use pointers. To do that, we're going to use the post-increment operator (*n*++) we discussed in Chapter 5.

Using the Increment/Decrement Operators with Pointers

Listing 7.5 is a modification of Listing 7.4. It is critical to remember that an *array name used in an expression "by itself" is identical to that array's lvalue.* Now, do a code walk-through on Listing 7.5 and what do you see?

Listing 7.5, Pointer version of Listing 7.4

```
void setup()
{
  char myLetter[] = {'A', 'B', 'C', 'D', 'E'};
  int myNumber[]  = {1, 2, 3, 4, 5};
  float myData[]  = {1.0, 2.0, 3.0, 4.0, 5.0};
  char  *ptrLet;
  int   *ptrNum;
  float *ptrDat;
  ptrLet = myLetter;      // Initialize pointers, 2100
  ptrNum = myNumber;      // 2200
  ptrDat = myData;        // 2300

  Serial.begin(9600);
  while (!Serial) ;

  for (int i = 0; i < 5; i++) {
    Serial.print(*ptrLet++);
    Serial.print("   ");
    Serial.print(*ptrNum++);
    Serial.print("   ");
    Serial.println(*ptrDat++);
  }
}
void loop() {
}
```

The output is exactly the same as before. Let's see why. Consider this statement:

```
ptrLet = myLetter;       // Initialize pointers
```

First, note that we are using the *myLetter[]* variable name "by itself"; there are no brackets being used in the assignment statement. If you verbalize this statement, it says: "Get the lvalue of *myLetter* (i.e., 2100), and make it the rvalue of pointer variable *ptrLet*." This works because using the *myLetter* array variable name without brackets is also the lvalue of *myLetter*. That's a syntax rule and you may as well memorize it. The other pointers are initialized the same way.

Now, we start marching through our *for* loop and run into this:

```
Serial.print(*ptrLet++);
```

Note that the expression being sent to the *print()* method uses two unary operators: the indirection operator ("*") and the post-increment operator ("++"). The code works because the rvalue is fetched via the indirection operator before the pointer is incremented. This expression says: "Get the rvalue of *ptrLet*, which is 2100, go to that memory address and fetch 'scalar-bytes' of data and display it on the Serial monitor". Since the pointer scalar for *ptrLet* is a *char*, it fetches one byte of data from address 2100. So, an 'A' pops up on the display screen.

Next, and this is the important part, the code processes the post-increment operator (++). What this expression does is increase the rvalue of *ptrLet* by "scalar bytes". Because the scalar for a *char* is 1 and the rvalue of *ptrLet* is 2100, the new rvalue for *ptrLet* is 2101. Guess what **ptrLet* will fetch next?

> *It is critical to understand that the post and pre-increment operators on pointers are <u>ALWAYS</u> adjusted by the pointer's scalar.*

Ok, since you understand the importance of pointer scalars, verbalize the next pointer expression:

```
Serial.print(*ptrNum++);
```

Again, the indirection expression is resolved first, so you can say: “Fetch the rvalue of *ptrNum*, which is 2200, go to that memory address, and fetch the scalar-sized rvalue stored there.” Because the scalar for an *int* (on an 8-bit processor) is 2, the code goes to memory address 2200 and retrieves 2 bytes of data and display it on the monitor. The number “1” pops up on the Serial display.

Now we process the post-increment operator. This time, however, because the pointer scalar is 2, the new rvalue for *ptrNum* is 2202. So, on the next pass through the loop, guess what *ptrNum* is pointing to?

I think you've got it, so explaining the next indirection on *ptrDat* turns this discussion into a dead-horse kicking contest. Walk through and verbalize the use of *ptrDat*, just for grins.

Can you see why understanding pointer scalars is so important? An understanding of pointer scalars is crucial to using pointers effectively. Let's hammer the concept home with one more example. Consider Listing 7.6.

Listing 7.6. A variation on using pointer scalars

```
void setup()  {
  char myLetter[] = {'A', 'B', 'C', 'D', 'E'};
  int myNumber[]  = {1, 2, 3, 4, 5};
  float myData[]  = {1.0, 2.0, 3.0, 4.0, 5.0};
  char  *ptrLet;
  int   *ptrNum;
  float *ptrDat;

  ptrLet = myLetter;        // Initialize pointers
  ptrNum = myNumber;
  ptrDat = myData;

  Serial.begin(9600);
  while (!Serial) ;

  for (int i = 0; i < 5; i++) {
    Serial.print(*(ptrLet + i));
    Serial.print("    ");
    Serial.print(*(ptrNum + i));
    Serial.print("    ");
    Serial.println(*(ptrDat + i));
  }
}
void loop() {
}
```

Listing 7.5 and 7.6 are identical, except for the shaded expressions in Listing 7.6. Let's look at the first shaded expression:

```
Serial.print(*(ptrLet + i));
```

Because the indirection operator (*) has higher precedence than the addition operator (+), we enclosed the *(ptrLet + i)* expression in parentheses so it is evaluated first. The expression says to get the rvalue of *ptrLet*, which is 2100 and add *i* to it. Because *i* is zero, the code performs an indirection on 2100 and fetches scalar-bytes (i.e., 1 byte since it's a *char*) of data from memory address 2100 and displays 'A' on the display. You should be able to convince yourself that similar things happen when using *ptrNum* and *ptrDat*. It's on the second pass through the loop, when *i* equals 1 that things get interesting.

We can synthesize what happens to the three pointer expressions like this:

```
*(ptrLet + i)→ *(ptrLet + i * scalar)= *(ptrLet + 1 * 1) = *
                (ptrLet + 1) = *(2101) = 'B'
*(ptrNum + i)→ *(ptrNum + i * scalar)= *(ptrNum + 1 * 2) = *
                (ptrNum + 2) = *(2202) = 2
*(ptrDat + i)→ *(ptrDat + i * scalar)= *(ptrDat + 1 * 4) = *
                (ptrDat + 4) = *(2304) = 2.0
```

Notice how *the final lvalue changes according to the scalar size of the pointer.* You can do pointer arithmetic on pointers with the add and subtract operators, but clearly you should not generate an lvalue that falls outside of the array boundaries.

Using a Pointer

Go back to Listing 7.1 and review the code there. That program pointed out that the scoping rules of a variable prevented the *SquareNumber()* function from changing the value of *val* in *loop()*. That is, *SquareNumber()* could not change *val* because it received a copy of the rvalue of *val*, not the "real" *val*. We also pointed out that the only way *SquareNumber()* could permanently alter the value of *val* was if the function had the lvalue of *val* back in *loop()*. Guess what the rvalue is of all initialized pointers?

The rvalue of a properly initialized pointer is the lvalue of a data item

An uninitialized pointer is whatever random bit pattern might exist at its lvalue. (Some compilers automatically initialize pointer variables to

NULL. In this context, a NULL pointer and a **void** pointer are the same thing. A *void* pointer means that pointer points to nothing useful.) Let the statement above sink in...

Initializing a Pointer

Perhaps the most common error made by beginning programmers with respect to pointers is that they try to use the pointer before it is properly initialized.

> *An uninitialized pointer points to garbage or NULL*

That is, if you don't initialize a pointer to the desired data item but then try to use it, you are going to be very disappointed. Okay, so how does one initialize a pointer?

First, think about a simple assignment statement:

```
myNumber = yourNumber;
```

If you use our lvalue/rvalue description of what's going on, an assignment operation reduces to moving the rvalue of *yourNumber* into the rvalue of *myNumber*. In other words, *a garden variety, default, assignment statement is an rvalue-to-rvalue exchange.*

Pointers are treated differently. We know pointers are different because we define them differently (i.e., we need the indirection operator, '*', as part of the definition). Therefore, the first step before using a pointer is to initialize the pointer. Using Listing 7.1 as a starting point, let's add the following new line to *loop()* just after the definition of *val*;

```
int *ptr;       // Define a pointer to int
```

The new statement defines an *int* pointer variable named *ptr*. As it stands now, you should assume that the rvalue of *ptr* is garbage equal to whatever random bit pattern happens to exist at the lvalue of *ptr*.

Let's visualize what's going on. When we ran the code for Listing 7.1, we saw that the lvalue of *val* was 2298. Let's assume that *ptr* is located at memory address 2100. So, SRAM would look like Figure 7.2 prior to the initialization of *ptr*. We have not filled in the rvalue for either variable because neither one

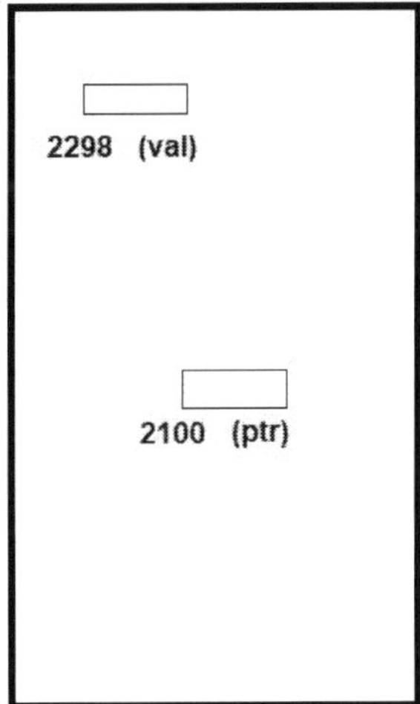

Figure 7.2. Memory map of SRAM for Listing 7.1.

has been assigned a value. They both just contain random bit patterns (garbage) at this point.

Now the magic happens. Let's initialize the pointer with this statement:

```
ptr = &val;        // Initialize pointer to point to val
```

Because pointers are different, we need to tell the compiler that this assignment is not the garden variety, rvalue-to-rvalue, assignment. Instead, *to initialize ptr, we use the address-of operator to get the lvalue of val from the symbol table, and assign that lvalue into the rvalue of ptr.* This operation is shown in Figure 7.3. Note how the rvalue of *ptr* is initialized and now points to the lvalue of *val*.

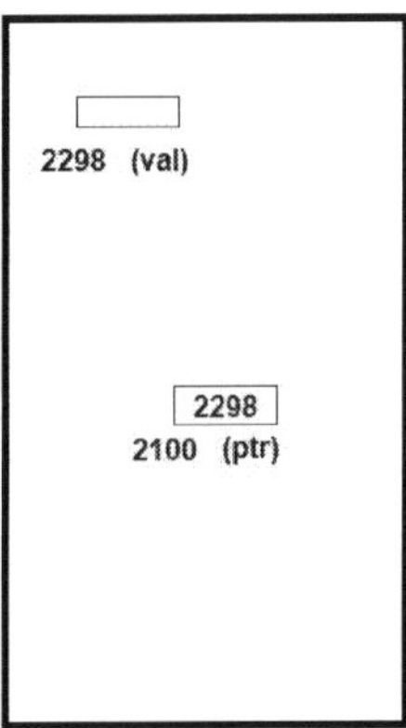

Figure 7.3. After initializing ptr to point to val

The original code in Listing 7.1 then assigned the value 100 into *val*, displays a message on the Serial monitor as to the value of *val* and then passes *val* as the argument to the *SquareNumber()* function.

Listing 7.7 shows the program code from Listing 7.1, but changed to use a pointer. The shaded statements show the changes made to Listing 7.1.

Listing 7.7. Change Listing 7.1 to use a pointer

```
void setup() {
  Serial.begin(9600);
}
void loop()
{
  int val;
  int *ptr;

  ptr = &val;       // Initialize ptr to point to val

  val = 100;
  Serial.print("Before function call, val = ");
  Serial.println(val);
  SquareNumber(ptr);
  Serial.print(" After function call, val = ");
  Serial.println(val);
}

/*****
  Purpose: To square a number

  Argument list:
    int *v       pointer to the number to square

  Return value:
    void

  CAUTION:
*****/
void SquareNumber(int *v)
{
  *v = *v * *v;           // Same as *v *= *v;
  Serial.print("   In SquareNumber(), *v = ");
  Serial.println(*v);
}
```

First, notice how we use the pointer (*ptr*) in the function call to *SquareNumber()*. When passing the pointer to the function, its lvalue gets put into your backpack and you jump to the *SquareNumber()* function. The function signature has also been changed, and the new parameter list has an asterisk in it, so the function knows it's been passed a pointer to an *int*. Therefore, the *SquareNumber()* function door opens, the hand shoots out, grabs your backpack and slams the door.

Call-by-Value versus Call-by-Reference

Because *SquareNumber()* knows the backpack contains a pointer, the function knows it must treat the information in the backpack a little differently. It knows that the data that it just received is the lvalue of an *int* data type. The function assumes the pointer has been properly initialized and that it has a valid lvalue.

Recall in our discussion of functions in Chapter 6 that function arguments were *copies* of the data that is passed to the function. That is, each function parameter has an rvalue that is a perfect copy of the value that variable has at the point from which the function was called. As mentioned earlier, this *passing a function an rvalue copy of a piece of data is* referred to as *Call-by-Value*. It simply means that a function is receiving a *copy* of a data value.

However, our new version of the function is passed a pointer variable (*ptr*) that was initialized to point to *val* using the address-of operator (*ptr = &val;*). The new function signature for *SquareNumber()* is changed to show that a pointer is being passed to the function in the temporary variable named *v*. Therefore, the code knows it was passed an lvalue, not a "standard" rvalue copy of a variable. This also means that *v* now contains a memory reference (i.e., an lvalue) to a variable defined elsewhere in the program. *Passing a function an lvalue for a piece of data is referred to as Call-by-Reference.* Any time you want a function to be able to permanently change one of its arguments, that argument must be a pointer.

Dereferencing a Pointer – The Process of Indirection

When an asterisk is used in an expression, like:

```
number = *v;
```

you should verbalize the operand on the right side of the assignment operator as: "Go to the lvalue of *v* (2100) and fetch its rvalue (2298), and then go to that lvalue (2298) and fetch scalar-bytes (i.e., 2) of data and assign that value (100) into *number*". *The process of using the lvalue stored in a pointer to fetch the rvalue of another variable is called indirection.* You will also hear this process called *dereferencing a pointer.* Using our lvalue/rvalue diagrams from Chapter 2, we can illustrate the process of indirection in Figure 7.4.

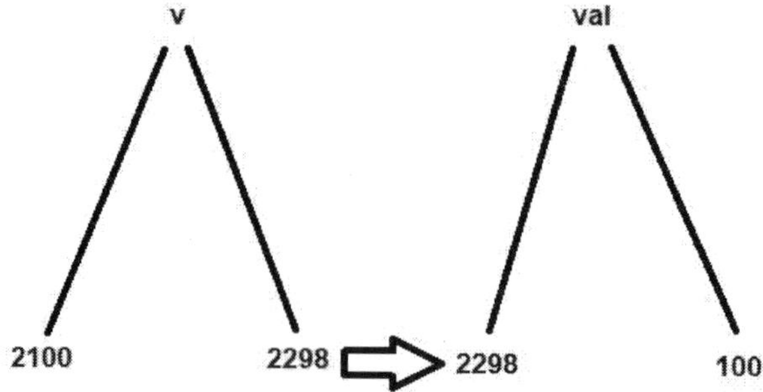

Figure 7.4. Illustrating the process of indirection.

In the expression in *SquareNumber()*, *v* is the *int* pointer variable that is passed to the function. The fact that *v* is a pointer to an *int* means that its scalar size is that of an *int*. Also note that scalar size always matches the "bucket size" of the data being pointed to. We changed the signature of *SquareNumber()* so it knows it's been passed a pointer. Therefore, *SquareNumber()* knows that the two bytes it grabbed from the backpack is actually an lvalue (i.e., memory address), not an rvalue.

So, *SquareNumber()* proceeds to resolve the statement within its function body. We have broken down that statement expression as indicated by the shaded areas of the statement:

```
*v = *v * *v;
```

Now, referring to Figure 7.4, the shaded expression above says: "Get the rvalue of *v* (2298), jump to that memory location and, because this is an *int* pointer, fetch the 2 scalar-bytes (100) from that memory location." (On the 32-bit processors, it would be 4 scalar-bytes to fetch an rvalue.) This is why the pointer's scalar is important. The pointer scalar tells the compiler how many bytes need to be fetched during the process of indirection. Because we have resolved the first part of the statement, we can now re-write our (intermediate) statement as:

```
*v = *v * 100;
```

The next shaded expression says exactly the same thing as the first: "Get the rvalue of *v* (2298), jump to that memory location and, because this is an *int* pointer, fetch the 2 scalar-bytes (i.e, the rvalue 100) from that memory location." Resolving this expression yields:

```
*v = 100 * 100;
```

or

```
*v = 10000;
```

The new shaded expression is a little different because it is on the left-hand side of the assignment statement. The assignment expression says: “Get the rvalue of v (2298), jump to that memory location, and assign the value 10000 as the new rvalue at memory location 2298.” In this case, we used the process of indirection to assign a new value into memory address 2298 instead of fetching a value.

That's it! That is all of the magic involved in using pointers.

Just remember:

& – the unary address-of operator (&) is used to get the lvalue of a variable
** – the unary indirection operator (*) is used to access the rvalue of the variable it points to.*

Common Pointer Mistakes

There are many interesting ways to blow your leg off with pointers. Here are some of the more common ones that beginning C programmers make.

Using an Uninitialized Pointer

It's common to find someone define a pointer and then do something like:

```
char letter;
char *ptr;

*ptr = 'A';
```

So, what lvalue is being used in the pointer assignment? Who knows? If the microcontroller starts and the random bit pattern for the rvalue of *ptr* happens to be 200, the compiler thinks that is the destination address for the assignment. You just wrote the letter 'A' at memory address 200, which could be in the middle of your bootloader. Most of the time, that is not going to be a good thing.

The rule is simple: *You must initialize a pointer before you use it.*

```
char letter;
char *ptr;
ptr = &letter;
*ptr = 'A';
```

Initializing a Pointer to the Wrong Data Type

If you did something silly like this:

```
int letter;
char *ptr;
ptr = &letter;
*ptr = "Me";
```

You are trying to initialize a *char* pointer (*ptr*) to the lvalue of an *int*. If you try to do that, the compiler issues an error message saying: "*cannot convert 'int*' to 'char*' in assignment*". You pound the heel of your hand into your forehead because you know the scalar of the variable and the pointer must match! So, you change variable *letter* from an *int* to a *char*.

```
char letter;
char *ptr;
ptr = &letter;
*ptr = "Me";
```

Notice that I changed the data type for *letter* to a *char*. Now when you compile the code, you look down at the statistics window and, voila! No error messages! You look a little further down and see no leg! Why is that? How many bytes of data can *letter* hold? Right, it's a *char* so it can hold 1 byte. And in the last statement above, what did you do? You went to *letter*'s lvalue and proceeded to pour 3 bytes of data (don't forget the *null*) into a 1-byte bucket! So now both your leg and 2-bytes of data are slopped all over the floor. This error also means that whatever data came after *letter* in memory just got trashed! There are some other errors here, too (i.e., you can't assign a string with that syntax). The really bad news is that the compiler doesn't help you very much in identifying this error. Even worse, you may not even know that some data got trashed. Really not good.

Forgetting to Dereference a Pointer

Remember: *The rvalue of a properly-initialized pointer is an lvalue.* So, doing this:

```
char letter;
char *ptr;
ptr = &letter;
```

```
*ptr = 'M';
Serial.print(ptr);
```

causes what to be displayed on the Serial monitor? If *letter*'s bucket has an lvalue of memory address 2800, and its rvalue is now 'M', the *Serial.print()* statement should display 2800. Why? The reason is because you told it to print out the rvalue of *ptr*, which is 2800, not its dereferenced value, **ptr*. What you meant to do was dereference *ptr*, displaying what the pointer *ptr* points to:

```
Serial.print(*ptr);   // Note the dereferencing
                      // asterisk operator
```

Now the statement displays 'M' on the monitor.

When I ran this program, it ran correctly with incorrect syntax. I wanted to figure out how it could do that, so I typed in:

```
void setup() {

  Serial.begin(9600);
  char letter;
  char *ptr;

  ptr = &letter;
  *ptr = 'X';

  Serial.println( (int) &letter);    // show the lvalue of letter
  Serial.println( (int) ptr);        // show the rvalue of ptr
  Serial.println(ptr);               // show the rvalue of ptr...WRONG
}
```

and the program displayed:

```
8698
8698
X
```

At first, I thought this was pretty cool. Now I don't. The reason is because the last print statement above should show the rvalue of *ptr*, but instead the compiler performs indirection *without me telling it to*! In other words, the GCC is so smart it knows from the definition of *ptr* that it should only be using *ptr* in the context of indirection when using the Serial object for displaying it. This is sorta like the silent cast thing and I'm not a fan of that, either. I don't like it when the compiler does things behind my back. Such things make debugging just a little bit harder.

Dereferencing a Pointer to a Non-initalized Variable

Consider this little code fragment:

```
int number;    int *ptr;

ptr = &number; // Initialize rvalue of ptr to lvalue of number
Serial.print(*ptr);  // Dereference and use the pointer
```

What is displayed on the Serial monitor? I have no clue. The reason is, even though I've done everything right with respect to the pointer, the content of *number* is going to be some random bit pattern that happens to exist when the program started! That is, you are (properly) dereferencing the pointer, but the variable itself is a pile of garbage. The fix is easy:

```
int number;   int *ptr;
ptr = &number;        // Initialize rvalue of ptr to lvalue of number
number = 2000;        // Give a meaningful value to number
Serial.print(*ptr);  // Dereference and use the pointer
```

The shaded statement above means that *number* now has the value we intended it to have. Question: Could I have initialized *number* to 2000 before I initialized *ptr*? Of course you can. I just did it this way because it's not as common to initialize a variable after you initialize its pointer. Still, either sequence works.

There are also some pointer errors that can happen with pointer arithmetic, but we'll cover those later. We have enough to chew on for the moment. Take the time to understand the mistakes shown here, as you will likely make the same mistakes until you get comfortable with pointers. You should expect to have a considerably flatter forehead after you've read this chapter...been there, done that...and so will you.

Function Variables and the Stack

The truth is, you don't need to use pointers with respect to function arguments if you're willing to define all of your variables so they have global scope. However, we've already explained why global variables are a bad idea. As a result, we encouraged you to define variables using function scope instead of global scope whenever possible. However, that has some potential drawbacks, too, especially with microcontrollers.

Back in Chapter 1, we talked about the various properties of the microcontrollers used in this book. One of those properties was the amount of SRAM each processor has. The amount of SRAM is very important because that is where *all* of the data you use in your program are stored. Indeed, if a program ever starts pressing on a processor's memory limits, it is almost always the SRAM limit, not the flash memory limit, that is the most worrisome. (Recall that flash memory is where the program statements reside and SRAM is where the data reside.) While there are some tricks that have been developed to lessen the impact of the SRAM scarcity (e.g., the *F()* macro, which is a clunky way to move string literals from SRAM into flash memory), the fact remains that SRAM can be a real bottleneck in program development.

Figure 7.5 is a snapshot of what the SRAM (i.e., the Stack) might look like when Listing 7.5 is run. (Figure 7.5 is a "teaching simplification" of what the stack actually looks like. The concepts are correct even though the mechanics taking place are more complex. We also assume that all variables with function or statement block scope are allocated on the Stack.)

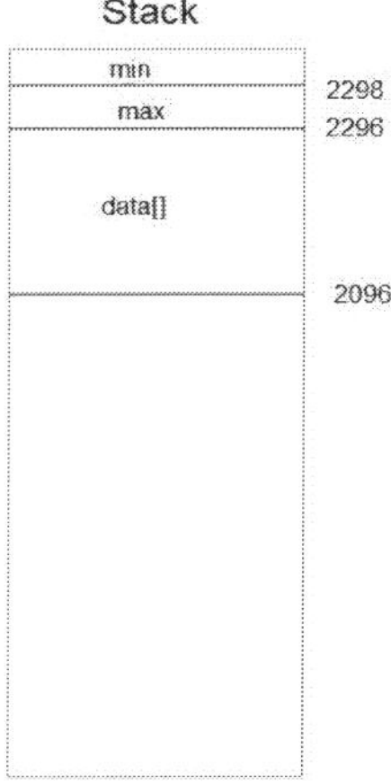

Figure 7.5. Simplified stack picture.

Think of the Stack as a salad plate dispenser in a restaurant. As the busboy brings out new plates and places them on the stack of plates, the old plates are pushed further down into the stack. Add enough plates and the plate space fills up and no new plates can be added. As customers go through the salad bar line and take a plate, the old plates start moving back up towards the top, leaving some space for new plates to be added.

Listing 7.8. Show the lvalues for three variables

```
void setup() {
  Serial.begin(9600);
```

```
}
void loop() {
  int data[100];
  int min;
  int max;

  Serial.print("\n   data has an lvalue of: ");
  Serial.println((int) data);
  Serial.print("     min has an lvalue of: ");
  Serial.println((int) &min);
  Serial.print("     max has an lvalue of: ");
  Serial.println((int) &max);
  delay(10000L);
}
```

The microcontroller SRAM is like the salad plate dispenser, except instead of plates, each item on the Stack is a byte of memory. So, when we defined *data[]* to hold 100 elements, and each *int* on an Uno takes 2 bytes, we pushed the top of the Stack down 200 bytes. Next, we defined *min* and *max*, each of which requires 2 bytes of memory. These two *int* variables push the stack of memory bytes further downward by 4 bytes.

After we compile the code in Listing 7.8, the Statistics Window for Listing 7.8 presents us with the following message (for an Arduino Mega2560):

Sketch uses 2368 bytes (0%) of program storage space. Maximum is 253952 bytes.
Global variables use 268 bytes (3%) of dynamic memory, leaving 7924 bytes for local variables. Maximum is 8192 bytes.

We're using about 0% of flash memory, but 3% of "Global" SRAM memory. But...but...Listing 7.8 does not define any variables with global scope, right?

Wrong!

What is the scope of *setup()* and *loop()*? Those two functions are not defined within a function — they *are* functions! Obviously, they are not defined within a statement block, so they do not have statement block scope, either. And, because there is only one source code file, they can't be inter-file scope. *All functions have global scope* and the Statistics Window tells us that the code size for those function variables and any "hidden" global definitions (e.g., the *Serial* object and other bootloader variables) is 268 bytes.

Now, go back to Listing 7.8 and bump up the *data[]* array to 400 elements and recompile/run the program. Look at the Statistics Window. After all, the bigger size for *data[]* chews up an additional 600 bytes of memory. So, what changed? Nothing! *The data in the Statistics Window is the same as before!* But, what happened to the lvalue of *data[]*? The *data[]* array is pushed much deeper into the stack than before and has an lvalue that is 800 bytes less than *max*.

When I ran the code using the larger element count for *data[]*, its lvalue changed to 1486. That seems to suggest that I have almost 1500 bytes left to play with, so let's bump the element count to *data[900]*. When I recompiled and ran the program, nothing happened. No program output...nothing. What happened?

Stack Crash

Okay, let's take stock of what we know. First, the Statistics Window tells us that global data use 268 bytes of memory. Where do those global variables get stored? A few pages ago I told you that *all* program data get stored in SRAM. Therefore, Figure 7.5 is misleading. The Stack picture actually looks like Figure 7.6.

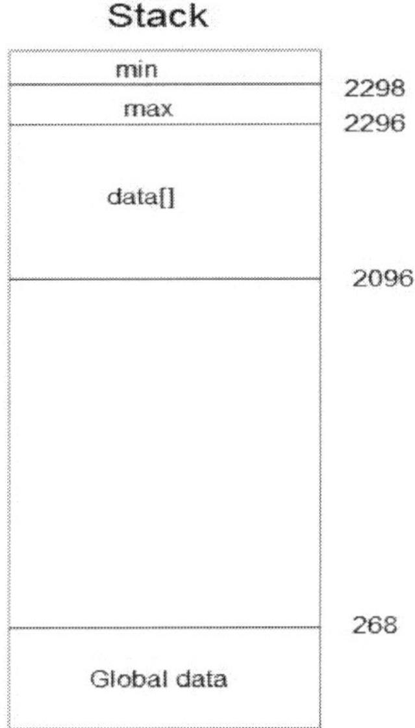

Figure 7.6. A Stack picture also showing global (Heap) data.

Figure 7.6 is a more honest representation of what SRAM looks like because global program data are also stored in SRAM. As a generalization, global data are stored "at the bottom" of the Stack in a section of SRAM often referred to as the Heap Space. *The Heap Space is that part of SRAM that is used by the program's global and static data.* Evidently, our program uses 268 bytes of Heap Space.

Guess what happened when you tried to pile on another 800 plates for the *data[900]* definition? The lvalue for *data[]* just crashed into the Heap Space, blowing some piece of global data out of the water! When data with non-global scope get allocated, they push the stack deeper and deeper. What happens if you stick in a bunch of function calls and each one of those functions has a bunch of their own function variables?

Runtime versus Compiletime Statistics

Each time your program executes and calls another function, if that new function has any variables with function or statement block scope, those new variables are allocated on the stack. (There are some additional overhead bytes required for each function call, too.) Therefore, those new variables cause the stack to go deeper and deeper. The good news is that, when program execution reaches the end of a function, what happens to all of the variables defined in that function? They go out of scope, which means they die. So, if a function defines 100 bytes of data for its own variables, when program control leaves that function, it's like 100 plates are removed from the stack. That is, the Stack reclaims those unused bytes. As a result, the bottom of the Stack “slides back up” towards the top by the amount of data that just “died”. In other words, the amount of *stack space* ebbs and flows as your program enters and leaves various functions.

Most programmers get tired of talking about variables with global scope, compared to variables with function scope, compared to variables with statement block scope. As a result, most programmers collapse function scope and statement block scope into a single term: local scope. Any variable defined within a function body has local scope. So, when you hear the term local scope, remember that local scope includes function and statement block variables, but excludes variables with global scope.

However, if your program code calls a function, and that function calls another function, and that function calls another function and each of the functions in that calling chain has its own set of variables, what else is taking place? The program is pushing the stack deeper and deeper with each new function call as the program executes. Given enough function calls and local variables getting defined, the Stack state of loop control variablespace collides with the Heap Space and your program branches into low-earth orbit...and that's if you're lucky! Sometimes there is a stack collision and you don't even know it because the data that just got clobbered isn't currently being used. Such bugs can be difficult to uncover. Not good.

It's important that you understand that the numbers you see in the Statistics Window are Compile-time numbers. That is, they reflect the program space the compiler needed for the program instructions (i.e., program storage space, or flash memory) plus the storage space for the global data, which the compiler places in the Heap Space. Therefore, *compile-time statistics are the numbers that exist when the program is compiled, not while it's running.*

As you may have guessed, *run-time statistics are the numbers that exist as the program executes*. The lvalues you see when the program in Listing 7.8 executes are run-time statistics.

Why can't the compile time statistics give us useful Stack space statistics? Well, consider this statement block:

```
if (sensorHeat > 70) {
   RunAirConditioner();
} else {
   RunHeatPump();
}
```

Let's further assume that the air conditioning function uses only 10 bytes of memory for local variables, but the heat pump function used 450 bytes of memory for its local variables. How can we know which function is called unless the code is running and we can see the value of *sensorHeat*?

We can't.

Therefore, we can't stand back at compile time and accurately measure the Stack usage at run time. (There are functions that you can use to insert calls to them at specific program execution points (see: https://learn.adafruit.com/memories-of-an-arduino/measuring-free-memory and https://arduino.stackexchange.com/questions/30497/how-to-measure-free-ram-on-an-arduino-due-inruntime), but I have not been able to find one that works for all 32-bit controllers.)

A rule of thumb on SRAM use is to *pay close attention to things when you see you've used up 70 percent or more of global space*. If you can, try to encapsulate more of your variables to minimize your use of the Heap space (and to ease your debugging burden).

Why Are Pointers Useful?

There are a number of reasons for using pointers. As you saw, pointers can make your code more bullet proof and also make it more flexible.

Enhanced Data Encapsulation

If there was only just one thing that makes pointers worth the effort it takes to master them, it would be that pointers lessen the need for global data. Remember in Chapter 5 how we had to declare *number* in a second file using the *extern* keyword? We had to do that because *number* was defined in one file but *MySquare()* needed to use it in another file. Using the *extern* keyword allowed us to declare and use *number* in the second file. That was the good news. The bad news was (and still is) that it required *number* to have global scope. Global data are subject to contamination by every statement in the file in which they are defined. True, using the *extern* keyword allows you to use the variable in a second (plus other?) source files in the project. However, that expanded ability also means you just increased the size of the pool in which any bug can swim. Not good.

However, now you can pass in *number* as a pointer variable and *MySquare()* can permanently change *number* within a function using indirection if you want it to. This allows you to define *number* in a way that gives it function scope instead of global scope. By not making *number* a global variable, data encapsulation is improved and, with that enhanced data encapsulation, the entire debugging process is simplified. That is a *huge* win!

Look Ma! No pointer!

In Listing 7.7, we used *ptr* to pass a pointer to the *SquareNumber()* function so we could permanently change *number*. Listing 7.9 is the same as Listing 7.7, except we commented out those statements that used *ptr*. However, look at the (shaded) statement where we call *SquareNumber()* in Listing 7.9.

Listing 7.9. Indirection with no pointer.

```
void setup() {
  Serial.begin(9600);
}
void loop()
{   int val;
//  int *ptr;

//  ptr = &val;       // Initialize ptr to point to val

  val = 100;
  Serial.print("Before function call, val = ");
  Serial.println(val);
//  SquareNumber(ptr);
  SquareNumber(&val);      // Send lvalue of val, not the rvalue
  Serial.print(" After function call, val = ");
  Serial.println(val);
}

/*****
  Purpose: To square a number

  Argument list:
    int *v       pointer to the number to square

  Return value:
    void

  CAUTION:
*****/
void SquareNumber(int *v)
{
  *v = *v * *v;          // Same as *v *= *v;
  Serial.print("   In SquareNumber(), *v = ");
  Serial.println(*v);
}
```

In Listing 7.4, we initialized *ptr* to hold val's lvalue. (See the commented-out statement in *loop()*.) Then we passed that pointer to *SquareNumber()*. Listing 7.9 does the same thing, but cuts out the middle man. Now in the call to *SquareNumber(),* we simply pass it the lvalue of *val* as the function parameter by using the address-of operator. In the function code, *SquareNumber()* knows it's been passed an lvalue because of the way *v* is defined to be an *int* pointer. In the Listing 7.7 code, *SquareNumber()* was passed the lvalue of *val* using *ptr.* Listing 7.9 says: "I don't need no stinkin' pointer! I'll just directly pass *val*'s lvalue to the function." You can completely do away with the *ptr* variable and simply use *val*'s lvalue directly! Getting rid of *ptr* saves you 2 (or 4) bytes of SRAM space. While that's not a huge SRAM savings, do that for enough variables and it might make a difference that allows you to compile a large program where otherwise you could not.

More Versatile Functions

Suppose you need to look through an array of data and find the minimum and maximum values in that data set. The function goal for writing good functions says that functions should solve one task and that each function be cohesive. In the strictest sense, then, we should have one function that finds the minimum data value and then a second function that finds the maximum value. After all, a function can only return one value anyway.

Well, come on. The code in the two functions is going to be virtually the same, plus two functions means plowing through the data array two times when we could do it in one pass through the array. Okay, so writing one function to find the minimum and maximum makes sense, but how are we going to return those two values when only one value can be returned from a function call? Think about the problem.

Let's start with a simple program to illustrate the problem. Listing 7.8 defines three data items and then displays their lvalues. That's all the program in Listing 7.8 does.

Because we wish to see the lvalue of each variable defined in *loop()*, we use the address-of operator before the variable name...sort of.

Using the address-of Operator...or What's in a Name?

Look at the *println()* statement for *data[]* in Listing 78:

```
Serial.println((int) data);
```

There is no address-of operator used with *data[]*. Why not? Remember: *using an array name by itself with no brackets is an expression that always resolves to the lvalue of that array.* In other words, *data* and *&data[0]* yield the same lvalue because *&data[0]* is where the array starts in memory. To drive that point home, try recompiling Listing 7.8, but add these new statements to the code in *loop()*:

```
Serial.print("data[0] has an lvalue of: ");
Serial.println((int) &data[0]);
```

Note the second new program statement uses *&data[0]*. When I ran the program, the output was:

```
    data has an lvalue of: 8495
     min has an lvalue of: 8697
     max has an lvalue of: 8695
 data[0] has an lvalue of: 8495
```

The exact numbers displayed when you run the program on your system will likely be different, but the important thing to notice is the lvalues for your *data* and *&data[0]* are identical. That is, *the name of an array, when used by itself, resolves to the lvalue of that array.* Because programmers don't like to type any more than necessary, they rarely would use *&array[0]* to find the lvalue of an array, preferring the shorter form of *array* instead.

The Min-Max Program

Let's write the full code for a program that finds the minimum and maximum values in an array. As you recall from Chapter 6, a function can only return a single value, as dictated by the function type specifier for that function. However, we need a function that finds both the minimum and maximum values in an array. Listing 7.10 presents that program.

The *setup()* function instantiates the Serial object and seeds the random number generator by an *analogRead(A0)* call. This seeds the random number generator with whatever value happens to be on the analog pin (noise?). If you remove the seed call, you get a repeatable sequence of "random" numbers, which can be useful when debugging. The limits.h header file is included because we use the hardware-defined minimum/maximums for an *int* on the host processor.

Listing 7.10. A Min-Max program.

```
#include <limits.h>

#define MAXCOUNT 100                // Elements in the array

void setup() {
  Serial.begin(9600);
  randomSeed(analogRead(0));        // Seed the random number
generator
}

void loop() {
  int data[MAXCOUNT];
```

```
  int min;
  int max;

  StuffArray(data, MAXCOUNT);        // Fill array with random
numbers
  FindMinMax(data, &min, &max, MAXCOUNT);   // Search the array
  ShowAll(data, min, max, MAXCOUNT);        // Show what you found
  delay(5000L);
}
/*****
  Purpose: To show the minimum and maximum value

  Argument list:
    int data[]       the array to fill
    int min          pointer to the minimum
    int max          pointer to the maximum
    int elements     the number of elements to inspect

  Return value      void

  CAUTION:
*****/
void ShowAll(int data[], int min, int max, int elements)
{
  Serial.println("\n=========");
  Serial.print("minimum = ");
  Serial.println(min);
  Serial.print("maximum = ");
  Serial.println(max);
  for (int i = 0; i < elements; i++) {
    if (i > 0 && i % 10 == 0) {        // Make 10 numbers/line
      Serial.println(" ");
      }
    Serial.print(data[i]);
    if (data[i] < 10) {          // Pad the spaces following the
      Serial.print("   ");       // number so they line up in
columns
    } else {
      if (data[i] < 100) {
        Serial.print("  ");
      } else {
        Serial.print(" ");
      }
    }
    Serial.print("  ");
  }
}

/*****
  Purpose: To find the minimum and maximum values in the array

  Argument list:
    int data[]       the array to fill
    int *min         pointer to the minimum
    int *max         pointer to the maximum
    int elements     the number of elements to inspect

  Return value
```

```
    void

  CAUTION:
*****/
void FindMinMax(int data[], int *min, int *max, int elements)
{
  int i;
  *min = INT_MAX;        // Set lowest value to a really large
value
  *max = INT_MAX * -1;  //     highest                    low
   for (i = 0; i < elements; i++) {
    if (data[i] >= *max) {          // Is this the largest we've
seen?
      *max = data[i];               // Yep.
    }
    if (data[i] <= *min) {          // The smallest value?
      *min = data[i];               // Yep.
    }
  }
}
/*****
  Purpose: To fill the array with random numbers

  Argument list:
    int *myStuff     the array to fill
    int MAXCOUNT     the number of elements

  Return value     void

  CAUTION:
*****/
void StuffArray(int *myStuff, int elements)
{
  int i;

  for (i = 0; i < elements; i++) {
    myStuff[i] = (int) random(0, 1000);
  }
}
```

In *loop()*, we define some local variables and then make the first function call to *StuffArray()*. The function arguments are *data* and *MAXCOUNT*, which we *#define*'d as 100. As we mentioned earlier, an array name by itself resolves to the array's lvalue. If we assume that the numbers in Figure 7.6 apply to this program, it means that our function call actually looks like:

```
  StuffArray(2096, 100);  // Assume array data start at 2096
```

The syntax is the same as you taking the numbers 2096 and 100, writing them down on a piece of paper, stuffing it into your backpack, and launching yourself to the sidewalk slab that sits in front of a black box with *StuffArray()* above the doorway. The hand shoots out through the door, grabs your backpack, and slams the door. This time, however, we are going to let you sneak inside the black box and watch what happens.

To better understand what is about to take place, look at the function signature defined for *StuffArray():*

```
void StuffArray(int *myStuff, int elements)
```

The guy with the impolite hand knows that he just received two numbers. The first number (2096) is associated with the first parameter (the *int* pointer named *myStuff*) and the second number (100) is the second parameter and dictates the size of the array we are going to use. So, the rude guy creates two new variables on the Stack named *myStuff* and *elements*. If we just look at the top of the Stack, it looks something like (we're assuming each integer takes 2 bytes as do memory addresses):

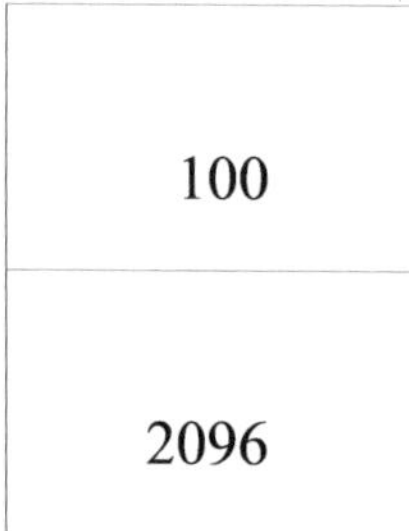

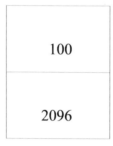

As you can see, the rvalue of *myStuff* is 2096 and *elements* has an rvalue of 100.

Wait a minute! What would happen if *myStuff* and the data array, *data[]*, were at the same scope level and I wrote this statement:

```
myStuff = &data[0];
```

or

```
myStuff = data;
```

Both expressions would resolve to the same thing: the rvalue of *myStuff* is 2096, which is the lvalue of *data[]* back in *loop()*. This means that we have initialized the pointer *myStuff* to point to *data[]* back in *loop()*! Therefore, *the rvalue of myStuff is actually the base address of the data[] array in loop()*. It is this identity between *data* and *&data[0]* that lets us write the *for* loop the way we did:

```
  for (i = 0; i < elements; i++) {
    myStuff[i] = (int) random(0, 1000);
  }
```

Notice that we use the array brackets in the shaded statement instead of the indirection operator with the *myStuff* pointer. When you run the program, the output looks something like this (your numbers will be different):

```
minimum = 13
maximum = 976
50     161    777    283    82     466    185    553    25     436
581    742    884    290    51     132    218    789    365    402
337    50     650    643    285    321    13     683    676    263
223    356    925    741    617    434    713    162    362    79
937    760    346    302    603    976    581    759    479    242
745    569    511    260    58     815    101    227    234    578
78     403    639    396    801    162    823    618    30     537
783    126    436    465    53     895    942    164    883    786
449    198    781    95     910    432    534    819    83     902
798    559    527    431    817    677    915    585    628    369
```

What would happen if I changed the *for* loop to:

```
  for (i = 0; i < elements; i++) {
    *myStuff++ = (int) random(0, 1000);
  }
```

Because the indirection operator is processed before the post-increment operator, the random number is written to the rvalue of *myStuff[i]* and then the pointer is incremented. End result: the array content is *exactly* the same as before.

What if I changed the *for* loop to:

```
  for (i = 0; i < elements; i++) {
    *(myStuff + i) = (int) random(0, 1000);
  }
```

In this case, the parentheses force us to add variable *i* to *myStuff* and *then* use indirection to change its rvalue. However, because *myStuff* points to an *int*, the offset added to the lvalue uses the pointer scalar (2) to get the correct memory address for the new value. All three uses (*myStuff[i]*, **myStuff*, and **(myStuff + i)*) are syntactically equivalent. When you read someone else's code listing, keep in mind that all three variations may be used but yield the same results.

Summary of Pointer Rules

To use a pointer correctly requires that you follow some basic rules.

1. Pointer variables must be defined using the *indirection operator* (int *ptr;)
2. Pointer definition's data type sets the pointer scalar and determines how each pointer is accessed (fetching an rvalue) or manipulated (e.g., ++ to get to the next element in an array)
3. A pointer must be initialized using the address-of operator (&) so the rvalue of the pointer is assigned the lvalue of the item being pointed to (e.g., *ptr = &myVariable*)
4. Use the indirection operator (*) to set/retrieve the rvalue of the data being pointed to (**ptr = 10*)

Please review these rules until they make sense to you. If you always follow these rules, you will never severely injure your leg.

Also remember that if you wish to print out the lvalue of a variable, you will likely need to cast the reference to the variable:

```
Serial.print("The memory address of myNumber is = ");
Serial.println( (int) &myNumber);
```

The reason is because memory address size may vary among microcontrollers that you might use for the program. The cast forces the address to be expressed as an *int*.

Conclusion

This chapter covers the most difficult aspect of C for beginning programmers to understand. Quite honestly, that's to be expected. Pointers are one of the most powerful features of C, so it only makes sense that understanding and using them correctly isn't going to be easy. But once that penny drops, man, is it worth it!

Please read this chapter more than once, even if you think you understand it. Also, make sure you do the exercises for this chapter to test that understanding.

Exercises

1. What is a pointer variable and how is it different from non-pointer variables?

2. Why is it important to initialize a pointer before using it? What might happen if you don't initialize a pointer before using it?

3. Discuss this statement: "Pointers allow you to permanently change variables that are not in scope."

4. How do you properly initialize a pointer?

5. Suppose a character string (e.g., *char myName[]*) contains "Jack Ourdum" in it. Use a pointer to correct the spelling error. (This means you need to change 'O' to 'P'--pay attention!)

6. Write a program that uses indirection via a pointer (*ptr*) to change the value of a variable (*yourNumber*) to 100.

7. Why are pointer scalars important? How do scalars relate to bucket sizes during the process of indirection?

8. Are there ways to use indirection without defining a pointer? If so, how?

Chapter 8 Using Pointers Effectively

This chapter is a continuation of the material discussed in Chapter 7. In that chapter, you learned what a pointer is and how to manipulate them in expressions. In this chapter, you will learn about:

- Valid pointer operations
- Pointer arithmetic
- Using pointers to functions
- The Right-Left Rule for deciphering complex data definitions
- Why using pointers can lead to more efficient code

When you have finished this chapter, you should be quite comfortable using pointers in your code.

Relational Operations and Test for Equality Using Pointers

Some C expressions make sense with almost any data type...except pointers. A partial reason this is true is because *a pointer should only have one of two types of rvalues: 1) a memory address or 2) NULL (i.e., '\0').* Any other type of data is going to result in an error of some form...sooner or later. Because the rvalue for pointer variables is thus constrained, some operators simply don't make sense with pointers. *Relational tests (e.g., >=, <=, > and <) on pointers are acceptable, but only when both operands are pointers and both point to the same data.* Therefore,

```
if (ptr1 < ptr2) {
   // other statements in if statement block
}
```

is acceptable *only* if both pointers *ptr1* and *ptr2* are initialized to point to the same object, but the expression:

```
if (ptr1 > 10) {
   // other statements in if statement block
}
```

is not allowed. This form is unacceptable because the relational test is against a constant, not a pointer. You can use a cast to dispel the error message you get when using constants in pointer relational tests, but that's almost never a good idea. Testing against a specific numeric memory address constant almost never makes sense.

Pointer Comparisons Must Be Between Pointers to the Same Data

You should not perform relational operations on two pointers if they do not point to the same data object. If you think about it, such comparisons simply don't make sense. (An exception is checking a pointer to see if it is *null*.) The problem, however, is that the Arduino C compiler does not catch this type of error. Consider the code in Listing 8.1:

Listing 8.1. Illegal Pointer test

```
void setup()
{
  char *ptr1;
  char *ptr2;
  char array[50];
  char name[10];

  Serial.begin(9600);

  ptr1 = array;
  ptr2 = name;                          // Initialize the pointers
  if (ptr1 > ptr2) {                     // Some RDC...
    Serial.println("Made it");
  } else {
    Serial.println("Didn't make it");
  }
}
void loop() {
}
```

The *if* test on the pointers in Listing 8.1 is nonsense and should be flagged as an error because you are comparing two pointers that point to different data objects. There is no way that two properly-defined arrays occupy the same memory space. It's difficult to imagine a use for such a comparison, too. The Arduino C compiler, however, lets this code slide by. (In all fairness, all C compilers allow the code in Listing 8.1 to compile without error.) Not flagging the test on the two pointers as an error (or at least issuing a warning) can make debugging a pointer problem more difficult than it should be. This is one of those situations where pointer comparison is syntactically correct, but makes no sense to do so.

Pointer Arithmetic

Some forms of pointer arithmetic are allowed, others are not. Confusing them is simply begging the train to leave the rails. You performed pointer arithmetic in Chapter 7, but probably didn't think much about it. Now, let's dig in and look closely at what happens when you use pointers in your code. Consider the code in Listing 8.2. Do a mental code walk-through for Listing 8.2 stating out loud what you expect to happen as you execute each statement line.

Listing 8.2. Using pointers.

```
#include <string.h>

void setup() {
  Serial.begin(9600);

  char buffer[50];
  char *ptr;                    // define a pointer
  int i;
  int length;

  strcpy(buffer, "When in the course of human events");

  ptr = buffer;                             // Initialize the pointer
  length = strlen(buffer);
  Serial.print("The length of buffer =  "); // How many chars?
  Serial.println(length);
  Serial.print("The lvalue for ptr is: ");
  Serial.print((unsigned int)&ptr);
  Serial.print(" and the rvalue is ");
  Serial.println((unsigned int)ptr);
  while (*ptr) {
    Serial.print(*ptr++);
  }
}
void loop() { }
```

The first thing to notice is that we are including a header file named *string.h*. (Actually, you could leave this preprocessor directive out and the compiler still compiles the program without errors.) If you read *string.h* with a text editor, you will find all kinds of functions designed to manipulate both strings and memory. Most of the function declarations you find in that header file are part of the System V Standard C Library that's been around for decades. If you are interested in learning more about any given library function (e.g., *memcmp()*), just use your Internet search engine on the function name and you will get more than enough information about the function. (A *memcmp()* search turned up over 300,000 hits!) As stated before, search the libraries before writing your own functions. There's a good chance what you need has already been written.

One of the function declarations in the *string.h* header file is:

```
extern char *strcpy(char * dest, const char *source);
```

which *appears* to copy the characters pointed to by the constant character pointer that is the second parameter (*source*) into the character array pointed to by the first parameter (*dest*). Because both arguments are pointers, this is one of those weird situations where we are copying the rvalue of the *source* pointer (which is a memory address, or lvalue) into the rvalue of another pointer variable (*dest*). The *const* data qualifier means that the function (e.g., *strcpy()*) should not alter the data pointed to by the second parameter (*source*). Because *strcpy()* knows the lvalue of the second parameter, it *could* alter its contents. The *const* qualifier tells the compiler not to let that happen. Therefore, the statement:

```
strcpy(buffer, "When in the course of human events");
```

copies the quotation into *uffer[]*.

The statement:

```
ptr = buffer;
```

simply initializes *ptr* to point to *buffer*. That is, it copies the lvalue of *buffer* into the rvalue of *ptr*. Remember: *an array name by itself is the lvalue of the array* (i.e., *buffer* is syntactically the same as *&buffer[0]*). Think about what's been said thus far until you're sure you understand what the last two sentences mean.

When you compile, upload, and run the program, your output for Listing 8.2 should look similar to that shown in Figure 8.1. You can tell from Figure 8.1 that *ptr* is stored at memory address 8697 and that *buffer* has an lvalue of 8647. (Question: What is the architecture of the processor used to produce the output seen in Figure 8.1?) The second line confirms that *ptr* does point to *buffer*. The code then enters a *while* loop to display the contents of *buffer*, using *ptr* to reference it.

Now, add the following lines of code to the program in Listing 8.2, just before the closing brace of *setup()*:

```
for (int i = 0; i < length; i++) {
  Serial.print(*(ptr + i));
}
```

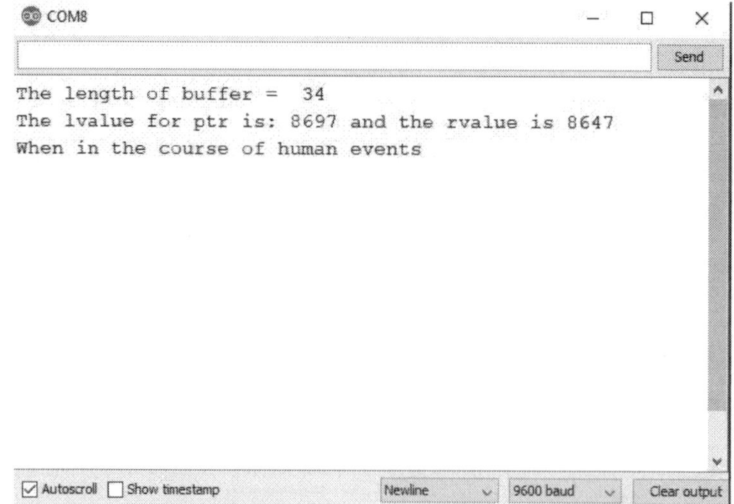

Figure 8.1. Output from pointer arithmetic program.

Now run the the modified code in Listing 8.2. The output when I ran the program is shown in Figure 8.2.

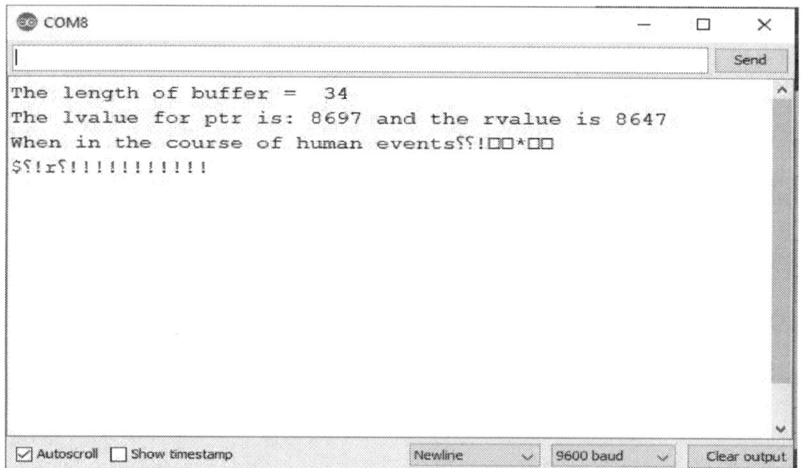

Figure 8.2. Output from pointer arithmetic program with for loop added.

What? What's all of the garbage in Figure 8.2 that follows the word "events" all about? In other words, what is the statement:

```
Serial.print(*(ptr + i));
```

printing? This variation of the program using pointer arithmetic worked in the last chapter, but isn't working here. Why?

To figure out the problem, look at the statement in Listing 8.2:

```
Serial.print(*ptr++);
```

that is controlled by the *while* loop. Now ask yourself: Why did the *while* loop terminate? The reason the *while* loop terminated is because *ptr* had been incremented so that it pointed to the *null* termination character for the quotation as stored in *buffer*. When *ptr* is pointing to *null*, the *while* loop expression evaluates to logic *False* and the loop ends. From the information in Listing 8.2 you know that *buffer* holds 34 characters plus one for the *null* character. When the *while* loop terminates, the rvalue for *ptr* must be 2277 (i.e., the starting lvalue for *buffer* of 2242 + 35) because you incremented *ptr* 35 times in the *while* loop. *As a result, ptr no longer points to the lvalue of the buffer*, but to its null termination character because you have been incrementing the rvalue of pointer in the *while* loop. After the *while* loop and the program code then falls into the new *for* loop you just added, the statement:

```
Serial.print(*(ptr + i));
```

Resolves to

```
Serial.print(*(2277 + 0));
```

which attempts to display whatever junk is stored in memory *after* the quotation that has been stored in the *buffer* array! This is going to be whatever garbage happens to be in SRAM at the memory location starting with 2277. Trust me, this is a Flat Forehead Mistake every C programmer has made at one time or another.

So, what's the fix? Very simple: reset the pointer any time you need to reuse it. In our case, add these lines before the new *for* loop code:

```
ptr = buffer;            // Reset the pointer back to &buffer[0]...
Serial.println("");      // So the output prints on a new line
```

and run it again. Now the output as shown in Figure 8.3 is as expected.

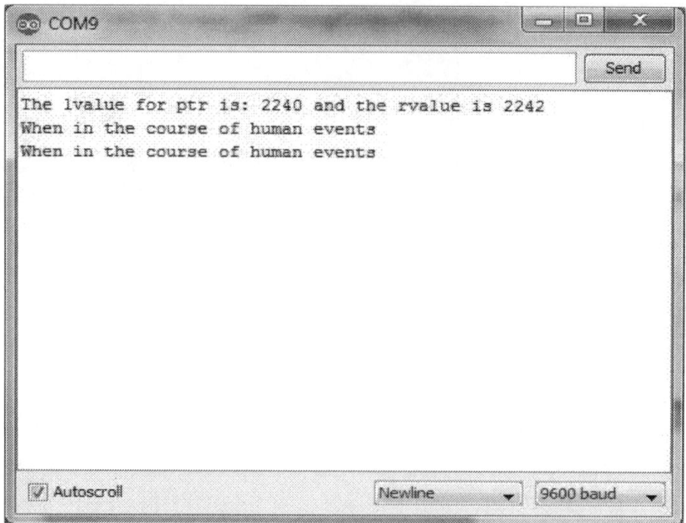

Figure 8.3. Program output after resetting ptr.

Always remember: *When you increment a pointer, it doesn't automatically reset itself.* Forgetting this simple rule has probably cost the programming world over a billion man-hours of wasted debugging time.

The statement controlled by the new *for* loop:

```
Serial.print(*(ptr + i));
```

shows how addition is one form of pointer arithmetic that is allowed. You learned in Chapter 7 that all pointer arithmetic is scaled to fit the data being pointed to. In this example, the scalar for a *char* data type is 1 byte, so each pass through the loop adds 1 to the rvalue of *ptr* and the code marches through the quotation. If *ptr* were pointing to *int* data, the expression:

```
(ptr + i)
```

in the *Serial.print()* statement would add 2 to the rvalue of *ptr* on each pass because the scalar for an *int* is 2 bytes (or 4 bytes if you're using a 32-bit microcontroller). Therefore, *the arithmetic operation of pointer addition is permissible and is automatically scaled for the type of data being used.*

Constant lvalues

You saw statements in Listing 8.2 that initialized the pointer, as in:

```
ptr = buffer;
```

and also the subexpression:

```
ptr + 1;
```

and both are perfectly acceptable expressions. The first statement simply initializes the pointer to point to *buffer* while the second statement adds one scalar unit to the pointer.

Now, using the variable named *buffer* from Listing 8.2, what happens when you try compiling the statement:

```
buffer = buffer + 1;
```

The compiler gets a tad cranky and issues an "incompatible types" error message. Why? Think about it. You know that, when an array name appears in a program statement by itself, it resolves to the lvalue of the array. Recall that it is the lvalue in the symbol table that allows the compiler to find where a data item resides in memory. The statement above, however, is attempting to change the *lvalue* by adding one scalar unit to it. If the compiler allowed you to change the lvalue, there would be no way to find where that variable is stored in memory. Therefore, the compiler must issue an error message when any statement attempts to change the lvalue of a variable. You can add an offset to an lvalue to access the elements of an array, but you cannot directly change its lvalue. That would be an attempt to change *where* the data item is stored in memory.

Two-Dimensional Arrays

Two-dimensional arrays are often used in programming to present tabular data. You might, for example, have a fire alarm system with 10 sensors per floor in a three story building. You could organize those sensors as:

```
int myFireSensors[3][10];
```

which could be used to store the current state of each sensor on all three floors. Obviously, you could also write the array as:

```
int myFireSensors[10][3];
```

Most programmers think of the organization for two-dimensional arrays in a row-column format, so this latter definition is "ten rows of sensors by three columns of floors". Which of the two forms is better? Doesn't matter. Pick one that makes sense to you and use it...but get rid of the magic numbers and make it clear. Place the symbolic constants in a header file and then use:

```
int myFireSensors[SENSORSPERFLOOR][NUMBEROFFLOORS];
```

Symbolic constants provide you a means by which you can make your code easier to read. Use them!

Let's write a short program that uses a two-dimensional array of characters. While you could write the program as a simple array of String-class variables, we organize the data as a *char* array instead. (I'm not a big fan of the String class as implemented on microcontrollers.) The code is presented in Listing 8.3.

Listing 8.3. Using a two-dimensional array of chars

```
#define DAYSINWEEK 7
#define CHARSINDAY 10   // Need char for null in Wednesday.
char days[DAYSINWEEK][CHARSINDAY] = {"Sunday", "Monday",
         "Tuesday","Wednesday","Thursday", "Friday", "Saturday"};
void setup() {
  int i, j;
  Serial.begin(9600);                   // Serial link to PC
  for (i = 0; i < DAYSINWEEK; i++)
  {
    Serial.print((int)days[i][0]);     // Show the lvalue
    Serial.print(" ");
    for (j = 0; days[i][j]; j++) {
      Serial.print(days[i][j]);        // Show each char
    }
    Serial.println();
  }
}
```

The character array is initialized by the statement:

```
char days[DAYSINWEEK][CHARSINDAY] = {"Sunday", "Monday",
  "Tuesday","Wednesday", "Thursday", "Friday", "Saturday"};
```

The reason *CHARSINDAY* is set to 10 is because Wednesday is the longest day name with nine characters. If we wish to view them as strings, you would need to define Wednesday with 10 characters, or nine characters plus the *null* termination character. The result is a table with seven rows and ten columns of characters. Note that the *days[][]* array in Listing 8.3 has global scope.

When I ran the sketch in Listing 8.3, this is what was displayed:

```
522 Monday
532 Tuesday
542 Wednesday
552 Thursday
562 Friday
572 Saturday
```

This shows that the seven strings are stored in low memory in SRAM and each lvalue is 10 bytes higher than the previous one. (Your actual numbers will likely be different.) Now, move the *days[][]* array so it is defined near the top and inside of *setup()* thus giving the array local scope and run the program. The output for me changed to:

```
8596 Sunday
8606 Monday
8616 Tuesday
8626 Wednesday
8636 Thursday
8646 Friday
8656 Saturday
```

Note that the memory addresses are much higher (but the differential remains the same at 10 bytes). The reason is because, by moving the definition of *days[][]* into *setup()*, you changed the scope of the array from global to local scope. Global data are allocated near the bottom of the stack. On the other hand, local data goes through the salad-plate mechanism we talked about earlier and is stored near the top of the stack. This also mean that when the *days[][]* array is defined in *setup()*, the *days[][]* array "dies" when control leaves *setup()*. This also means that the stack space used in the *setup()* function is reclaimed for use later in the program (i.e., the salad plates slide up towards the top.) This is what we mean when we say the amount of SRAM used ebbs and flows as the program runs and enters and exits the functions in the program.

The static keyword

Now, while still keeping the definition of *days[][]* in *setup()*, add the keyword *static* in front of its definition:

```
static char days[DAYSINWEEK][CHARSINDAY] = {"Sunday", "Monday",
"Tuesday", "Wednesday", "Thursday", "Friday", "Saturday"};
```

Now recompile and run the program. When I did this, the output was:

```
512 Sunday
522 Monday
532 Tuesday
542 Wednesday
552 Thursday
562 Friday
572 Saturday
```

Look familiar? (The reason they are the same is because of the array's placement in the code.) It should look familiar because the lvalues are almost exactly what they were when we defined the array with global scope. Why?

By using the *static* storage modifier for data with local scope, the compiler allocates that data in the Heap space rather than on the Stack. This means the memory is allocated at compile time rather than run time. It also means that *static* data can retain its value between calls. Consider Listing 8.4.

Listing 8.4. Displaying a local variable in a function

```
int DummyFunction()
{
  int i = 0;

  i++;
  return i;
}
void setup() {
  Serial.begin(9600);     // Serial link to PC     \
  while (!Serial) ;
}
void loop() {
  Serial.println(DummyFunction());  // Show the lvalue
}
```

If you run the code in Listing 8.4, it displays an endless series of 1's in the Serial monitor. Okay, now add the word *static* in front of the definition of *i* in *DummyFunction()*:

```
static int i;
```

and recompile/run the program. What happens? Now, instead of the endless stream of 1's, you get a series of numbers where each is 1 greater than the previous value. In other words, *the static modifier used inside a function allows you to "remember" its value between function calls*! This means you get the *data persistence* of a variable defined with global scope, but it remains hidden (encapsulated) within its function so code in other functions can't mess with it. This is a win-win in many cases.

What happens when you place the keyword *static* in front of a variable with global scope. In that case, that data item cannot be seen across other files that might be part of the sketch. This gives you a somewhat restricted visibility for a global variable.

Here's one more thing about the static keyword that will make more sense when we talk about Object Oriented Programming (OOP) and classes. If you define a class member using the *static* keyword, that data item is only allocated once in memory, even if you create a 1000 objects of that class. For example, if you have a *days[][]* array like we did in Listing 8.3, do you really need to repeat that array 1000 times? Probably not, because the 1000 objects can share that array.

Using the *static* storage qualifier is a great way to save some data bytes when the information can be shared. You need to keep in mind that you are not programming a PC that has a megamunch of memory available to you. When it comes to data space, you might only have 2Kb of SRAM available and you may have to use some tricks to shoehorn your data into that limited space. The *static* storage modifier might help you do that.

How Many Dimensions?

Our sample program in Listing 8.3 uses a two-dimensional array. Each dimension is called a *rank* so Listing 8.3 uses a rank 2 array. So, how many ranks does Arduino C allow you to use? Well...how many do you need? You might use a rank 3 array if you are doing 3D graphics, storing the coordinates for x, y, and z. If you're writing a game where those graphics change in relation to time, you might use a rank 4 array. I've tried to think of a good rank 5 example and all I got was a headache. While I thought the old ANSI X3J11 spec stated a maximum rank of 256, I cannot find that limitation in print. I do know that the Arduino can compile a rank 5 array. I read where some theoretical physicists now believe there are 11 dimensions. If that makes sense to you, you probably don't need this book. I can't think of any reason to go beyond rank 4. If you need more, write the code and try to compile it. If it compiles, you should then send me a copy of the code...I need a good example of a rank N program.

Two-Dimensional Arrays and Pointers

Can you rewrite the code in Listing 8.3 to use pointers? Sure, but it takes a little more thought. The modified code appears in Listing 8.5.

Listing 8.5. Modified two-dimensional array program to use pointers.

```
#define DAYSINWEEK 7
#define CHARSINDAY 10

void setup() {
  Serial.begin(9600);
}
void loop() {
  static char days[DAYSINWEEK][CHARSINDAY] = {"Sunday", "Monday",
          "Tuesday", "Wednesday","Thursday", "Friday",
"Saturday"};
  int i, j;           // Note dual definitions in one statement
  char *ptr, *base;   // Some programmers hate them. Your choice.

  base = days[0];     // Different for N-rank arrays where N > 1
  for (i = 0; i < DAYSINWEEK; i++) {
    ptr = base + (i * CHARSINDAY);
    Serial.print((int) ptr);          // Show the lvalue
    Serial.print(" ");
    for (j = 0; *ptr; j++) {
      Serial.print(*ptr++);           // Show one char
    }
    Serial.println();
  }
  Serial.flush();
  exit(0);
}
```

The first thing to notice is that there are two *char* pointer variables now, *ptr* and *base*. In the code, *ptr* is used to march through the character array while *base* is used to keep track of where the array begins in memory. Recall from the previous program that when you ran the program back-to-back without resetting the pointer, random garbage ended up being displayed. The *base* pointer is used in Listing 8.3 to prevent the same problem.

The next difference is how the *base* character pointer is initialized to point to the array. The statement:

```
base = days[0];
```

is necessary because this is a rank 2 array. A one-dimensional array resolves to a pointer to *char*, so the name of the array *is* the lvalue for the array. However, with two-dimensional arrays, what you have is a pointer to an array, not a pointer to a pointer. For that reason, you need to show “rank - 1” array brackets. You can make this even more explicit if you wish by using

```
base = &days[0][0]; // Clear we are initializing a rank-2 array
```

If you have a rank 3 array, you would need to use: *array[0][0]* or *&array[0][0][0]* in the *base* pointer initialization. You could force the syntax using a cast, but that seems to be an artificial way to do it. Inside the *for* loop controlled by variable *i*, the statement:

```
    ptr = base + (i * CHARSINDAY);
```

initializes *ptr* to point to the element of the array that you wish to display next.

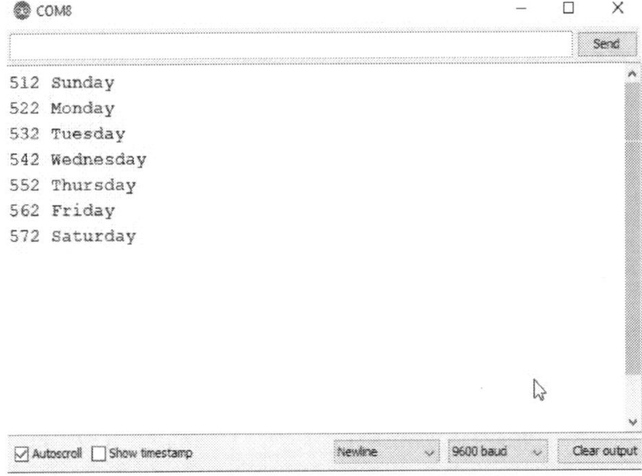

Figure 8.4. Output of Listing 8.5

Looking at Figure 8.4, the *days[][]* array starts at memory address 512. Because you initialized *base* to point to the starting address of the first element of the array, *base* equals 512. So, on the first pass through the *i* loop, the expression resolves to:

```
    ptr = base + (i * CHARSINDAY);
    ptr = 512 + (0 * 10);
    ptr = 512 + 0;
    ptr = 512;
```

which is exactly what we want. On the second pass through the *i* loop, *ptr* resolves to:

```
    ptr = base + (i * CHARSINDAY);
    ptr = 512 + (1 * 10);
    ptr = 512 + 10;
    ptr = 522;
```

which agrees with the value displayed in Figure 8.4. You should be able to convince yourself that each pass through the *i* loop results in an lvalue for *ptr* that is 10 bytes larger than the previous value...exactly as expected. Note that the base pointer is never changed. That's because all of the calculations are indexed from the beginning of the array.

Inside the *for* loop controlled by variable *j*, the statement:

```
Serial.print(*ptr++);     // Show one char
```

simply causes the code to march through the array, displaying each character until the *null* termination character is read. When *ptr* has been incremented to the *null* termination character, *expression2* of the *for* loop terminates (the loop code interprets the *null* as a logic *false* condition), and the *j* loop ends. An end-of-line character is displayed so the next display line appears on a new line. The program then increments variable *i* and the next pass through the *i* loop is made.

Treating the Two-Dimensional Array of char's as a String

If you just want to print out the contents of the array as strings, you can simplify the program even more. Remove the two *for* loops and replace them with the following single *for* loop:

```
for (i = 0; i < DAYSINWEEK; i++) {
  Serial.println(days[i]);
}
```

If you compile and run this modified version of the program, the days of the week are displayed. How does that work? The operation of the program becomes clear when you realize (using the lvalues from Figure 8.4) where the starting bytes are located. That is, days[0][0] marks the 'S' in "Sunday":

```
days[0][0] = 'S';  // lvalue = 512
days[1][0] = 'M'   // lvalue = 522
days[2][0] = 'T';  // lvalue = 532
// more elements...
```

Therefore, each time variable *i* is incremented by 1, the compiler adds an offset to the base index of the array name (512) that is equal to the size of the second element for the array (i.e., 10) times its scalar size. For a character array, the scalar is 1, so the offset is always 10. This is why the lvalue that is used to display the string is always 10 larger than the previous address. What if the array is defined as:

```
float myData[5][10];
```

What is the scalar for each increment of *i* in:

```
for (i = 0; i < 5; i++) {
  Serial.println(myData[i]);
}
```

Because the scalar for a *float* is 4, each increment on *i* advances the lvalue address by 40:

```
40 = sizeof(float) * second element size
40 = 4 * 10
40 = 40
```

As an exercise, you could change the code in Listing 8.5 to work with the *float* data type and display the lvalues to verify this conclusion is correct.

Pointers to Functions

Remember back in Chapter 4 when I told you about getting fired from a consulting job because I pointed out in a code walk-through that the cascading *if* statement for each day of the month was the best example of RDC I had ever seen? The code was something like:

```
if (today == 1) {
        DoFirstDayOfTheMonth();
 } else {
    if (today == 2) {
        DoSecondDayOfTheMonth();
    } else {
        if (today == 3) {
             DoThirdDayOfTheMonth():
        } // ...and so on...
```

We changed this example of RDC to SDC by using a *switch/case* statement block. The code change was an improvement because a *switch/case* creates a jump table that allows us to use *today* as an index into the jump table. That change was a vast improvement over the cascading *if* statement block...but still not the best we can do, now that you understand pointers.

Improved though it is, the *switch/case* block code still has to compile over 90 statements to generate the jump table, plus you are still going to be looking at those 90+ statements in the *switch* block any time you are debugging and testing its code.

Listing 8.6 is a non-pointer version of the banking code, but only showing 6 of the possible 31 daily functions. We've simply placed a *print()* method call in each function so you can see what the output looks like.

Listing 8.6. Non-pointer stripped down version of Bank problem

```
void DoFirstDayOfTheMonth() {
  Serial.println("Function1 call to Day 1");
}
void DoSecondDayOfTheMonth() {
  Serial.println("Function2 call to Day 2");
}
void DoThirdDayOfTheMonth() {
  Serial.println("Function3 call to Day 3");
}
void DoFourthDayOfTheMonth() {
  Serial.println("Function4 call to Day 4");
}
void DoFifthDayOfTheMonth() {
  Serial.println("Function5 call to Day 5");
}
void DoSixthDayOfTheMonth() {
  Serial.println("Function6 call to Day 6");
}
void setup() {
  Serial.begin(9600);
   for (int i = 0; i < 6; i++)
   {
    switch (i) {
      case 0:
        DoFirstDayOfTheMonth();
        break;
      case 1:
        DoSecondDayOfTheMonth();
        break;
      case 2:
        DoThirdDayOfTheMonth();
        break;
      case 3:
        DoFourthDayOfTheMonth();
        break;
      case 4:
        DoFifthDayOfTheMonth();
        break;
      case 5:
        DoSixthDayOfTheMonth();
         break;
      default:
        Serial.print("Shouldn't be here. i = ");
        Serial.println(i);
        break;
```

```
    }
  }
}
void loop() {
}
```

The output of the program looks like:

```
Function1 call to Day 1
Function2 call to Day 2
Function3 call to Day 3
Function4 call to Day 4
Function5 call to Day 5
Function6 call to Day 6
```

No surprises here and it functions as expected. I compiled this using an Arduino ATMega2560 which used 2000 bytes of flash memory and 332 bytes of SRAM. Like I said before, this is SDC because we can improve it several ways.

When I first started learning C over 40 years ago, I wanted to write a computer version of the game Monopoly. I started out with a very messy 64+ *switch/case statements.* After I learned about pointers to functions, I changed the *switch/case* blocks to use pointers to functions. The resulting code was significantly easier to test and debug.

While pointers to functions look a little intimidating at the start, it's the old how-do-you-eat-an-elephant problem. You start with the first bite. Once you understand the power function pointers affords, with a little imagination, you'll find many instances where function pointers offer a perfect solution to an otherwise messy code structure. This is especially true if you find your *switch/case* blocks reduced to a simple function call. Let's see how function pointers work.

The code in Listing 8.7 is almost the same as Listing 8.4 except we've modified it to use pointers to

Listing 8.7. Using a Pointer to Function

```
void DoFirstDayOfTheMonth() {
  Serial.println("Function1 call to Day 1");
}
void DoSecondDayOfTheMonth() {
  Serial.println("Function2 call to Day 2");
}
void DoThirdDayOfTheMonth() {
  Serial.println("Function3 call to Day 3");
}
```

```
void DoFourthDayOfTheMonth() {
  Serial.println("Function4 call to Day 4");
}
void DoFifthDayOfTheMonth() {
  Serial.println("Function5 call to Day 5");
}
void DoSixthDayOfTheMonth() {
  Serial.println("Function6 call to Day 6");
}

void (*functionPointers[])() = {&DoFirstDayOfTheMonth,
&DoSecondDayOfTheMonth,&DoThirdDayOfTheMonth,
&DoFourthDayOfTheMonth,&DoFifthDayOfTheMonth,
&DoSixthDayOfTheMonth
                                };

void setup() {
  Serial.begin(9600);
  for (int i = 0; i < 6; i++)
  {
    (*functionPointers[i])();
  }
}
void loop() {
}
```

functions. The list of the six dummy function remains the same, but then we introduce the first 800 pound gorilla in the room:

```
void (*functionPointers[])() = {&DoFirstDayOfTheMonth,
&DoSecondDayOfTheMonth, &DoThirdDayOfTheMonth,
&DoFourthDayOfTheMonth, &DoFifthDayOfTheMonth,
&DoSixthDayOfTheMonth
                                };
```

This looks pretty intimidating, but it really isn't. We will show you how to "unwind" this complex data definition using my *Right-Left Rule* in the next section. For now, you can verbalize this data definition as; "*functionPointers* is an array of pointers to functions that return a *void* data type." (If you ever want to impress a group of people at a party, spring that mouthful on 'em.)

Look at the initializer list of the array and think about what you're reading. *The functionPointers[] array is really nothing more than a list of the lvalues where each function "lives" in memory.* Remember when we said that an array name without brackets resolves to its lvalue? The same is true for functions. *A function name that omits the function's parentheses resolves to the lvalue for that function.* Referring back to our function discussions in Chapter 6, the function pointer array holds the "sidewalk slab numbers" where we jump to when we call a function.

Epiphany time! Guess what the next statement does if *today* is the current day of the month:

```
(*functionPointers[today])();
```

Presto-chango! The 90+ lines of code using the *switch/case* reduces to two statements! Compare that to the rats' nest of the cascading *if* statement block and its inefficiencies and you'll see how simple all of this really is.

To be honest about it, the pointer to function code uses 2 more bytes of flash memory and 12 more bytes of SRAM. Not good. But, not bad either. Up to this point, I've always argued in favor of lower memory resources, but I'm shying away on this one. The reason: The pointer to function code is shorter and easier to read. While you may not feel that way right now, that's only because you're just being introduced to pointers to functions. With a little more coding and debugging experience, I think you'll see the light.

Pointers to Functions with Arguments

Okay, but what if each of the day functions has an argument and the function returns a data type? Listing 8.8 is the same as Listing 8.7, except for the function body statements.

Listing 8.8. Using a Pointer to Function with Arguments

```
long DoFirstDayOfTheMonth(long num) {
  Serial.print("num = ");
  Serial.print(num);
  Serial.print("  Function1 call to Day 1");
  return num * 10L;
}
long DoSecondDayOfTheMonth(long num) {
  Serial.print("num = ");
  Serial.print(num);
  Serial.print("  Function2 call to Day 2");
  return num * 10L;
}
long DoThirdDayOfTheMonth(long num) {
  Serial.print("num = ");
  Serial.print(num);
  Serial.print("  Function3 call to Day 3");
  return num * 10L;
}
long DoFourthDayOfTheMonth(long num) {
  Serial.print("num = ");
```

```
  Serial.print(num);
  Serial.print("  Function4 call to Day 4");
  return num * 10L;
}
long DoFifthDayOfTheMonth(long num) {
  Serial.print("num = ");
  Serial.print(num);
  Serial.print("  Function5 call to Day 5");
  return num * 10L;
}
long DoSixthDayOfTheMonth(long num) {
  Serial.print("num = ");
  Serial.print(num);
  Serial.print("  Function6 call to Day 6");\
  return num * 10L;
}
long (*functionPointers[])(long) = {&DoFirstDayOfTheMonth,
                                    &DoSecondDayOfTheMonth,
&DoThirdDayOfTheMonth,
                                    &DoFourthDayOfTheMonth,
&DoFifthDayOfTheMonth,
                                    &DoSixthDayOfTheMonth};
void setup() {
  long retVal;
  long testValues[] = {10, 20, 30, 40, 50, 60}; // U test
arguments.
  Serial.begin(9600);

  for (int i = 0; i < 6; i++) {
    retVal = (*functionPointers[i])(testValues[i]);
    Serial.print("   retVal = ");
    Serial.println(retVal);
  }
}
void loop() {
}
```

Listing 8.8 is really little changed from Listing 8.7. The changes in the functions are just so we can pass in an argument and display it. Each function has identical changes, so just looking at the first function is all you need to study.

The definition of the *functionPointers[]* array is changed to allow you to pass in an argument and return a value. If you need to pass in a second argument, say an *int*, just use a comma-separated list of the arguments:

```
int (*functionPointers[])(long, int)
```

Of course, you need to alter the way you call the function to include the new argument:

```
retVal = (*functionPointers[i])(testValues[i], newVal);
```

Everything else remains the same.

The Right-Left Rule

What went through your mind when you saw:

```
long (*functionPointers[])(long) = {&DoFirstDayOfTheMonth,
       &DoSecondDayOfTheMonth, &DoThirdDayOfTheMonth,
       &DoFourthDayOfTheMonth, &DoFifthDayOfTheMonth,
       &DoSixthDayOfTheMonth};
```

Alas, after seeing that definition, many people probably close the book, and pick up a Basic or Java programming book. That's really sad, because, once you know C, you're going to throw rocks at any other language you may know.

Definitions like the one for *functionPointers[]* are called complex data definitions because they involve more than a simple data type specifier and a variable name. Let's take this definition and remove the initializer code that appears between the braces, and just concentrate on what's left:

```
void (*functionPointers[6])()
```

(I used 6 for the array size because that's the number of functions we wanted to use in Listing 8.8 and we need to supply that size if the initializer list is missing.) The question is: What does this definition do? Alternatively, how can you verbalize this definition? Actually, it's pretty simple when you use the *RightLeft Rule* I published almost 40 years ago.

The Right-Left Rule:

> *Locate the identifier in the definition (e.g., functionPointers) and then spiral your way out of the definition in a right-to-left fashion.*

Figure 8.5 shows the steps to follow to verbalize the definition. We explain each step as you follow the Right-Left Rule. During the process, *definition tokens* that you find in data definitions are verbalized as shown here:

Token Verbalize:

*	pointer to
()	function that returns
[n]	array of n (do for *all* ranks)

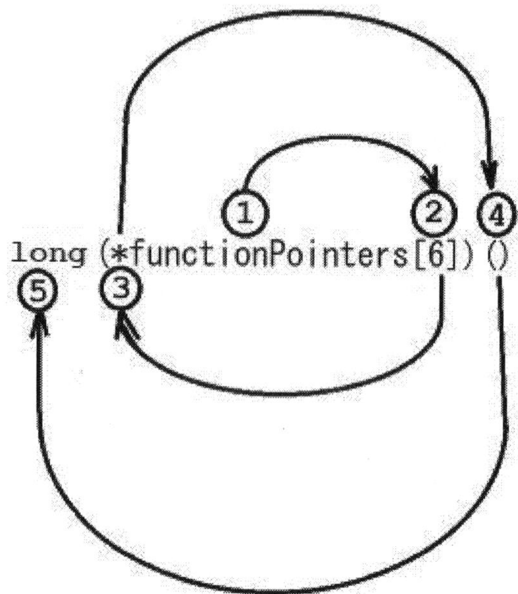

Figure 8.5. Using the Right-Left Rule

Step 1: Locate the identifier (i.e., variable name) used in the data definition. In this example, it is *functionPointers*.

Step 2: Look to the right for the next attribute closest to the identifier. In this example, it is "[6]". Because brackets are used with array dimensions, we now have: "*functionPointers* is an array of 6".

Step 3: Look to the left for the next attribute closest to the identifier. The attribute is an asterisk "*". Because asterisks represent pointers in data definitions, now we have: "*functionPointers* is an array of 6 pointers to".

Step 4: Look to the right for the next (unused) attribute closest to the identifier. In our example, it is "()". In data definitions, functions are denoted using parentheses. Therefore; we now have: "*functionPointers* is an array of 6 pointers to functions that return".

Step 5: Look to the left for the next (unused) attribute closest to the identifier. In this case, it's the keyword *long*. So, we know that each function is designed to return a *long* to the caller. That is, *long* is the function type specifier for the functions in the array.

Because we don't have any more unused attributes, now we can verbalize our full data definition: *functionPointers is an array of 6 pointers to functions returning long.*

If you look at the code in Listing 8.6, that is precisely what *functionPointers* is.

In what follows, *cover up everything on the right side of the page* and see if you can use the Right-Left Rule to verbalize the following data definitions correctly.

`int *mySensors[100][101];`	mySensors is a 100 by 101 array of pointer to ints.
`MyStructure (*myDisplay[2])();`	myDisplay is an array of 2 pointers to functions that return MyStructure objects
`byte *(*port11)();`	port11 is a pointer to function that returns a pointer to a byte.
`int (*functionPointers[6])(long);`	functionPointers is an array of 6 pointer to function with a long function parameter that returns an int.
`char (*(*myData)())[7][15];`	myData is a pointer to a function that returns a pointer to a 7 by 15 array of chars.

As you can see, you can construct some pretty complex data types if you need them. Indeed, that's one of the strengths of C: it's flexible and extensible.

Conclusion

Pointers are one of the most powerful features in the C language. In this chapter, we expanded your understanding of pointers and showed how pointers to functions can simplify your code. We have one more "pointer topic" to cover, but that is reserved for Chapter 9.

Alas, pointers are also one of the most difficult concepts for beginning programmers to understand. However, because you understand how data are represented in memory and what pointers are designed to accomplish, with a little practice you will soon be using them all the time in your own code. It really does take practice writing code to get comfortable with pointers. Yet, they are just too useful not to use them.

Exercises

1. What is the difference between *memcpy()* and *strcpy()*?

2. Write a program that properly uses the function *strtok()*. You should look it up on the Internet to see what its parameters are. (This is an incredibly useful function!)

3. Is *strtok()* destructive? (Try an example that prints out the original string.)

4. Suppose you have a 2x16 LCD display and you want the second line to be able to scroll long messages from right to left. How would you write it?

5. It's common to see the days of the week defined like

```
char days[7][10] = {"Monday", "Tuesday",
        "Wednesday", /* and so on */};
```

The problem is that you must size the array for the largest day (i.e., 10 characters for "Wednesday") when other days require less memory. How would you define the array to fix this waste?

6. Suppose you have a huge list of first and last names all stored in an array that looks like: "George Washington", "Adam Smith", "John Keynes", etc. After you've written the program and generated a list of 1,000,000 names, your idiot boss looks at it and says: "You need to add their middle names". How would you fix this? (And, no, you can't quit.)

7. What is the Right-Left Rule?

8. If you define a pointer to a function, what is the pointer's rvalue if it is properly initialized?

Chapter 9 Structures, Unions, and EEPROM

In this chapter, we examine C structures, unions, and the different ways our microcontrollers work with EEPROM storage. While there are some syntactic topics covered in this chapter, these new topics give you a new way of thinking and organizing your program data. We start with structures first, since some of the syntactic rules for structures spills over into the area of unions.

Structures

To appreciate what structures bring to the table, you have to consider the types of problems they can help solve. Some time ago I was asked to write a program that required storing information about people/companies who performed services for homes. Those services could be lawn maintenance workers, pool cleaners, in-house duties (i.e., watering plants, checking the air conditioning settings, etc.), and others. The project was based in Florida and the project was geared for people who lived in Florida on a part time basis. The project required storing a service company's ID number, Name, password, time in and out, and phone number. (Actually, more data was required, but this is good enough for our purposes.) From a data point of view, such disparate data poses a number of problems, not the least of which is how you "tie together" such differing data elements. You could define the data something like:

```
int  serviceID;
char serviceName[20];
char servicePW[10];
long serviceArriveDepart[2];
long servicePhone;
```

In this example, we attempt to link the data together by using the word "service" in the names of the data. This is a clumsy attempt and adds clutter to the variable names that really aren't necessary. While better than nothing, such an approach doesn't really "tie" the data together and allow us to manipulate it as an integrated unit of information.

The problem of grouping dissimilar data items together is solved in C by using a structure. A *structure organizes different data items so they may be referenced by a single variable name.* A structure normally holds two or more data items, usually of differing data types.

Declaring a Structure

The syntax for declaring a structure is:

```
struct structureTagName {
      // Structure Member List
};
```

If we wanted to declare a structure for our service program, we might declare it as:

```
struct serviceCompany {
  int  ID;
  char Name[20];
  char PW[10];
  long arriveDepart[2];
  long Phone;
};
```

Note that this is a data *declaration*; we have an attribute list of the structure and that serves as a model of how we "build" a structure. Think of a structure declaration as a set of blueprints for building a house. While the blueprints allow you to visualize the house based on the items (attributes) shown in the blueprints, you can't "move into" a set of blueprints. Those blueprints must be turned over to a contractor who actually builds (instantiates and defines) the house. Stated differently, a structure declaration creates a list of the structure attributes in the symbol table, but there is no lvalue yet for the structure. Figure 9.1 labels the various parts of the structure declaration.

```
Type Specifier      Structure Tag

      struct serviceCompany {
           int  ID;
           char Name[20];
           char PW[10];                  Structure Members
           long arriveDepart[2];
           long Phone;
      };
```

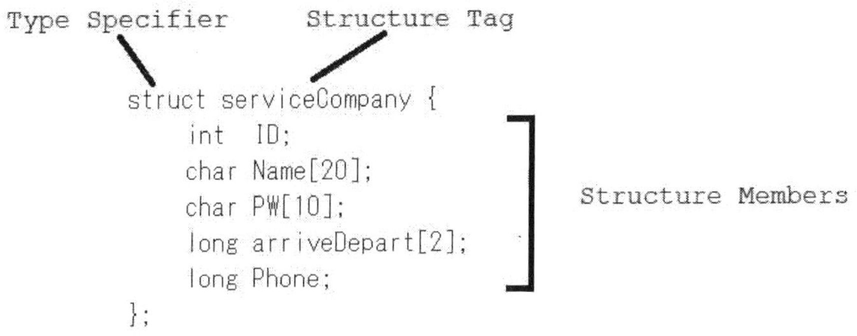

Figure 9.1. Parts of a structure declaration.

The type specifier is our new data type named struct, the *structure tag* simply gives this form of structure a name so we can differentiate it from any other structures we might have in the program, and finally, a pair of opening and closing braces encompasses the members of the structure. The *members of a structure are simply the variables that comprise the structure*. Note that we don't actually have a structure variable yet. We need to define a *struct* variable to do that.

Defining a Structure

You have two ways that you can define a structure: 1) declare the structure and then define a structure variable, or 2) declare and define the structure at the same time. Here's an example of the first approach:

```
struct serviceCompany {
    int  ID;
    char Name[20];
    char PW[10];
    long arriveDepart[2];
    long Phone;
};
struct serviceCompany veroBeachNeighborhood[100];
```

The last statement is really like any other data definition. The definition names a data type specifier (*struct*), the structure tag (*serviceComany),* and the name of the variable you want to define (*veroBeachNeighborhood []*). In this example, it appears like the company developing the software expects to have around a hundred customers in the Vero Beach area so we define an array of the *serviceCompany* structure. (A friend of mine named Kim Brand once called structure arrays "arrays for adults" and it's a good name. Where normal arrays are collections of identical data sharing a common name, structure arrays can hold different data types under a single name.)

If you apply the Right-Left Rule to the last statement above, you have: *veroBeachNeighborhood* is an array with 100 elements of the *serviceCompany* type of *struct*. Pretty simple!

Wait a minute! If each structure on a Nano takes 44 bytes and we want 100 of them, how do we jam 4400 bytes of data into a microcontroller that has a total of only 2048 bytes of SRAM? Short answer: We don't. If we hope to work with this many clients, we need to put on our Big Boy pants and switch to one of the other microcontrollers, paying attention to its SRAM limits when making the selection. Chapter 1 should help you decide. (As I'm writing this, PJRC just announced the Teensy 4.1 with 8 megabytes of flash and 1 *megabyte* of SRAM. That's some Huge Boy pants!)

While the code above does declare and define an array of structures, most C programmers prefer the slightly abbreviated second form, seen here:

```
struct serviceCompany {
   int  ID;
   char Name[20];
   char PW[10];
   long arriveDepart[2];
   long Phone;
} veroBeachNeighborhood[100];
```

This code block also defines the same array, but does so as part of the structure declaration. If you need more than one array of structures, then:

```
struct serviceCompany {
   int  ID;
   char Name[20];
   char PW[10];
   long arriveDepart[2];
   long Phone;
} veroBeachNeighborhood[100], palmRiver[30];;
```

All you need to do is create a comma-separated list of the new structure variables you want to define.

Why Use a Structure?

What's the big deal? We can use the "old style" data definitions for the members of the structure like we did at the beginning of the chapter:

```
int  serviceID;
char serviceName[20];
char servicePW[10];
long serviceArriveDepart[2];
long servicePhone;
```

and, if we use meaningful names, we can keep them "verbally together". True, but at what scope level are you going to define those members? Truth is, you're going to define them with global scope because you will quickly learn that local scope means passing in five variables to any function that you want to have access to the data. You already know what that means in terms of debugging. Also, you can pass a single structure pointer to a function and you're done.

If you place that data into a structure, you have to use a very purposeful syntax to assign a value into the member of a structure. That syntax makes it more difficult to mistakenly make an assignment to one of the structure members. Okay, so how do we access the members of a structure?

Accessing Structure Members

Remember our discussion of functions where you walked down a sidewalk and there were black, windowless boxes for each function? Each black box was like a house, except there were no windows. Just a door that a rude hand shot out of.

I want you to think of structures in the same way. Each structure is a black, windowless box with a locked door. Above the door is the name of the structure (*veroBeachNeighborhood[100]*). You cannot access the black box without a key to the door. That key comes in the form of a new operator, called the dot operator.

The Dot Operator

The *dot operator is actually just a period that appears between the structure's variable name and the structure member you want to access.*

```
StructureVariableName.StructureMemberToAccess
```

Notice the dot between the structure variable and its member. For example, suppose you want to give your first client an identification number of 200. The statement to do that is:

```
veroBeachNeighborhood[0].ID = 200;
```

Notice the placement of the dot operator. What this statement is saying is: Go to the black box structure with the name *veroBeachNeighborhood[0]* over the door, stick the dot operator key into the keyhole, twist the key, open the door, and walk inside. The room has five people sitting in chairs, each of whom is wearing a name tag (e.g., ID, Name, PW, etc.). You walk over to the person with the ID name tag on it, open your backpack, take out the value 200, and hand it to the ID person. After doing that, there's a flash of light and you're back on the sidewalk looking at the sidewalk slab for the instruction on what to do next.

Suppose that later in the program you need to take the first client's ID and assign it to a variable named *billingID*. The syntax to do that is:

```
billingID = veroBeachNeighborhood[0].ID;
```

Try to verbalize the statement above. It says: Find the structure black box with the name *veroBeachNeighborhood[0]* over the door, stick the dot operator key into the keyhole, twist the key, open the door, and walk inside. Look for the person sitting around wearing a name tag with ID on it. Walk over and copy down the number you see sitting in their lap (200). Place the paper with the number on it in your backpack and leave the black box. There's a flash of light whereupon you see *billingID* standing there with his hands out. You hand him the piece of paper and *billingID* immediately goes to his (lvalue) bucket in memory and places 200 in the bucket for its new rvalue. Piece of cake.

Listing 9.1 A simple program using a structure

```
struct serviceCompany {          // Declare a structure
  int  ID;
  char Name[20];
  char PW[10];
  long arriveDepart[2];
  long Phone;
};
                                 // Define and initialize the
structure
struct serviceCompany veroBeachNeighborhood[10] = {
  {10000, "Jack Purdum",         "myHouse",   0L, 0L, 2222222L},
  {10010, "Jerry & Barb Forro", "yourHouse", 0L, 0L, 3333333L},
  {10020, "Al & Jeanie Peter",  "someHouse", 0L, 0L, 1234567L}
};

void setup() {
  Serial.begin(9600);

  for (int i = 0; i < 3; i++) {
    Serial.println(veroBeachNeighborhood[i].Name);
  }

  Serial.print("\n          Name = ");
  Serial.println(veroBeachNeighborhood[0].Name);
  Serial.print("         phone = ");
  Serial.println((long) veroBeachNeighborhood[0].Phone);
  strcpy(veroBeachNeighborhood[0].Name, "Jill Purdum");
  Serial.print("Revised name = ");
  Serial.println(veroBeachNeighborhood[0].Name);

  Serial.print("size of one element of structure  = ");
  Serial.println(sizeof(veroBeachNeighborhood[0]));
}
void loop() { }
```

Listing 9.1 is just a simple example of using a structure. The program begins with a structure declaration and then defines an array of the structures, also showing how to initialize members of a structure as part of its definition. A *for* loop then prints out the names in the structure array. The program ends with showing how many bytes are taken by each structure element. That is 44 for an Arduino, but different for the other microcontrollers. Notice how we can use *strcpy()* to copy a new name over an old name. (Yep...I have a twin sister named Jill. If I had a nickel...)

Using Structures with Functions

When you think about it, passing a structure to a function is kind of a sneaky way to pass multiple arguments in one tidy package wrapped in a single argument. Listing 9.2 is almost the same as Listing 9.1, except we moved all of the display code into a function and made a few minor changes in *setup()*.

Listing 9.2. Passing a structure to a function

```
struct serviceCompany {
  int  ID;
  char Name[20];
  char PW[10];
  long arriveDepart[2];
  long Phone;
}; struct serviceCompany veroBeachNeighborhood[10] = {
  {10000, "Jack Purdum",         "myHouse",   0L, 0L, 2222222L},
  {10010, "Jerry & Barb Forro", "yourHouse", 0L, 0L, 3333333L},
  {10020, "Al & Jeanie Peter",  "someHouse", 0L, 0L, 1234567L}
};

void setup() {
  Serial.begin(9600);
  Serial.println("Original data\n");
  ShowSomeStructureStuff(veroBeachNeighborhood[0]);
  strcpy(veroBeachNeighborhood[0].Name, "Jill Purdum");
  Serial.print("\nRevised data\n");
  ShowSomeStructureStuff(veroBeachNeighborhood[0]);
}
/*****
  Purpose: To display the Name and phone number of the members of
           the structure and the size of one structure element.

  Argument list:
    struct serviceCompany s      the structure to display

  Return value:
      void
*****/
void ShowSomeStructureStuff(struct serviceCompany s) {
  Serial.print("                  Name = ");
  Serial.println(s.Name);
  Serial.print("                 phone = ");
  Serial.println(s.Phone);
  Serial.print("size of structure  = ");
```

```
  Serial.println(sizeof(s));
}
void loop() { }
```

Do a code walk-through and verbalize out loud what's going on. When you've finished, answer this one question: What is displayed on the Serial monitor? The output of Listing 9.2 is as follows:

Original data

```
            Name = Jack Purdum
           phone = 2222222
  sizeof structure = 44
```

Revised data

```
            Name = Jill Purdum
           phone = 2222222
  sizeof structure = 44
```

The code does show how easy it is to change the data of a structure member. However, it also shows a little bit of RDC as well. Note the size of the data that is passed to the function. We're pushing 44 bytes on to the stack each time we call the function. Why?

Using Structures with Pointers

We can write the program presented in Listing 9.2 and make it a little more efficient by using a structure pointer. Listing 9.3 is almost identical to Listing 9.2, except we are using a structure pointer. *elementToEdit*.

Listing 9.3. Passing a struct pointer to a function.

```
struct serviceCompany {
  int  ID;
  char Name[20];
  char PW[10];
  long arriveDepart[2];
  long Phone;
};
struct serviceCompany veroBeachNeighborhood[10] = {
  {10000, "Jack Purdum",         "myHouse",   0L, 0L, 2222222L},
  {10010, "Jerry & Barb Forro", "yourHouse", 0L, 0L, 3333333L},
  {10020, "Al & Jeanie Peter",  "someHouse", 0L, 0L, 1234567L}
};         portrait

void setup() {
  struct serviceCompany *elementToEdit;   // Define a struct
pointer
  Serial.begin(9600);
```

```
  elementToEdit = &veroBeachNeighborhood[0]; // Initialize the
pointer
  Serial.println("Original data\n");         // Show original data
  ShowSomeStructureStuff(elementToEdit);     // ...show using
pointer
  strcpy( (*elementToEdit).Name, "Jill Purdum");  // Change the
name
  Serial.print("\nRevised data\n");          // Show, but using
array
  ShowSomeStructureStuff(&veroBeachNeighborhood[0]);
}

/*****
  Purpose: To display the Name and phone number of the members of
           the structure and the size of one structure element.

  Argument list:
      const struct serviceCompany *s    a pointer to the structure
                                        to display

  Return value:
      void
*****/
void ShowSomeStructureStuff(const struct serviceCompany *s)
{
  Serial.print("              Name = ");
  Serial.println( (*s).Name);
  Serial.print("             phone = ");
  Serial.println( (*s).Phone);
  Serial.print("size of structure = ");
  Serial.println(sizeof(s));
}
void loop() {
}
```

Note the new signature for the *ShowSomeStructureStuff()* function. Because the function is only concerned with displaying the structure members, I have used the *const* keyword in the function's signature. In other words, I have defined the function as a “read-only” function that does not have the rights to alter anything in the function argument. This prevents me from doing something silly later on like adding code that alters the contents of the structure. Of course I can make such a change, but I would then have to edit the function signature and prototype. Such changes are quite purposeful and not likely to be made “in a hurry” without proper forethought. Quite honestly, I don't use this bulletproofing approach as often as I should. However, you should (e.g., do as I say, not as I do!).

The interesting change takes place in the *ShowSomeStructureStuff() function*. Notice that we are using the structure pointer that we defined back in *setup()*. When you run the program, the output becomes:

Original data

```
               Name = Jack Purdum
              phone = 2222222
   sizeof structure = 2
```

Revised data

```
               Name = Jill Purdum
              phone = 2222222
   sizeof structure = 2
```

Note that we have gone from using 44 bytes in the function to only 2 bytes. (Obviously I'm running the code on an Arduino because the pointer is only 2 bytes instead of 4 bytes.) Okay, so what is this statement in the function all about:

```
Serial.println( (*s).Name);
```

Well, because we are using a pointer, we have to use indirection on the structure pointer, *s*, to access the structure data. The problem is that the dot operator has higher precedence than the indirection operator, so we need to parenthesize the pointer first, and then use the dot operator to access the *name[]* data.

The Arrow Operator, '->'

So, just how lazy are we C programmers? Lazy enough to create a special operator for using indirection on pointers to structures and unions. (You can also use it with C++ object pointers. More on that in Chapter 12.) The *arrow operator, '→', is formed by combining the minus sign ('-') and the "greater than" ('>') symbols (i.e., ->) and is used to dereference a structure or union member when used with a pointer.*

Replace these lines in the *ShowSomeStructureStuff()* function from Listing 9.3:

```
Serial.print("              Name = ");
Serial.println( (*s).Name);
Serial.print("             phone = ");
Serial.println( (*s).Phone);
```

with these lines:

```
Serial.print("              Name = ");
Serial.println(s->Name);
Serial.print("             phone = ");
```

```
Serial.println(s->Phone);
```

Note how we are now using the arrow operator to access the contents of structure members *Name[]* and *Phone*. A new operator just to save two keystrokes! Yeah, but does the arrow operator use less memory. Nope. Both flavors use exactly the same flash and SRAM. Either form works fine, but you'll be more likely to be asked to join other C programmers for a beer after work if you use the arrow operator. Your choice.

Escape Sequences

Okay, so what this all about?

```
Serial.println("Original data\n");
```

This statement uses the Serial monitor to cause a new line to be displayed on the monitor. The '\n' character is called the *newline character* and it creates a new line for the next set of output characters. The newline character is but one of a number of escape sequences available to you. Escape sequences are used to cause specific action to take place on the output stream. While we use these escape sequences most often in displaying data on the Serial monitor, they can also be written for other output devices, like text files and printers. These escape sequences are shown in Table 9.1.

Table 9.1. C escape sequences

Escape Sequence	ASCII Value	Description
\a	7	Alarm, bell, buzzer
\b	8	Backspace
\f	12	Formfeed
\n	10	Newline
\r	13	Carriage return
\t	9	Tab
\v	11	Vertical tab
\\	92	Backslash
\'	39	Single quote mark
\”	34	Double quote mark

While you may not need to use escape sequences often, they can come in handy. Listing 9.4 shows an example using the tab escape sequence.

Listing 9.4. Using the tab escape sequence

```
void setup()
{
  Serial.begin(9600);

  Serial.println("There was an input error.");
  Serial.println("\tThere was an input error.");
}
void loop() {
}
```

Notice the tab escape sequence at the start of the second string. (If you just wanted to output an escape sequence by itself, you can use single quotes.) The output looks like:

```
There was an input error.
        There was an input error.
```

Most tab controls are set to 8 characters, so the second sentence appears 8 characters to the right of the first sentence. The number of spaces isn't etched in stone, so you need to experiment with other output device.

Structures are a very useful tool to hang on your programming belt. If you think about it, structures are perfect if you're working with data that have the look of a database record. In other languages that don't support structures, the programmer often resorts to parallel arrays that share similar names. C structures allow you to avoid that ambiguity.

Typedefs in C

In a sense, C structures allow you to define a new, complex data type if you choose to do so. The keyword *typedef* in C allows you to give new names to existing C data types, including structures. The *typedef* can be very simple, or complex, depending upon your needs. The basic syntax for a *typedef* is:

```
typedef expression1 expression2
```

where *expression1* is the existing name for the data type and *expression2* is the new name, or alias, that you wish to use for *expression1*. For example, suppose you have two variables named frequency1 and frequency2 that you wish to define as *unsigned long* variables. Let's further assume you don't want to have to type in *unsigned long* each time you define such a variable. Instead, you would like to refer to them as *ulong* variables. You could do this with:

```
typedef unsigned long ulong;
ulong frequency1, frequency2;
```

A more common use is to typedef a C structure. Using our earlier service example as a base, we could do this (note the *typedef* keyword at the top of the structure):

```
typedef struct serviceCompany {
  int  ID;
  char Name[20];
  char PW[10];
  long arriveDepart[2];
  long Phone;
} customerRecord;          // This is the alias
```

Now you have an alias name of *customerRecord* that you can use to define a structure variable (or an array of them):

```
customerRecord veroBeachNeighborhood[10];
```

Another interesting property of *typedefs* is that *the alias applies to all variables defined in the current statement*. For example, this statement:

```
char *s, c;
```

defines variable *s* as a pointer to *char*, but *c* is just a simple *char* variable. However:

```
typedef char* cPtr;
cPtr s, c;
```

defines both *s* and *c* to be *char* pointer variables! You need to be mindful of this little syntax nuance. I would have a lot more rounded forehead if I hadn't forgotten this little detail more often than I'd care to admit. Indeed, it's because of this that I probably don't use *typedefs* as often as I should.

Symbolic Constants (#defines) versus typedefs

At first blush, it may appear that a *typedef* is just another way of using a symbolic constant that you create using a *#define* directive, but that interpretation is not correct.

First, a *typedef* can only be constructed using defined data types. Symbolic constants, on the other hand, are often used to assign numeric values to the constant. Indeed, we frequently use symbolic constants to get rid of "magic numbers" in the code. You can't do that with a *typedef*.

Second, symbolic constants are simple *textual* substitutions that are performed on the source code. All of the work is done by the C preprocessor, not the C compiler. A *typedef*, however, is processed by the C compiler itself and is responsible for its interpretation.

A *typedef* is a good way to create an alias for a complex data type, so it's worthwhile remembering them.

Unions

I think unions are an extremely useful data structure that C makes available to you. That said, you don't see unions used all that often. Part of the reason for their limited use is because they have a narrowly-defined purpose. Their syntax looks very similar to that of structures, but they serve an entirely different purpose. *A union is a small chunk of memory that is capable of holding different data types.* Like a structure, there are two ways to define a *union*. The first is to have a *union* declaration followed by its definition, as in:

```
union mystery {                   // declare the union...
   char bytes[8];                 // These are union members...
   int num;
   long bigNum;
   float fpNum;
};

mystery myUnion;                  // define a union variable
```

Or, you can combine the declaration with a definition:

```
union mystery {
    char bytes[8];
    int num;
    long bigNum;
    float fpNum;
 } myUnion;
```

Both versions yield you a *union* variable named *myUnion*. The *union members* of *myUnion* are *bytes[]*, *num*, *bigNum*, and *fpNum*. Just like structures have a structure tag which you use to identify which structure you are using, *union*s have a *union tag* that serves the same purpose. In our example, *mystery* is the *union* tag for *myUnion*. You can omit the *union* tag if you are just defining a single *union* variable and won't be using that variable in a function call. I prefer to always have a *union* tag even if it is redundant. If nothing else, a *union* tag helps document the *union*'s use if the tag name is selected well.

Memory Used by a union

Given the definition of the *myUnion* variable, it would appear that, for an Uno, the *union* requires 18 bytes of memory (8 bytes for the *byte* array *bytes[]*, 2 for *num*, 4 for *bigNum*, and 4 for *fpNum).* Wrong! (You know me well enough by now to know that I wouldn't have made such a big deal about *myUnion*'s size in memory if the answer was that obvious.) *The Bucket size for a union always equals the storage required for largest data member that is contained within the union.* For *myUnion*, the *bytes[]* array requires the most memory for storage (i.e., 8 bytes), so that is how big the *myUnion* bucket is in memory. What? How useful is it if the *myUnion* can only hold 8 of 18 required bytes?

Ok, that's not the purpose of a *union*. A *union* is a small storage place (i.e., a buffer) that is capable of holding a single, *different,* data type. True, you could define all of the *union* members as simple data types, but then you'd be using 18 bytes where you might be able to get away with only 8 bytes with a *union*. When you're programming microcontrollers, 10 bytes might be important. An example might help.

The Endian Problem

Our microcontrollers all have EEPROM capability for storing data. However, some of the EEPROM *write()* functions (e.g., the Arduino's) are byte-oriented. That is, they can only write one byte at a time to a specific EEPROM memory address. An assignment to a *union* has the same syntax you used for a structure, using the dot operator. So, suppose we have this code
fragment:

```
int sensorState = 1;
// ...some code...
myUnion.num = sensorState;
```

Now the union holds the *int* value of *sensorState*. If we want to store the *int* value of *sensorState*, but can only write one byte at a time to EEPROM, how do we do that? The problem is complicated by the fact that the binary representation for the *int* as stored in memory could be either

```
00000000 0000001 // Big endian-from most significant byte to
                 // least significant byte
```

or

```
00000001 0000000 // Little endian—from least significant byte to
                 // most significant byte
```

With a Big Endian organization, the 16-bit *int* is stored with the first byte holding bits 8-15 and the second byte holding bits 0-7. With Little Endian, the first byte is bits 0-7 and the second byte is bits 7-15. If the *int*s "endianess" gets messed up, what should have the decimal value of 1 ends up with the decimal value of 256 because the organization is wrong. Not good.

The good news is that, with a *union*, we don't need to worry about the "endianess" of the data as long as we write and read the EEPROM data consistently. Given a byte-oriented *EEPROM.write()* function:

```
for (int i = 0; i < sizeof(int); i++) {
      EEPROM.write(memoryAddress + i, myUnion.bytes[i]);
}
```

would work fine. The *for* loop writes the *int* value of *sensorState* to EEPROM. We do this by assigning *myUnion.num* the *int* value of *sensorState*, but we extract the data from the *union* one byte at a time using the *bytes[]* array! The *union* could care less about what you do with the *union* data, but it does assume you know what you're doing because *union* error messages are few and far between.

Suppose that sensorState equals 1 and the data are stored in Little Endian format starting at memory address 0 (i.e., *memoryAddress* = 0). Going through the *for* loop passes, we would see:

```
EEPROM.write(0, 0b00000001); // write MSB first, myUnion,bytes[0]
EEPROM.write(1, 0b00000000); // ...then LSB, myUnion,bytes[1]
```

The result would be an *int* stored in EEPROM. Note how we used the *union*. We stored the *int* into the union with *myUnion.num*, but we extracted that *int* one byte at a time from the buffer space using the *bytes[]* array. It is the programmer's responsibility to keep track of what is actually in the *union*.

Now, if we want to retrieve that EEPROM data, we would use:

```
for (int i = 0; i < sizeof(int); i++) {
      EEPROM.read(memoryAddress + i, myUnion.bytes[i]);
}
sensorState = myUnion.num;
```

In this example, we byte-read from EEPROM memory into the *union* placing each byte we read into the *bytes[]* array After the loop finishes reading the data, we then extract it from the *union* as an *int* (*myUnion.num*), which we then assign into *sensorState*.

Note that we don't need to worry about the endianess of the data as long as we write/read them in a consistent manner. We do this virtually any time we need to write data to EEPROM. Some SD card libraries are byte-oriented, too, so the *union* would be useful there as well.

The Arduino IDE uses the GCC compiler and it is the compiler's code generator that determines which endian style it uses. As it turns out, GCC is a Little Endian compiler. The advantage of using a *union* is that, if we take this code to a different compiler that uses Big Endian data organization, our code will still work. It works because the *union* allows us to abstract from the endian problem.

The rules for using a *union* are pretty simple: whatever is placed into the *union* can be withdrawn in whatever manner makes sense. Unions are useful for temporarily storing different data values without having to define a temporary variable for each data type necessary. Unions can save you some memory.

Data Logging-- Secure Data (SD) Cards

In another beginning C book I wrote, I suggested using EEPROM data and a *union* for storing data. On reflection, that is an RDI (i.e., Really Dumb Idea). The use of a *union* is okay, but using EEPROM for data logging is not. The reason is because: 1) on-chip EEPROM data is usually very limited (e.g., 1024 bytes on an Uno), 2) reading and writing EEPROM data is usually slower than flash memory, 3) most EEPROM chips have a limited write-cycle life of about 100,000, and 4) some forms of EEPROM can only hold their state for 10 years at room temperature.

Also, while 100,000 sounds like a lot, if you were storing samples from a sensor every second and storing them in EEPROM, your data could start going wonky after only 1.15 days! (You just did the math, didn't you?) Perhaps a better idea for data logging is to use a Secure Data (SD) card.

SD storage is kinda neat because you have a variety of ways to use the SD card. Figures 9.2 through 9.4 show some of the options. The board shown in Figure 9.2, which uses the SPI interface, costs under $3. The SD holder in Figure 9.3 is integral to the TFT SPI display, and most such displays cost

Figure 9.2. SD card board using SPI interface.

Figure 9.3. TFT display with SD card holder. (Note SD pinouts on left side.)

Figure 9.4. Teensy 3.5 with integrated micro SD card holder.

less than $10. As the labeling on the display states, it too uses the SPI interface. You can see the SD access pins on thc lcft side of Figure 9.3.

The SD holder in Figure 9.4 shows a Teensy 3.5 (T3.5) which has an onboard SD card holder. The T3.5 costs about $25, but has pretty impressive specs (32-bit ARM Cortex-M4 running at 120MHz, 512K of flash memory, 256K of SRAM, and 4K EEPROM). The first program we test uses the T3.5 and its onboard SD card socket. The Teensy 4.1 was just introduced and, unlike the Teensy 4.0, it also has an SD holder on it. (While the T4.1 costs about $27, it also supports Ethernet connections and 8Mb of flash memory and 1Mb of SRAM.)

Testing an SD Card

To test either the Teensy 4.1 (T4.1) or the Teensy 3.5 (T3.5), simply insert the micro SD card into the slot and load the code shown in Listing 9.5. The program begins with two *#include* preprocessor directives to establish the code for using an SD card with the Teensy. The *theInvitation[]* array is a long quote from my favorite poem. Recall that the newline character ('\n') causes a carriage return/line feed to occur when being displayed, so what follows after that character appears on a new line.

Everything takes place in *setup()* in the demo program shown in Listing 9.5. The call to *SD.begin(BUILTIN_SDCARD)* attempts to initialize the SD card and issues an error message if the initialization fails. The most likely cause of failure is using an unformatted SD card. (There are plenty of resources online that tell you how to format your SD card.) The call to *RemoveFile("POEM.TXT")* deletes the file. We did this so we don't keep appending new copies of the poem to the file as we test it. If you do want to append to the existing file, simply comment out the *RemoveFile()* call.

The statement:

```
myFile = SD.open("POEM.TXT", FILE_WRITE);
```

opens the text file for writing. If the file does not exist, it creates it. From this point on, all action with respect to the file is done through a FILE handle named *myFile*. The statement:

```
myFile.write(theInvitation,sizeof(theInvitation));//write to file
```

does the heavy lifting, writing the contents of the *theInvitation[]* array to the SD card. (To show how tired I am, I spend almost 5 minutes looking for the file on my development hard drive. Another flatforehead moment–the search is a lot faster if you look on the SD card!)

Listing 9.5. Using Teensy 3.5 with onboard SD socket

```
#include <SD.h>
#include <SPI.h>

const int chipSelect = 4;      // Change for your board/SD card
int RemoveFile(char *fileName);

File myFile;
        // Excerpt from The Invitation by Oriah Mountain Dreamer
char theInvitation[] = {"It doesn't interest me\nto know where you
live or how much money you have.\nI want to know if you can get
up\nafter the night of grief and despair\nweary and bruised to the
bone\nand do what needs to be done\nto feed the children.\n\n"};

void setup()
{
  char c;
  int flag = 0;

  Serial.begin(9600);
  while (!Serial) {
    ;                  // Serial object instantiate...
  }

  Serial.print("Initializing SD card...");
  if (!SD.begin(chipSelect)) {
    Serial.println("initialization failed! Card in place?");
  } else {
    Serial.println("initialization done.");

    flag = RemoveFile("POEM.TXT");// Comment out to append to file

    myFile = SD.open("POEM.TXT", FILE_WRITE);

    if (myFile) {                     // If we could create/write...
      myFile.write(theInvitation, sizeof(theInvitation)); // write
      myFile.close(); // close the file:
      Serial.println("Done writing.\n");
    } else {
      Serial.println("No file handle for POEM.TXT");         //
oops...
```

```
    }

    myFile = SD.open("POEM.TXT");  // reopen for reading
    if (myFile) {
      Serial.println("\n\tPOEM.TXT:");

      while (myFile.available()) { // Something to read?
       c = (char) myFile.read();
        if (c == 0x5C)                              //Backslash?
          Serial.println(" ");
        if (c == 0x0A || c == 0x0D) {    // Look for LF or CR
          Serial.print('\n');
        } else {
          Serial.print(c);\
        }
      }
      myFile.close();                              //We're done
      Serial.println("\nDone reading.");
    } else {
      Serial.println("Can't open POEM.TXT");      // if open failed
    }
  }
}

void loop()
{  }

/*****
  Purpose: To delete the file from the SD card. This prevents
           appending the test message to the file each time the
           program is run.

  Argument list:
    char *fileName      the name of the file to remove

  Return value:
    int                 0 on error, 1 on success

  CAUTION: Assume the SD class object exists
*****/
int RemoveFile(char *fileName)
{
  return ((int) SD.remove("POEM.TXT"));
}
```

Once the file is written, we close the file, re-open it, and then proceed to read the contents of the file and write it to the Serial object one character at a time. When there are no more characters to read, we close the file and we're done. Do a code walk-through to make sure you can follow what's being done.

Non-Teensy SD Card Holders

One of the nice things about having an onboard SD card socket is you don't need to concern yourself with wiring the socket for the desired interface. As you might guess from the *#include* in Listing 9.5, we're using the SPI (Serial Peripheral Interface) to access the SD card. As always, the heavy lifting is done for us using the Teensy's SD library. That's also pretty easy for the other microcontrollers, but with the other microcontrollers it is a little more difficult because pin placement on the SD boards is not in the least bit standardized.

If you're using an Arduino Uno, there are many Uno SD shields that plug directly into the Uno header sockets on its board. Again, this means no wiring of the SD socket to the board. The shields can be purchased online for less than $2. You can also purchase an Arduino Nano shield like the one shown in Figure 9.5 for about $5. The SD socket is on the "under" side of the board. Note that the board has a socket for the Nano and a holder for a button battery to power a Real Time Clock (RTC) and a level converter to manage the 5V to 3.3V needed for the SD socket. The software for the Uno or Nano can be

Figure 9.5. An Arduino Nano SD shield.

taken from the *File-->Examples-->SD* menu option in the IDE.

Warning!

The ESP32 and STM32 can use an SD board similar to those shown in Figure 9.2. *However*, I had one of these boards in my junk drawer for who knows how long. I pulled it out, attached it to the STM32 using the SPI interface, and proceeded to spend an embarrassingly long time getting it *not* to work. I kept checking my wiring and rechecking my wiring...no joy.

I then suspected that I needed to update my SD library, so I searched and installed new libraries. Still no joy. Finally, I put a scope on the card and noticed that data pins either weren't changing state or, at best, the pulse chain was "mushy". Only then did it dawn on me that this old board was intended for 5V operation only, but I was feeding it 3.3V. As stupid as that sounds, it's common for boards not to specify the voltage (just Vcc) but I assumed it needed 3.3V. Yeah, I know...pretty dumb, *but*...if I had fed it the 5V the SD board wanted, that would have put those 5V on the STM32/ESP32 I/O pins (which expect 3.3V) and I likely would have created a silicon brick. Moral: Don't make assumptions about the board like one idiot I know. Instead, make sure you know the operating voltage of your SD board.

As we mentioned in Chapter 1, the ESP32 can have as few as 30 pins and as many as 38. Even if we can agree that pin GPIO23 is the MISO pin for the SPI interface, the physical location for that pin could be physical pin 15 on one board and physical pin 18 on another. I've also seen one ESP32 board where GPIO23 was also used for the onboard LED, where most other boards often use GPIO02 for the LED pin. Because of this "non-standard" pin assignments, making a "generic" PCB for all ESP32's is difficult. Just like non-standard rail gauges for early railroad lines hindered US rail development, I think that this "pin disparity" has hurt the adoption of the ESP32 family despite some impressive resources on the ESP32 board.

The ESP32 has some different ways of doing things, too. For example, their spec sheet says:

> ESP32-WROOM-32 integrates a 4 MB SPI flash, which is connected to GPIO6, GPIO7, GPIO8, GPIO9, GPIO10 and GPIO11. These six pins cannot be used as regular GPIOs.

This is why many ESP32 boards don't even make GPIO pins 6-11 available on their board. It is probably less confusing to just leave them off the board than trying to support a board that makes them available. (Most 38-pin boards do bring those pins out.)

Despite all of these limitations, the ESP32 has features other boards don't bring to the table. Virtually all of the ESP32 boards support WiFi and Bluetooth connectivity plus a 180-240MHz clock, 1Mb (or more) of flash memory and usually 300+Kb of SRAM. Because of the non-standard pinouts for the ESP32 boards, most vendors provide a diagram of the pinout for the board you ordered. (You should ask your vendor if they supply such a pinout map before you buy.) *In all ESP32 code you see in this book, check to make sure your board pin maps to the pin shown in any source code listing.*

Using an SD card with Arduino Nano

A common use for an SD card is to record data that need to be saved for some reason. We thought we'd present an example of writing a Comma Separated Variable (CSV) file to the SD card. (See: https://en.wikipedia.org/wiki/Comma-separated_values) The reason for using a CSV file is because there are a lot of programs that can import a CSV file (e.g., Excel) for further analysis, charting, and a variety of other data uses.

The format for a CSV file is usually in tabular form, with column headers for the variables and the rows representing the observations (or cases) for those variables. In our simple example, we're going to record a golfer's name, their 18-hole score, and the course that was played. The raw data are "dummied" in the project's source code file:

```
int scores[]     = {88, 78, 82, 82, 94, 72};
char *columns[] = {"Player", "Score", "Course"};
char *player[]  = {"Katie", "Jack", "Al", "Stu", "Jane", "John"};
char *course[]  = {"CCI", "Augusta", "Legendary", "Pinehurst",
                   "Bunker Hill", "Pine Valley"};
```

Using the Right-Left Rule, you can see that the *columns[]* array is an array of pointers to *char*. The *players[]* array and the *course[]* are also arrays of pointers to char. The *scores[]* array is simply an array of *int*s. You can tell that the data are constructed "in parallel" in this example. That is, there are three variables (Player, Score, and Course) and there are six observations for each variable.

The format for a CSV file is simple, but strict. First, the data in CSV files are typically stored as plain ASCII text, which makes reading them very simple. Second, the first row of data in the file contains the column headers (i.e., variable) names, or the *columns[]* array in our example. Third, each value in the table is separated from the next variable by a comma character. Fourth, each data row ends with a newline character ('\n'). That's it! Now, let's see the code that does this. The complete program is presented in Listing 9.6.

First, we establish the Serial object and inform the user we are initializing the SD reader. If something goes wrong (e.g., they forgot to put a formatted card in the reader), we inform the user and call the *MyExit()* function to end the program. (The *exit()* function would normally be called here, which returns control to the operating system. However, since we don't have an operating system, I just wrote a routine that enters an infinite *while* loop. It's inelegant, but I don't know a better alternative that doesn't involve interrupts.)

If the SD can initialize successfully, the call to *OpenDataFile()* is made to acquire a file handle for referencing the file (*myFile*). If *myFile* is non-null, the file was created successfully (or opened for appending) and we write the column headers to the CSV file with a call to *WriteColumnHeaders()*. The code:

```
   for (i = 0; i < col; i++) {
       myFile.write(columns[i]);
       myFile.write(",");
  }
  myFile.write("\n");
```

is typical for writing CSV data. The ASCII string for the column name (e.g., *columns[i]*) is written, followed immediately by a comma, followed by the next column name. This continues until all variable names are written to the file. The final *write()* method call writes a newline character ("\n") to the file which serves as an end-of-row marker.

Listing 9.6. Writing a CSV file to an SD card.

```
/*
  Write a CSV file to an SD card for an Arduino Nano
  Ver 1.0, June 14, 2020, Jack Purdum. Start program */

#include <SPI.h>
#include <SD.h>

#define CHIPSELECT  10    // Works for the Arduino Nano. See
pinout for microcontroller
// and the pin for chip select CS of SPI interface
File myFile;

int scores[]     = {88, 78, 82, 82, 94, 72};
char *columns[] = {"Player", "Score", "Course"};
char *player[]  = {"Katie", "Jack", "Al", "Stu", "Jane", "John"};
char *course[]  = {"CCI", "Augusta", "Legendary", "Pinehurst",
                   "Bunker Hill", "Pine Valley"};
//====================== Prototype ======================
void MyExit();
```

```
int  OpenDataFile(char *fileName);
int  WriteColumnHeaders(char *columns[], int col);
int  WriteDataFile(char *player[], int scores[], char *course[],
int row);

void setup() {
  int flag;

  Serial.begin(9600);
  while (!Serial) {
    ;          // wait for serial port...
  }
  Serial.print("Initializing SD card...");
  if (!SD.begin(CHIPSELECT)) {
    Serial.println("\n\nInitialization failed!");
    Serial.println("Make sure formatted SD card is inserted.");
    MyExit();                              // Bail out
  }
  Serial.println("Initialization completed successfully.");
  flag = OpenDataFile("Scores.csv");        // Open new data file
  if (flag) {
    flag = WriteColumnHeaders(columns, 3);  // Do CSV column
headers
    flag = WriteDataFile(player, scores, course, 5); // Write data
    myFile.close();                                  // We're done
    Serial.println("File write completed.");
  } else {
    Serial.println("Cannot open Scores.csv");       // Not good...
  }
}
void loop()
{
}

/*****
  Purpose: To prevent further program execution. A clunky way of
           ending a C program in an environment where there is no
            OS.

  Argument list:
    void

  Return value:
    void
*****/
void MyExit()
{
  while (true) {
    ;
  }
}

/*****
  Purpose: To write the column headers for a CSV file

  Argument list:
    char *columns[]   the column heads for the table
    int col           the number of columns
```

```
  Return value:
    int               0 on error, 1 okay
*****/
int WriteColumnHeaders(char *columns[], int col)
{
  int i;
  for (i = 0; i < col; i++) {
    myFile.write(columns[i]);
    myFile.write(",");
  }
  myFile.write("\n");
}

/*****
  Purpose: To open an SD card for file writing

  Argument list:
    char *fileName    The name of the data file

  Return value:
    int               0 on error, 1 okay
*****/
int OpenDataFile(char *fileName)
{
  myFile = SD.open(fileName, FILE_WRITE);
  if (myFile == 0) {
    Serial.print("error opening ");
    Serial.println(fileName);
    return 0;
  }
  return 1;
}

/*****
  Purpose: To write a list of data to the data file

  Argument list:
    char *player[]    The names of the players
    int scores[]      The 18 hole scores
    char *course[]    The course where played
    int row           the number of entries

  Return value:
       int            0 on error, 1 okay
*****/
int WriteDataFile(char *player[], int scores[], char *course[],
int row)
{
  char buff[5];
  int j;
  for (j = 0; j < row; j++) {
    myFile.write(player[j]);
    myFile.write(",");
    itoa(scores[j], buff, DEC);      // Need to convert to ASCII
    myFile.write(buff);
    myFile.write(",");
    myFile.write(course[j]);
```

```
    myFile.write("\n");
  }
}
```

After the variable names are written to the file, we call *WriteDataFile()* to write the rows of data to the file. The code is very similar to that for the column headers, except for:

```
    itoa(scores[j], buff, DEC);       //convert to ASCII
    myFile.write(buff);
```

The *itoa()* function converts the *int* data in *scores[]* to their ASCII equivalent and stores it temporarily in *buff[]*. The contents of *buff[]* is then written to the file. The conversion is necessary because the *scores[]* array holds binary data, but we want to have only ASCII data in the file. After all row data have been written, the file is closed and the program ends.

If we did things correctly, we should be able to directly load the CSV file into any program that can import a CSV data file. In our case, I opened Excel and read the file. The result is seen in Figure 9.6.

I20

	A	B	C	D
1	Player	Score	Course	
2	Katie	88	CCI	
3	Jack	78	Augusta	
4	Al	82	Legendary	
5	Stu	82	Pinehurst	
6	Jane	94	Bunker Hill	
7	John	72	Pine Valley	
8				

Figure 9.6. The CSV file displayed using Excel.

The program changes required for the using other microcontrollers are minimal, especially for the Teensy since the SD card holder is on the board for the T3.5 and the T4.1. Using the Serial Peripheral Interface (SPI) greatly simplifies using an SD card in your programs. Table 9.2 shows the pins you can use for the SPI interface for the various microcontrollers. (Keep in mind the difference in the pin voltage tolerance for each microcontroller.) When you do interface your SD holder to the microcontroller, check to see if there is a special SD library for that microcontroller (e.g., STM32SD).

Table 9.2. SPI pins for various microcontrollers

SPI Pin	Nano[1]	Teensy 4.1[2]	STM32[3]	ESP32[4]
SS	10	10	PA4	GPIO5
MOSI	11	11	PA7	GPIO23
MISO	12	12	PA6	GPIO19
SCLK	13	13	PA5	GPIO18

1. See Figure 1.9.
2. See Figure 1.10. (Has 2 SPI ports)
3. See Figure 1.11. (Has 2 SPI ports)
4. See Figure 1.13. (Has 2 SPI posts)

Using EEPROM

We talked about EEPROM memory in Chapter 1. Perhaps the most frequent use for EEPROM is to store "settings" type of data that are rarely changed, but needed in the program. The type of data stored could be anything, from the default room temperature for a thermostat to the foreground color for text in a program. (Some people are color blind, you know.) The point is, EEPROM data allows customization for certain program parameters that don't get changed very often. Typically, EEPROM data are read as part of the Step 1, Initialization Step of a program.

Only the Arduino family has "real" EEPROM storage. The other microcontrollers emulate it using a dedicated chunk of flash memory instead of standard EEPROM. We will take a look at the Arduino EEPROM code first. A program to read and write to EEPROM is presented in Listing 9.7.

I wrote this so you'd get some practice using a *union* and also using pointers. Truth be told, you could redo the EEPROM *Read??()* functions to return the data type that you're interested in, but I wanted you to use pointers instead. You can use the return value versions later; stick with the pointer practice for now.

Note how I use symbolic constants for offsets into the EEPROM memory space. I think symbolic constants make it easier to read and understand what's going on. Also, note how I use the *sizeof()* operator when defining the constants to make the code more portable between 8-bit and 32-bit controllers. It's okay to have "holes" in the address space. For example, if I write my name into EEPROM, it takes 12 bytes (including the space and null), but the room temperature value is written at address 21. This leaves an 8-byte "hole" in the EEPROM space. Yes, I am wasting some EEPROM space, but I've never fully used the available EEPROM space anyway, so I'm not going to worry about it. You could "pack" the addresses if you want, but if the owner's name changes, you may need to rewrite the entire EEPROM space. To me, that's not worth the effort.

Listing9.7. Write/read EEPROM to Arduino Nano

```
/*
  Write a CSV file to an SD card for an Arduino Nano
  Ver 1.0, June 14, 2020, Jack Purdum. Start program
*/
#include <EEPROM.h>

#define OWNERNAMEADDRESS      0  // Set the EEPROM offset
addresses
#define TEMPERATUREADDRESS    21
#define MILEAGEADDRESS        TEMPERATUREADDRESS + sizeof(int)
#define MAXNAMELENGTH         20

union settings {         // Declare the union member list...
  char buffer[MAXNAMELENGTH];
  int smallNumber;
  float bigNumber;
} myUnion;               // ...and define one

//=========== Write EEPROM Routines ==========================
/*****
  Purpose: To store the owner's name in EEPROM

  Argument List:
    char *name      pointer to owner's name

  Return value:
    void
*****/
void WriteOwnerName(char *name)
{
  int index;
  int nameLength = strlen(name);
  for (index = 0; index < nameLength; index++) {
    EEPROM.write(OWNERNAMEADDRESS + index, name[index]);
  }
}
```

```
/*****
  Purpose: To store the default room temperature in EEPROM

  Argument List:
    union settings myUnion

  Return value:
    void
*****/
void WriteRoomTemp(union settings myUnion)
{
  int index;
                                          // Abstract Endian issues away
  for (index = 0; index < sizeof(int); index++) {
    EEPROM.write(TEMPERATUREADDRESS + index,
myUnion.buffer[index]);
  }
}
/*****
    Purpose: To store the car mileage in EEPROM

    Argument List:
      union settings myUnion

    Return value:
      void
*****/
void WriteCarMileage(union settings myUnion)
{
  int index;

  for (index = 0; index < sizeof(float); index++) {
    EEPROM.write(MILEAGEADDRESS + index, myUnion.buffer[index]);
  }
}
//============== Read EEPROM Routines ============================
/*****
  Purpose: To read the owner's name in EEPROM

  Argument List:
    char *name      pointer to owner's name

  Return value:
    void
*****/
void ReadOwnerName(char *name)
{
  int index;
  for (index = 0; index < MAXNAMELENGTH; index++) {
    name[index] = EEPROM.read(OWNERNAMEADDRESS + index);
    if (name[index] == NULL)
      break;
  }
}

/*****
  Purpose: To read the default room temperature in EEPROM
```

```
  Argument List:
    union settings myUnion    the union structure for extraction
    int *temp                 pointer to the temp from setup()

  Return value:
    void
*****/
void ReadRoomTemp(union settings myUnion, int *temp)
{
  int index;
  for (index = 0; index < sizeof(int); index++) {
    myUnion.buffer[index] = EEPROM.read(TEMPERATUREADDRESS +
index);
  }
  *temp = myUnion.smallNumber;      // Copy temp to pointer
}
/*****
  Purpose: To store the car mileage in EEPROM

  Argument List:
    union settings myUnion    the union structure for extraction
    float *miles              pointer to mileage in setup()

  Return value:
    void
*****/
void ReadCarMileage(union settings myUnion, float * miles)
{
  int index;
  for (index = 0; index < sizeof(float); index++) {
    myUnion.buffer[index] = EEPROM.read(MILEAGEADDRESS + index);
  }
  *miles = myUnion.bigNumber;
}

void setup()
{
  char owner[20];
  int roomTemp;
  float mileage;
  Serial.begin(9600);

  WriteOwnerName("Jack Purdum");    // Write owner's name
  myUnion.smallNumber = 74;         // The default room
temperature
  WriteRoomTemp(myUnion);
  myUnion.bigNumber = 58908.5;      // Car mileage as a float
  WriteCarMileage(myUnion);
  Serial.println("Data written to EEPROM. Now reading back...");
  delay(1000L);                     // Wait a second...
  ReadOwnerName(owner);             // Now read everything back...
  ReadRoomTemp(myUnion, &roomTemp);
  ReadCarMileage(myUnion, &mileage);
  Serial.print("\nOwner:            ");
  Serial.println(owner);
  Serial.print("Room temperature: ");
  Serial.println(roomTemp);
  Serial.print("Car mileage:      ");
```

```
  Serial.println(mileage);
}
void loop()
{
}
```

The *Write?()* EEPROM functions are similar in that they pass in the union as the function argument. *WriteOwnerName()* is different in that it writes and passes the owner's name in directly as a *char* array. The function should check to make sure the length of the name isn't longer than 19 bytes (still need that null character at the end). That's left as an exercise for the reader.

The other two functions pass in the *union* and write the numeric data one byte at a time from the *union*. This gets around the Endian issue discussed earlier in the chapter. Note how we use the *sizeof()* operator to determine the number of bytes to write from *buffer[]*. Hard-coding the size of an *int* would make the code non-portable between 8-bit and 32-bit architectures.

The *Read?()* EEPROM functions simply reverse the write process, reading the data back from EEPROM from the appropriate offset. Obviously, we didn't need to use the *union* or pointers to the numeric variables to *roomTemp* or *mileage*. Rather, we chose to do it that way to illustrate using *unions* and pointers. You could write an *int ReadEEPROMInt()* and *float ReadEEPROMFloat()* functions, pass in the proper offset, and then return the value that was read.

The EEPROM library supports *EEPROM.put()* and *EEPROM.get()* which can be used to write and read primitive data types (e.g., *char*, *int*, etc.) to EEPROM. You may want to experiment with those methods, too.

The Teensy EEPROM reading and writing is the same as for the Arduino family, except it is done without using actual EEPROM memory. Instead, a chunk of flash memory is dedicated as a blocked EEPROM address space. To the user, the difference isn't noticeable.

STM32 and ESP32 EEPROM

Both of these microcontrollers also use a block of flash memory, but unlike the Teensy, you are responsible for defining where that block of pseudo-EEPROM is to reside. For the STM32F103 series, I use the following function:

```
/*****
  Purpose: The STM32 does not actually have any EEPROM, so we have
           to fake it with flash memory. This code defines where
           the page in flash memory resides that is used as EEPROM

  Argument list:
    void

  Return value:
    Void
 *****/
void DefineEEPROMPage()
{
   EEPROM.PageBase0 = 0x801f000;      // EEPROM base address.
   EEPROM.PageSize  = 0x400;          // 1024 bytes of EEPROM
 }
```

In this example, I defined the base EEPROM address to be 0x801F000 and set aside 1024 bytes to be treated as EEPROM. Once this is done, the read and write routines for EEPROM are the same as they are for the Arduino and Teensy microcontrollers. Obviously, you need to call *DefineEEPROMPage()* before you attempt to use any other EEPROM calls.

The ESP32 is similar in that is also uses flash memory, but it only reserves a maximum of 512 bytes for EEPROM use. You can reserve less if you wish using the syntax:

```
EEPROM.begin(100);        // Reserve 100 bytes of flash as EEPROM
```

This statement sets 100 bytes of flash for EEPROM use. Once the amount of EEPROM has been reserved, the read and write functions are similar *except* when writing to EEPROM:

```
EEPROM.write(0, 'X'); // Save letter X to first EEPROM address
EEPROM.commit();      // Tell 'em you really mean it!
```

When you write data to EEPROM on the ESP32, you must call the *EEPROM.commit()* function after the *EEPROM.write()* call. This is a little less convenient than the other versions, but it works. Also, because you can only write a byte at a time, the max value for any byte is 255. This means you may have to use a *union* for multi-byte data.

Conclusion

This chapter covered structures, *typedef*s, and *union*s, using SD cards, and then presented a discussion of EEPROM memory as a replacement for SD card storage. Understanding structures and the advantages they represent is important, as it is conceptually a fundamental aspect of Object-Oriented Programming (OOP) and C++. The advantage of grouping disparate data under a single variable ID is a real boon to programmers. A *typedef* simply gives you the ability to alias simple or complex C data types under a new name. In a real sense, an SD card is a more versatile way of using a microcontroller as a data logging platform. We showed you how to write a CSV file which can then be imported into other programs for whatever need you may have. For limited program environmental variables, EEPROM is fine and may obviate the need for SD storage. Still, knowing how to use both types of storage can enhance the performance of our applications.

Exercises:

1. In two sentences or less, what is a C structure? What is a structure tag?
2. What is a structure declaration and how does it differ from a structure definition?
3. Take the golf example program and modify it to use a structure.
4. What is a *typedef*? Give an example that uses one. Why did you select that example to implement a *typedef*?
5. How is a *typedef* different than a symbolic constant?
6. Write a sample phone book that records the person's name, phone number, a birthday. You should use a structure in the code and save the data to an SD card in CSV format.
7. What is the purpose of using the *const* keyword with a function parameter in its signature?
8. Why is this statement:

```
myFile.write("\n");
```

used in the writing of the SD data?

Chapter 10 The C Preprocessor

If you go back far enough in C's history, you will find that the preprocessor wasn't even part of the C compiler. Rather, it was a separate pass that inspected the source code for preprocessor directives and made the textual substitutions associated with each directive. A *preprocessor directive is simply an action that results from an instruction that is to be processed by the preprocessor.* All C preprocessor directives have two things in common:

1. The directive is introduced by the sharp (#) sign
2. The directive is terminated by an invisible newline character. This means there is no semicolon at the end of a preprocessor directive.

You've used several preprocessor directives earlier in this book. The purpose of this chapter is to show some of the other directives that are available to you.

#define

We have discussed the *#define* directive before, and it is probably the easiest directive to understand. (Also, there are some flavors of the *#define* that we have not discussed, but will in this chapter.) We used the #define directive to create symbolic constants for a program. In many cases, the symbolic constant was introduced so we could get rid of "magic numbers" in the code. Hard-coding numbers makes the code less flexible and makes it more difficult to change those constants in the program. For example:

```
#define MAXELEMENTS 50

// Several hundred lines of code later...

  int myScores[MAXELEMENTS];
  // Some more code...
  for (index = 0; index < MAXELEMENTS; index++) {
    // do something...
  }
```

Here we are using *MAXELEMENTS* as a symbolic constant for the number of elements in an array. By convention, we define symbolic constants using uppercase letters. This makes them easy to spot when reading the source code. While you can use lowercase letters for symbolic constants, we don't think that's a good idea. You want the symbolic constants to stand out in the code listing.

Keep in mind that *symbolic constants are a textual substitution in the source code made by the preprocessor.* Symbolic constants are not variables. Because the preprocessor pass does *not* work in concert with the C compiler, symbolic constants *never* appear in a symbol table and they never have an lvalue. Indeed, the compiler never even "sees" them. Therefore, for a code block like:

```
for (index = 0; index < MAXELEMENTS; index++) {
    // do something...
}
```

what the compiler actually sees is:

```
for (index = 0; index < 50; index++) {
    // do something...
}
```

Again...the preprocessor simply does a textual substitution to the source code before the compiler gets its turn to read the code.

The advantage of symbolic constants is that it makes changes to the source code much easier and less error prone. If program demands change and you find you need 100 elements for the array, the change only requires a one-statement change:

```
#define MAXELEMENTS 100
```

When you recompile the program, the preprocessor finds every instance of MAXELEMENTS and substitutes 100 for its value. In theory, there could be dozens of places in the source code where MAXELEMENTS is used, but one simple change and a recompile "fixes" everything for the new array size.

Why not just do a global search-and-replace of "50" for "100" on the program code and be done with it? The answer is because, just as sure as you're sitting there reading this, you will have something like this in your code:

```
delay(5000);                // Pause for 5 seconds
```

With a global search-and-replace on the source code, you'd end up with:

```
delay(10000);                   // Pause for 5 seconds
```

which is probably not what you wanted. Using a symbolic constant avoids this kind of mistake and helps keep a nice round shape for your forehead.

#define as a Parameterized Macro

You can also use the *#define* directive to perform some other types of work for you. Consider Listing 10.1. Look at the *#define* on the first line of Listing 10.1. If you verbalize this directive, it tells the preprocessor: "Anytime you see *ELEMENTS(x)* in the source code, substitute the expression *(sizeof(x)/sizeof(x[0])*". If you use a variable within a *#define*, it is called a parametized macro definition. In other words, we are passing a parameter to this macro and letting the compiler handle its final expansion. Let's walk through the *for* loop in Listing 10.1:

```
for (index = 0; index < ELEMENTS(myArray); index++) {

             // After the processor
for (index=0;index<(sizeof(myArray)/sizeof(myArray[0]);index++) {
for (index = 0; index < (80/4); index++) {
for (index = 0; index < (20); index++) {    // The compiler sees
```

When the preprocessor finishes its pass, the source code looks like the second line above. We ran this program on the ESP32, so the size of an *int* is 4 bytes. Therefore, the *sizeof(myArray)* expression is 80 bytes (20 elements times 4 bytes each), as seen in the third line above. Because an *int* is 4 bytes, the expression *sizeof(x[0])* is 4 bytes. Dividing 80 by 4 gives 20, which is exactly the dimension of *myArray[]*.

So what?

You're thinking: "I know there are 20 elements in *myArray[]* so why not just code the test: *index < 20*?" You could, but suppose there are dozens of similar loops scattered throughout the program. Now you're back to the search-and-replace alternative which is fraught with all kinds of potential mischief as we've pointed out before. Suppose you increase *myArray[]* to 50 elements. Then the macro expansion becomes:

```
for (index = 0; index < ELEMENTS(myArray); index++) {
             // After the processor
for (index=0;index<(sizeof(myArray)/sizeof(myArray[0]);index++) {
```

```
for (index = 0; index < (200/4); index++) {
for (index = 0; index < (50); index++) {    // The compiler sees
```

Note how the preprocessor automatically adjusts the element count in the *for* loop (i.e., the shaded number). With the parametized macro, if you changed the number of elements in *myArray[]*, just recompile the program and any change is automatically factored into the program.

Listing 10.1. Using a parametized macro to figure out array sizes

```
#define ELEMENTS(x)  (sizeof(x)/sizeof(x[0]))

void setup() {
  int myArray[20];
  int index;

  Serial.begin(9600);
  while (!Serial) {
    ;                // Waste time until Serial is instantiated...
  }
  for (index = 0; index < ELEMENTS(myArray); index++) {
    myArray[index] = index * 10;
    Serial.println(myArray[index]);
  }
}
void loop() { }
```

Parameterized Macros versus const

Some programmers argue that they don't need a parametized macro. They point out they could use a *const* qualifier for the definition instead:

```
const int ELEMENTS = 50;
```

and use *ELEMENTS* in the second *for* loop expression. Yep, you could do that, but that's SDC to me. The reason is because using *const int* as part of the definition of *ELEMENTS* means that it can only be properly used in *int* expressions. This is because *ELEMENTS* appears in the symbol table with the attribute of *int*. Because of the *int* for ELEMENTS in its attribute list in the symbol table, if you don't want to draw a warning (or error) message from the compiler, you need to define one of these constants for every data type in the program. Not good.

The parametized macro, on the other hand, is *typeless*. That is, the textual substitution takes place before the compiler even sees it. *Because it doesn't have a data type attribute, you can use it in any expression.*

There are lots of parametized macros that we've used before, we just never told you about them. What looks like the *toupper()* "function" is actually a parametized macro. (See ctype.h.)

#define must be on a single line...sort of

All preprocessor directives are terminated by the (invisible) newline character ('\n'). In the IDE, the editor inserts a newline character each time you press the Enter key. Therefore, the preprocessor directive must be completely defined on the line where you are entering the directive.

Fortunately, that rule is not etched in stone. For example, many sorting algorithms require you to swap two values during the sort process. You could write a *swap()* function, but more often it is implemented as a parametized macro. Consider Listing 10.2

Listing 10.2. The swap() parametized macro

```
#define swap(x, y) {   \
     (x) ^= (y);       \
     (y) ^= (x);       \
     (x) ^= (y);       \
  }

void setup() {
  long a = 5L;          // Use storage modifiers to make it clear...
  long b = 10L;         // Overkill, but do it anyway.
  Serial.begin(9600);
  Serial.print("a = ");
  Serial.print(a);
  Serial.print("    b = ");
  Serial.println(b);
  swap(a, b);
  Serial.print("a = ");
  Serial.print(a);
  Serial.print("   b = ");
  Serial.println(b);
}
void loop() {
}
```

At the top of Listing 10.2 is a parametized macro that defines the *swap()* macro. To make it easier to read, I spread the macro definition over several lines even though I could have written it on a single line. Note the backslash character ('\') at the end of each line. The *backslash tells the preprocessor that this macro definition is continued on the next line*. Note that the last line (i.e., the closing parenthesis for the macro) does not have the continuation character. Also note that the macro does not have a semicolon at the end of the line, which helps to identify it as a macro.

You might be saying: "Okay, but I thought C statements had to end with a semicolon." They do, but always keep in mind that preprocessor directives are textual substitutions and that they are performed before the compiler is even loaded. This means the preprocessor directives themselves are not parsed by the compiler's error checking routines. Therefore, when the preprocessor sees the shaded line in Listing 10.2 (i.e., *swap(x, y)*), it replaces those shaded characters with the macro definition. Note that the semicolon is "already there", so when the preprocessor is done, that section of the code looks like:

```
    {
(x) ^= (y);
(y) ^= (x);
(x) ^= (y);
    }; // This semicolon not part of the macro but in source code.
```

to the compiler. The shaded part of the statement in Listing 10.2 is replaced with the shaded expansion shown above. Note that the semicolon is not shaded because it is not part of the macro definition.

Good news, bad news

First, the bad news. Every time the preprocessor sees the *swap()* macro, it replaces it with the block of code shown above. If you wrote a *swap()* function instead of a parameterized macro, then the code would only appear once in the generated code. In other words, parametized macros may bloat the code a bit because their code is inserted at every point in the program where the macro is used. If you use the macro in a lot of different places throughout the program, the bump up in code size may become important.

The good news is that, because it is a macro, it is typeless. That means you can pass different integral data types to the macro and it will work. (Because of the XOR operator, the macro will not work on floating point data.) If you were swapping *byte, char, int, long, unsigned int, unsigned long, long long*, or *unsigned long long* variables and using functions instead of the macro, you would need to write a *swap()* function for each of those different data types to avoid using casts or ignoring warnings. In that case, the memory savings might even be negative! You may gain a little speed because the overhead of a function call is avoided.

#undef

Just as you can *#define* a symbolic constant, you can also undefine the constant by using *#undef*. If the symbolic constant is in scope, *the #undef has the effect of removing that symbolic constant from the directive to the end of the source file*. While I have used *#undef* a few times over the years, I find it confusing to *#undef* something in the middle of a file. If I want to remove a constant from a program, I simply delete its *#define* or, if I think I'll put it back in the code later (like with *#define DEBUG*), I'll just do a single-line comment pair to remove the symbolic constant. Your choice.

Other Macros

There are many other macros hiding in various header files, some masquerading as functions. The short program in Listing 10.3 illustrates some that might be useful to you in other programs.

Listing 10.3. Using Other predefined macros

```
void setup() {
  Serial.begin(9600);
  Serial.print("line     = ");
  Serial.println(__LINE__);
  Serial.print("file     = ");
  Serial.println(__FILE__);
  Serial.print("function = ");
  Serial.println(__FUNCTION__);
  Serial.print("time     = ");
  Serial.println(__TIME__);
  Serial.print("date     = ");
  Serial.println(__DATE__);
}
void loop() {
}
```

When I ran the code, the output looked like:

```
line     = 6
file     = D:\CForMicros\Chap10\PredefMacros\PredefinedMacros.ino
function = setup
time     = 17:06:43
date     = Jun 17 2020
```

With a little thought, I'm sure you can find uses for these macros. Note that these macros all use two underscore characters before and after the macro name.

The inline Keyword

A related topic is the use of the *inline* functions in C. If you have a short C function that needs to execute as fast as possible, consider using an *inline* function. Recall from Chapter 6 that a lot of things need to happen each time a function is called. These "things" are the *function overhead* that is associated with calling a function (e.g., saving the instruction pointer, pushing/pulling parameters from the stack, etc.). The *inline* keyword allows you to replace the function code with inline code. For example:

```
inline int printable(char x) {
  if ( (x) < 32)
    return 0;
  else
    return 1;
}
// ...a bunch of code, and then:

flag = printable('a');
```

which means the compiler can replace the *printable()* function call with the *inline* code for that function. The benefit is that *inline* functions avoid the function overhead associated with a function call. The bad news is that it's up to the compiler to decide if it wants to make the substitution or not. In other words, using the *inline* keyword is like you on your knees begging for an *inline* substitution, but the compiler can ignore you if it wants. If there are multiple calls to the inline function, program code size will increase.

So, how can you tell whether the compiler likes you or not? I'm not sure. I wrote a small test program on the ESP32 and Nano that used multiple calls to a test function, using the *inline* modifier and without it. No matter which form I used, the code size did not change. This suggests that the compiler ignored my *inline* request and used a function call each time.

#include

This directive seems to confuse people, but it really shouldn't. The confusion arises because there are two flavors of the *#include* that can be used:

```
#include <myFile.h>     // Look in default include path
#include "yourFile.h"   // Look in project directory first
```

So, what's the difference? Well, this is one of those questions where there is a short answer and a *really* long answer. Let's do the short version first.

```
#include <filename.h> // Look in the default path...
```

This means that the compiler looks in the default include path name to find *filename.h*. The *include* path is usually the same as the default path for the *libraries* subdirectory. Let's say you installed the IDE at the root directory on drive C. This means, for example, the IDE executable file is located at:

```
C:\Arduino1.8.12
```

This also means that the default *libraries* path is:

```
C:\Arduino1.8.12\libraries
```

as that is where the compiler expects to find the IDE's libraries.

If you use:

```
#include "myHeader.h"    // Look in the project directory first
```

the compiler first looks in the *default projects directory* for the header file. If your program is at the root directory with the name *MyProject*, then the compiler expects to find:

```
C:\MyProject\MyHeader.h
             MyProject.ino
```

in that project directory. This also means that the IDE will have two source code tabs showing above the Source Code window. However, if the compiler does not find the header file in the project directory, it will look in the default libraries directory (e.g., C:\Arduino1.8.12\libraries). Using double quotes allows you to keep special project headers where they belong: with the project.

A Complication

There are a bunch of other header files that the compiler knows about and can call upon if it needs to. If you want to see them, try looking at this path (my root directory for the IDE is C:\Arduino1.8.12):

```
C:\Arduino1.8.12\hardware\arduino\avr\cores\arduino\
```

and you will see over three dozen header/source files listed. The IDE is free to use these headers as needed. Sometimes you will see code that, by design, includes some of these files, too.

Now, here's the wrinkle: Suppose you installed the Teensy software patch we mentioned in Chapter 1. If so, look down this path:

```
C:\Arduino1.8.12\hardware\teensy\avr\cores\teensy4
```

and you will see over 100 header/source files listed! Indeed, each patch you installed is free to add as many header and supporting source code files as it deems necessary to its own core. And if that's not enough to confuse you, look at:

```
C:\Arduino1.8.12\hardware\teensy\avr\libraries
```

and you will see the header files the Teensy uses by default! In other words, just like the Arduino family has a *libraries* subdirectory, so does the Teensy, but it's below the *teensy* subdirectory! The same will be true for the STM32 and the ESP32 if you installed them, too.

OK, so what?

Well, if you are using the Teensy microcontroller for a project and use this preprocessor directive:

```
#include <Adafruit_GFX.h>
```

in your program, the default search path becomes:

```
                                        // Default include path for Teensy
C:\Arduino1.8.12\hardware\teensy\avr\libraries

C:\Arduino1.8.12\libraries      // Default include path for Nano
```

like it would if the code is compiled for the Arduino Nano board. This is just another reason why it is so important to specify the correct board you are using when you compile a program.

Please Help Others

Other than a tall grass fire, the thing that burns my butt the most are programmers who use a specialty library, but don't bother telling you where to find it. For example, these lines are from the JackAl source code main header file:

```
#include <RA8875.h>  //http://hamradiodesigns.com/index.php/content/
#include <Rotary.h>  // https://github.com/brianlow/Rotary
```

Both of these header files introduce *non-standard libraries*. That is, neither library is distributed with the Arduino IDE or any of the patch libraries. What makes matters even worse is that there are multiple libraries out there that use the name Rotary for their library name. Chances are, if you select the wrong one, your code isn't going to work properly. By making the download URL known, users can download and install the non-standard library.

The rule is this:

> *If you are using a non-standard library in your project, put its download URL as a comment on the line that includes the library.*

There are a lot of programmers who don't do this and that's a crime, especially if you let others use your code.

#if and variants

There are a boatload of variations of the simple *#if* preprocessor directive. They are: *#if, #else, #elif, #endif, #ifdef,* and *#ifndef.* In this section, we discuss how those might be used in your programs, starting with a directive you've seen before.

#ifdef

Another preprocessor directive we've used earlier is the *#ifdef.* The general syntax is:

```
#ifdef  expression
    statement(s)
 #endif
```

We used the *#ifdef* in this context:

```
#define DEBUG   // Comment out this line to turn off Serial object
// a bunch of code....
void setup()
{
#ifdef DEBUG
  Serial.begin(9600);
#endif
 // more code in setup(), perhaps defining x and y for screen size
#ifdef DEBUG
  Serial.print("screen width = ");
  Serial.print(x);
  Serial.print("   height = ");
  Serial.println(y);
#endif
```

Because the symbolic constant *DEBUG* is defined in the program, the *#ifdef* expressions are all logic *true*, so the statements between each *#ifdef* and *#endif* pair are compiled into the program. When you are finished debugging the program, you don't want those debug statements chewing up your precious memory, so you comment out the first line above that defines the DEBUG symbolic constant. Doing that makes all of the subsequent *#ifdef* expressions logic *false*, so all of the debug statements are no longer compiled into the program. We referred to this type of code as *scaffolding code*. Scaffolding code can save you a lot of retyping if (when?) a new bug rears its ugly head.

One complaint about scaffolding code is that it results in a lot of unwanted *Serial.print()* output for those sections where the bugs have been fixed. The complaint is that this clutters up the useful print statements. It's a valid complaint.

So, is there an easy way to solve the problem? Obviously there is or I wouldn't have raised the question! Suppose you're tired of seeing the screen sizes each time the program starts up.

Clearly, you could simply erase the lines, but that defeats the purpose of scaffolding code. Instead, try this:

```
#ifdef DEBUG1          // Note the '1' at the end of the constant
   Serial.print("screen width = ");
   Serial.print(x);
   Serial.print("   height = ");
   Serial.println(y);
#endif
```

Now what happens when you recompile the code? Because *DEBUG1* is not *#define*'d in the program, the compiler would never even see the enclosed *Serial* method calls. This has the effect of removing these particular debug statements, but keeps all of the others alive in the program. You can do this for all of the other debug statements in the program. When you are confident that you have killed all the bugs, you can do a global search on DEBUG1 and replace it with DEBUG, and then comment out the DEBUG preprocessor directive. Note, I still don't do global search-and-replace; just global search and then replace those after I've read each one that is found. The reason is because the search function can ignore case if it wants to, and you may have a variable with the unfortunate name *myDebug1*.

#ifndef

The general syntax for the *#ifndef* (i.e., if not defined) is similar to the *#ifdef*:

```
#ifndef  expression
  statement(s)
#endif
```

but with the logic reversed. We've already shown the advantage of using multiple source code files in a project. Suppose a project has three files: testproject.ino, testproject.h and support.cpp. Now suppose we defined an *int* variable named *veryImportant* in testproject.ino, but we want to use it in support.cpp. This is a problem because any global defined in testproject.ino goes out of scope when the end of that file is reached. This means that support.cpp can't use *veryImportant* even though it needs to. Here's what we have:

testproject.ino	support.h	testproject.h
`int veryImportant;`	`if (veryImportant == true) {`	

This code is untenable because *veryImportant* simply is invisible in support.cpp. Now suppose we change the code in the files as follows:

testproject.ino	support.cpp	testproject.h

`#ifndef BEENHERE`
`#include "testproject.h"`
`#endif`
	`#ifndef BEENHERE`
	`#include "testproject.h"`
	`#endif`
		`#ifndef BEENHERE`
		`#define BEENHERE`

		`extern int veryImportant;`
	`if (veryImportant == firstOne) {`	
`int veryImportant;`		`#endif // Last statement in file`

The Arduino compiler reads the INO file first (i.e., the file with *setup()* and *loop()* in it). So when the first line in testproject.ino is read, BEENHERE is not defined, which means the first line in the file is logic *true* for the preprocessor. Because the first line is logic *true*, the *#include "testproject.h"* preprocessor directive causes the testproject.h header file to be immediately read into the program.

The first thing done in the header file is to *#define BEENHERE*, so it becomes defined for the rest of the files in the project. It also provides a *declaration* for *veryImportant* by using the *extern* keyword. This means the attribute list for *veryImportant* is now part of the symbol table and available everywhere in the project. There are likely other things in the header file, but we just close it out with the paired *#endif* as required by the first line in the header file (*#ifndef*).

Eventually, the preprocessor finishes reading the .ino file. Note that this also means that *veryImportant* is now defined in the program, too. The preprocessor then checks if there are any more files that need to be processed in the project. Yep, there are: support.cpp. When the preprocessor reads the first line of support.cpp, *BEENHERE* is now defined, which makes the directive logic *false*. Therefore, the *#include "testproject.h"* directive is skipped. Note how this technique makes it possible to avoid "double-reading" the header file. Also notice that, because *veryImportant* is now defined in the symbol table via the *extern* declaration in the header file as well as its definition in testproject.ino, the compiler can use the symbol table information to generate the code for the *if* statement block in support.cpp.

Because header files can make some aspects of programming easier, I have a general format I use when writing a new header file. I'll assume that there are multiple source code files in the program.

```
/*                              Development history:
  Version 0.02, Sep  1, 2020, Jack Purdum, Edit of header
  Version 0.01, Jun 17, 2020, Jack Purdum, Start of test project
*/

#ifndef BEENHERE                // Start "double-read" protection...
#define BEENHERE

#define DEBUG                   // Comment out for distribution
#define VERSION    0.02         // Version number for code development

//============= #include files go here =======================

//============= remaining symbolic constants go here ==========

//============= function prototypes go here ===================

//============= extern data declarations go here ==============


#endif                          // End "double-read" protection
```

#if, #endif

These two preprocessor directives are exactly what you think they are: a conditional way to have the code appear in different ways to the compiler. For example, perhaps you're working with a colleague who is color blind and can see green text, but not red. You might have something like:

```
#if colorBlind == true
  tft.setTextColor(GREEN);
#endif
```

This is just a simple way of having an if statement block seen by the preprocessor in a way that changes the code the compiler actually generates. Note that every *#if* must be followed at some point by a *#endif.*

#if, #else, #elif, #endif

Extending the preprocessor's conditional directive, you can also have the equivalent of an *ifelse* statement block: For example, perhaps you have a PC or a tablet that you're talking to and the device has a very slow COM port. However, other machines are substantially faster. In that case, you might have something like:

```
       #if device == SLOW
```

```
        Serial.begin(9600);
    #else
        Serial.begin(115200);
    #endif
```

If the output device is marked SLOW, the baud rate is set to 9600, otherwise it defaults to 115200 baud. I'm sure you can think of dozens of other examples where setting the Step 1 environment variables would make sense.

Sometimes you need to test more than one expression and the #elif can make this easier. For example, look at Listing 10.4.

Listing 10.4. Preprocessor if-else block.

```
#define WINDOWS 1
//#define LINUX 1

void setup() {
  Serial.begin(9600);

#if WINDOWS
  Serial.println("Using Windows");
#else
  #if LINUX
   Serial.println("Using Linux");
  #endif
#endif

}
void loop() {
}
```

The code in Listing 10.4 displays "Using Windows" because we *#defined* it at the top of the program. (Because we are using a *#if* instead of a *#ifdef*, we need to have the symbolic constant associated with a value.) The important thing to notice is that we need to use two *#endif* directives at the bottom of the code block to satisfy the syntax requirements of *#if*. Suppose we change the code slightly to that shown in Listing 10.5:

Listing 10.5. An if-else block using #elif

```
#define WINDOWS   1
//#define LINUX   1

void setup() {
Serial.begin(9600);

#if WINDOWS
Serial.println("Using Windows");
```

```
#elif LINUX
Serial.println("Using Linux");
#endif
}
void loop() {
}
```

If you run the code for Listing 10.5, the output is exactly the same as for Listing 10.4. So, if the output is the same, which one should you use? Because both versions are pretty easy to read, I would always opt for the one that takes fewer keystrokes. Selecting the option with fewer keystrokes is not just because I'm lazy. Fewer keystrokes also mean less chance to make a typing error. *Ceteris paribus*, always go with the few keystroke option if the code is equally readable. If shorter code makes it harder to read, go with the longer code version. Program code will likely change very little, if at all. The only time you would not make that choice is when fewer keystrokes makes it significantly more difficult to read and understand the code.

Conclusion

The C preprocessor has many tasks that it is designed to address, but most programmers don't take full advantage of them. Everyone knows about the *#include* and *#define* directives, but many overlook the control directives that can be used to control the code before the compiler even sees it. Also, if you're going to take advantage of the compiler's ability to do incremental compiles, you need to know how to properly use multiple project files...it's worth the effort.

Exercises

1. What does the preprocessor pass do with symbolic constants?
2. What does the preprocessor cause to happen when it encounters a #include directive?
3. What are the two syntax forms for a #include directive and how are they different?
4. What advantage does a symbolic constant have over using a similar *const* data definition?
5. Why is global search-and-replace a bad idea in program code?
6. Suppose your code needs to read MyHeader.h if the code is being compiled using the STM32 processor, but include YourHeader.h if it is being compiled on an ESP32. How would you cope with those needs?

7. Write an *isdigit()* macro. Of course you included the minus and plus signs, didn't you?
8. Suppose a complete beginner asks you: “What's the difference between the C preprocessor and the C compiler?” How would you answer them?

Chapter 11 Polling, Interrupts, and Bitwise Operators

We have mentioned several times that programs that acquire input data directly from humans appears as a very slow process to a microcontroller. Programs that wait for the user to type something into the Serial monitor spend a lot of time just twiddling their digital thumbs. Given the design of such programs, that slowness is not a real problem. It's expected.

Processing Speed and Program design

However, there are other programs that we would like to have respond as quickly as possible. A program that reads a motion sensor in order to record a high-speed camera image wants to react as quickly as possible. Alarms, chemical processing systems, and crash-avoidance systems are just a few examples where quick response times makes a difference. As always, however, there's more than one way to address the need for a response to a given event. We investigate two of those options in this chapter:

1. Polling
2. Interrupts

Both approaches often provide satisfactory results, but the means of accomplishing those results relies on significantly different software.

Before we get to the polling/interrupts debate, we need to set a frame of reference within which such comparisons take place. We really haven't spent much time with programs that take advantage of the *loop()* function that is provided as part of every Arduino C program. That's about to change.

Listing 11.1 shows a short program that counts how many passes through a simple *for* loop each processor can make in 1 second. First, let's take a look at the code.

At the top of the listing is a *#define* for *MAXSAMPLES*, which I've set to 10. The reason is because I expect there to be small variations on the loop counter on each pass through the loop. Because of this expected variation, the code makes *MAXSAMPLES* (i.e., 10) passes through the loop to use in constructing the average pass count. These samples are saved in an *unsigned long* array named *timeSamples[]*. The array needs to be an *unsigned long* because the measured time slice is determined by the *millis()* function, which returns an *unsigned long* data type. We want to make an apples-to-apples assignment any time we can. A second symbolic constant, named *TIMETARGET*, is set to 1000UL. This defines the number of milliseconds for each pass through the timing loop as determined by calls to the *millis()* function.

I collapsed the *setup()* function to fit on one line so that I could display the code in one screen shot. As you've seen before, the *Serial.begin(9600)* function call defines (i.e., instantiates) the *Serial* object for the program. The *while (!Serial)* statement block sets up an empty *while* loop that spins around until the task of instantiating the *Serial* object is complete. (We use a simple alternative to this approach later in the chapter.) Some of the microcontrollers are so fast that they would spin through *setup()* before the Serial object was usable in *loop()*. Usually, this wastes less than a second.

Near the top of *loop()*, we define a number of working variables and then create a *for* loop that is repeated *MAXSAMPLES* times. The *millis()* function returns the number of milliseconds that have passed since the program started. If you run this program nonstop for about 50 days, *millis()* overflows the range of an *unsigned long int* and its internal counter resets to 0. Hopefully, this isn't a problem. Note that on each 1 second pass through the loop we display a number for the pass just completed. I did this so the user doesn't think the code is "locked up".

We use a *while* loop starting at line 18 to make the 1 second loop pass. Just before entering the loop, we initialize *start* with the current *millis()* count. Let's say that start gets initialized with the value 12000. The expression that controls the *while* loop continually calls *millis()* and compares its present value to *start* to see if we've wasted 1 second. So, if *millis()* returns 12750, the *while* expression is logic *true* (i.e., 12750 – 12000 = 750 which is less than *TIMETARGET)*. As long as the *while* test expression is logic *true*, the code increments *count* and keeps trucking through the *while* loop.

Eventually, the elapsed time exceeds *TIMETARGET*, making the *while* test expression logic *false*, and the *while* loop block no longer executes. Line 21 takes the value of *count* and stores it in the *timeSamples[]* array. Line 22 simply prints out the current pass count (variable *i*) on the Serial monitor to inform the user the code is running as it should.

Program control then loops back up to Line 15 to make the next pass through the *for* loop. Note how *count* and *start* are reset before we enter the *while* loop. Eventually, the loop control variable (*i*) will equal *MAXSAMPLES*, at which time the *for* loop block is no longer executed.

At this point, *timeSamples[]* holds the count for each 1 second pass through the loop. Line 26 is another *for* loop that does double-duty. First, it shows you the 10 sample counts on each pass through the loop. Second, Line 31 takes each individual pass values and adds it to *average*. After all 10 samples have been displayed, the second expression of the *for* loop (*i* < *MAXSAMPLES*) becomes logic *false*, and we end the loop. Line 34 then displays the timing average for all ten passes through the loop.

A single pass for the Arduino Mega2560 looks like:

```
timeSamples[0] = 7074
timeSamples[1] = 7555
timeSamples[2] = 6877
timeSamples[3] = 7555
timeSamples[4] = 6876
timeSamples[5] = 7555
timeSamples[6] = 6876
timeSamples[7] = 7555
timeSamples[8] = 7555
timeSamples[9] = 7555

Average loop passes = 7303
```

This shows that the Arduino Mega2560 can make about 7300 passes per second through the loop shown in Listing 11.1. (I cannot explain the "4 frequency dips" that appear for the loop counts, clustering around 6900 and 7550. Someone with deeper EE understanding than I have might be able to explain it.)

Listing 11.1. Loops per second for four microcontrollers

```
#define MAXSAMPLES     10                            // Number of timing passes
#define TIMETARGET     1000UL                        // Time slice, 1 second

unsigned long timeSamples[MAXSAMPLES];

void setup() {  Serial.begin(9600);   while (!Serial) ; }

void loop()
{
  int count;
  int i;
  unsigned long int average;
  unsigned long int start;

  for (i = 0; i < MAXSAMPLES; i++) {
    count = 0;
    start = millis();
    while (millis() - start < TIMETARGET) {          // Has a second passed yet?
      count++;                                       // Nope
    }
    timeSamples[i] = count;                          // Save the count and show progress
    Serial.println(i);
  }
  Serial.println("-------");
  average = 0UL;
  for (i = 0; i < MAXSAMPLES; i++) {                 // Show what happened
    Serial.print("timeSamples[");
    Serial.print(i);
    Serial.print("] = ");
    Serial.println(timeSamples[i]);
    average += timeSamples[i];
  }
  Serial.print("\nAverage loop passes = ");          // Show the average
  Serial.println(average / MAXSAMPLES);
}
```

Table 11.1 shows the pass counts for all of the microcontrollers. As you

Table 11.1. Passes through loop code per second

Microcontroller	Passes per second
Arduino Mega2560	7,303
STM32F103	5,185,815
ESP32	862,449
Teensy 4.0	199,979,425

can see, there is quite a bit of variation across microcontrollers. You can also see the impact that a 600MHz clock has compared to a 16MHz clock. While the Mega2560 looks pretty slow compared to the others, slow is a relative term. Ask yourself this: How many times can you press a button in 1 second? My guess is that it's less than 7 thousand times per second. Even fewer people can approach 200 *million* presses per second. (My button press rate is less than that.) The point is that even the slowest microcontroller scoots along at a pretty healthy clip.

Okay, so why did I spend time on this sample program? The reason is to give you a frame of reference for the rest of this chapter. Keep in mind that the cost of each microcontroller varies and there is little reason to buy a blazingly fast microcontroller when the application spends most of its time waiting for the user to type something into the program.

Human Reaction Time

The vast majority of the sample programs you write for this text aren't concerned with high-speed response times to some external event or sensor. More often the code is responding to human input, perhaps typing something into the program using the Serial monitor, pressing a push button switch, or turning a rotary encoder. Let's connect a simple push button switch to a microcontroller to see what your reaction time is. That reaction time in conjunction with Table 11.1 should give some insight into making a selection between polling and interrupts.

To run the reaction time program, you need to wire a push button switch to your microcontroller. The idea is that the program generates a random delay of between 0 and 5 seconds. Once that delay passes, the microcontroller's onboard LED is turned on. That's the user's signal to press the push button as fast as they can. A call to the *millis()* library function returns an *unsigned long* that is assigned into *startTimer*. The code then waits for a button push and, upon sensing the closure, calls *millis()* and saves its value in *endTimer*. The difference between *endTimer* and *startTimer* is your reaction time. As a frame of reference, my reaction times centered around 190ms. Dead people clock in at about 225ms.

Figure 11.1 shows the circuit I used for testing on an STM32F103 board, although you can use any of the microcontrollers for the experiment. The top of the pushbutton is connected to 3.3V. The other end of the switch is connected to ground through a 10KΩ resistor. The digital pin I used to check for a button press was PB9. You can set this pin to whatever digital pin you wish for the microcontroller you are using. (Check your pin map for your microcontroller, because not all pins are GPIO pins.) You can also leave the resistor out of the circuit if you wish. (Discussed in the *pinMode()* section below.)

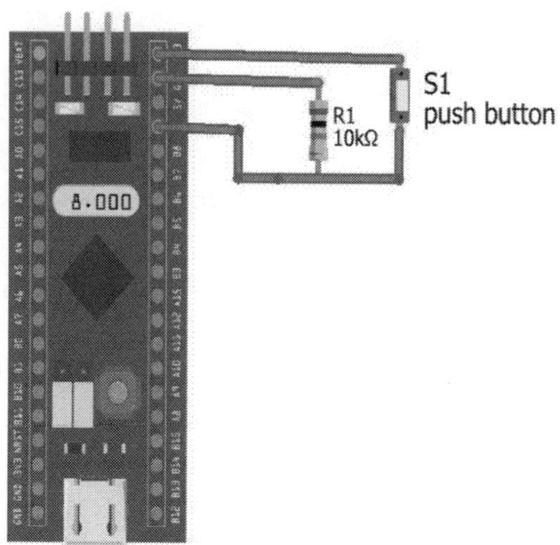

Figure 11.1. STM32 wiring for reaction time.

The reaction time program code is presented in Listing 11.2. At the top of the listing you should select the *#define* that applies to your microcontroller board. If you have an Arduino Nano or Uno or a Teensy, you don't have to use a *#define* as those are the default controllers. We use a *#if* preprocessor block to set the requisite symbolic constants that are to be used.

LEDPIN is the onboard LED that all of the boards have. The Uno, Nano, and Teensy all use pin 13 for the LED, but the ESP32 has to be different going with pin GPIO2. The STM32 uses a different physical pin, but uses PC13 for its symbolic constant.) Oddly, many of the board images you find on the Internet do not identify the LED pin for that board. If you're using a board other than what is specified here, a little Internet digging should identify the proper LED pin for you. Trial-and-error also works.

The RANDOMPIN should be an analog pin because they can generate values between 0 and 1023. (The 1023 value is for a 10-bit ADC. However, the 32-bit microcontrollers have 12-bit ADC's, so the range increases to 4095. See Table 1.1.) Usually there is some random "noise" value on the pin that we use to seed the *pseudo-random number generator.* It is a pseudo-random number generator because, if you don't seed it with a different value, the generator produces the same sequence of random numbers. The numbers are randomly distributed, but without the seed, they are repeated. The fact that the sequence is repeatable is not all bad. During testing and debugging sessions, a randomly distributed, but repeatable, sequence of numbers can be quite useful.

ACTIVESTATE is the logic state that we are using in this program. It could be set to high or low, depending upon how you wire and sample the circuit. We are using the circuit shown in Figure 11.1. Technically, we don't need to set three values for ACTIVESTATE. Because the values are all equal, one definition is all we really need.

Listing 11.2. Push button reaction time.

```
//#define ESP32      true           // Comment out for all but ESP32
#define STM32      true             // Comment out for all but STM32

#if (STM32 == true)
#define LEDPIN          PC13        // For STM32F103
#define PUSHBUTTON      PB9
#define RANDOMPIN       PA0
#define ACTIVESTATE     LOW         // low or hi on push? Low here
#elif (ESP32 == true)               // For ESP32
#define LEDPIN          2
#define PUSHBUTTON      GPIO25
#define RANDOMPIN       GPIO4
#define ACTIVESTATE     LOW
#else                                // Defaults to Arduino or Teensy
#define LEDPIN          13
#define PUSHBUTTON      7
#define RANDOMPIN       A0
#define ACTIVESTATE     LOW
#endif

void setup()
{
  Serial.begin(9600);
  delay(1000UL);                     // Wait for Serial instantiation
  pinMode(LEDPIN,          OUTPUT); // Set modes and states
  pinMode(PUSHBUTTON,      INPUT);
  digitalWrite(PUSHBUTTON, HIGH);
  digitalWrite(LEDPIN,     HIGH);
  randomSeed(RANDOMPIN);             // Seeds random number generator
  Serial.println("Press switch as fast as you can when LED comes
                on.");
}
void loop() {
  long rnd;
  unsigned long startTimer;
  unsigned long endTimer;
  rnd = random(0, 5);
  delay(rnd * 1000UL);      // Wait a few seconds...then
  digitalWrite(LEDPIN, LOW);       // ...turn LED on
  startTimer = millis();           // Start timer
  while (true) {
    if (digitalRead(PUSHBUTTON) != ACTIVESTATE) {
      endTimer = millis();         // Stop timer
      break;
    }
  }
  digitalWrite(PUSHBUTTON, HIGH);        // Reset pushbutton
```

```
  digitalWrite(LEDPIN, HIGH);          // ...turn LED off
  Serial.print("\nYou took ");
  Serial.print(endTimer - startTimer);
  Serial.print(" milliseconds to respond.");
  Serial.println("\nYou will have more than 5 seconds to the next
                 test.");
  delay(5000UL);
}
```

pinMode()

The *pinMode()* function call is used to prepare a given I/O pin for its use in the program. The signature for the function is:

```
void pinMode(int whichPin, int whatMode);
```

Obviously, *whichPin* is the identifier for the pin that is to have its mode set. This can be a "pure" number (e.g., 13 on a Nano or Uno) or it can be a symbolic constant (e.g., PC13, GPIO4, etc.).

The *whatMode* argument recognizes three states for this variable:

OUTPUT. In this state, the impedance on the pin is low, which means it can provide a relatively large amount of current to the attached circuit. While the documentation for the microcontrollers we are using says the pins are capable of 40mA of current, I feel more comfortable shooting for about half that amount.

INPUT. When pins are set for the INPUT state, the pins are configured so that they present a high impedance at the pin, which means they don't load down any external circuit they are tied to and make very small current demands on that circuit. To the outside circuit, the pin looks similar to a 100MΩ load. This also means that it takes very little current to register a change in the state (HIGH, LOW) of the pin. On the downside, if you define a pin to be an INPUT pin, but connect nothing to it, a *digitalRead()* of that pin may be subject to seemingly random values as the pin "floats" between states. You can add 10K pullup or pulldown resistors to set the pin to a known state.

INPUT_PULLUP/INPUT_PULLDOWN. If you use either of these two symbolic constants, you are using the resistors that are internal to the microcontroller to set the pin to a known state (pullup is to +5 or +3.3V, or 0V for pulldown, depending upon the microcontroller). If you don't use one of these two constants, there's a chance that the pin could “float” with a value between 0.0V and +3.3V (or +5V on the Arduinos). Which one to use depends upon how you connect the external device. For example, if you want a pushbutton switch to read 0V when closed, you want it to be +3.3.C (or +5V) when it is open. The Arduino family does not make a pulldown network available to you. However, the Teensy 4.0 (core_pins.h). STM32F103 (io.h), ESP32 (esp32-hal-gpio.h) all define the INPUT_PULLDOWN symbolic constant in their header files. It appears that between 10K and 50K are the values of the internal resistors.

In my circuit, I used my own external 10KΩ resistor. Since it appears on the ground side of the switch, you view its function as a pulldown resistor, which means the pin does not float, but has the value of 0V when the switch is open. When the switch is pressed, the positive voltage is sensed (HIGH) on the PUSHBUTTON pin.

The code in *loop()* is pretty straightforward. A call to the *random()* function returns a random number in the domain of 0 through 4. Note that the second argument to *random()* sets the upper limit and is *not* included in the distribution of numbers. The *delay()* function call takes the product of the random number, *rnd*, multiplies it by 1 second (1000UL), and pauses the program for that length of time. Because of the second *delay(5000UL)* call at the bottom of *loop()*, you are guaranteed of at least a 5 second delay between tests.

After the delay, the code lights the onboard LED and starts the *startTimer* and the user's button press sets the *endTimer* value. The rest of the code does little but display the difference between the two timers.

The heart of the processing takes place in the *while* loop:

```
while (true) {
  if (digitalRead(PUSHBUTTON) != ACTIVESTATE) {
    endTimer = millis();                    // Stop timer
    break;
  }
}
```

As you know, if a *while* expression evaluates to logic *true*, the *while* statement block is executed. By using the constant *true* for the *while* expression, we create an infinite *while* loop. The *if* statement block tests to see if the push button has been pressed. In essence, the test is saying: If the PUSHBUTTON digital pin is logic LOW, we continue spinning around in the *while* loop. When the user does push the button, the *digitalRead()* call returns a logic HIGH which triggers the call to *millis()* to get the *endTimer* value. The *break* statement transfers control out of the infinite *while* loop and the code displays the results.

Note that this code is polling the *PUSHBUTTON* pin with a *digitalRead(PUSHBUTTON)* each time we make another pass through the infinite *while* loop. Can the code miss your button push while it's spinning around that while loop? Unless you can push that button faster than 7300 pushes per second, chances are pretty good it's going to catch the button press without a problem.

Given that fact, let's look at polling with another example and show a situation where polling might not be the best choice.

Polling

Suppose your company is bidding on a contract to install fire alarms in the Empire State building. Your company sells and installs a system of fire sensors that can sense and report the presence or absence of a fire within a 10' radius in less than 1 second. You get the blueprints for the building and, given its structure, your bid details the installation of 100 fire sensors on each floor of the building.

The software is designed to sample each of the fire sensors, checking for the presence of a fire. If there is a fire, the sensor reports the fire to the controller, and its software sounds an alarm throughout the building, turns on the sprinkler system, dials and reports the fire to the closest five fire stations, and informs the Mayor's office.

The sensor reading process begins on the first floor with a variable, *sensorVisit* with its value set to 1, and the program reads the status of sensor 1. Within a second, the sensor reports back its status (1 = fire, 0 = no fire). If there is no fire, *sensorVisit* is incremented to 2 on the first floor and that sensor is read and reports back fire/no fire. This continues to sensor 100. If there still is no fire, it reports its state back to the control unit. However, since sensor 100 is the last sensor on the first floor, the floor counter variable (e.g., *floorCounter*) is incremented by 1 and *sensorVisit* is reset to 1. This causes sensor 1 on the second floor to report back. This process continues to the top-most floor, after which it starts all over again on the first floor.

This is how polling works. You poll a device or sensor following some scheduled sequence. You could very easily adapt the program in Listing 11.1 to emulate this polling process. All you'd really need to do is change MAXSAMPLES to MAXFLOORS, and add a second *for* loop that would spin through 100 fire sensors. You could simulate the 1 second needed to read the sensor with a *delay(1000UL)* function call.

There's one problem, however.

Suppose you are a really unlucky person and just as you move from sensor 100 on the first floor to sensor number 1 on the second floor, sensor 100 on the first floor bursts into flame! By the time your software finishes reading the sensors on the top floor, the fire has had almost a 3 <u>hour</u> head start on your alarm system! You'd be surprised how cranky people get when they have to wade through 10 floors of fire on their way to lunch!

Hmmm...maybe we need a trip back to the drawing board.

Interrupts

Anyone who has raised a two-year old knows what an interrupt is, and software interrupts work much the same way here. An *interrupt is an event that interrupts whatever the microcontroller is currently doing and immediately transfers program control to a software routine written to process that interrupt.* The routine that is written to process the interrupt is called the *Interrupt Service Routine*, or *ISR*.

In our fire alarm system, instead of polling each fire sensor and reporting its status, we select a different type of sensor, each of which has the ability to call the ISR which processes the message, perhaps sending a message to the control unit which screams: "I'm on fire!" If a sensor isn't saying anything, we assume that everything's okay. Using an interrupt design for the fire system, worst case there's only about a 1 second delay between sensing a fire and reporting it to the control unit. (You would probably need a *SensorTest()* routine that would periodically check to see that each sensor in the system is functioning properly.)

Clearly, interrupts are a must for things where elapsed time is an important consideration. In the next section, we will implement a rotary encoder using both polling and interrupts. These two programs will give you a better idea of how each system might be used.

Rotary Encoders

Rotary encoders are used as input devices for many microcontroller projects. Rotary encoders typically are available in two basic flavors: 1) mechanical, and 2) optical. Figure 11.2 shows a common mechanical rotary encoder. Rotating the encoder shaft sends out a pulse chain on pins A and B in Figure 11.2. By reading the pulse chain, we can determine whether the shaft is moving

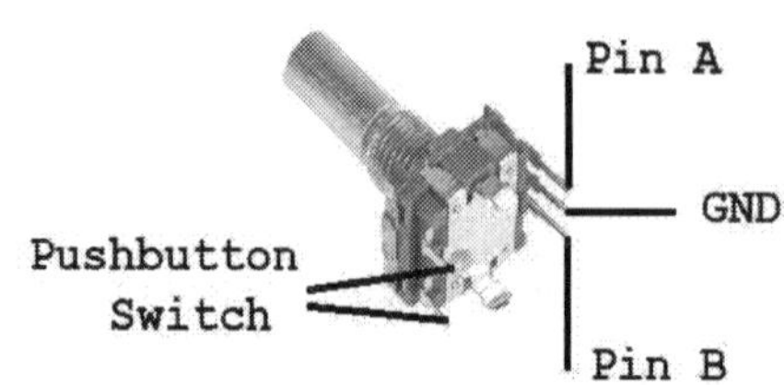

Figure 11.2. Common mechanical rotary encoder.

clockwise or counterclockwise. Your program code can then interpret that encoder movement as you see fit. Perhaps you are increasing/decreasing the value of some input variable. Or you might use the information to move a highlight cursor on a display. The encoder pictured in Figure 11.2 has pins for a pushbutton that is connected internally to the encoder shaft. When the user has highlighted the desired menu item, they can push the encoder shaft which closes the switch. The program code can then interpret the switch closure as selecting that menu item and react accordingly. Encoders are incredibly useful devices.

A lot of the projects I build are rather small and do not have enough mass to allow an encoder switch press without holding onto the project's case. For that reason, many of the encoders I purchase now do *not* have switches built into them. If I need a switch for the encoder to work properly, I add a separate NO (Normally-Open) pushbutton switch which takes a lot less force to activate. The “switchless” encoders look similar to Figure 11.2, but without the two switch pins. Usually I can buy 20 pulses per revolution (*ppr*, see below) encoders for about $1.50 or less, depending upon quantity. Also, be careful when you order, because lot of encoders do not have threads on the mounting shafts or matching hardware, making them more difficult to mount in a project case.

The Encoder Pulse Chain

So, how does an encoder create the pulse chain for our program code to read and interpret? While the actual construction is different, think of the encoder shaft as being connected to a circular disk. Radiating from the center of the disk are raised ridges that look like “speed bumps”. Inexpensive encoders typically have about 16 to 24 of these speed bumps radiating outward from the center. When you go to buy an encoder, one of the specifications is the *pulses per revolution* (ppr). You can think of the ppr as the number of speed bumps the encoder has for a 360 degree rotation.

Now envision a thin metal arm with a ball bearing soldered on the end of it. The arm extends from outside the encoder disk towards the center of the disk and is connected to pin A in Figure 11.2. Floating above the first disk is another plain flat metal disk. As you rotate the encoder shaft, the speed bumps push the ball bearing contact upwards until it contacts the disk above. This movement completes a circuit which creates a pulse that we can then read on pin A. Now imagine a second contact arm (pin B) that is 90 degrees out of phase with the first contact. The second contact arm can also send a pulse out on pin B. Figure 11.3 shows what these two pulse chains might look like as we rotate the encoder shaft. Notice how the pulse chain for pin B is one time period (90 degrees) “behind” the pulse chain for pin A.

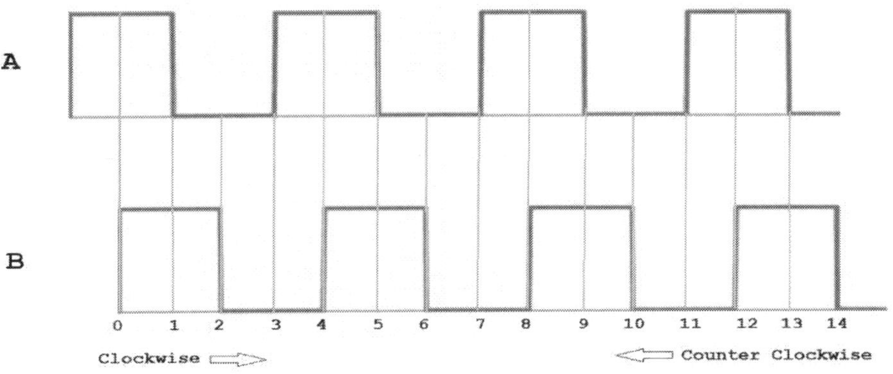

Figure 11.3. The rotary encoder pulse chain on pins A and B.

A complete pulse cycle for an encoder pin can be divided into four equal parts, as shown in Figure 11.3. Looking at pin A, the movement from position 0 to position 4 completes one complete pulse cycle. The width of each speed bump is such that each pin remains HIGH for 2 units of time and then switches to LOW for 2 units of time. When contact arm A first contacts a speed bump, the pulse rises from 0 to 1 (i.e., going from 0V to 3.3V or 5.0V). You can see this movement at position 3 in Figure 11.3 for pin A. Pin B makes the same transition, but at position 4 (90 degrees later).

The encoding scheme used here is called *quadrature phase shift encoding*. (This is a great icebreaking phrase at cocktail parties.) All this means is that the two signals coming from the encoder are phase-shifted by a quarter of a period (i.e., 90 degrees). The signals are gray coded to ensure that neither signal can change state at the same time. Optical encoders work much the same, but use slots cut into the disk with LED's creating the pulses instead of a contact arm. Optical encoders don't have the feedback feel that you get with the speed bumps (detents) of a mechanical encoder. As a result, optical encoders provide a much smoother feel when they are rotated. The downside is that optical encoders are often up to 20 times more expensive.

Now recall that pin B uses the same pulse parameters, but is 90 degrees out of phase with pin A. This means that when pin A is transitioning from HIGH to LOW at position 1 in Figure 11.3, pin B is in the middle of its HIGH pulse. Look at the movement for pin A from position 3 to position 4. Pin A goes high, followed by pin B going high at position 4. This sequence requires a clockwise movement. That is, if pin A transitions to HIGH before pin B, the movement must be clockwise. If pin B goes high before pin A (e.g., going from position 11 to position 10), that sequence only occurs when movement is counterclockwise. The arrows in Figure 11.3 show the pulse directions.

Suppose we use 2 bits to represent the current state of pins A (lsb) and B (msb), and we tack on two more bits to represent the two pins at the next state. For example, in Figure 11.3, consider the move from position 3 to position 4. At position 3, both pins are LOW, or binary 00. However, moving from position 3 to position 4 sees pin B remain LOW, but pin A transitions to HIGH. Therefore:

Position 2		**Position 3**		**Transitio n**
Pin B	Pin A	Pin B	Pin A	
0	0	0	0	0000
Position 3		**Position 4**		**Transitio n**
Pin B	Pin A	Pin B	Pin A	
0	0	0	1	0001

If we trace all possible BABA states shown in Figure 11.3, we can construct the table shown in Table 11.1.

Table 11.1. Table of Rotary Direction for Transition States

Previous BA, Next BA	**Directio n**	**Array coding**
0000	?	0
0001	CW	1
0010	CCW	-1
0011	?	0
0100	CCW	-1
0101	?	0
0110	?	0
0111	CW	1
1000	CW	1
1001	?	0
1010	?	0
1011	CCW	-1
1100	?	0
1101	CCW	-1
1110	CW	1
1111	?	0

How do you read Table 11.1? Consider the state change 0001 (i.e., row 2), which is from where both pins A and B are 0 to a state where B is 0 but A is one. You only find that transition from positions 3 → 4, 7 → 8, and 11 → 12. This only happens when moving from left to right in Figure 11.3, so it is a clockwise movement. Now look at row 3 where you start with both pins 0 but transition to B is 1 and A is zero. That transition only occurs at positions 11 → 10, 7 → 6, and 3 → 2. This pattern only happens when moving from right to left in Figure 11.3, which is a counter-clockwise movement. The third column simply assigns numeric values to unknown state (? or 0), CW (1), or CCW (-1). We can initialize an array to hold these states and use it to determine rotation direction.

Note that reading the encoder means we must compare the previous reading with the current reading to determine the direction the encoder is moving. While we can do the necessary pin reading and resultant manipulation mathematically, it is much easier to use the C bitwise operators.

Bitwise Operators

C is famous for bit-twiddling. I kinda put off learning about the bitwise operators because we never really needed them. Now we do. The bitwise operators allow you to inspect and otherwise manipulate individual bits of data within a variable (or operand). All of the bitwise operators save one (one's complement operator) are binary operators requiring two operands. The bitwise operators can only be used on integral data types. This means you can use the bitwise operators on the integral data types, but not floating point numbers.

Bitwise AND (&)

The bitwise AND operator is a single ampersand character (&). A common mistake is to use a logical AND operator (&&) where you really wanted a bitwise operator (&). As sure as we're sitting here, there will come a time where such confusion will put another dent in your now-flatter forehead. Learn from it and move on. Semantics tells the compiler what's right.

A bitwise AND between two bits results in a 1 bit only if *both* bits are 1. For example:

```
myNumber     0101    1111    0010    1010
myBitMask   &0001   &0100   &1111   &0101
            -----   -----   -----   -----
   result    0001    0100    0010    0000
```

The bitwise AND operator lets you examine the value of one or more bits in a data item. Quite often individual bits in a data byte are used to indicate the status of something. If, for example, you have a sensor where bit 0 must be 1 for it to be stable enough to read, and bit 2 is the status of FIRE (1) or NOFIRE (0), you could do this:

```
result = sensorByte & 0b0101;      // Note the bitwise operation

switch (result) {
  case 0:                            // No data or not stable
    KeepReading();                   // react as necessary (read
again?)
    break;
  case 1:                            // Sensor is stable
    NoFire();
    break;
  case 4:                            // Read again
    KeepReading();
    break;
  case 5:                            // Oh-oh...Not good!
    Fire():
    break;
  default:
    Serial.print("Shouldn't be here. result = ");
    Serial.println(result);
    break;
}
```

The value 0b0101 in the code fragment above means that we are only interested in masking off bits 0 and 2 to see what the sensor contains. If the *sensorByte* has bits 0 and 2 set to 0, either the sensor is not stable enough to read or there is no fire. If bit 0 is 1 and bit 2 is 0, the result is decimal 1 which means the sensor is stable enough to read and bit 2 is 0 so there is no fire. If bit 2 is 1 and bit 0 is 0 (decimal 4), we need to wait for the sensor to stabilize before we call the fire department. If a subsequent read shows both bits 0 and 1 are 1, we have a fire.

Remember when we wrote a program to see if the number entered was odd or even? We used the modulo operator to provide the answer. What if we wrote this:

```
byte userInput;
int bitMask = 1;            // some code to get a number from the user
if (userInput & bitMask) {
  Serial.println("odd");
} else {
  Serial.println("even");
}
```

What happens here? Suppose the user enters 5. Then *userInput* would contain 0b0000 0101. When applied using the bitwise & with *bitMask*, we get:

```
0b0000 0101   userInput
0b0000 0001   bitMask
     ------------------
0b0000 0001   result
```

and the code fragment would display "odd". Now try using an even number and see if it still works.

Bitwise OR, (|)

The bitwise OR operator (aka inclusive OR) uses the vertical bar, or pipe symbol (|). The bitwise OR returns 1 if *either* bit in the operands is 1. The only time a logic *false* is returned is when *both* bits are 0. Using the same examples from the bitwise AND discussion above:

```
myNumber       0101      1111      0010      1010
myBitMask    | 0001    | 0100    | 1111    | 0101
           -------- --------  -------  --------
 result        0101      1111      1111      1111
```

As you can see from the examples, the bitwise result always has the same or more bits turned on than the bitwise mask does. Some sensors have an initialization byte that requires certain bits to be turned on before the sensor can be used. For example, suppose you must have bits 0, 3, 4 and 7 turned on upon power-up. We might do this as shown here:

```
sensorStatusByte     0000 0000    // query the sensor's state
sensorInit         |  1001 1001    // these bits on at startup
                   -------------
     result          1001 1001
```

which turns on the required bits.

Bitwise Exclusive OR, XOR

The bitwise XOR operator symbol is the carat or circumflex (^). The result of an XOR operation is such that *the result is 1 only when the two bits are different*. Using our previous examples:

```
myNumber        0101      1111      0010      1010
myBitMask     ^ 0001    ^ 0100    ^ 1111    ^ 0101
            --------    ------    ------    ------
  result        0100      1011      1101      1111
```

A lot of graphics programs use XOR operations for animation purposes. However, a fairly common coding practice is to swap two variables; sorting routines do this all the time. Usually you would write an integer swap routine as:

```
        temp = firstValue;      // temporarily hold first value
  firstValue  = secondValue;    // swap values
  secondValue = temp;
```

If you do a code walk-through on this code snippet and substitute the value 5 for *firstValue* (0101) and 3 for *secondValue* (0011), you can see that their values are exchanged. You can accomplish the same thing using bitwise operators:

```
//    5  ^    3  = 0110 = firstValue
firstValue  = firstValue ^ secondValue   // 0101^0011=0110=firstValue
secondValue = firstValue ^ secondValue   // 0110^0011=0101=secondValue
firstValue  = firstValue ^ secondValue   // 0110^0101=0011=firstValue
```

The comments show the progression of the values as the statements are executed. As you can see, the ending value for *firstValue* is 3 (0011) and *secondValue* is 5 (0101).

Okay...so what?

There are a couple of advantages gained when using the XOR swap. First, you do not waste memory with a temporary variable (i.e., *temp*). The memory savings are pretty small, but a savings nonetheless. Second, and more importantly, the swap can be done in registers with no need to do multiple fetches from memory. The bitwise operators are usually directly supported by the microcontroller so the instructions are extremely fast. About the only downside is that, the first time you see such a swap, it takes you a while to recognize what's taking place.

One's Complement Bitwise Operator

The bitwise one's complement operator is the tilde (~) and it is the only unary bitwise operator. The one's complement operator changes all 1 bits to 0 and all 0 bits to 1. When you run this example:

```
byte value = 5;
byte newValue = ~value;

Serial.print("   value = ");
Serial.println(value);
Serial.print("newValue = ");
Serial.println(newValue);
```

the program displays 5 for *value* and 250 for *newValue*. Recall that the binary representation of 5 is 0b00000101, so if we apply the one's complement operator, *newValue* becomes 0b11111010. This result is because a byte is an unsigned number. If we use a data type that allows signed values, the one's complement equals -(N + 1). So, if *value* is an int, *newValue* would be -6. (I really don't want to get bogged down in why this happens. If you're interested, search for "2's complement arithmetic".)

Honestly, other than as a programming exercise, I've only used the one's complement operator for one use. I was working on a graphics program and tried a new TFT color display and all of the colors were way off. I took one of the colors and looked at its binary representation on the new display and then used the same color on the older display. The new value appeared to be a one's complement of the original value. I changed the header file that defined the colors:

```
#define CYAN            0x07FF
```

to

```
#define CYAN            ~0x07FF
```

and the two display colors were the same. The one's complement operator is rarely used, but on rare occasions, it can save your bacon.

Bitwise Shift Left Operator

The bitwise shift left operator is a binary operator and using the << symbol. We discussed both the shift left and shift right operators briefly in Chapter 3. The general syntax is:

```
operand1 << operand2
```

where operand1 is the value to be shifted and operand2 is the number of places to shift the bits leftwards. So, if we evaluate this expression:

```
byte val = 2;          // 0000 0010
val = val << 3;        // 0001 0000
```

the new value for *val* is 16. Any bit in the MSB of the data being shifted "falls off the end" of the data. (While there are assembler instructions for "rotate left with carry", that does not apply to the bitwise shift operators.)

Bitwise Shift Right Operator

The bitwise shift right operator is a binary operator and indicated with the >> symbol. The syntax for the bitwise shift-right operator is;

```
operand1 >> operand2
```

where operand1 is the value to be shifted and operand2 is the number of places to shift the bits to the right. For example,

```
byte val = 128;       // 1000 0000
val = val >> 3;       // 0001 0000
```

again resulting in the value 16. As you can see from these examples, each leftward shift by one bit position results in a multiply by 2. Conversely, a rightward shift by one bit position is a divide by two operation.

So, why the discussion of the bitwise operators at this point in the book? The reason is because you will use them to figure out how to properly work with a rotary encoder.

Using a Rotary Encoder with Polling

Listing 11.3 presents code that allows you to test a rotary encoder. You should be able to use this code unchanged with any of the microcontrollers. There are two aspects of the program that

Listing 11.3. Program code to test rotary encoder

```
#define DEBUG

#define ENCODERPINA        18    // I used an ESP32 for this program
#define ENCODERPINB        19
#define PULSEPERDETENT      4

void setup() {
#ifdef DEBUG
  Serial.begin(9600);
  while (!Serial)          // Waste time until Serial is created
    ;
#endif
  pinMode(ENCODERPINA, INPUT_PULLUP);
  pinMode(ENCODERPINB, INPUT_PULLUP);
}

void loop() {
  int encoderDirection;

  encoderDirection = ProcessEncoder();   // Use the encoder?
```

```
  if (encoderDirection) {
    Serial.print("Direction is ");
    if (encoderDirection > 0)
      Serial.println("CW");
    else
      Serial.println("CCW");
  }
}                                         // Yep...

/*****
  Purpose: Read the rotary encoder for encoder movement based on
           encoder states

  Parameter list:
    void

  Return value:
    int8_t        according to array value
*****/
int8_t ReadEncoder()
{
  static int8_t enc_states[] = {0, -1, 1, 0, 1, 0, 0, -1,
                               -1, 0, 0, 1, 0, 1, -1, 0};
  static uint8_t old_AB = 0;
  old_AB <<= 2;                          //remember previous state
  old_AB |= (digitalRead(ENCODERPINB) << 1) |
            digitalRead(ENCODERPINA);       //add current state
  return (enc_states[( old_AB & 0x0f )]);
}

/*****
  Purpose: Process encoder movement

  Parameter list:
    void

  Return value:
    int           1 on CW, -1 on CCW, 0 on no movement
*****/
int ProcessEncoder()
{
  int8_t result;
  int localDir;
  static int val = 0;

  while (val != PULSEPERDETENT) {
    result = ReadEncoder();
    if (result == 0) {
      return 0;                     // Nothing going on...go home.
    } else {
      if (result == 1)
        val++;                      // Clockwise          (CW)
      else
        val--;                      // Counter-clockwise  (CCW)
                          //PULSEPERDETENT pulses per rotation
      if (val == PULSEPERDETENT || val == -PULSEPERDETENT) {
        if (val > 0) {              // CW??
```

```
          localDir = 1;
        } else {                          // Nope, CCW
          localDir = -1;
        }
        val = 0;
       return localDir;
      }
    }
  }
}
```

benefit from a more detailed explanation. The first section to discuss is the code found in the *ReadEncoder()* function. In particular, consider these three statements:

```
  old_AB <<= 2;                          //remember previous state
                                                  //add current state
  old_AB |= (digitalRead(ENCODERPINB) << 1) |
                 digitalRead(ENCODERPINA);
  return (enc_states[( old_AB & 0x0f )]);    //return array code
```

When the program starts and you have not touched the encoder, the initial value of *old_AB* is 0000. This corresponds to the first row in Table 11.1. This starting position can also be viewed as position 3 in Figure 11.3. Now let's suppose you rotate the encoder CW to position 4 in Figure 11.3. This means that pin A is now 1, but pin B remains at 0. (Keep in mind that Table 11.1 is organized as bits BA, not AB.) Therefore, we can take the second statement and fill it in with the pin values:

```
  old_AB |= (digitalRead(ENCODERPINB) << 1) |
digitalRead(ENCODERPINA);   //add current state
  old_AB |= (0000 << 1) |    0001;
  old_AB |= 0000        |    0001;
  old_AB |= 0001;
```

Because the "|=" operator is just shorthand notation for OR'ing the operand on the left side of the assignment operator with the expression on the right, we get:

```
 old_AB |= 0001;
 old_AB = old_AB | 0001;
 old_AB = 0000 | 0001;
 old_AB = 0001;
```

The final statement can be expended to

```
 return (enc_states[( old_AB & 0x0f )]);
 return (enc_states[( 0001 & 0x0f )]);
 return (enc_states[( 0001 & 1111 )]);
```

```
return (enc_states[(0001)]);
return (enc_states[1]);
return 1;
```

which is interpreted as a clockwise (CW) movement for the encoder. Therefore, we know the user rotated the encoder clockwise.

Okay, so what's all this about:

```
while (val != 4) {
  result = ReadEncoder();
  if (result == 0) {
    return 0;                           // Nothing going on...go home.
  } else {
    if (result == 1)
      val++;                            // Clockwise          (CW)
    else
      val--;                            // Counter-clockwise  (CCW)
    if (val == 4 || val == -4) {        // 2 pulses to make a rotation
      if (val > 0) {                    // CW??
        localDir = 1;
      } else {                          // Nope, CCW
        localDir = -1;
      }
      val = 0;
      return localDir;
    }
  }
}
```

Not all encoders are made the same. The encoder I happened to be using returns a four-pulse chain for each encoder detent (where a detent is a "speed bump"). Some return a single pulse, and some return two pulses. If you see multiple print statements for a single detent move, your encoder also sends out multiple pulses. If you need to move your encoder 4 detents before you see a message displayed, your encoder probably only puts out a single pulse. You may have to change the *ProcessEncoder()* function to work properly with your encoder.

For most of the microcontrollers, the polling code presented in Listing 11.3 will work fine since it is designed to work with human input turning the encoder. However, you can just about bet that someone will put a weighted, large diameter knob on the encoder and use it as a tuning knob for a radio. Further, they will likely "strum" the knob when they want to make a fast frequency change. Depending upon how much other stuff you have going on in *loop()*, polling might not be able to keep up. When that happens, you need to consider using interrupts on the encoder.

Using a Rotary Encoder with Interrupts

Using polling to react to encoder movement can get kinda sluggish. Usually encoder sluggishness is because polling normally occurs in the *loop()* function which often has a lot of other stuff going on. When slow response gets noticeable, it might be time to investigate using interrupts instead of polling for the encoder. Also, keep in mind that there are rotary encoder libraries available to you.

Some ISR Rules

If you do decide to use interrupts, there are some things you need to consider when you are designing your program.

First, some digital pins are better to use for interrupts than others. It's not that the pins don't support interrupts. Rather, some pins have other uses that you may want to keep intact. For example, pins 0 and 1 on the Arduino family are used as the RX and TX lines for the COM port you use between your microcontroller and your PC. Also, pins 2 and 3 on the Uno and Nano are the only external hardware interrupt pins. Some pins (6 through 11) on the ESP32 are designed for specific purposes, of which interrupts isn't one of them. Check the pin map for your microcontroller to make sure it is a general purpose I/O pin. Also, make sure the pins aren't used for some other purpose (e.g., using an I/O pin for an interrupt, but which also is the only SPI MISO pin left.) Simply stated, look at the resources the microcontroller brings to the table and plan accordingly.

Second, when an interrupt occurs, control is *immediately* transferred to the ISR that you provide. Because an ISR cannot return a value, chances are pretty good you're going to use a global variable in the ISR to track the state of some variable. For example, you might use an *int* variable named *encoderDirection* as the variable that ultimately gets set to the encoder's direction of change. If that's the case, you need to define the variable as:

```
volatile int encoderDirection;
```

The keyword *volatile* tells the compiler to load a fresh copy of the variable each time it is referenced in the program. The reason for defining the variable using *volatile* is because of the way optimizing compilers work to enhance performance. When generating the program code, compilers often keep a heavily-used variable in a microcontroller register so it doesn't have to venture out across the data bus to memory, retrieve the rvalue, and trundle back to the microcontroller. The process of tucking variables away in a register is called *caching*, and it is meant to improve the performance of the routine(s) using that variable. The problem is that the code might be one instruction away from updating the cached value of *encoderDirection* when the interrupt occurs. Now we have a situation where the cached value is out of sync with the new "correct" value. The keyword *volatile* tells the compiler not to cache the variable, but use the most-current value from memory instead.

Third, keep the code in the ISR as short as you possibly can. The reason is because the microcontroller cannot recognize any other interrupts until it is finished processing your ISR. Large, cumbersome, ISR's run the risk of delaying the processing of other (more important?) interrupts. Even if you don't have any other active interrupts in your program, it's just good coding practice to keep them short and crisp.

Fourth, don't try passing a parameter to your ISR...you can't. If you think about the purpose of an interrupt, this makes sense, because you never know at what execution point the interrupt will occur. The same is true for trying to return a value from an ISR. Where would it return to? The interrupt could occur at any point in the code, so there's no "return function call" assignment waiting to take place. You're sprinting to the ISR as fast as you can and you can't be bogged down with carrying a backpack on the way there. The same logic probably explains why Olympic sprinters don't wear backpacks.

Finally, do not use blocking functions in your ISR. A *blocking function* is a function that calls its own ISR to accomplish its own interrupt-driven task. Common blocking functions are *Serial.print()* or *Serial.println()* and *delay()*. If you use a blocking function in your ISR, the microcontroller is going to attempt to finish your interrupt before theirs since it can only process one interrupt at a time. A sloppily written function with its own ISR could cause a lockout while the blocking function waits for the first function to finish.

Okay, with those caveats tucked away, let's write an interrupt-based encoder program.

Using a Graphics Display with an Encoder

I've gone back and forth on this choice in my mind for over a week. The wishy-washiness is because adding a TFT graphics display opens up a very large can...no, bucket...of worms. First, there are a lot of display sizes from which to choose. You can buy a TFT display as small as 1.8" up to 7", ranging in price from $8 to about $50. Also, the resolution for TFT displays varies from as little as 128x160 pixels up to 1280x400 pixels. And if that isn't confusing enough, each display has its own driver chip that likely is not compatible with other displays. That means that you need to find a graphics library that works with the display. I have a true dilemma: Two choices, both bad.

I decided to include a TFT graphics program under the assumption that discussing one graphics device is better than no discussion at all. There are enough similarities among displays and libraries, that you can probably figure out how to correctly identify and use the proper display/library combination.

I2C and SPI Interfaces

Before we can use a graphics display, we need to consider how a microcontroller communicates with devices that are more complex than controlling them with just a simple ON/OFF signal.
While there are many possible communication protocols that you can use, perhaps the two most common in the microcontroller world at the present time are the *Inter-Integrated Circuit*, or I2C, interface and the Serial Peripheral Interface, or SPI. There have been books written on each of these interfaces and there is no way I can do justice to either one here. Rather, this section gives a quick overview which may provide some impetus to study one or both in greater detail.

I2C Interface

The I2C interface was developed by Phillips in 1980 as a protocol that would allow integrated circuits to communicate with one another. Usually, I2C is implemented as a pure master/slave communications protocol using a two-wire communication system. One wire is used for data transfer (SDA) and the other wire carries the clock signal that controls the data flow. Pull up resistors are connected to both the SDA and SCL lines. These wires use a wire-AND configuration which allows multiple nodes to be used on the same bus.

Any communication across the I2C bus starts with the master sending a start bit followed by the slave address, which will be unique for each slave that shares the I2C bus. The slave device sends an acknowledgment bit and the communication between the two can commence.

SPI Interface

The *Serial Peripheral Interface* (SPI) interface often is used to communicate between a microcontroller and some external device. The SPI also uses a clock (SCK) and data (SD0) line along with other control lines used to select the proper device to receive the data. Only one side of the communications link generates the clock signal and that side is considered the master while the other side is the slave. For our purposes, the microcontroller is the master and the device is the slave. Data that is sent from the master to the slave appears on the "*Master Out Slave In"* line, or *MOSI*. Data flowing from the slave to the master appears on a different line called the "*Master In Slave Out*" line, or *MISO*. This means that the SPI bus is capable of full duplex communications. The "Slave Select", or SS, line is used to wake up the slave device that is to communicate on the SPI bus. When working with an SPI TFT display, data are generated in the microcontroller and transferred to the slave, which means using the MOSI line for data.

Okay, so which interface should you use? Obviously, the answer varies and each has its own place. Table 11.2 shows a comparison of the two interfaces.

In the next section, I am using a 3.5" TFT display with 480x320 pixel resolution which is driven by a ILI9488 graphics controller using the *Serial Peripheral Interface (SPI).* Make sure you buy one with the SPI interface, as there are less expensive displays using *the High Definition Multimedia Interface (HDMI*). The Raspberry Pi comes with an HDMI interface, which may explain why these

Table 11.2. Comparison of SPI and I2C interfaces

Interface	Advantages	Disadvantages
	Higher speed	Short transfer distances
	full duplex	does not verify data

SPI	Multiple slaves easy	more data lines
		more susceptible to noise
	Fewer lines	slower
	good compatibility for protocol	uses more power
I2C	verifies data	requires known device address
	fairly inexpensive	
	longer data runs	
	less susceptible to noise	

In the next section, I am using a 3.5” TFT display with 480x320 pixel resolution which is driven by a ILI9488 graphics controller using the *Serial Peripheral Interface (SPI)*. Make sure you buy one with the SPI interface, as there are less expensive displays using *the High Definition Multimedia Interface (HDMI*). The Raspberry Pi comes with an HDMI interface, which may explain why these are less expensive due to RP's popularity. The microcontrollers we are using do not have HDMI interfaces. The 3.5” SPI displays will suit our needs just fine. These displays are large enough for old people to read, but still fairly small, lightweight, and available for less than $15.

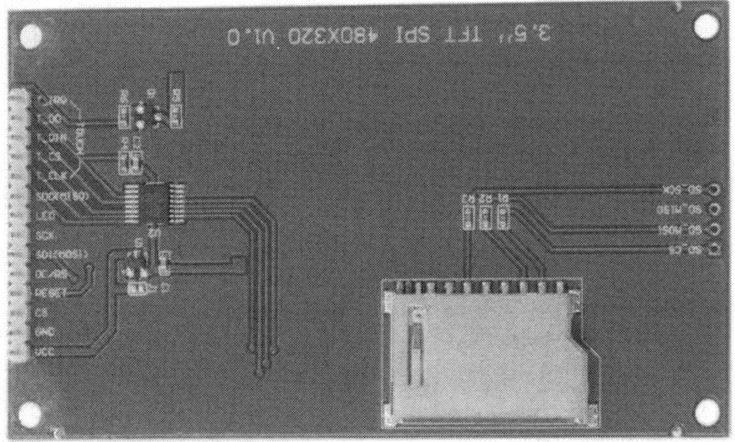

Figure 11.4. Typical 3.5” 480x320 TFT SPI display.

If you plan on using an Uno for the project, you can find such displays with an Uno shield configuration so they plug directly into the header pin sockets on the Uno. Otherwise, I suggest you look for a display with a pin configuration that looks like that shown in Figure 11.4. Many of the displays come with a micro Secure Digital (SD) card socket, as shown in Figure 11.4. The five pins on the top left are for the resistive touch screen feature of the display. The remaining pins on the left are used to interface the display with the microcontroller via the SPI interface.

Program Design

The program we are about to build uses a dummy menu system and presents the user three menu options: Read, Test, Config. The menu options can read a set of sensors, test those sensors, and set/change the configuration of the sensors. We won't actually implement a system of sensors because I don't know what your interests are or the cost you might face adding sensors that do interest you. You might, for example, create a weather station that reads inside and outside temperature, humidity, wind direction, rain detection, etc. The specifics aren't what's important. Rather, the goal here is to show you how you might implement an encoder-based menu system on a graphics display that allows the user to activate different elements of the program you want to design.

The program we are about to build is not trivial, as it uses a TFT graphics display, rotary encoder, plus the normal syntactic glue to hold everything together. These program elements make it a good candidate for showing you how to break up a larger program into its component parts for easier writing, testing, and debugging. Rather than chunking everything into one large *.ino source code file, we will break it up into a controlling *.ino file (which *must* hold *setup()* and *loop()*), plus a header file, plus supporting *.cpp (C++) files.

Multiple Source Code Files...why?

Lots of students shudder when I say we're going to use *.cpp files. There's absolutely no reason to feel that way. We are not going to use any C++ code in the support files. We only use the *.cpp file extension because you could use C++ in these files if you wanted to. (Indeed, I would probably write C++ classes for the display and encoders, and we do discuss that in Chapter 12.) Why break up the program into multiple source code files? After all, the single *.ino file has worked just fine up to this point. True, but there are a number of benefits that you gain by fracturing the program into smaller parts.

First, you can break the program into source code files that have meaning in a macro sense. For example, if we call this program *WeatherStation*, then the primary file must be named *WeatherStation.ino*. This *.ino file must contain the source code for *setup()* and *loop()*. However, we also know the program uses a TFT display as well as a rotary encoder, so I will name those files as *DisplayManagement.cpp* and *EncoderManagement.cpp*. My program style is to have a single header file (*.h) that controls global variables, symbolic constants, function prototypes, and external libraries we may need. I usually use a name for the header file that reflects the project's purpose. In this example, I named the header file *Weather.h*.

Note, a lot of very talented programmers have a separate *.h header file for each *.cpp file. I have had, on a few occasions, multiple header files, but I don't think I've ever done a project where I had a one-to-one relationship between header and cpp files. You do what makes sense for your projects.

Okay, so we've deconstructed the program into logical components...so what? I recently worked on a large program with over 10,000 lines of source code, all crammed into the *.ino file. Just moving from the start of that file to its end was a monumental waste of time. Breaking the file into smaller parts makes it easier to just navigate around in the program's source code.

Second, breaking the program source code into functional sections simplifies finding a given section of code. If something is messed up with the TFT display, I know which file is likely causing the problem and can quickly move to that piece of code.

Third, multiple source files can speed up the development process. When I was working on the JackAl Project, the program involved almost 12,000 lines of code. I broke the code into 19 separate source code files. Each morning when I started a programming session, I would start with a fresh compile of the source code. Even though I was working on a multi-core PC with a mega-munch of memory and a 3.8GHz clock, it would take over a minute to compile the project. Now, suppose some part of the menu system had a bug. I would tab to the file with the “buggy” code in it and look for the bug. I'd make a source code change to that file and recompile the program. However, instead of over a minute to compile the code, it only took a few seconds. Why?

The reason is because the Arduino compiler supports *incremental compiles*. When I did the first compile in the morning, the compiler kept the compiled version of each source code file tucked away (i.e., *cached*) for later use. Now when I made changes to just that one source code file, the Arduino IDE set a "dirty flag" on that source code file which tells the compiler that source code file has been changed and needs to be recompiled. The other 18 files have been cached and don't need to be recompiled. Therefore, the IDE compiles the one file and then merges it with the other 18 pre-compiled files to create the executable file that gets downloaded to the microcontroller. This saved me about 30 seconds each time I needed to recompile the code during development. If you do 50 compiles a day, that's 25 minutes less thumb-twiddling I have to do during the day. Multiply that times the number of development days, and that might add up to a two week vacation!

Simply stated, multiple source code files make sense for all but the most trivial programs and you need to know how to create and use them properly.

The Weather.h Header File

After I create the project's *.ino file, the next file I create is the project's main header file (there could be more than one). You can see the sequence of steps used to create the Weather.h project header file in Figure 1.7, 1.9, 1.10, and 1.11 in Chapter 1. When you are done, you will have a new tab in the IDE named Weather.h. The first thing I add to this file is the following set of preprocessor directives:

```
#ifndef BEENHERE
#define BEENHERE
    // The header file contents goes in this blank space
#endif
```

For our mock weather project, we need to draw from several extra library files, so I usually add those next:

```
#ifndef BEENHERE
  #define BEENHERE

  #include <SPI.h>              // Shipped with the patch
```

```
  #include <TFT_eSPI.h>        //https://github.com/Bodmer/TFT_eSPI
  #include <Rotary.h>          // https://github.com/brianlow/Rotary
#endif
```

The SPI.h header file is distributed with each software patch you installed, designed to “fit” each particular microcontroller. However, the additional two other library files are not standard install libraries. In those cases, you can use the Library Manager in the IDE to install the new library, or you can go to the URL I've placed in the comments and download/install them yourself. (We cover library installation in Chapter 13. If you don't have the two libraries mentioned here already installed and are not familiar with the process, read the Installation section of Chapter 13.)

So how does this header file setup work? Look at the first two directives we have in the file and the last one. What those directives say is: “If the symbolic constant *BEENHERE* is *not* defined, define that constant now and then process every remaining statement in this file.” At the top of every other source code file in the program we have:

```
#ifndef BEENHERE
  #include "weather.h"
#endif
```

which guarantees that the header file contents are available to that file. If the *.ino file is read first by the compiler, the content of the header file is now known to *.ino file.

Now suppose the compiler reads those three lines in the *DisplayManagement.cpp* file. Because *BEENHERE* was defined when the *.ino file read the header file, the *#ifndef BEENHERE* prevents us from re-reading everything in the header file. There's no reason to read it a second time, because the IDE already knows about everything there is in the header file. In other words, *those three preprocessor directives prevent us from double-reading the contents of the header file.*

Why Have a Header File?

Why is it important to not read the header file a second time? Well, let's ask the more important question first: Why do we even need a header file? Consider your TFT display. It's probably true that different elements of the program are going to need to know the pixel resolution of your display. So somewhere in the code you need these definitions;

```
int height = 320;
int width  = 480;
```

(You could make them constants using the *const* data qualifier, but I don't. The reason for not defining them as constants is that using them in assignment statements should properly use a cast, to avoid a silent cast, which I don't like.) Now here's the problem. There's a good chance that the *DisplayManagement.cpp* file needs to have access to these variables, but it's probably equally likely that *WeatherStation.ino* also needs access to them. If we define these variables with global scope in one file, their scope ends with the last statement in the file in which they are defined. A header file lets us solve this problem. We do this as follows:

Weather.h

```
#ifndef BEENHERE
#define BEENHERE
// a bunch of lines we have omitted from the header file...

 extern int height;       // Declare them in the header file so
 extern int width;        // they have an attribute list.

 #endif
```

WeatherStation.ino

```
 #ifndef BEENHERE
   #include "weather.h"
 #endif
 char *menuChoices[] = {"  Read  ", "  Test  ", " Config "};

 int height = 320;     // Define them here so they have an lvalue
 int width  = 480;
```

By placing a *data declaration in the* header file, all source code files have access to the attribute list of the variable. This means the compiler has enough "attribute list" information about the variable to use it in any file. However, only the *.ino file contains the *data definition* for the variable, so we don't get any "multiply-defined" error messages.

Note that *you cannot initialize a variable declaration*. For example, that means we cannot set the pixel sizes for *height* and *width* in the header file. Those values can only be assigned at the point of definition, not declaration. Being able to only set initial values at the point of definition makes a lot of sense if you think about it. The purpose of an initializer value *is* so that variable starts its life with a known rvalue. However, it is only after a variable is defined that it has a known lvalue. How can you initialize the rvalue of a variable if you don't know its lvalue? Hint: You can't! Therefore, header files cannot contain initializer lists for variables.

For those *.cpp files that use a specific variable, the linker fills in the lvalue for each variable and all is right with the world. Listing 11.4 shows a skeletal form I use for my header files. It's only a suggestion and you are free to modify it as you see fit.

Listing 11.4. Skeletal header file.

```
#ifndef BEENHERE
#define BEENHERE

//================ Symbolic constants ========================
#define DEBUG          // Comment this line out for production

//================ Globals ====================================
extern char *menuChoices[3];
 extern int height;
 extern int width;

//================ Instantiate ================================
 extern Rotary rotary;
 extern TFT_eSPI tft;

//================ Function prototypes ========================
 void Rotate();
 void Splash();

#endif
```

As I add more global variables/objects, write new functions, or add new symbolic constants, I place them in the project's header file. I also tend to place things in the header file in alphabetical order within data types. While it does make things easier to find in the file, it's probably more of an OCD thing.

SPI Display I/O Lines

Most inexpensive TFT displays support the SPI interface. It is for that reason that I am using a 3.5" SPI TFT display in this program. You can do the same, but the SPI connections to your microcontroller may well vary from those I'm using with an ESP32 microcontroller. Table 11.3 shows the SPI I/O lines that you can use with different microcontrollers. Note that your microcontroller may have more than one set of SPI control lines. Use whatever is convenient.

Table 11.3. SPI control I/O pins

Pin	SPI	Nano	STM 32	ESP32	Teensy 4.0
SDO (MISO)	Bus read data signal	D12	PA6	19	12

LED[1]	Backlight. If not controlled, connect 3.3V for always bright	5V	5V	3.3V	Vin
SCK	Bus clock signal	D13	PA5	18	13
SDI (MOSI)	Bus write data signal	D11	PA7	23	11
DC	Register/data signal. HIGH:register, LOW:data	D9	PA1	2	9
RESET	Reset signal (LOW reset)	D8	PA0	4	8
CS	Chip Select (LOW enable)	D10	PA2	15	10
GND	Ground	GN D	GND	GND	GND
Vcc	Voltage input, 5V, 3.3V	5V	3.3V	3.3V	3.3V

1. *Most connect the LED pin to the Vcc pin through a dropping resistor (e.g., 100Ω).*

Splash Screen

One of the first things I do with a new display program is write a Splash screen. This is really little more than displaying the name of the program and who wrote it. Many programmers also display a software version number. When I first started writing this program, I knew it was going to feature a menu system, so that was my temporary title for my Splash screen. My testing Splash screen is shown in Figure 11.5. For me, the Splash screen serves a secondary purpose besides having something to say about the program. It gives me a chance to experiment with the display and its supporting graphics library. Listing 11.5 shows the code for my Splash screen.

Figure 11.5. Menu testing Splash screen.

Listing 11.5. Splash screen source code.

```
/*****
  Purpose: A brief signon message

  Parameter list:
    void

  Return value:
    void
*****/
void Splash()
{
  tft.fillScreen(TFT_BLACK);       // in essence, a clear screen
  tft.setTextColor(TFT_MAGENTA, TFT_BLACK);
  tft.setTextSize(5);
  tft.setCursor(90, 50);
  tft.println("Menu System");
  //  tft.print("1234567890123456789012345678901234567890");
  tft.setTextColor(TFT_YELLOW, TFT_BLACK);
  tft.setTextSize(2);
  tft.setCursor(218, 150);
  tft.println("by");
  // tft.print("1234567890123456789012345678901234567890");
  tft.setTextColor(TFT_GREEN, TFT_BLACK);
  tft.setTextSize(3);
  tft.setCursor(150, 200);
  tft.println("Jack Purdum");
  //  tft.print("1234567890123456789012345678901234567890");
  delay(SPLASHDELAY);
  tft.fillScreen(TFT_BLACK);
}
```

The first statement clears the screen to black. My guess is you can guess what the rest of the statements do. The *setTextColor()* method sets the text color to magenta on a black background. The next statement adjusts the text size to 5. Next the display cursor is set to column 90 on row 50. Finally, the code displays “Menu System” using the attributes that have been previously set. You can see the combined effect in Figure 11.5.

But what's the commented-out line with all the numbers about?

Because this was a new display for me and I had not used the graphics library before, I wanted to know how many characters fit on a display row using the different font sizes. Because these libraries use fixed fonts, by counting the number of characters displayed on a row and dividing that into the pixel width (480), I know the pixel width required for each letter for each font size. Using the Splash screen and the “number rows”, I constructed the Table 11.4. It's pretty obvious that a one unit increase in the font size adds about 6 pixels to each character's width. Such a table

Table 11.4. Font size and pixels per character

Font Size	Pixels Per Character
2	12
3	18
4	24
5	30

makes it easier to place text on the screen at a specific row/column location. You can figure out the number of pixels for a character height by just printing a bunch of rows and dividing that into the pixel height (320) of the display. Also not in Listing 11.5 is the use of the SPLASHDELAY symbolic constant. I typically set this to 4000L when the code is done, but something like 500L during development so I don't have to sit there waiting for the Splash screen to go away.

Listing 11.6 shows the content of the WeatherSystem.ino file. Near the top we initialize the *menuChoice[]* array. I've padded with spaces so each option uses 8 character spaces. I think that makes the menu look better by providing equal spacing for each menu regardless of the characters in that menu option. If you use a lot of menu options, you may not have enough room to pad the options. Any remaining variables that are declared in the header file are defined in this *ino* file.

Listing 11.6. WeatherSystem.ino.

```
#ifndef BEENHERE
  #include "weather.h"
#endif
char *menuChoices[] = {"  Read  ", "  Test  ", " Config "};

int currentMenuChoice;  // Which menu option is currently 
highlighted?
int currentMenuLevel;   // We only have one, but you can add more
int height = 320;       // display stuff
int width  = 480;

volatile int encoderDirection;  // Used in the ISR

//================== Instantiate objects 
=========================
Rotary rotary = Rotary(ENCODERPINA, ENCODERPINB);// Encoder object
TFT_eSPI tft  = TFT_eSPI();                     // graphics display
//================== Program start 
================================
void setup()
{
#ifdef DEBUG
  Serial.begin(9600);
  while (!Serial)       // Waste time until Serial is created

  tft.init();                   // Pay attention to caveat in book
  tft.setRotation(1);           // Orient to 480 wide and 320 tall
  pinMode(ENCODERPINA, INPUT_PULLUP);   // Encoder pins are inputs
  pinMode(ENCODERPINB, INPUT_PULLUP);
                             // Trigger an interrupt ON state changes
  attachInterrupt(ENCODERPINA, Rotate, CHANGE);
  attachInterrupt(ENCODERPINB, Rotate, CHANGE);

  Splash();
  currentMenuChoice = 0;
  currentMenuLevel  = -1;
}

void loop() {
  if (currentMenuLevel < 0) {
    ShowMainMenu();                   // Display menu row...once
  }
  if (encoderDirection) {
    UpdateMainMenu(encoderDirection); // Update menu if encoder 
moved
    encoderDirection = 0;
  }
}
```

In *setup()*, the code establishes the working environment for the program. It initializes the graphics display via the call to *tft.init()*. The *setRotation(1)* call allows you to print with the text set with different orientations. You can use 1 through 4 for the function argument, which rotates the text presentation 90 degrees.

Next we set the pin mode for the encoder pins, using the *INPUT_PULLUP* symbolic constant. In essence, this adds pullup resistors to the pins which prevents them from having "floating values". We want digital I/O pins to be either 0 or 1 (i.e., 0V or 3.3V or 5V, depending on microcontroller), and not float with some wishy-washy intermediate value.

attachInterrupt()

It is the *attachInterrupt()* function calls that set up the encoder pins for interrupt use. In the call:

```
attachInterrupt(ENCODERPINA, Rotate, CHANGE);
```

the code is setting up *ENCODERPINA* for use as an interrupt pin. The second function argument, *Rotate*, is the name of the ISR that processes the interrupt. Recall that a function name without parentheses resolves to that function's lvalue in memory. The final argument tells what triggers the interrupt. Here, you have 4 choices:

LOW – trigger whenever the pin is low (position 2)
CHANGE – trigger whenever the state of the pin changes (0 → 1)
RISING – trigger when the pin transitions from low to high (2 → 3)
FALLING – trigger when the pin transitions from high to low (4 → 5)

The numbers at the end of the descriptions above are positions for the A signal in Figure 11.3 when moving from left to right. In our code, any time the state of one of the encoder pins changes, the ISR function named *Rotate()* is called. Okay, so what happens when a change triggers the call to *Rotate()*?

Actually, as you can see in Listing 11.7, not much.

Listing 11.7. The ISR function Rotate().

```
/*****
  Purpose: ISR to process encoder interrupt

  Parameter list:
    void

  Return value:
    void
*****/
void Rotate()
{
  unsigned char result = rotary.process();

  encoderDirection = 0;
  switch (result) {
```

```
    case 0:            // No interrupt
      return;
      break;

    case DIR_CW:         // clockwise
      encoderDirection = 1;
      break;

    case DIR_CCW:         // clockwise
      encoderDirection = -1;
      break;

    default:
      encoderDirection = 0;
      break;
  }
}
```

We are using the Rotary library written by Brian Low (see the weather.h header file and the #include for his library) to call the *process()* method of the *rotary* object to see which direction the encoder was moved. If the encoder is not moving, *process()* returns a zero. Including this capability means we could use this library for polling use, too. (We have a case 0, although we don't need it. Why would you need it if you used polling instead? Think about it.) The symbolic constants *DIR_CW* and *DIR_CCW* indicate the direction of change and we set the global variable *encoderDirection* accordingly.

As you can see in Listing 11.6, a non-zero value for *encoderDirection* causes us to call *UpdateMainMenu(encoderDirection)*. Listing 11.8 shows the *UpdateMainMenu()* code. The first thing we do is determine how many menu options are in the *menuChoice[]* array by using the macro named *ELEMENTS()*. That macro is defined in the header file so all files have access to it.

The only tricky part about updating the *menu choices* as the user scrolls through them is to remember that you must restore the menu option they *didn't* choose before you move to a new menu choice and highlight it.

Listing 11.8. The UpdateMainMenu() source code.

```
/*****
  Purpose: to display the main menu options

  Argument list:
    int direction        // Which direction is it changing

  Return value:
    void
*****/
```

```
void UpdateMainMenu(int direction)
{
  int numberOfChoices = ELEMENTS(menuChoices);  // How many
options?
  tft.setTextColor(TFT_GREEN, TFT_BLACK);       // green on black
  tft.setCursor(MAINMENUSPACING * currentMenuChoice, 0);
  tft.print(menuChoices[currentMenuChoice]);   // turn off last
                                               // option
  currentMenuChoice += direction;
                                        // The new menu option
  if (currentMenuChoice < 0) {          // Did we go too far left?
    currentMenuChoice = numberOfChoices - 1; // Yep, wrap to last
  } else {
    if (currentMenuChoice > numberOfChoices) { // Too far right?
      currentMenuChoice =  0;         // Yep, wrap to first choice
    }
  }
  tft.setTextColor(TFT_BLACK, TFT_WHITE);
                                       // Make active menu option
  tft.setCursor(MAINMENUSPACING * currentMenuChoice, 0);
  tft.print(menuChoices[currentMenuChoice]);
  currentMenuLevel = 0;                // Set to top menu level
}
```

Figure 11.6 illustrates what we mean. If the user wants to move from the Read menu option to

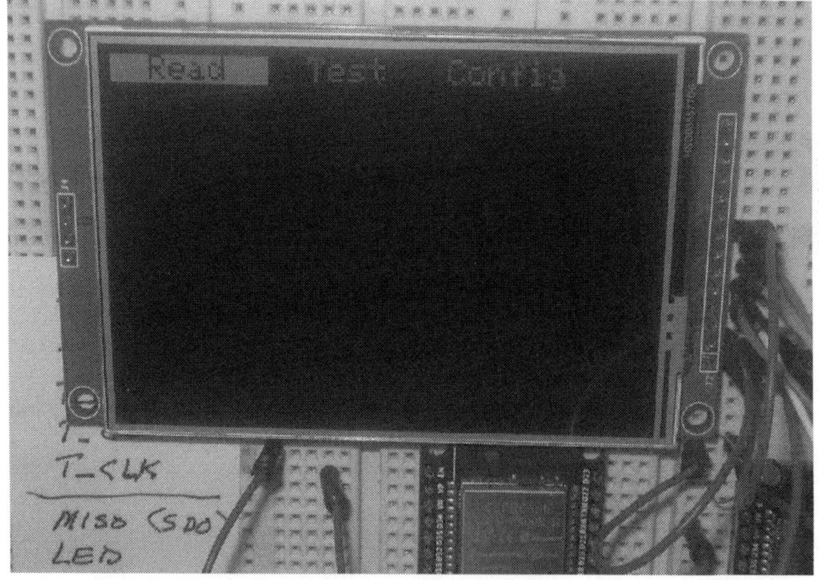

Figure 11.6. The main menu

the Test menu option, we need to redraw Read with green letters on a black background and then move to Test and display it with black letters on a white background. If you read Listing 11.8 carefully, you'll see that's exactly what the code does. Indeed the second three statements restore the Read menu choice to green letters on a black background.

Next, the variable *currentMenuChoice* is changed by the statement:

```
currentMenuChoice += direction;   // The new menu option
```

Think about what this does. If *currentMenuChoice* is 0, as it is in Figure 11.6, and the user rotates the encoder CW, *direction* equals 1, which bumps up *currentMenuChoice* to 1. The *if* statement block just checks to see if we are at an "endpoint" in the menu. For example, if Config was highlighted and the user turned the encoder CW, there are no more menu choices, so we "wrap around" to the first menu choice (Read). If we are on Read like in Figure 11.6 and then rotate the encoder CCW, we "wrap" the other direction and highlight Config. The remaining statements in *UpdateMainMenu()* simply redraw Test as black letters on a white background.

By the way, if you look near the lower-left corner of Figure 11.5, you can see a white piece of paper with MISO (SD0) written on it. Actually, that is a description of each of the display pins when looking at them from the viewing side of the display. I usually tape such a sheet on the breadboard when I'm working with a new display. Otherwise, you'll find yourself flipping the display back and forth about a bazillion times while you hook up the data lines.

As simple as this program is, it provides all the basics you need to write a display-based menuing system. All you need to do is write code that reads the encoder selection (a switch connected to an I/O pin) and then branch to the section of code that processes the menu selection.

Conclusion

The purpose of this chapter was to see the differences between using polling or interrupts when writing the user interface for a program. In those programs that have the program input coming from the user via keystrokes or button presses, polling is usually going to be fast enough for program use. In other situations where quick response is critical, interrupts are the way to go. You also learned how to use the bitwise operators to shift or mask data bits to accomplish a given task. Finally, we introduced a simple menuing system that uses an interrupt-driven encoder for menu selection.

Now you need to experiment with what was covered in this chapter. Working the exercises at the end of this chapter is a good place to start. However, you have enough C under your belt to strike out on your own. Think of a program you'd like to write and give it a go. It's a great way to learn.

Exercises

1. Why did I use a symbolic constant for TIMETARGET when I could have used:

```
unsigned long timeTarget = 1000UL;
```

2. In four sentences or less, explain the difference between polling and interrupts.

3. Use a symbolic constant in the *ProcessEncoder()* function to get rid of the magic number “4” in Listing 11.3.

4. What do the symbolic constants INPUT_PULLUP and INPUT_PULLDOWN do?

5. Assume that a pushbutton switch is connected to pin I/O 12 of your microcontroller. How would you write the code to see if it was pressed?

6. What does w equal?

```
byte x = 0b11111111;
byte w = 0b10101010;

w = x >> 2;
```

7. What is the return data type on an ISR?

8. What does the keyword *volatile* do and when should you use it?

9. What is a blocking function?

10. Suppose in Figure 11.6 that when you press the switch to select the Read menu option, the user should be presented with a submenu that appears directly below it:

Read Test Config

Temperature
Humidity
Barometer

Write the code that would present the submenu below Read if they select that option.

Chapter 12 A Gentle Introduction to C++ and Object Oriented Programming

Why C++?

It may seem strange for an introductory text on C to tackle a discussion of C++. However, it really isn't that strange when you think about it. First, Object Oriented Programming (OOP) has a number of very useful concepts buried in the C++ language that we can use in plain old C.

Second, every library I've used in the Arduino IDE environment is written in C++. Indeed, I think that one reason you hear so much about the Arduino programming platform is because of its robust and deep library pool. Experienced programmers know that good libraries allow them to offload a lot of programming work onto those libraries, making their job easier. However, to be able to use those libraries effectively requires you to know a little bit about how they are written.

Third, knowing how libraries are written and organized can come in handy should you need to put your code on a diet to fit the microcontroller's limited resources. I know of one amateur radio product with software that simply wouldn't "fit" as it was written. However, one programmer was able to venture into the library's source code and chop out those elements of the library that were not needed so the code fit within the memory resources available.

Finally, thinking in terms of programming objects forces you to view things in another light. Two perspectives are almost always better than one. The material presented in this chapter will help you to better_ understand-how libraries work and result in you writing better programs.

Object Oriented Programming (OOP)

I've heard other programmers refer to C++ as a "beefed-up" version of C. I asked them to define "beefed-up", but really didn't get an answer. I'm not surprised since the C++ feature set doesn't lend itself well to a simple two-sentence description. I was at the Software Development Conference in San Francisco (1987??) and heard Bjarne Stroustrup, the father of C++, give his keynote address "C with Classes". (It wasn't even called C++ yet.) I remember 750 of us filing into the auditorium to hear his presentation. About an hour and a half later, 749 of us filed out saying "What the hell was that all about?" I did not understand what Object Oriented Programming was about or what advantages it brought to the table and I'm pretty sure I wasn't alone in that feeling.

Fast forward about five years ~~to~~ when I was part of a consulting team that was using C++. Despite five years of investigating C++, I still "didn't get it". I could "use" it, but I still didn't understand it. Then one night as I was trying to fall asleep, so help me, there was a flash of light and I suddenly understood what OOP and C++ was all about! It was the only epiphany I've ever had, but well-worth the wait. While I don't have the hubris to think that this chapter is going to lead to your epiphany moment, I do hope it gives you some insight to the power that OOP affords.

And don't think for a moment that OOP or C++ is too difficult to understand and use. The fact is, if you've compiled and run at least one program that used Serial.print(), you've already used C++. This chapter just wants to build on that limited experience and flesh in some missing details.

We start our OOP discussion using C++ libraries as the focal point. As we stated earlier, virtually all of the Arduino IDE's libraries are written in C++ and you need to learn how to read, understand, and use the nuggets of gold that are available in those libraries.

What is a Library

A C library is a collection of code that is designed to address one particular aspect of a programming *task*. For example, the Rotary library is designed to let you use rotary encoders in your programs. The Adafruit company has dozens of libraries tailored to specific uses, like the AdafruitLiquidCrystal library to be used with an LCD display. They also have the Adafruit_GFX library that contains graphics functions for drawing on various graphics displays. There are libraries written for TFT displays, OLED displays, and specialty libraries, like a Fast Fourier Transform library. This source, https://www.arduinolibraries.info, shows that there are over 2800 contributed libraries available for you to use...for free! Every one of these libraries means you get to stand on the shoulders of others and use their work in your own programs. Indeed, just becoming aware of all of the library choices you have is a large, but worthwhile, effort.

How to Think About Libraries

Before we talk about the library code, let's consider how they are used by the compiler to make your work easier. Let's suppose that you want to use the Adafruit graphics library. You already learned in Chapter 10 that you make this library known to the compiler using the *#include* preprocessor directive:

```
#include <Adafruit_GFX.h>
```

If you load the Adafruit_GFX.h header file into a text editor, about 60 lines down you'll see something like:

```
void drawCircle(int16_t x0, int16_t y0, int16_t r, uint16_t
                color);
void drawCircleHelper(int16_t x0, int16_t y0, int16_t r,
                uint8_cornername, uint16_t color);
void fillCircle(int16_t x0, int16_t y0, int16_t r, uint16_t
                color);
void fillCircleHelper(int16_t x0, int16_t y0, int16_t r,
                      uint8_t cornername, int16_t delta, uint16_t
                      color);
void drawTriangle(int16_t x0, int16_t y0, int16_t x1, int16_t y1,
                int16_t x2, int16_t y2, uint16_t color);
void fillTriangle(int16_t x0, int16_t y0, int16_t x1, int16_t y1,
                int16_t x2, int16_t y2, uint16_t color);
void drawRoundRect(int16_t x0, int16_t y0, int16_t w, int16_t h,
                int16_t radius, uint16_t color);
void fillRoundRect(int16_t x0, int16_t y0, int16_t w, int16_t h,
                int16_t radius, uint16_t color);
void drawBitmap(int16_t x, int16_t y, const uint8_t bitmap[],
                int16_t w, int16_t h, uint16_t color);
```

These are function prototypes you learned about in Chapter 6 for just some of the graphics methods that you can use in your programs from the Adafruit_GFX graphics library. (Technically, these are *method prototypes* since they come from a C++ library.) If you use the *drawCircle()* method in your program, the compiler places that method name in its symbol table so the linker knows to pull that code from the library into your program.

Pull that code? How does that work? While this discussion is a simplification, think of a library as a single book. If you open that book and look at its Table of Contents (TOC), instead of seeing a chapter title and page number, you might see something like:

```
drawCircle....................231,145
drawCircleHelper..............580,331
fillCircle.....................25,87
fillCircleHelper............1010,1285
```

and so on for all of the methods in the library. (A C++ *method* is very much like a C function. However, C++ calls them methods to distinguish them from C functions in programming discussions. More on this later in the chapter.)

Let's suppose you use the *drawCircle()* method in your program. The compiler left an entry for that method in the symbol table, as well as some question marks in the code where you call *drawCircle()*. Now the linker comes along and sees *drawCircle()* in the symbol table. The linker opens the TOC for the library, finds the *drawCircle()* entry, and knows that it needs to skip over the first 231 bytes in the library file and copy the next 145 bytes into your program. It then records the lvalue of where it placed *drawCircle()* code in memory. The linker then "back-fills" all of the question marks where the *drawCircle()* method was called and replaces them with that method's lvalue. (Yes, this description is a simplification, but close enough to get the idea across.)

Libraries, therefore, are a bunch of pre-written, tested, and debugged chunks of code that can make your programming life a whole lot easier. Most of your work is providing the syntactic glue to hold all that library code together. What we need to do now is understand the framework upon which those libraries are built.

Objects in C++

C++ is based on the concept of objects. Indeed, that's what Object Oriented Programming (OOP) is all about. *C++ objects are models or simplifications of things* we see around us. There are plastic model airplanes based upon the Boeing 777 aircraft that a 10 year old child can assemble. We can look at that model and get some appreciation and understanding of what a 777 plane is. However, instead of assembling the 6 million parts that actually make up the 777, our understanding is derived from a few dozen parts. That simplification of reality is what a C++ object is: simplifications of things around us.

C++ objects can be reduced to two elements:

properties (attributes) *that describe the object*
methods (actions) *that the object does or can support.*

C++ Properties

Sticking with our 777 example, we know there are really over 6 million parts in a 777, but we might simplify it to a fuselage type and length, wings, engines, landing gear, tail assembly, number of passengers and crew, and cockpit. These simplified parts are the properties, or attributes, of a 777. *Properties are variables that belong to the class which describe the object*. For example, the fuselage type might be a 777-200, so we might see the following properties defined for a 777-200 object:

```
char fuselageType[]  = "777-200";
float fuselageLength = 63.1;       // in meters
float wingspan       = 60.9;
```

However, if we changed the fuselage type to the extended range 777-300ER, these properties change to:

```
char fuselageType[]  = "777-300ER";
float fuselageLength = 73.9;       // in meters
float wingspan       = 64.8;
```

It is the properties of an object that allows us to describe what the object looks like or what information the object contains. It is the properties that allow us to distinguish one object (e.g., a 777-200) from another (a 777-300ER). In that sense, class properties are the "nouns" of an object which can be used to build an *attribute list* (e.g., image) of that object.

C++ Methods

The primary purpose of a 777 is to move people and cargo between two locations. Therefore, one of the methods we need is a *cruise()* method. However, we also need other methods for the 777 object to do its job. We probably need:

```
int airComsCheck();
int airsurfacesCheck();
int baselegCheck();
int boardCrew();
int boardPassengers();
int cruise();
int deplaneCrew();
int deplanePassengers();
int electricalSystemsCheck();
int finalApproach();
int galleyCookMeals();
int land();
int preflightCheckSequence();
int purgeWasteTanks();
int takeoff();
int takeoffRunUpCheck();
int towerCheck();
```

and probably a thousand other things I don't know about. If this were an actual prototype list, it is quite likely that each method would have one or more parameters in its signature. For example, the cruise() method would likely pass speed in the desired cruising speed and (perhaps) altitude. The point is that an object's *methods tell us what the object does and how to do them.* A C++ method is almost identical to a C function, except object methods are buried *inside* of the object instead of having global scope like a function has. Just like C functions, methods usually take on the connotation of a verb, describing some action that the object can do.

Collectively, the properties and methods of an object comprise what is called a C++ class

What is a C++ Class?

A C++ class is a group of properties and methods that collectively describe what an object is and what it can do. Think of a class as a set of *blueprints* for an object. A skeletal view of a class appears in Listing 12.1. (There are other possible (e.g., *protected*) parts of a class, but we don't need to worry about them here.)

Listing12.1. The basic parts of a C++ class

```
class Plane777
{
   public:                    // Make available outside the class

   private:                   // Make available only within the class
};
```

The *class* keyword is used to denote that we are about to declare a class object. The class identifier is the name you wish to use for this class declaration (e.g., Plane777). Everything between the opening brace ('{') of the class and its closing brace ('}') contains the properties and methods for this class object.

Within the class braces is the public keyword. The public keyword is an access specifier and means that any property or method with the *public* specifier can be accessed from outside the object. The *private* keyword is also an access specifier, but means that access is limited to only those properties and methods in the class. I think of anything with the *private* keyword as something secret that we don't want exposed outside of the class itself. In our 777 example, a *private* property might be *blackBoxPassword* and a *private* method might be *readBlackBox()*.

Adding some flesh to our skeletal Listing 12.1 yields Listing 12.2.

Listing12.2. A C++ class with some details

```
class Plane777
{
  public:          // Make available outside the class
    char fuselageType[15];
    float fuselageLength;
    float wingspan;

    int airComsCheck();
    int airsurfacesCheck();
    int baselegCheck();
    int boardCrew();
    int boardPassengers();
    int cruise();
    int deplaneCrew();
    int deplanePassengers();
    int electricalSystemsCheck();
    int finalApproach();
    int galleyCookMeals();
    int land();
    Plane777();
    int preflightCheckSequence();
    int purgeWasteTanks();
    int takeoff();
    int takeoffRunUpCheck();
    int towerCheck();

  private:         // Make available only within the class
    char blackBoxPassword[50];
    char *readBlackBox();
};
```

Listing 12.2 tells us that all of the properties and methods within the class declaration, with the exception of *blackBoxPassword[]* and *readBlackBox()* are accessible for external use.

Listing 12.2 is, therefore, is a guideline for creating a 777 object. That is, the *class Plane777* is a <u>*declaration*</u> for creating a 777 plane object. In that sense, it's like a set of blueprints for a house. The blueprints tell you how to build it, but the house doesn't yet exist. You can't “move into” a set of blueprints. You need to hire a contractor to build the house. In similar fashion, you can't fly a *Plane777* declaration to London. You need to create a *Plane777* object in order to use it.

Object Instantiation

The process of using a class declaration shown in Listing 12.2 to define a class Plane777 object is called object instantiation. Until you instantiate an object of a class, you do not have anything that you can actually use in your program. Without object instantiation, all you have is a set of dusty blueprints for the object that are of absolutely no use to you.

To have an object that you can actually use in your program requires you to instantiate it. The syntax for instantiating an object is:

```
objectClassName  objectName;
```

or

```
Plane777 myPlane;
```

where *Plane777* is the *class* identifier and *myPlane* is the object being instantiated. This single statement takes your set of the *class Plane777* blueprints and carves out a chunk of memory big enough to hold the *myPlane* object. Just like any other data definition, *myPlane* now has an lvalue in memory that serves as your go-to place for using your *myPlane* object.

Class Constructors

Let's take a peek at what happens when you instantiate (define) a class object. Without you really knowing it, the compiler automatically created a method called a constructor. The *constructor* contains some smoke-and-mirrors stuff that sets things up correctly in memory so you can use the object. *The constructor method always has the same name as the class itself.* If you look back at Listing 12.2, you'll see that I sneaked in a method named *Plane777()*. That's the constructor for this class. You are free to create a *Plane777()* class constructor yourself if you want to. However, if you don't, the compiler automatically creates a constructor for you which is then used as part of the instantiation process for the object. The source code for a default constructor is not visible in any of your source code files, but nonetheless exists for your program.

Why do you need a class constructor? If you think about it, doesn't a *class* look similar to a *struct*? A major difference, however, is that structures can only contain variables, but a *class* can contain variables *and* methods. It's pretty simple for the compiler to look at a list of variables declared in a *struct*, add up the number of bytes, and set aside that many bytes for the *struct* when you define it. However, setting things up for a class is a different story because the compiler has to figure out lvalues for every property *and* method that you declare in the class. Having *public* and *private* attributes just adds to the complexity. There are other reasons for the presence of a constructor, but just accept the fact that every object has a constructor that is automatically called when you instantiate a *class* object.

There are several constructor rules you must follow if you decide to write your own constructor.

> *First, it must share the same name as the class.*
> *Second, the constructor cannot return a value.*
> *Third, you can pass arguments to your constructor if you wish.*

Passing arguments to a constructor is a convenient way to set default value(s) for a class property. For example, a church organization once_ asked me to create a membership management program for them. Since virtually every member lived in Indianapolis, my constructor set the *City* and *State* properties to "Indianapolis" and "IN" when a member object was instantiated. In essence, these became the default values for the City and State properties of the object.

Wait a minute! Where's all the code for the class methods? So far, we've only talked about the class header file that declares the class. As a general rule, header files should not contain executable code, so where is the method code?_To find the class source code, you need to look in the class CPP file.

Class *.cpp Files

We talked earlier about the Adafruit_GFX library. One of the public methods listed in the Adafruit_GFX.h header file is:

```
void fillCircle(int16_t x0, int16_t y0, int16_t r, uint16_t
                color);
```

The method prototype tells us that a 16-bit integer sets the X/Y coordinates for drawing a circle with a 16-bit integer radius of *r* and ~~to~~ draws it using a 16-bit color specified by *color.* However, as we_just mentioned, header files normally don't have code in them. The method code is placed in the *.cpp file(s).

Scope Resolution Operator (::)

Okay, so we look in the Adafruit_GFX.cpp file and we find:

```
void Adafruit_GFX::drawCircle(int16_t x0, int16_t y0, int16_t r,
                              uint16_t color)
{
      // the code for this method
}
```

Uh-oh. What's that double-colon all about? (See shaded block above.) The double colon (::) is called the *scope resolution operator*. You can verbalize the scope resolution operator as: "...class has a method declared as...". In this example, then, you can say: "The Adafruit_GFX class has a method declared as *drawCircle()*". In other words, the scope resolution operator links a specific method to its class. Some programmers might also say: "*drawCircle()* is a member of the Adafruit_GFX class." (When used in this fashion, the adjectives "property" and "method" are implied by the word "member" rather than explicitly stated.) The scope resolution operator is like a pedigree certificate in that it tells you where the method came from.

*Using the *.h and *.cpp Files as Information Sources*

When you install a new library, one of the first things you need to do is understand how to use the methods that are embodied within the library. The place to start that understanding is with that library's header file. As we showed in the 777 example, the header file contains prototypes for the methods in the library. For example, with the Adafruit_GFX library, you will find:

```
drawCircle(int16_t x0, int16_t y0, int16_t r, uint16_t color);
```

in its header file. Programmers are notoriously stringy when writing documentation, but the prototype for the *drawCircle()* method is clear enough for us to guess that the center of the circle is placed at the *x0* and *y0* pixel coordinates, *r* is the radius of the circle, and *color* is the line color used to draw the circle. Other times, the method prototypes aren't all that helpful, often because they use cryptic names for the parameter list. In that case, you should look in the corresponding class_*.cpp file to read the full description and the source code for the method. Alas, sometimes even that is not very much help. When that happens, about the best you can do is examine any example program files to see if they use the method(s) you're interested in.

Thinking about objects

Okay, you now have some background information about objects, but you need to adjust the way you look at things when you use OOP versus "conventional" programming. I want you to think of a programming object as a windowless, boxy, black house that only has a front door. If you manage to get into the house, you look around and you see a bunch of people in a large room with name tags like *fontSize, foregroundColor, backgroundColor, width, height*, etc. Surrounding the room are doors with labels on them, like *setCursor(), print(), clear()*, etc. The people in the room represent the class properties of the object and the rooms contain the code for the class methods of the object.

The interior of the_object's room might look something like Figure 12.1.

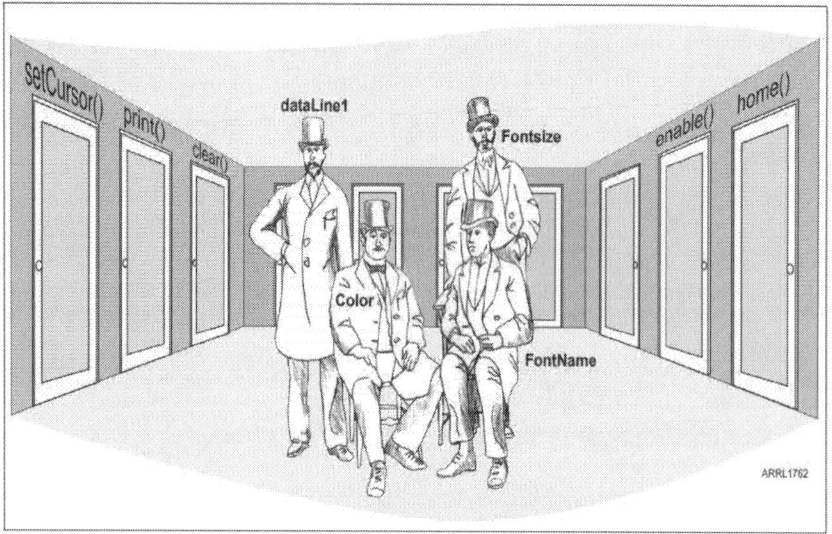

Figure 12.1. Inside an object black box.

Some of the side rooms don't have names above them. Those are the *private* methods outsiders can't use. There may well be some *private* properties, too, but those people are also invisible to us outsiders.

Question: How did you "get inside" the object in the first place? You can't just open the object's front door and walk in. Just like the dot operator was the key to access the members of a structure, so is the dot operator the key that opens the door of an object. For example, suppose you are using an ESP32 board and the TFT_eSPI graphics library. You could instantiate a graphics object with the following statement:

```
TFT_eSPI tft = TFT_eSPI();   // Instantiate graphics object
                             // using constructor call
```

This statement calls the *TFT_eSPI()* constructor (note how the constructor method identifier shares the same name as the class) and instantiates a graphics object named *tft*. Because you have instantiated the object, when the statement finishes, *tft* now has an lvalue and you are now free to use it in your program.

Let's suppose you need a method to clear the graphics display. A clear screen usually clears the screen to black, so you would call the proper graphics method using:

```
tft.fillScreen(TFT_BLACK);
```

The *syntax for gaining access to an object* is always the same: the object's identifier (or name)_followed by the dot operator. In preparation for the method call, you place a copy of the symbolic constant TFT_BLACK's value (i.e., 0xFFFF) onto a piece of paper and stuff it into your backpack. The call causes program control to go to the memory address (lvalue) where the *tft* object is stored. You insert your dotoperator key into the object's keyhole, turn the key, and walk in. You look around and it look's similar to Figure 12.1, but with more people and doors.

You look for the door with *fillscreen()* on it. Because it is a *public* method, you can see the *fillscreen()* nameplate above the door, across the room. You walk across the room, look down, and notice a doormat with a number on it. (That doormat number corresponds to that method's own lvalue.) You knock on the door, and the door flies open, a hand shoots out and grabs your backpack, withdraws back into the room, and slams the door. A few milliseconds later, the door opens again, the hand shoots out with your backpack, drops it on the floor, and retreats back into the room, and slams the door. There's a flash of light and you and your backpack are instantly transferred back to the next instruction after the *tft.fillscreen() method* call. (Because *fillscreen()* is a *void* method, your backpack is empty.) Everything pretty much looks the same, except now the display screen is completely black.

public Object Properties can be Read/Write

Many objects created from libraries have their properties defined in the *public* section of the class. This means you can both read and write their values. For example, I wrote an electronic keyer for use by amateur radio operators for sending Morse Code. One of the class properties was *wordsPerMinute*. Because not all radio operators use the same speed for sending code, the keyer needed to be able to read and write the *wordsPerMinute* property. You might see a statement like this:

```
currentWPM = myKeyer.wordsPerMinute;
```

Verbalizing the assignment expression above, we'd say: "Go to the *myKeyer* object, insert your dot operator key into the lock, walk into the room and look for a person named *wordsPerMinute.* Walk over to that person and ask for a copy of the value that they are holding in their lap. The person writes down a number and sticks it into your backpack and you are instantly transferred back to the point in the program that made the property call to get the object's *wordsPerMinute* value. Once you've returned, you take the number out of your backpack and hand it to *currentWPM.* The variable *currentWPM* takes that number, speeds across the data bus to its lvalue memory location, and dumps that number into the bucket it finds there. The *currentWPM* variable now has the current keyer speed as its rvalue. This is how you *read an object's property.* This is also called *getting* an object's property. *Reading an object's property means that object operand always appears on the right hand side of the assignment operator.*

If you want to set the object's property, you simply switch sides on the assignment expression:

```
myKeyer.wordsPerMinute = currentWPM;
```

Changing an object's property means the object operand always appears on the left hand side of the assignment operator. Such *an object assignment also means you have changed the state of the object*. I want you to verbalize what you see in the statement above, using words like lvalue, rvalue, bucket, bus, backpack, lap, property, state, and dot operator for both expression operands given above. Humor me.

What can mess up these assignment rules? Well, if you've defined a property using the *const* storage modifier, that class property is a read-only property. If the property appears in the *private* section of the class, as an outsider, you're not even supposed to know about it. There are additional (bizarre) things you can do to make properties behave in non-standard ways, but this is good enough for our purposes.

Again...Why C++?

Okay, so you've got a basic understanding of what an object is and how to get or set it. Still, you may be sitting there scratching your head and wondering why the authors of the libraries used C++ and not C. Honestly, that's a fair question, and one I grappled with for five years. Let's step back out of the trees and take a look at the OOP forest.

The OOP Trilogy

The philosophy of OOP (and the benefits it brings to the programmer's table) can be summed up in what's called the Object Oriented Programming Trilogy. The Trilogy is Polymorphism, Inheritance, and Encapsulation. While all three concepts form the heart of the OOP Trilogy, it was Encapsulation that made the penny drop for me. Let's take a quick look at each element of the Trilogy.

Polymorphism and Method Signatures

The word polymorphism roughly translates to "many shapes". In Chapter 6, we discussed the concept of a function signature. As we mentioned earlier, *method signatures* in C++ have the same general interpretation and purpose as function signatures. The component parts of a signature remain the same and convey the same information, regardless of whether you're discussing functions or methods. A method signature tells you the return data type, the method's identifier (or name), and a list of the parameters that you want to pass to the method.

A major difference between function and method signatures, however, is that methods exist *within* objects while functions exist by themselves outside of any object. Indeed, C doesn't let you define a function within another function. Think about what this means. *Functions have global scope* and are everywhere visible in the file in which they are defined. Methods, on the other hand, have their scope confined to the object in which they are defined. This means that, if you defined your object within a function, that object has function scope. Because methods are buried within the object, this also means that those methods within that object have the same function scope. The result is that you can only access an object's method through a very purposeful use of the object's dot operator from within the function in which you defined it.

So what?

Think about this: You have used these object methods in a number of sample questions:

```
char myName[]       = "Jack";
int wordsPerMinute = 25;

Serial.println(myName);
Serial.println(wordsPerMinute);
```

Did you ever stop and ask yourself: “Wait a minute! How can a method named *println()* display a characters string and the *same* method display an integer value? What does that method's signature look like?” It would seem to be a conflict that the *println()* method has a parameter list that magically changes the type in its method signature. Yet, that's sorta what happens.

Do a disk search for the Print.h header file that is shipped with the Arduino IDE. About 60 lines into that file you'll see this list of method prototypes:

```
size_t print(const __FlashStringHelper *);
size_t print(const String &);
size_t print(const char[]);
size_t print(char);
size_t print(unsigned char, int = DEC);
size_t print(int, int = DEC);
size_t print(unsigned int, int = DEC);
size_t print(long, int = DEC);
size_t print(unsigned long, int = DEC);
size_t print(double, int = 2);
size_t print(const Printable&);
```

You might be saying: “What!? Eleven method prototypes with exactly the same method name? In Chapter 3 you told us that function names had to be unique within the first 31 characters. Is this another thing you lied about to us?”

No.

A C++ compiler embraces the concept of *polymorphism*, which means that *method names can be “reused”* *as long as their parameter lists are different*. Different parameter lists mean the method signatures are different. In other words, as long as the parameters the method uses are different, the compiler is smart enough to pick the right one for the task at hand even though there are multiple methods with the same name. If you look at the prototypes from the Print.h header file, you'll see they all obey this rule.

Think what this brings to your programming table. Now you can use a single method name (e.g., *print()*) but pass it eleven different data types without having to memorize a different method name for each data type! This same concept can be extended to other methods, too. For example, if you have a list of names (e.g., *char[]*), their ages (e.g., *int*), and their salaries (e.g., *float*), you can use the same method name, *sort()*, for the three different data sorts:

```
sort(char name[]);
sort(int age);
sort(float wage);
```

You don't need to contend with different method names because their data are different. Indeed, you might even discover that one type of sort (e.g., a Shell sort) works better on a certain type of data than does a different sort (e.g., Insertion sort) so the implementation code can be different as needed. Good stuff!

Inheritance

Inheritance is a feature of C++ that allows you to declare a set of common denominator properties and methods for one class and use those properties and methods to create new subclasses. For example, some time ago I was asked by a real estate investor to write a program that would track their real estate holdings. The investor has three basic types of buildings: residential, commercial, and apartments. Each type of rental property had its own special considerations. While the number of bedrooms affected both residential and apartment properties, it had no impact on the commercial properties. Likewise, commercial properties had to have so many parking places per 100 square feet of building space, of which some fraction had to be for handicap parking. Also, bathroom facilities in commercial properties were affected by the square footage of the building. There were even snow removal restrictions that varied by property type as well as township location. So, how do you minimize the complexity of the software?

You can reduce the complexity by looking for features that are common to all property types, and worry about the details a little later. For example, each property has a number of properties in common: *address, propertyTaxes, purchasePrice, purchaseDate, insuranceCost, mortgageLender, mortgageAmount*, etc. We could create variables for these common_properties of a building and place them in something called a building class. That is, we can take all of the properties that are common to all buildings and hide them in the black, windowless, house named building as shown in Figure 12.2. These class properties become the "people" living within the black "building"_house. In the figure, building holds all of the properties and methods (e.g., *payMortgage(), payInsurance(), collectRents()*, etc.) that are common to all three property types.

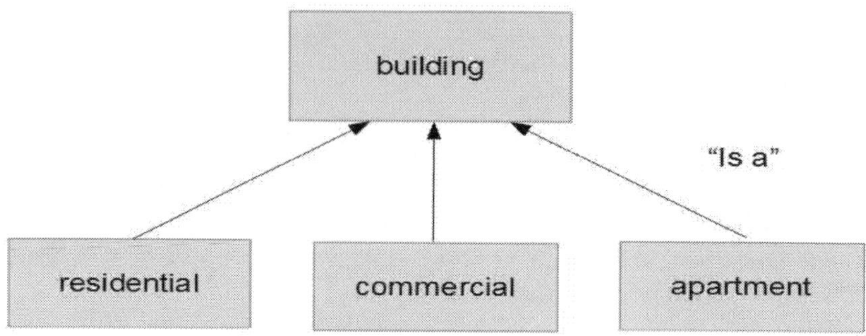

Figure 11.2 Inheritance from building.

We now create three new "subclasses", one for each property type (i.e., residential, commercial, apartment). Each new class holds those properties and methods that make it a unique building and differentiates it from the other building types. For example, the residential class might have an attribute named *squareFeetInFinishedBasement*, which likely does not apply to the other two subclasses. Likewise, a commercial property might have an attribute named *handicappedParkingSlots* that doesn't apply to the other subclasses.

What Figure 12.2 illustrates is that residential, commercial, and apartment buildings are all a special type of the base class called *building*. In other words, these three special types of building "inherit" all of the basic elements shared in common for all buildings. The arrows pointing from the three specific building types to the common building type is called an "is a" relationship and says that each of those special building types inherits all of the traits (i.e., properties and methods) of *building* class. That is, a *residence* "is a" type of *building,* as are *commercial* and *apartment* buildings.

Base and Sub Classes

OOP jargon often refers to *building* as the *base class* and the three building types as *subclasses* of the base class. (Some programmers prefer to call the base class the *parent class* and the subclasses as *child* classes. Pick whatever makes sense to you...the meaning is the same.)

So, what does inheritance bring to the party? Note that, instead of writing all of the program code needed to track property taxes, mortgages, addresses, and other common attributes for each type of building, we can push all of the code for those common attributes and methods into a "common denominator" class (i.e., the base class) and simply let each subclass inherit and use those members variables from the base class. The same is true for many of the methods that are common to all properties (e.g., *payMortgage()*, *payInsurance()*, *payPropertyTaxes()*, *payBribes()*, etc.) This can cut down the duplicate source code by as much as two-thirds. Less code to manage is a good thing.

Perhaps another example would help. You could have a base class named *clsCookieCutter* and subclasses named *clsStar, clsWreath, clsChristmasTree*, and *clsCandyCane*. Each cookie cutter has a metal frame, sharp metal edges, and a handle of some sort affixed to it. While each subclass shares these attributes, the angles of the metal are different for each one and they are constructed slightly differently. Those unique attributes and methods belong in the subclasses.

However, until you take the desired class cookie cutter (e.g., *clsStar*) and push it into the cookie dough (i.e., memory), only then have you instantiated a cookie that you can bake and, ultimately, eat. It is through the act of instantiation that you define something you can use (or eat!).

By using inheritance from the base class, you've reduced the number of lines of program code for tracking those variables and methods by two-thirds of what they would be otherwise. Reducing the lines of code you have to write also means fewer lines to test, debug, and maintain...that's a good thing.

In truth, we don't use inheritance much, perhaps because we don't need the features inheritance makes available. Still, it's good for you to know about it just in case a situation arises for you where it might provide a simpler solution to the task at hand.

Encapsulation and Scope

To me, encapsulation alone makes learning a little C++, and OPP in general, well worth the effort. Also, encapsulation is the one aspect of the OOP Trilogy that you can practice using plain old C. Practicing the tenets of encapsulation in *any* language is going to make you a better programmer. Encapsulation was what gave me my epiphany moment.

Simply stated, *encapsulation is the practice of data hiding*. Data hiding makes it more difficult for other parts of the program to "contaminate" the data. The concept of encapsulation works hand-in-hand with the concept of program scope that you studied in Chapter 6. Encapsulation, however, gives the programmer some options they didn't have before.

The Fight Between Encapsulation and Global Scope

Usually, there's a fist fight going on between the goal of encapsulation and global scope. The fact is, encapsulation makes it much easier to test and debug a program. We talked about this in Chapter 6. If you stop defining variables with global scope and, instead, define them with function or block scope, you significantly reduce the time it takes to isolate a given program bug. It is bug isolation that takes time. Bug fixes are pretty easy once you've isolated the bug._With global scope, the bug could be anywhere the buggy data is used. With function scope, at least you've ruled out every other function in the program as the source of the bug. You can concentrate your sleuthing to that single function. That's the good news.

The fight breaks out because now, if you define a variable with function scope, but_want to use that data in another function, you must explicitly pass that data as a parameter in the function call. This means more typing and coding for the programmer. The best solution: Write perfect, bug-free code every time and use global data. Probably not going to happen.

C++ attacks the problem by encapsulating all of the object's data in the object. That way, it requires a very purposeful use of the dot operator to access the data. Some languages (e.g., C#) even require you to write "Getter" and "Setter" methods to read or write an object's property. (This isn't a bad idea, since this is the ideal place to write data validation code for reading/writing the property.) "Pure C" can't really encapsulate the data in an object. However, it can come close by using a structure. While C can't wrap things up in a nice single place called an object, at least we can hide the data in C. Just moving the data from global to function scope would help. However, unlike C++ methods, C functions are still out there hanging in the breeze, perhaps operating on data they shouldn't be using.

I don't know how to referee this fight. I truly admire the concept of encapsulation and all of the good things that it represents. On the other hand, I've assumed that you are just getting started in programming and forcing the full force of C++ on you at this point would be like throwing a drowning person an anvil. If you can simply make a concerted effort to keep your global data to a minimum by whatever means makes sense to you, that's a good start. As you gain experience, other encapsulation techniques will help you minimize the need for global data.

Installing Libraries

I think one of the most frustrating experiences for beginning programmers is the installation of a new library for use by the IDE. Let's examine two ways that you might use to install a "non-standard library" for use in the Arduino IDE.

First, by "non-standard library" I'm referring to any library that is not part of the Arduino IDE installation or one of its patch installations (i.e., an install for the ESP32, STM32, or Teensy 4.0). For the Arduino standard libraries, they end up being installed in the *libraries* subdirectory. For example, my latest Arduino installation is on drive C_is in directory Arduino1.8.12, so my default libraries are in the *libraries* subdirectory as seen in Figure 12.3.

› Local Disk (C:) › Arduino1.8.12 ›

Name	Date modified	Type	Size
drivers	6/10/2020 11:42 AM	File folder	
examples	6/12/2020 10:18 PM	File folder	
hardware	6/23/2020 11:13 PM	File folder	
java	6/10/2020 11:42 AM	File folder	
lib	6/12/2020 10:18 PM	File folder	
libraries	7/9/2020 10:25 AM	File folder	
reference	6/10/2020 11:42 AM	File folder	
TempSketches	7/16/2020 3:38 PM	File folder	
TempSketchesLib	7/11/2020 11:00 AM	File folder	
tools	6/10/2020 11:42 AM	File folder	
tools-builder	6/10/2020 11:42 AM	File folder	
arduino.exe	6/10/2020 10:14 AM	Application	395 KB
arduino.l4j.ini	6/10/2020 10:14 AM	Configuration sett...	1 KB
arduino_debug.exe	6/10/2020 10:14 AM	Application	393 KB
arduino_debug.l4j.ini	6/10/2020 10:14 AM	Configuration sett...	1 KB
arduino-builder.exe	6/10/2020 10:14 AM	Application	15,971 KB
libusb0.dll	6/10/2020 10:14 AM	Application exten...	43 KB
msvcp100.dll	6/10/2020 10:14 AM	Application exten...	412 KB
msvcr100.dll	6/10/2020 10:14 AM	Application exten...	753 KB
revisions.txt	6/10/2020 10:14 AM	TXT File	93 KB
wrapper-manifest.xml	6/10/2020 10:14 AM	XML Document	1 KB

Figure 12.3. The default IDE library directory.

Let's assume that you are experimenting with the ESP32 microcontroller and you want to install a library you heard about named ACAN2517. How can you install this non-standard library and make it available for use in your programs?

Installing a Non-standard Library using the Library Manager

First, load the Arduino IDE. Then select the Tools → Library Manager menu option. This causes the Library Manager (LM) dialog box to be displayed. The LM is shown in Figure 12.4. If you look across the top of the LM, you will see that I have elected to list All libraries covering All Topics. However, the third text box shows that I typed in ESP32. This tells the LM to limit its listing to only those libraries that are compatible with the ESP32. If you've done other Windows programming, what's being done here is a little different than what you might be used to. Most Windows libraries end up as Dynamic Link Libraries (DLL's) which are in binary format and not "human-readable" by us mortals. Arduino libraries, on the other hand, are Open Source, which means these libraries provide the source code for the library. So when the library manager displays a list of libraries for the ESP32, that does not mean those libraries are in a binary-compatible format. Instead, it means that those libraries have source code that can be compiled and then linked into your program by the IDE's built-in linker.

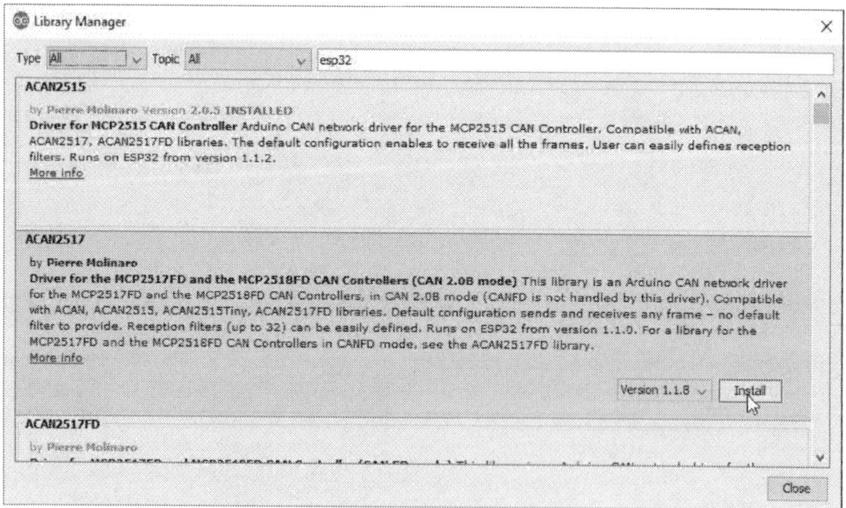

Figure 12.4. The Library Manager dialog box.

By scrolling down to the library I want to install, I simply click on the Install button and the LM copies the selected library into your IDE.

Really? Copies it where?

It depends. The STM32, ESP32, and the Teensy provide their own *libraries* subdirectory on their paths under the *hardware* subdirectory you can see in Figure 12.3. However, if you do a non-standard patch install, it's possible for the patch to put their libraries somewhere else. For example, on the ACAN2517 library I just installed, the LM put the new library in a new subdirectory named *libraries* below my *TempSketchesLib* directory seen in Figure 12.3. Why did it do that? Don't know, but it did.

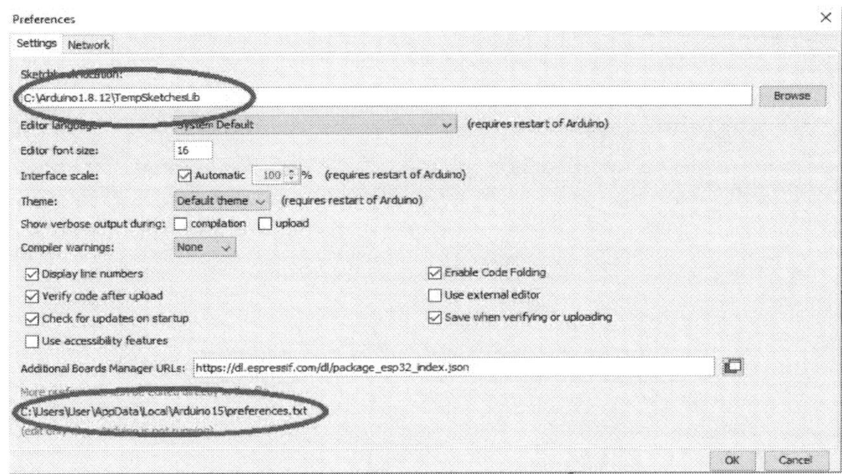

Figure 12.5. The Preferences dialog box.

Look at your Preference data by using File → Preferences in the IDE. My Preferences data looks like that presented in Figure 12.5. When the LM got done copying the new library, I could see it on the *TempSketchesLib/libraries* path. The root of that path is the upper circle in Figure 12.5. To confirm that's what happened, I erased the library and the path name in text box at the top of Figure 12.5. I then use the LM to reinstall the same library.

For a while, I couldn't find the new library, but I finally found it on the path given in the second circled texts box in Figure 12.5. Anyway, the end of the story is that installing a new library using the LM could end up almost anywhere on your system. If you're not sure, use your OS's disk search facility (e.g., Windows Explore) to see where the new library was placed. Your Preferences text box is a good place to start your search looking in the two "circled" text boxes in Figure 12.5. Obviously, the IDE knows where the new library is, and that's really all that matters. Still, I kinda like to know such details.

When you are done with the library installation, you need to restart the IDE so the new library is known to the system.

Manual Library Install

Most of the time I don't use the LM to install a new library. Quite often I discover a new library that's available and want to install it on my system. Many times, the article where I heard about the library includes a download URL for getting the library. Other times, I use Duck-Duck-Go to find the download address. Usually, the download is from the GitHub.com web site, which is a popular repository for Open Source library code. Figure 12.6 shows what a common GitHub download page looks like.

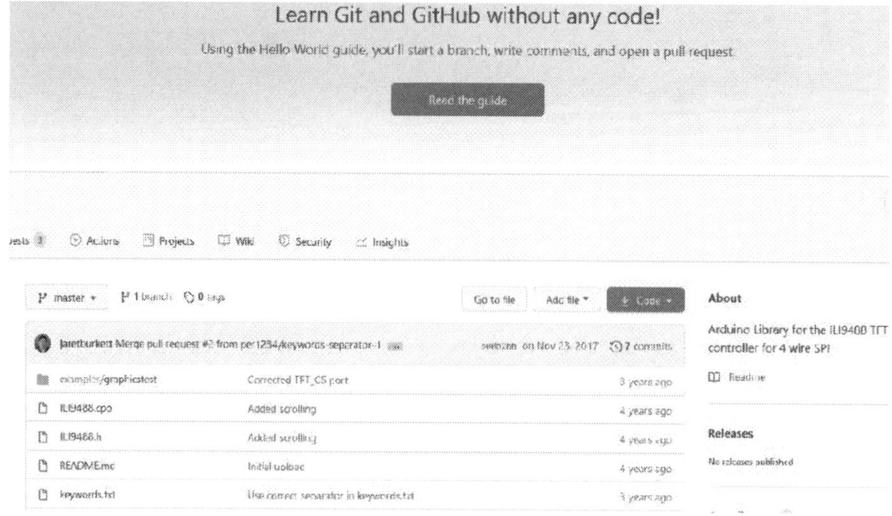

Figure 12.6. Typical GitHub *download page.*

When you click on the "Code" button in Figure 12.6, you are given the standard Save file dialog box, similar to that shown in Figure 12.7. In this example, I am downloading the ILI9844 graphics library.

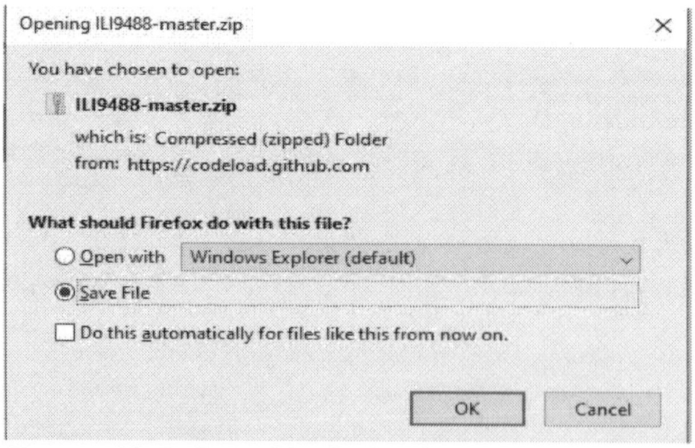

Figure 12.7. Save file dialog box.

The name for the download ZIP file is *ILI9488-master.zip*. I usually copy this ZIP file directly into my Arduino IDE's *libraries* subdirectory (e.g., C:\Arduino1.8.12\libraries). I then double-click on the ZIP file and extract the library contents from the ZIP file directly into the *libraries* subdirectory.

It's at this point in the process where the train leaves the rails for a lot of people. Look at the extraction path shown at the top of Figure 12.8. What actually happens is that the extracted files end up in the libraries subdirectory defined by the path: *libraries\ILI9488-master\ILI9488-master.* The underlined part of that path name is wrong for two reasons.

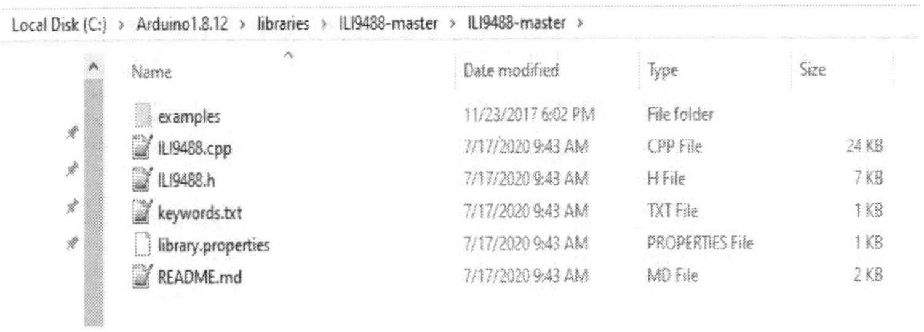

Local Disk (C:) › Arduino1.8.12 › libraries › ILI9488-master › ILI9488-master ›

Name	Date modified	Type	Size
examples	11/23/2017 6:02 PM	File folder	
ILI9488.cpp	7/17/2020 9:43 AM	CPP File	24 KB
ILI9488.h	7/17/2020 9:43 AM	H File	7 KB
keywords.txt	7/17/2020 9:43 AM	TXT File	1 KB
library.properties	7/17/2020 9:43 AM	PROPERTIES File	1 KB
README.md	7/17/2020 9:43 AM	MD File	2 KB

Figure 12.8. Library files after ZIP extraction.

First, the actual library files we need to use from the library (i.e., ILI9488.h and ILI9488.cpp) are too far down the subdirectory path. The IDE won't find them. The files need to be in their own subdirectory *immediately* below the *libraries* subdirectory. That is:

C:\Arduino1.8.12\libraries\ILI9488-master\ILI9488-master

is wrong. It should be:

C:\Arduino1.8.12\libraries\ILI9488

which gives rise to the second problem.

Second, there is a very strict naming convention used by the IDE for imported libraries. If I had nickle for every time I've had to tell someone this library naming convention, I could be drinking a G&T on my chalet porch overlooking the Swiss Alps. So, here are the *rules for the manual installation of library files:*

1. The new library must be in its own subdirectory immediately below the IDE's libraries subdirectory.
2. The *name of that library subdirectory must be the same as the primary file name of the header file for the library being installed.*

Rule #2 has seen thousands of trains crash into the valley below the chalet I'd like to buy. When you get finished with the manual installation, this is what you end up with:

```
C:\Arduino1.8.12\libraries\ILI9488-master\ILI9488-master\examples
                                                          ILI9488.cpp
                                                          ILI9488.h
                                                          Keywords.txt
                                                          library.properties
                                                          Readme.md
```

This is *NOT* going to work because Rule #2 has been ignored. The shaded components in the directory path above are wrong. To fix this so the IDE can find the new library, you must change the path so it reads as follows:

```
C:\Arduino1.8.12\libraries\ILI9488\examples
                                   ILI9488.cpp
                                   ILI9488.h
                                   Keywords.txt
                                   library.properties
                                   Readme.md
```

In the path above, the new library's subdirectory name (ILI9488) matches the primary file name of the libraries C++ source file (i.e., ILI9488.cpp, so it follows Rule #2). Obviously, the shaded parts of the directory path above will vary according to the name of the new library being installed. In all cases, however, the IDE does *not* like the word “master” in a library path name.

Note that almost all libraries have an *examples* subdirectory that contains source code illustrating how to use the library. The examples found in that directory are a learning gold mine...make use of them.

You still have two things to do before the installation of the new library is complete. First, erase the ZIP file that is in the IDE's *libraries* subdirectory. It's done its job and leaving it there just adds clutter to the *libraries* subdirectory. Second, you must close and restart the IDE before the new library can be used in a program. Once those two steps are completed, you're ready to use your installed library.

Conclusion

As I stated at the start of this chapter, you do not need to know the full details of C++ to write Arduino programs. However, understanding the principles of OOP and what C++ brings to the table can help you write better program code, even if it's all “pure C” code. Understanding how polymorphism works should help you understand how methods can have the same name but address different tasks. Encapsulation is a concept that applies to all languages and the more you encapsulate your data, the less time you will have to spend fixing bugs. Actually, inheritance is used in some of the Arduino libraries, but those details are buried in the library code.

Always remember that there are literally thousands of Open Source libraries out there to help you with your programming endeavors. Indeed, any time you start a non-trivial programming task, do an Internet search on the topic first. No offense meant, but it's likely that someone else has already traveled down that same road, affording you the opportunity to stand on their shoulders. There's nothing “sissy” about shoulder-standing...it just makes good sense to do so.

Exercises

1. What is Object Oriented Programming? How would you convince a beginning Arduino programmer that knowing something about OOP is a good idea?

2. What is the difference between a *class* and an object?

3. What is the major distinction between a C *struct* and a C++ *class*?

4. In two sentences or less, explain the dot operator as it pertains to an object. Do the same for the scope resolution operator, “::”.

5. What is the OOP Trilogy? Explain each pillar of the trilogy in three sentences or less.

6. Using the simple menuing system presented in Chapter 11, write the header file for a menu class of your own design.

7. Go to the Internet and look for an SPI TFT LCD display device. (Careful, as a lot of them are for the Raspberry Pi only.) Now determine the driver chip that display uses (e.g., ILI9486, ILI9488, ILI9341). Finally, find a graphics library for the driver chip you selected and manually install it.

> (You don't have to actually purchase a display, but they are kinda fun to play with.)

8. Assume a friend calls you and says he having trouble installing a new library. What questions would you ask in order to help him fix the problem?

Chapter 13 Creating Your Own Classes

When I first started thinking about the content of this chapter, I wanted an example that: 1) was a little complex, 2) illustrated some commonly-used hardware components, and 3) would illustrate useful coding practices. Given those goals, I started thinking about what the example might be.

At first, I thought I would interface a Real Time Clock (RTC) module with one of the microcontrollers. I did an Internet search on that topic for an Arduino and found 1.72 *million* posts. Since that topic had been done to death, I thought about a temperature/humidity sensor, as those sensors are also fairly inexpensive. That is a little less common, with only 1.09 *million* results! If you're interested in either one of those projects, pick one and give it a try. You know enough C now to get almost anything up and running.

During my topic search, one other thing I noticed was that, if I specified a non-Arduino chip in the searches, the search result numbers fell off a cliff. This was more true for the ESP32, which is sad because it has a deep resource pool.

In the process of looking for a chapter topic, I found Bodmer's TFT_eSPI graphics library for the STM32 and ESP32 (https://github.com/Bodmer/TFT_eSPI) microcontrollers. The library includes drivers for wide range of inexpensive SPI displays (i.e., ILI9341, ILI9163, ST7735, S6D02A1, ILI9481, ILI9486, ILI9488, HX8357D, ST7789 and ST7796). What really pushed me over the edge, however, was an example program named TFT_Meters.ino.

Figure 13.1 is a picture of the program as I modified it for this chapter. The program output uses a 3.5" TFT display. The original display example output is animated, with the analog meter needle moving between the endpoints while the linear meters in the lower section have pointers that move in concert with a sine wave. The output shown in Figure 13.1 is my modification where the two meters move together and are controlled by a rotary encoder. I was using an ESP32 at the time and there aren't a lot of good sample programs out there for it, so I thought using the library would be a good exercise in program development. Although written for the STM32 and ESP32, it easily should be adaptable to the Teensy and Arduino family, too.

Figure 13.1. The TFT_Meters.ino display output.

There are all kinds of uses for both analog and linear meters. I concentrated on the analog meter as it serves as a good example of connecting a rotary encoder to a circuit and showing its value on the meter. To that end, I thought I could extend its "teaching usefulness" by building it into a Meter class. A perfect closing example!

Well, maybe not.

When I looked at the source code, there were magic numbers all over the place. All of the coordinate spaces were hard coded pixel locations, which means the meter can only be positioned in the upper-left corner of the display screen as seen in Figure 13.1. Not good.

A little more reflection and I thought it might still be a good learning example, provided I modified it so the user could move the meter around on the display surface. Long story short, we are going to build an analog meter class based on Bodmer's example meter code, but allow the user to move the meter location on the display. I have not done anything with the linear displays that are part of the example code. If you can work your way through the analog meter code, writing code for the linear displays should be fairly easy.

Analog Meter Design Considerations

My objective was to design a simple class that allows you to move the analog meter shown in Figure 13.1 to a different location on the display. The first step is to look at Figure 13.1 and try to construct a list of class properties that we might wish to change. The only property that I must change is the row/column location of the meter. However, there are some other properties that we might also wish to experiment with. Table 13.1 presents some properties that I think might be useful for the class.

Table 13.1. Class properties for the analog meter.

Class Property	Description
char label[]	The name for the data displayed on the meter (e.g., "Volume")
char *tickLables[]	Labels for the major tick marks on the display (e.g., "0", "25", "50", etc.)
int fontSize	What font size is being used
int height	What is the pixel height of the meter
int meterBorderColor	The color of the bezel on the outside of the meter
int maxDisplayHeight	The height of the TFT display in pixels (e.g., 320)
int maxDisplayWidth	The width of the TFT display in pixels (e.g., 480)
int meterFaceColor	The face (i.e., background) color for the meter
int needleEndpointMin	The minimum value shown on the meter
int needleEndpointMax	The maximum value shown on the meter
int showNeedleValue	A toggle that allows you to show or not show the needle's current value
int old_analog	The previous value plotted
uint16_t osx	The old x coordinate space
uint16_t osy	y
int ticklength	The length of the major tick marks for the *tickLables[]* positions
int width	The width of the meter in pixels
int x	The column coordinate for the meter, in pixels
int y	The row coordinate for the meter, in pixels
float ltx	The needle origin

The list of properties presented in Table 13.1 are the "people" you saw in Figure 12.1. Because I've decided to give this class the clever name of *Meter*, if I instantiate a *Meter* object named *myMeter*, then I could set the *height* property with the statement:

```
myMeter.height = 140;
```

which would set the *height* property of the *myMeter* object. You learned how to do that in Chapter 12. However, suppose my display is a 480x320 pixel display and I try to assign ***height*** a value of 350? There's nothing inherent in the class design that prevents that. While we want to make our code as bullet proof as possible, allowing us to make this kind of assignment surrounds the code in silk rather than Kevlar. How can we fix this problem?

One solution is to do something like this:

```
if (newHeight > 0 && newHeight <= myMeter.maxDisplayHeight)
   myMeter.height = newHeight;
```

The *if* code block allows us to perform error checks on the value *before* we try to assign it into a class property. This is a form of input error checking mentioned in Chapter 2 when we talked about the Five Program Steps. So, the good news is that the code block above can check for legitimate property values for the class members before we commit to them. The bad news is that there could be multiple places in the program where the *height* property might be changed. This means we'd need to duplicate the error checking code at each of those assignment blocks in the code. Not good. Less code is always better than more code if the two versions perform the same.

Getters and Setters

C++ lets you change the *public* properties of a class any way you see fit, including the silk assignment shown above. Other languages (e.g., Microsoft's C#), however, force you to use getter and setter methods when reading or writing a class property. A *getter method* is used to retrieve the value of a class property for use in the program. A *setter method is used to assign a value to a class property.*

Hmmm...using getters/setters might not be a bad idea. For example, using a setter method would allow us to place any error checking code in the class setter method and not have to scatter that same code all over the place in the program. Likewise, a getter method would allow us to perform any processing of the property that might be necessary before exposing it to the outside world. For example, to save memory, suppose you have an array of 150 sample weight measures that can vary between 0.10 and 1.99 pounds. You could store those 150 values in a *float* array, but that would take 600 bytes of scarce SRAM memory. Instead, store it as a *byte*, but have the getter method cast the array value to a *float* and then divide by 100.0 before the getter returns the value. That would save 450 bytes of data space! The other win is that you don't have to duplicate the scalar code at every point in the program that fetches a new array value. (Also, us older programmers don't have to *remember* to scale the data before using it!)

Okay, but how can I "force" someone to use a property getter or setter method in a class? Simple. Just move that property out of the *public* section of the class declaration to the *private* section of the class. Presto-chango! That property is now invisible (i.e., out of scope) outside of the class. (Look at Listing 12.1 in Chapter 12 if you've forgotten about the *public* and *private* keywords.) Moving the property to the *private* section of the class means that no statement outside the class itself has access to that property. Cool! Another level of encapsulation of your data and that's a good thing!

The downside of getters and setters is that you have to write the class code to support them. But, is it really a burden? I think not, because you should be checking the data before you use it anyway, so why not do it once and be done with it? Why scatter those checks throughout the program when you can contain the code size? If error checking is not necessary for a property, just leave that property in the *public* section of the class declaration. If the class properties are *public*, you just get or set their values in your code using the object's dot operator; no getter/setter methods are required.

So, how do you decide when to use getters/setters? There really is no fixed answer to that question. For me, I look at it from a cost/benefit approach. If a property is wrong and it immediately manifests itself in the output of the program, I can isolate the bug pretty quickly in most cases. If the property is but one element in a complex algorithm, then it might be better to use getters/setters and perform whatever error checking makes sense for the data. Another consideration is how often is the property subject to change. For example, if a display is 480x320, chances are I will set it once (probably in *setup()*) and not change it again. Data that don't change much as the program executes probably benefit less from bullet proofing. It really does depend upon the nature of the data and how that data are used in the program. You're writing the program...your call.

Our Meter Class Declaration

The first task I usually take on is the class declaration that goes into the header file for the class. Because the library is designed to work with such a variety of display devices, the author of the TFT_3SPI graphics library decided to use a separate header file for the user to set the characteristics for their display. You need to configure the header file for your particular display before you can use it. (I assume you have already installed the TFT_eSPI library.)

Setting User_Steup.h

In the library's User_Setup.h header file, around line 38, you will see this code fragment:

```
// Only define one driver, the other ones must be commented out
//#define ILI9341_DRIVER
//#define ST7735_DRIVER     // Define additional display parameters
//#define ILI9163_DRIVER    // Define additional display parameters
//#define S6D02A1_DRIVER
//#define RPI_ILI9486_DRIVER // 20MHz maximum SPI
//#define HX8357D_DRIVER
//#define ILI9481_DRIVER
//#define ILI9486_DRIVER
#define ILI9488_DRIVER      // WARNING: Do not connect ILI9488
                                                 display
                            // SDO to MISO if other devices
// share the SPI bus (TFT SDO does NOT tristate when CS is high)
//#define ST7789_DRIVER     // Full configuration option, define
                  // additional parameters below for this
                                   // display
//#define ST7789_2_DRIVER   // Minimal configuration option,
// define additional parameters below for
                // this display
//#define R61581_DRIVER     //#define RM68140_DRIVER
//#define ST7796_DRIVER
```

I am using a 3.5" display that employs the ILI9488 driver, so that is the line in User_Setup.h that I uncommented. (See shaded entry in code fragment above.) Okay, that tells the library which driver my display is using, but it still needs to know the SPI pins I'm using for the display. The following code fragment begins around line 190 in the same User_Setup.h file:

```
// For ESP32 Dev board (only tested with ILI9341 display)
// The hardware SPI can be mapped to any pins
```

```
//#define TFT_MISO 19
//#define TFT_MOSI 23
//#define TFT_SCLK 18
#define TFT_CS   15  // Chip select control pin
#define TFT_DC    2  // Data Command control pin
#define TFT_RST   4  // Reset pin (could connect to RST pin)
//#define TFT_RST  -1  // Set TFT_RST to -1 if display RESET is
connected to ESP32 board RST
```

I removed the comment characters from the start of the shade lines above, which sets those pins for use with the SPI interface. You need to make sure that you wire the TFT display using these pins. (Check Table 9.2 for help using your microcontroller. Most displays label the CS, DC, and RST pins on the back of the display.)

I then saved the User_Setup.h header file. Any time I make a change to a library, I usually reload the IDE to make sure the changes are in use by the IDE. Now that the library knows how to talk to my display, let's look at the header file that controls the Meter class.

The Meter Class Header File

The Meter class header file is presented in Listing 13.1.

Listing 13.1. The Meter.h header file

```
//==================================================================
// CAUTION: Make sure you select the right display pins and driver
// in User_Setup.h file in the library.
//
// The display will not work properly if these items are not set!
//==================================================================
#ifndef BEENHERE
#include "TFTMeter.h"
#endif

#define MAXLABELLENGTH    8  // Max label length on meter face

class Meter {
  public://========== Class Properties ====================
    char label[10];          // string for meter label
    char *tickLabels[11];

    int meterBorderColor;
    int meterFaceColor;
    int maxDisplayHeight;
    int maxDisplayWidth;
    int needleValueColor;
    int needleEndpointMin;
    int needleEndpointMax;
    int old_analog;          // Value ensures they are reset when
run
    uint16_t osx;            // Saved x & y coords
    uint16_t osy;
```

```
    int showNeedleValue;      // Display needle: 1 = true, 0 =
false
    int tickLength;           // For meter marking
    int tickMarkScalar;       // 100 divided by this scalar
    float ltx;                // x coord bottom needle (not pivot)

    //================ Class Methods ====================
    void analogMeterInit();
    void analogMeterInit(int x, int y, int w, int h,
                         char *tm[], char *fl);
    void drawAnalogMeter();
    void plotLinear(char *label, int x, int y);
    void plotNeedle(int value, byte ms_delay);
    void plotPointer(void);
    void setLocation(int x, int y);
    void setDisplaySize(int maxXPixels, int maxYPixels);
    void setMeterColors(int face, int border);
    void setMeterHeightSize(int h);
    void setMeterLabel(char *lbl);
    void setMeterSize(int w, int h);
    void setMeterWidthSize(int w);
    void setNeedleDisplayValue(int toggle);
    void setNeedleLimits(int min, int max);
    void setNeedleValueColor(int color);
    void setScalarMajorTickmarks(int number);
    void setTickLabels(char *tm[]);
    void setTickLength(int tic);

  private:    //====== Class Private Properties ============
    int height;            // Display height in pixels
    int width;             // display width in pixels
    int x;                 // pixel column location for meter
    int y;                 //         row
};
```

There are no surprises in Listing 13.1. I placed most of properties in the *public* section of the class. I did this because most of them are of the set-and-forget nature and don't change as the program executes. Also, for the most part, they don't lend themselves to or need error checking. Some of the properties (*height, width, x, y*) are in the *private* section of the class declaration. Honestly, they don't need to be *private*, but I wanted to show you an example of the placement of a *private* property.

I have placed all of the class methods in the *public* section, which means all of the methods are available for use anywhere in the program via the instantiated *myMeter* class object and the dot operator. Most of the methods are *set?()* methods used to change some aspect of the meter display. There are no *get?()* methods because none of the properties benefit from error checking and the meter is “read-only”.

Note how I have followed the normal *class style convention* and made all of the method names start with a lowercase letter. (Any functions [i.e., not object methods] that I write have names that start with an uppercase letter.) I also tend to place properties and methods in alphabetical order, as I find that makes it easier to find things in the file should I need to do so. Obviously, such ordering is just my preference and is not required.

Finally, note the preprocessor directive at the top of the Meter.h class header file:

```
#ifndef BEENHERE
  #include "TFTMeter.h"
#endif
```

We explained what this does in Chapter 10, but it illustrates that most programs have a program, or sketch, header file (e.g., TFTMeter.h) along with a header file for each class that is defined in the program (e.g., Meter.h).

The Project Header File, TFTMeter.h

Listing 13.2 shows the project's header file, TFTMeter.h. The contents of the listing should look pretty familiar by now. The extern keyword is used to declare any global variables and objects used in the program. These declared variables and objects are always defined in the main project file (i.e., the *.ino file that contains the *setup()* and *loop()* functions). Also note that I have declared two meter objects. The function prototypes for the function I wrote that are not part of the Meter class appear near the bottom of the header file. Again, this allows the compiler to perform type checking on those function calls.

Listing 13.2. The project TFTMeter.h header file

```
#ifndef BEENHERE         // Make sure we only read header file once
#define BEENHERE

#include <SPI.h>            // Part of normal IDE libraries
#include <TFT_eSPI.h>       // https://github.com/Bodmer/TFT_eSPI
 //
https://github.com/buxtronix/arduino/tree/master/libraries/Rotary
#include <Rotary.h>
#include "Meter.h"          // Our custom Meter class header file

#define PIXELWIDTH        480      // Our 480x320 TFT display
#define PIXELHEIGHT       320

#define ENCODER1PINA      13       // Encoder pins
#define ENCODER1PINB      12
```

```
              // Overkill since a float doesn't have this
precision
#define RADIANSPERDEGREE  0.0174532925
#define MAXLABELLENGTH    8

//================== declare variables ==========================
extern char *tickNames[];

extern volatile int encoderDirection;   // Used in ISR's
extern volatile int encoderCounter;

//================== declare objects ============================
extern Rotary rotary;
extern TFT_eSPI tft;
extern Meter myMeter1, myMeter2;

//================== non-class function prototypes ==============
void Rotate();
void MyDelay(unsigned long millisWait);

#endif
```

The Rotary Encoder File, Encoder.cpp

Now let's look at the Ecoder.cpp file, which is also the ISR for the encoder interrupt. It's very simple with just a single (ISR) function call in it. The code is presented in Listing 13.3. We are using Ben Buxton's encoder library, which you can download from the URL presented in the TFTMeter.h header file. The code records which way the rotary encoder was turned.

Listing13.3. The *Ecoder.cpp* code file.

```
#ifndef BEENHERE
#include "TFTMeter.h"
#endif

/*****
  Purpose: ISR to process encoder interrupt

  Parameter list:
    void

  Return value:
    void
*****/
void Rotate()
{
  unsigned char result = rotary.process();

  encoderDirection = 0;
  switch (result) {
    case 0:                    // Should not get here with
interrupts
```

```
      return;                         // Just go home...
      break;                          // Needed for syntax

    case DIR_CW:                      // clockwise
      encoderDirection = 1;
      break;

    case DIR_CCW:                     // counter-clockwise
      encoderDirection = -1;
      break;

    default:
      encoderDirection = 0;
      break;
  }
  encoderCounter += encoderDirection; // Works for either
                                      // direction
  if (encoderCounter < myMeter1.needleEndpointMin)   // Check
                                                     // overshoot
    encoderCounter = myMeter1.needleEndpointMin;
  if (encoderCounter > myMeter1.needleEndpointMax)
    encoderCounter = myMeter1.needleEndpointMax;

  myMeter1.plotNeedle(encoderCounter, 0);          // First meter
  myMeter2.plotNeedle(encoderCounter, 0);          // Second
meter
}
```

The encoder library returns 0 if the encoder was not turned, *DIR_CW* when the encoder is turned clockwise and *DIR_CCW* when turned counter-clockwise. You must use the symbolic constants or code the values appropriately (CW = 16 = 0x10, CCW = 32 = 0x20). You cannot test directly against 1 and -1. The variable *encoderCounter* tracks the value of the encoder and is used to display the encoder value on the display if the user wishes to do so. Otherwise, *encoderCounter* is used as part of the code that plots the meter needle. Because *encoderDirection* and *Rotate()* have their external declarations and prototypes are detailed in the TFTMeter.h header file, there is no reason for the encoder file to have a header file of its own.

Note that I am using a single ISR as I only have one encoder connected to the ESP32. However, I have two Meter objects, *myMeter1* and *myMeter2*. Because the ISR calls the *plotNeedle()* method using the same encoder counter, the two meters move together as you turn the encoder shaft. If you wish to use the meters independently, simply write a second ISR routine for the second encoder and use the *attachInterrupt()* routine to attach the ISR to the second encoders set of pins.

You may be thinking: "Wait a minute! If we are using an ISR for the encoder, why do we need to check the return value from the call to *rotary.process()* for 0? After all, an interrupt is only generated when the encoder is turned." Well...sort of. First, recall our "speed bump" discussion of how mechanical rotary encoders work. The fact is, the internal encoder contact arm can vibrate after passing over a speed bump and that vibration can send a false pulse chain to the software. Having a *case 0* allows us to ignore the false pulse chain that may result. (You might find it interesting to place a *Serial.print()* statement in each of the *case* blocks in the *Rotate()* function. That's a no-no in production code because *Serial.print()* uses its own interrupt and, therefore, is a blocking method.) Second, if we placed a call to *Rotate()* in the *loop()* function and removed the *attachInterrupt()* calls from *setup()*, you could use the code in a polling process to read the encoder rather than using interrupts. Therefore, when the encoder is stationary, we would see a 0 value from the encoder code. I'm not sure why you would want to use polling, but you could.

The TFTMeter.ino Main Project File

The main project source code file is always the *.ino file that holds *setup()* and *loop()*. Listing 13.4 presents the TFTMeter.ino code. (When I use someone else's software, I leave the main header comment unchanged even if there are spelling errors.) The first thing that is processed is the preprocessor directive to include the TFTMeter.h header file. Because that header file also includes the reading of the Meter.h header file, all of the header files have been read by the end of the preprocessor directive.

Next come the definitions of the *extern* variables from the TFTMeter.h header file. There are more elegant ways to initialize the *tickNames[]* array, but this one is direct and easy to find. Using the RightLeft Rule, you can see that *tickNames[]* is an array of pointers to *char*. These become the identifiers for the tick marks on the meter. The other definitions are global variables and objects that are used in the program. I tend to place object definitions at the end of the definition list because...I don't have a reason, I just do.

The *rotary* object is defined just before the *MyDelay()* function call, as are the *tft* and *myMeter* objects. The rotary object expects you to pass the encoder pins as part of the rotary object's call to its constructor. Note how the constructor's method name matches the Rotary class name.

Listing 13.4. The TFTMeter.ino Main Project File.

```
/*
  Example animated analogue meters using a TFT LCD screen

  Originanally written for a 320 x 240 display, so only occupies
half  of a 480 x 320 display.
```

```
  Needs Font 2 (also Font 4 if using large centered scale label)


###################################################################
#######
  ###### DON'T FORGET TO UPDATE THE User_Setup.h FILE IN THE
LIBRARY ######
###################################################################
#######
*/
#ifndef BEENHERE
#include "TFTMeter.h"
#endif

//======== global definitions ==============================
char *tickNames[MAXLABELLENGTH] = {"0", "25", "50", "75", "100",
""};
                                // Empty entry at end list end
volatile int encoderDirection;
volatile int encoderCounter;
// ======= objects =========================================
Rotary rotary = Rotary(ENCODER1PINA, ENCODER1PINB);  // Encoder
object
TFT_eSPI tft  = TFT_eSPI();  // Invoke custom graphics library
Meter myMeter1, myMeter2;    // My meter class object

//================================================================
/*****
  Purpose: to cause a delay in program execution. This is not
         a blocking function like delay is.

  Parameter list:
    unsigned long millisWait     milliseconds to wait

  Return value:
    void
*****/
void MyDelay(unsigned long millisWait)
{
  unsigned long now = millis();      //ms now since program start?
  while (millis() - now < millisWait)  // If time left to waste...
    ;                                  // Twiddle thumbs...
}

//==============================================================
void setup(void)
{
#ifdef DEBUG
  Serial.begin(57600);       // For debug
  while (!Serial)            // Wait for Serial object
    ;
#endif
  tft.init();   tft.setRotation(1); // Results in "landscape"
display
  tft.fillScreen(TFT_BLACK);
  pinMode(ENCODER1PINA, INPUT_PULLUP); // no "floating" pins
```

```
  pinMode(ENCODER1PINB, INPUT_PULLUP);
  attachInterrupt(ENCODER1PINA, Rotate, CHANGE);    // Use
interrupts
  attachInterrupt(ENCODER1PINB, Rotate, CHANGE);
  encoderCounter = 0;                          // Starting scale value
  myMeter1.setDisplaySize(480, 320);
                                               // See text discussion
//  myMeter1.analogMeterInit(0, 0, 240, 140, tickNames, "Slice
1");
  myMeter1.setMeterLabel("Slice 1");
  myMeter1.analogMeterInit();
  myMeter2.setDisplaySize(480, 320);
                                               // See text discussion
//myMeter2.analogMeterInit(235, 150, 240, 140, tickNames, "Slice
2");
  myMeter2.setLocation(235, 150); // Upper-left corner meter
placement
  myMeter2.setMeterLabel("Slice 2");
  myMeter2.analogMeterInit();
}
//===================================================================
void loop() {
}
```

I always use the *MyDelay()* function shown in Listing 13.4 instead of the more common Arduino library *delay()* function because mine is non-blocking. As you'll recall, *delay()* uses its own interrupts which could block my interrupt, so I use my own version instead.

The program then enters the *setup()* function. The first thing I do there is establish the *Serial* object. I could have surrounded it with the *#ifdef DEBUG* directive you've seen in previous examples and I would probably do that if I was going to ship this out for distribution. However, since I'm just using it for testing purposes, I have permanently included it. Its presence does not impact the performance of the code.

The *tft.init()* call is required by the display library before you can do anything with the display. The *tft.setRotation()* call allows you to configure the display for different viewing angles. There are four possible values (0-3) for the argument passed to the *setRotation()* method. An argument value of 0 sets the display in "portrait" mode. In this mode, the narrow edge (320 pixels) is at the top of the display and the wide edge (480 pixels) is at the side. The "landscape" mode (i.e., 1) is what I'm using and has the wide edge at the display top and the narrow edge on the sides. The other two modes simply "invert" the first two modes. I guess these inversions could be useful if you wired the display into the circuit "upsidedown". The *tft.fillScreen(TFT_BLACK)* simply erases the screen using black as the background color.

The *pinMode()* function call is required any time you wish to use an I/O pin. While we talked about this before, here I'll provide a little more detail about this function. The first argument specifies which pin you are setting. Actually, this can be confusing because there is sample code that uses absolute pin numbers while other examples use symbolic constants. For example, the Blink code uses pin 13 for the LED pin, but you can use PD6 on the Teensy 2.0 or 13 on the Teensy 4.0. (Most processors recognize the LED_BUILTIN symbolic constant for their onboard LED.) Also, some pins on the ESP32 cannot be used as GPIO pins. (See Table 1.2 in Chapter 1.) We are using the symbolic constants for the pins as defined in the TFTMeter.h header file in the *pinMode()* function calls.

The second argument to the *pinMode()* call dictates how you want to use the pin I've repeated the three modes that can be used with the *pinMode()* function:

> **INPUT** – In the *INPUT* mode, the pin is placed in a high impedance state, which is like placing a 100mΩ resistor in front of the pin. This prevents the pin from large demands on the circuit being sampled.

INPUT_PULLUP – In the INPUT_PULLUP mode, the pins are pulled up using internal resistors rather than external pullup resistors. This places the pin in a known state and guarantees the pin is not "floating" between a 0 or 1 interpretation.

OUTPUT – This places the pin in a low impedance state which means the pin can provide current to an external circuit. Most of the microcontrollers can supply as much as 40 mA of current, but you should shoot for about half that amount if you can.

In our application, we are using the INPUT_PULLUP mode to sense when there is a change in the encoder pin's state.

We've talked about the *attachInterrupt()* function before. Subject to the GPIO pin warnings about the ESP32 in Table 1.2, you can use any general-purpose pin for the interrupt. We are using symbolic constants for the ESP32 pins (12 and 13) for the interrupt pins. The interrupt service routine (ISR) for the encoder pins is the *Rotate()* function presented in Listing 13.3. The third parameter in the *attachInterrupt()* call means we want to call the ISR any time the state of the pin changes. The ESP32 is sufficiently fast (180Mhz to 240MHz) that encoder and meter movement is very smooth. (In fact, we delay the response a little so it looks like a smooth change rather than an abrupt, jerky, change.)

Near the bottom of *setup()* is a call to the *setDisplaySize()* method of the Meter class, which simply sets the pixel resolution for the display I'm using. The last method call is to *analogMeterInit()* which passes in information needed for the meter to construct itself properly. The first two parameters are the row/column (x/y) coordinates for the upper-left corner of the analog meter. In this example, I'm placing the meter at the extreme upper-left. The next two parameters are the width and height of the meter in pixels. The last parameter is the array of pointers to *char* that serve as labels for the tick marks on the display. That array is initialized near the top of Listing 13.4.

The two commented-out statements show how you could call *analogMeterInit()* with parameters. Because the meter location is unknown as is the meter label, those class methods need to be called in *setup()* before the *init()* method. Listing 13.5 below shows how the "no parameter" version works.

That completes the code in the *setup()* function.

The *loop()* function has nothing in it! What? All this for nothing? Well, not really. Because we are using interrupts, turning the encoder does cause the meter needle to move, but that's done by the code in the Meter.cpp file, not code in *loop()*. If we were using polling instead of interrupts, then you would have calls in *loop()* to Meter methods to handle the processing.

As it stands right now, all that the program does is reflect the new needle position on the meter as you turn the encoder. I am using just the one encoder to move the two meter needles together. However, with the encoder connected to an appropriate circuit, you could use the encoder to set the volume of a radio, the drip rate of a garden watering system, reposition a solar panel via a stepper motor, adjust a motorized window shade, release dog food into a bowl...a little imagination and a perceived need and I'll bet you can think of something that the encoder could control.

The Meter.cpp Code

Obviously, everything we've discussed so far is more concerned with establishing the environment in which the meter works than with manipulating the meter itself. In this section we want to discuss some of the factors that need to be considered when coding a non-trivial class. I am not going to spend time discussing the trigonometric functions involved in drawing an arc on a TFT color display. There are all kinds of tutorials for that. Instead, I want to concentrate on the issues that need to be considered when drawing *anything* that is animated on a display. There are a number of nettlesome details that need to be addressed when working with a TFT display. Solving those details is what the remainder of this chapter is all about. The starting point for the discussion is instantiating the class Meter object.

Meter Instantiation and Initialization

As you know, the instantiation of any object is done by the class constructor. I opted to use the default constructor that is automatically supplied by the compiler. However, once the object is instantiated, I use the common library technique of using an *init()* (or *begin()*) method to set the default values for the meter. I chose to overload the *analogMeterInit()* method and provide two versions: 1) a lazyprogrammer version, and 2) a choosy-programmer version. Listing 13.5 presents the lazy-programmer

Listing 13.5. The lazy-programmer init() method.

```
/*****
  Purpose: The default settings to draw an analog meter

  Argument list:
    void

  Return value:
    void
*****/
void Meter::analogMeterInit()
{
  setMeterColors(TFT_WHITE, TFT_GREEN);
  setNeedleValueColor(TFT_BLACK);
  setTickLength(15);
  setMeterWidthSize(240);
  setMeterHeightSize(140);
  setNeedleLimits(0, 100);     // End points for needle values
  setScalarMajorTickmarks(6);
  showNeedleValue   = 1;       // Display needle value
  old_analog = -999;           // Value ensures they are reset when
run
  ltx  = 0.0;                  // Saved x coord (not pivot point)
```

```
  setTickLabels(tickNames);    drawAnalogMeter();
}
```

version which shows that the *analogMeterInit()* version which does not use a parameter list. Instead, the method selects default values for the Meter class properties. The end result after the *analogMeterInit()* method call is a "garden variety" analog meter. Note that there is no label displayed on the meter face, so we don't even have a clue as to what we're looking at in terms of meter values.

Because we are writing the code in Listing 13.5 for the Meter class, you can reference any property or method of the class without using the class name. For example, you could write the call in Listing 13.5 as:

```
Meter.setMeterColors(TFT_WHITE, TFT_GREEN);
```

but there's no need to do so because the method call being defined (i.e.,M *Meter::analogMeterInit()*) is part of the Meter class code definition. Again, programmers always seem to use the shorter version.

If the user wants to display the name of what the meter is measuring, they can call the setMeterLabel() method. This method is a fairly standard way of writing a "setter" method, as shown in Listing 13.6. I choose to limit

Listing 13.6. The setter method for the meter label.

```
/*****
  Purpose: Set the label to display on meter face

  Argument list:
    char *lbl      the label

  Return value:
    void

  CAUTION: The label length is limited to
MAXLABELLENGTH characters.
           Anything longer is truncated
*****/
void Meter::setMeterLabel(char *lbl)
{
  if (strlen(lbl) > MAXLABELLENGTH) {       // Is
label too long?
    strncpy(label, lbl, MAXLABELLENGTH);    // Yep
  } else {
    strcpy(label, lbl);                     // Nope
  }
}
```

the length of the label that appears on the meter face to MAXLABELLENGTH (i.e., 8) characters.

When I first wrote the Meter class, I did do a little bit of a non-standard library placement of the symbolic constant by placing it in the TFTMeter.h header file instead of the Meter.h header file where it would normally be found. I did this because I tend to look in the project's header file for symbolic constants rather than in a library header file. I knew I shouldn't do it that way because it's important to keep any symbolic constants for a class within the class header. Being old and fairly set in my ways, I thought: Anyone who wants to take me to the shed for a lesson in respecting convention is welcome to do so and place their constant in the library header file. Then the bullheadedness faded a bit and I placed the symbolic constant in the Meter.h header file where it belongs. There's no reason for me to teach you my bad habits.

The real lesson to be learned here, however, is that we perform a basic error check on the parameter *before* assigning it to the class property. Most of the error checks performed in the Meter class work in similar fashion.

Because you are not a lazy programmer, you need to see the other *analogMeterInit()* method. Again, there's no problem "reusing" the same method name because the two class methods have different signatures. Listing 13.7 shows the other overloaded *analogMeterInit()* method. The difference between the two methods is the changed signature because of the passing of parameters to the method.

Listing 13.7. Parameterized init() method.

```
/*****
  Purpose: The user settings to draw an analog meter

  Argument list:
    int x            meter column pixel position
    int y                    row
    int w            pixel width of meter
    int h                 height
    char *tm         tick name labels
    char *fl         meter face label

  Return value:
    void
*****/
void Meter::analogMeterInit(int x, int y, int w, int h, char
*tm[],
                              char *fl)
{
  old_analog = -999;          // Value ensures they are reset when
run
```

```
  ltx   = 0.0;// Saved x coord of bottom of needle (not pivot
point)
  setDisplaySize(PIXELWIDTH, PIXELHEIGHT);
  setMeterColors(TFT_WHITE, TFT_GREEN);
  setNeedleValueColor(TFT_BLUE);
  setMeterWidthSize(w);
  setMeterHeightSize(h);
  setLocation(x, y);
  setMeterLabel(fl);
  setNeedleLimits(0, 100);
  setTickLength(15);
  setTickLabels(tm);
  setNeedleDisplayValue(1);
  drawAnalogMeter();
}
```

In Listing 13.7, the parameter list allows the user to override the default values for the meter's location, size, tick labels, and faceplate label. All of the other class properties necessary to draw the meter use default property values. You can, of course, change any default values by calling the appropriate class setter method. Obviously, the parameterized version of the *analogMeterInit()* method gives you greater latitude in making the meter look the way you want it to look.

Note at the bottom of the *setup()* listing (Listing 13.4) after the meter is drawn, you must call *myMeter.plotNeedle()* to see the needle and its label displayed. If you don't perform that call in *setup()*, the meter is drawn without the needle or the faceplate label. The reason is because most of the time we only want to redraw the meter if the encoder is turned. Therefore, we place the call to update the needle in the *Rotate()* method so it is only called when the encoder it rotated.

The drawAnalogMeter() method

I don't want to get bogged down in the specifics of drawing the meter face, but there are some aspects of the method that need clarification. Listing 13.8 shows the code for the *drawAnalogMeter()* method.

Listing 13.8. The drawAnalaogMeter() method

```
/*****
  Purpose: Draw the analog meter on the display

  Argument list:
    void

  Return value:
    void
*****/
void Meter::drawAnalogMeter()
```

```
{
  uint16_t x0, y0, x1, y1;
  int halfWidth = width / 2;
  int minorTickLength;
  int x2, y2, x3, y3;
  float sx, sy, sx2, sy2;

                                                  // Draw background block
tft.fillRect(x, y, width + 9, height + 6, meterBorderColor);
                                                  // Overlay meter face
  tft.fillRect(x + 5, y + 3, width height, meterFaceColor);

  tft.setTextColor(TFT_BLACK);                    // Text color
                     // Draw ticks every 5 degrees from -50 to +50
  for (int i = -50; i < 51; i += 5) {
    // degrees (100 deg. FSD swing)
    sx = cos((i - 90) * RADIANSPERDEGREE);  // Coord long tick
marks
    sy = sin((i - 90) * RADIANSPERDEGREE);
    x0 = sx * (100 + tickLength) + halfWidth + x;
    y0 = sy * (100 + tickLength) + height + y;
    x1 = sx * 100 + halfWidth + x;
    y1 = sy * 100 + height + y;
                           // Coordinates of next tick for zone
fill
    sx2 = cos((i + 5 - 90) * RADIANSPERDEGREE);
    sy2 = sin((i + 5 - 90) * RADIANSPERDEGREE);
    x2 = sx2 * (100 + tickLength) + halfWidth + x;
    y2 = sy2 * (100 + tickLength) + height + y;
    x3 = sx2 * 100 + halfWidth  + x;
    y3 = sy2 * 100 + height + y;
    if (i >= 0 && i < 25) {                     // Green zone limits
      tft.fillTriangle(x0, y0, x1, y1, x2, y2, TFT_GREEN);
      tft.fillTriangle(x1, y1, x2, y2, x3, y3, TFT_GREEN);
    }
    if (i >= 25 && i < 50) {                    // Orange zone limits
      tft.fillTriangle(x0, y0, x1, y1, x2, y2, TFT_ORANGE);
      tft.fillTriangle(x1, y1, x2, y2, x3, y3, TFT_ORANGE);
    }
    if (i % 25 != 0)          // ignore ticks half major tick length
      minorTickLength = tickLength / 2;
    x0 = sx * (100 + tickLength) + halfWidth + x; //if tick
changed
    y0 = sy * (100 + tickLength) + height + y;
    x1 = sx * 100 + halfWidth + x;
    y1 = sy * 100 + height + y;
    tft.drawLine(x0, y0, x1, y1, TFT_BLACK);           // Draw tick
    if (i % tickMarkScalar == 0) {  // Check if labels should be
drawn
                                             // Calculate label positions
      x0 = sx * (100 + tickLength + 10) + halfWidth + x;
      y0 = sy * (100 + tickLength + 10) + height + y;
      switch (i / tickMarkScalar) {
        case -2:
          tft.drawCentreString((const char *)tickLabels[0],
                               x0, y0 - 12, 2);
          break;
        case -1:
```

```
            tft.drawCentreString((const char *)tickLabels[1],
                                      x0, y0 - 9, 2);
            break;
          case  0:
            tft.drawCentreString((const char *)tickLabels[2],
                                     x0, y0 - 6, 2);
            break;
          case  1:
            tft.drawCentreString((const char *)tickLabels[3],
                                     x0, y0 - 9, 2);
            break;
          case  2:
            tft.drawCentreString((const char *)tickLabels[4],
                                     x0, y0 - 12, 2);
            break;
        }
      }
                                     // Now draw the arc of the scale
      sx = cos((i + 5 - 90) * RADIANSPERDEGREE);
      sy = sin((i + 5 - 90) * RADIANSPERDEGREE);
      x0 = sx * 100 + halfWidth + x;
      y0 = sy * 100 + height + y;
      if (i < 50)                        // don't draw the last part
        tft.drawLine(x0, y0, x1, y1, TFT_BLACK);
    }
  }
```

First, the code for drawing the meter as taken directly from the TFT_eSPI library examples was filled with magic numbers. All I did was to make some of those magic numbers go away so you can move the meter around on the display. (I have more to say about this towards the end of the chapter.)

The *tft.fillRect()* method is used to draw the meter face and its border on the display. We replaced the hardcoded numbers with Meter class properties. It doesn't show up well in Figure 13.1, but there is a border color surrounding the meter face. The code uses the following statement to draw the border:

```
// Draw background block
 tft.fillRect(x, y, width + 9, height + 6, meterBorderColor);
```

which means that we are drawing a fairly large rectangle for the border and then overlaying that rectangle with a second rectangle drawn using:

```
// Overlay with meter face
tft.fillRect(x + 5, y + 3, width, height, meterFaceColor);
```

Note what this means. If we are drawing the meter in the upper-left corner of the display, *x* and *y* are both 0. The third parameter, *width + 9*, bloats the desired meter width by 9 pixels. The fourth parameter, height + 6, bloats the height by 6 pixels. The end result is an oversized "meter face" drawn using the border color.

The second rectangle method call positions the corner of the meter face 3 pixels to the right of the left edge of the display, and 3 pixels down from the top. Because we now don't bloat the width and height of the meter like we did in the first rectangle call, you end up overlaying the meter face on top of the border rectangle you drew first. You now have drawn a meter that has a border drawn using *meterBorderColor* color and a meter drawn using the *meterFaceColor* for its face.

Why not just draw a line around the meter face and be done with it? Actually, it takes more code to draw the four line segments it would take to draw a border than just using the *fillrect()* method. In terms of speed, it might be faster to draw four line segments, but is the added complexity worth it? You're talking about a human's reaction to something drawn on a display screen. If the more complex code saves you 20 milliseconds or less, to me, it's not worth the effort.

Virtually all of the rest of the code in the method is used to draw the tick marks and arc of the meter. The last three statements are used to write the meter face label. The method call:

```
tft.drawCentreString(label, x + halfWidth, y + height / 2, 7);
```

is unusual in that it is not found in all graphics libraries. All of the other method used in the Meter class are part of almost any graphics libraries. The purpose of the method is to center the string passed to it (i.e., *label*) in the x/y coordinate space. The last argument is the font size to use when drawing the label. If you are forced to use a library that doesn't have a *drawCentreString()* method, it wouldn't be to the method are the value to be plotted and the delay in milliseconds for the redraw of the needle. The delay is to make the needle appear to be moving smoothly from one point to the next. The method compares the current value to the previous value to make sure they are different. If they are the same, there's no reason to redraw the needle so execution is returned from the method call. that hard to write your own version.

The plotNeedle() method

Once the meter face and its graduations are drawn, you can draw the needle on the meter face. That's the purpose of the *plotNeedle()* method. The code is presented in Listing 13.9. The parameters passed

Listing 13.9. The plotNeedle() method

```
/*****
```

```
  Purpose: Draw the needle indicator on the meter

  Argument list:
    int value           the value to plot on the meter
    byte ms_delay       the delay to make the move look like a
                        smooth change rather than a jump

  Return value:
    void

  CAUTION: This function is blocking while needle moves, time
           depends on ms_delay 0ms minimizes needle flicker if
           text is drawn within needle sweep Smaller values OK
           if text not in sweep area, zero for instant movement
           but does not look realistic... (note: 100 increments
           for full scale deflection)
*****/
void Meter::plotNeedle(int value, byte ms_delay)
{
  char buf[13];
  int halfWidth = width / 2;
  static int oldEncoderCount = -1;
  float sdeg;
  float sx;
  float sy;
  float tx;

  if (value < needleEndpointMin)    // Limit value for needle end
stops
    value = needleEndpointMin;
  if (value > needleEndpointMax)
    value = needleEndpointMax;
  if (showNeedleValue) {  // Show the needle value on meter face?
    tft.setTextColor(needleValueColor, TFT_WHITE);  // Yep...
                        // To erase "left-overs" from previous
number
    itoa(value, buf, DEC);     strcat(buf, "   ");
    tft.drawString(buf, x + width * 0.45, y + height * 0.85, 4);
    tft.setTextSize(1);
  }
  oldEncoderCount = value;            // Update counter for next
pass
  while (!(value == old_analog)) {    // Move needle to new value
    if (old_analog < value) {
      old_analog++;
    } else {
      old_analog--;
    }
    if (ms_delay == 0) {          // Update immediately id delay is
0
      old_analog = value;
    }                                  // Map value to angle
    sdeg = map(old_analog,needleEndpointMin,
               needleEndpointMax,-140, -40);
    sx   = cos(sdeg * RADIANSPERDEGREE);  // tip of needle coords
    sy   = sin(sdeg * RADIANSPERDEGREE);
    tx   = tan((sdeg + 90) * RADIANSPERDEGREE); // needle x delta
```

```
    if (value != 0) {     // Draw new needle 3 pixels wide putting
                          // magenta in center "thicken" it
      tft.drawLine(x + halfWidth + 20 * ltx - 1, y + height - 20,
                   osx - 1, osy, meterFaceColor);
      tft.drawLine(x + halfWidth + 20 * ltx,     y + height - 20,
                   osx    , osy, meterFaceColor);
      tft.drawLine(x + halfWidth + 20 * ltx + 1, y + height - 20,
                   osx + 1, osy, meterFaceColor);
    }
    tft.setTextColor(TFT_BLACK);      // Redraw label on meter face
    tft.drawCentreString(label, x + width / 2, y + height / 2, 4);
    ltx = tx;              // Store needle end coords for next erase
                                     // Draw new needle 3 pixels wide
    osx = x + sx * 98 + 120;      osy = y + sy * 98 + 140;

    tft.drawLine(x + halfWidth + 20 * ltx - 1, y + height - 20,
                 osx - 1, osy, TFT_RED);
    tft.drawLine(x + halfWidth + 20 * ltx,     y + height - 20,
                 osx    , osy, TFT_MAGENTA);
    tft.drawLine(x + halfWidth + 20 * ltx + 1, y + height - 20,
                 osx + 1, osy, TFT_RED);
    if (abs(old_analog - value) < 10) {     // Makes smooth mover
      ms_delay += ms_delay / 5;
    }
    MyDelay(ms_delay);               // This does not block
interrupts
  }
}
```

Because the value of the encoder counter is done in the encoder's ISR, the code checks the new value to make sure it does not fall outside of the meter's end limits. Any extreme value is set to the proper end point value. The code then uses *showNeedleValue* to determine if the current needle value is to be displayed on the meter face. If so, convert the current needle value to an integer number using *itoa()* and then display the value on the meter face. The string is padded with extra spaces so that the previous number is completely erased.

The code then figures out where the current needle value is compared to where the new needle value is. It then erases the old needle on the display via the calls to the *tft.drawLine()* method. There are 3 calls, each offset by a pixel, so that the needle is 3 pixels wide. Because the color used to draw the lines is the same as the meter face (i.e., *meterFaceColor*), this has the effect of erasing the current needle shown on the display. The code then determines where the new needle should be drawn and uses 3 new *tft.drawLine()* calls to repaint the needle using red and magenta. The original author used magenta for the center of the needle as he felt it made the needle easier to see. I didn't see much difference, but stuck with the author's colors. The last three statements simply determine the pause between the drawing in order to make the needle movement smoother.

That's it. Once the meter face is drawn using the *drawAnalogMeter()* call, the rest of the program is only concerned with updating the needle movement based upon what comes back from the encoder's ISR routine. In a complete program, the *loop()* function would contain code that would use the encoder counter to perform some processing task(s).

That's Odd

On my machine, the TFTMeter program compiled and produced the following statistics:

Sketch uses 262309 bytes (20%) of program storage space. Maximum is 1310720 bytes. Global variables use 16052 bytes (4%) of dynamic memory, leaving 311628 bytes for local variables. Maximum is 327680 bytes.

(Most of that program size is the ESP32 bootloader, not the program code we wrote. A completely "empty" program with nothing but *setup()* and *loop()* uses 206423 bytes of flash and 14556 bytes of SRAM on the ESP32, so our program is actually pretty small.) I then went back and removed all references to the *meter2* object and recompiled the code. The program size dropped to 262209 and the SRAM use decreased to 15932.

What?

Adding a second meter object to the program only bumped the program size up 100 bytes and the SRAM use 120 bytes. Given all of the code you've seen in the Meter.cpp file, how is that possible?

The reason is because it is the properties of the class that make one object different from another. The methods in the class could care less about what *describes* the object (i.e., its properties), only about how to *process* the object (i.e., what the methods do). This means, while we need to create a second property list for each object, those objects can "share" the class methods. (Sometimes you'll hear this code-sharing ability referred to as "*re-entrant code*".) Therefore, adding additional class objects to a program often adds only marginal increases in the memory demands.

Improvements

There are a lot of things in the Meter class that you may want to change to make it more useful. A starting point might be the following ideas:

1. Add a property to draw or not draw a border for the meter.

2. Add a property that allows the programmer to omit the "green zone" on the display.

3. Add a property that allows the programmer to omit the "red zone" on the display.

4. Add start and end points for drawing green and red zones. As the code exists now, they are in a
fixed coordinate space.

5. Add properties that allows the programmer to use colors for the zones other than green and red.

6. Allow variable data range. As it is currently, the meter range is fixed from 0 to 100. That might be fine for many things, but not all.

7. Allow the number of tick marks to vary according to the data range. It currently is fixed at one tick mark for every 5 units of the 100 point scale.

8. Add a less clunky way to label the major tick marks. There should be some synergy between this goal and #7 above.

9. Remove the remaining magic numbers and replace them with class properties. Many of them are related to the current (fixed) size of the meter itself, and those should be changeable.

These are the immediate changes that would make the meter more useful in a wider variety of uses. However, the point of this exercise was to show you the general format that a class assumes when you design your own class.

Conclusion

In this chapter, you took a very nice analog meter example and made it more useful by expanding its class properties and methods to give it more flexibility. I also introduced you to the concept of getters and setters. While we buried the getters and setters in a class, there is no reason why you can't apply their principles to straight C code without using classes. By forcing variable changes through a function (or method) call, you can perform error checking on the variable in one place without the need for duplicating that code elsewhere in the program. Also, we spent some time discussing how the meter is drawn. Many of the processes discussed here apply to other applications where display data are updated. Finally, we suggested some areas that would further enhance the utility of the class.

By now, you should be fairly comfortable reading just about any C code that is placed in front of you. However, always keep in mind that reading some else's code is always easier than writing your own from scratch. It would be beneficial for you to think up a project or two that you'd like to write and give it a try. You have enough tools on your belt now to take on that task.

Exercises

1. Add a property to the Meter class that lets the user display a meter with or without a border. How does that impact other methods?

2. Write your own *drawCenterString()* method. (Notice the two are spelled differently.)

3. Explain in two sentences or less what a setter is. What is a getter?

4. Why are getters and setters a good idea, even outside of C++?

5. Write a function that takes a string and centers it within start/end coordinates (e.g., x1/y1 and x2/y2). Use the *setCursor()* method to test your code.

6. What is the difference between *public* and *private* entities in a class?

7. In chapter 12 I talked about writing a program for a real estate investor. Write a building.h header file for the building class. (I'm not asking for the method code, just the *public* and *private* properties and methods found in the class.)

8. Design a real time clock class. Use the DS3231 RTC module as the basis for your design. (Hint: some people just want to look at a display and see the time, while many other applications want to log a sensor observation and record the date and time of the observation.)

Appendix A Suppliers and Special Products

Parts Suppliers:

For microcontrollers themselves, with the exception of the Teensy which is sold primarily by PJRC directly, I shop online looking for the best price. I prefer domestic sellers mainly because of the time to receive the products. If time is important to you, make sure you check the "Expected delivery date". Many foreign sellers have drop-ship addresses in the US, but are still actually shipping from outside the US. I also tend to buy microcontrollers, encoders, switches, and TFT displays in lots of 5 as it often makes a noticeable difference in price. Also, I seem to use a lot of these parts.

https://www.arrow.com It was my go-to place for parts as they would ship overnight for free. That has ended unless you order over $50. Still a good source for most parts.

https://www.digikey.com Perhaps the largest parts vendor in the US, yet will still sell quantity 1 on most items. Good source for encoders, SMD parts, and all electronic parts.

https://www.mouser.com Large parts vendor and will sell quantity 1 on many items. Good service and wide selection.

https://www.surplus-electronics-sales.com This is a new small family company and I have ordered from them several times. Really good prices on many items and excellent service. I often check their site first as their prices are good and I like supporting small companies.

https://www.surpluscenter.com This company sometimes has really good prices on "odd" and "unusual" parts you might need for a project.

https://www.taydaelectronics.com I have used this company for parts for several years and am happy with their service. Prices are good and they have a distribution warehouse in the US so orders are reasonably quick on commonly-used parts.

Products

I got my amateur radio license in 1954 and have been licensed ever since. Most of the microcontroller projects I build are for my amateur radio hobby and I know that many of you share the same interest. What follows is a list of products/suppliers who have good products at reasonable prices. Microcontrollers lend themselves to many amateur radio projects, especially for lower power (i.e., QRP) use.

MyAntenna EFHW-8010-1K ™ Multi-Band End Fed Half Wave Antenna

This is the antenna I use at my home. This is an End-Fed Half-Wave (EFHW*) antenna for 80/40/30/20/17/15/12 and 10m bands and does not require the Antenna Tuner to operate. It is a resonant Half wave on 80m (3.5MHz) therefore also resonant on second, third, and fourth harmonics, etc. Various installations such as horizontal, vertical, as inverted V, as inverted L, zigzag, etc. are possible. Measured VSWR in the gallery are taken with the antenna in an inverted V shape with the center of wire at 20 feet and ends a few feet above the ground, your values could vary with way and height of installation.

https://myantennas.com
Price: $180
Sales Contact: https://myantennas.com/wp/contact

Seeeduino-XIAO-Arduino-Microcontroller

This controller became available just a few weeks before this book was finalize. There is a small software patch (see: https://wiki.seeedstudio.com/Seeeduino-XIAO/) that is installed after which the XIAO comes up in the Board and Port menus. I have a few projects that I'm going to use with this controller. Seeeduino XIAO is the smallest Arduino compatible board in Seeeduino Family. Seriously, you can see in the photo that it's about twice the size of a USB type C connector. It is an Arduino IDE compatible microcontroller that is embedded with the SAMD21 microchip. Apart from the strong CPU, Seeeduino XIAO has 256Kb of flash, 32Kb of SRAM, and is clocked at 48MHz. It has 14 GPIO PINs, which can be used for 11 analog PINs, 11 digital PINs, 1 I2C interface, 1 UART interface, and 1 SPI interface. Some PINs have various functions, A1/D1 to A10/D10 Pins have PWM

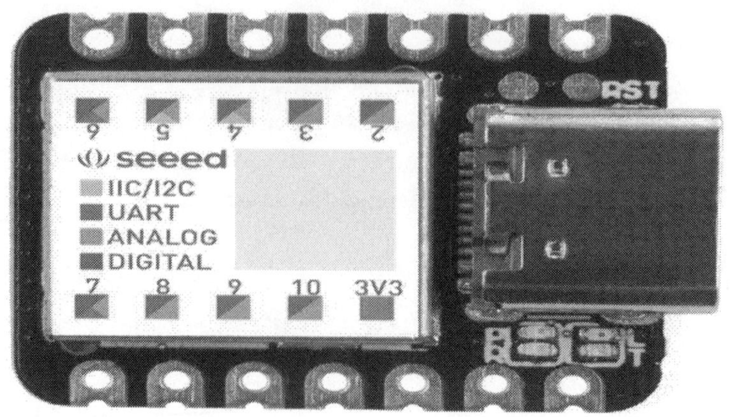

functions and Pin A0/D0 has a function of DAC which means you can get true analog signals not PWM signals when you define it as an analog pin, that's why 14 GPIO PINs can realize more I/O PINs and interfaces. You can also use Grove Shield for Seeeduino XIAO to extend more possibilities.
https://www.seeedstudio.com/Grove-Shield-for-Seeeduino-XIAO-p-4621.html
Price: $4.90
Sales contact: order@seeed.cc

C

Q

R

S

T

Made in the USA
Las Vegas, NV
30 November 2023